THE
INDIANA WAY

THE

INDIANA
WAY

A State History
JAMES H. MADISON

INDIANA UNIVERSITY PRESS
Bloomington and Indianapolis

INDIANA HISTORICAL SOCIETY
Indianapolis

This book is a publication of

Indiana University Press
601 North Morton Street
Bloomington, IN 47404-3797 USA

http://www.indiana.edu/~iupress

Telephone orders 800-842-6796
Fax orders 812-855-7931
Orders by e-mail iuporder@indiana.edu

First Midland Book Edition 1990

© 1986 by James H. Madison

The paper used in this publication meets the minimum
requirements of American National Standard for Information
Sciences–Permanence of Paper for Printed Library Materials,
ANSI Z39.48-1984.

Manufactured in the United States of America

Library of Congress Cataloging-in-Publication Data

Madison, James H.
The Indiana way.

Bibliography: p.
Includes index.
1. Indiana—History. I. Title.
F526.M22   1986   977.2   85-45071
ISBN 0-253-32999-X
ISBN 0-253-20609-X (pbk.)

6   7   8   9   10   05   04   03   02   01   00

For Julia and John

CONTENTS

INTRODUCTION   xiii

PART I   Before There Was a State

i   Peoples and Empires before the Americans   3

     Prehistory and Prehistoric Peoples, 3
     The Land, 7
     Contests for Empire, 10
     The British Empire in the West, 1763–1776, 18

ii   The American Nation and the West, 1776–1800   20

     The American Revolution in the West, 1776–1783, 20
     The New Nation and the Northwest Territory, 1783–1800, 27

iii   Indiana Territory and Statehood, 1800–1816   36

     Treaties and Conflicts with Indians, 37
     Government and Politics in Indiana Territory, 1800–1810, 46
     Statehood and the Constitution of 1816, 50

PART II   Pioneer Indiana, 1816–1850

iv   On the Indiana Frontier   57

     Migration and Settlement Patterns, 58
     Land and the Frontier Family Home, 62
     Food, Clothing, and Health, 66

v   The Evolving Pioneer Economy   74

     Rivers and Roads, 75
     Canals and the System of 1836, 82
     Merchants, Bankers, and Manufacturers, 86
     Town Building, 93

vi   Pioneer Community Life   98

     The Protestant Frontier, 98

Morality, Social Order, and Reform, 104
Pioneer Education, 108
The New Harmony Communities, 115

vii Pioneer Government and Politics   121

Land Acquisition and Indian Removal, 122
Government and the General Welfare, 126
Pioneer Politics, 131
The Constitutional Convention of 1850–1851, 138
The Pioneer Legacy, 140

PART III   *Indiana in Transition, 1850–1920*

viii Making a Living, 1850–1920   145

Life on the Farm, 147
The Railroad Age, 153
Industrialization and the Rise of Big Business, 158
Labor and the Workers' World, 163

ix Hoosiers Together, 1850–1920   168

Black Hoosiers, 169
Ethnic Hoosiers, 173
Urban and Small-Town Hoosiers, 175
Educating Hoosiers, 179
Religious Hoosiers, 185
Culture and Leisure, 187

x The Politics of the Civil War Era, 1850–1873   193

The Politics of the 1850s, 194
A Civil War at Home, 197
Reconstruction, 1865–1873, 205

xi The Indiana Way of Politics, 1873–1920   208

Politics, Indiana Style, 1873–1896, 208
The Politics of Moderate Reform, 1890–1916, 218
A Golden Age? 228

Contents

PART IV   Continuity and Change since 1920

xii   The People since 1920   233

Many Kinds of Hoosiers, 234
Black Hoosiers and the Civil Rights "Revolution," 241
The Continuing Challenges of Public School Reform, 247
Basketball and Other Forms of Leisure and Culture, 253

xiii   The Economy since 1920   262

Agriculture and Farm Life, 263
The Automobile Age, 268
The Industrial Economy, 274
Government, Labor, and the Economy, 281

xiv   The Politics of a State   288

The Klan and the Politics of Mediocrity: The 1920s, 289
Liberalism, Ambition, and the New Deal: The 1930s, 295
Party Politics since 1940, 302
State Government since 1940, 308

xv   Hoosiers Past and Present   318

APPENDIXES   323
NOTES   333
A GUIDE TO FURTHER READING   352
INDEX   355

Illustrations

Angel Mounds / 6
"Summer Evening in Vincennes" / 14
"The Capture of Fort Sackville" / 25
Fort Wayne in 1812 / 32
William Henry Harrison / 38
"Death of Captain Wm. Wells" / 42
Capitol at Corydon / 52
Log cabin / 65
Flatboats and steamboat on the Ohio River / 78
Cannelton Cotton Mill / 93
Frontier circuit rider / 101
Abraham Lincoln's sumbook / 109
New Harmony / 118
Second Indiana statehouse / 128
Oliver plow / 148
Indiana state fair / 150
Interurban service / 158
Studebaker factory, South Bend / 161
Evansville's German Day parade / 174
Richmond, 1859 / 178
Golden age authors / 188
Oliver P. Morton / 199
Morgan's Raiders, Salem / 204
Indiana statehouse / 210
Orange County courthouse / 216
One-room schoolhouse, Clinton County / 248
Basketball, Nashville / 254
New state parks / 257
Wes Montgomery / 260
A new plow / 264
Early auto travel, Kendallville / 270
Women workers at Eli Lilly and Company / 275
Boom times at Gary Works, United States Steel / 278
Ku Klux Klan departing church services / 292
Democratic smiles in 1932 / 296
The state song / 320

List of Maps

1. Physiographic Regions / 8
2. Forts and Settlements in the 1750s / 16
3. Indian Treaties / 39
4. Indiana, 1817 / 48
5. Early Routes of Transportation / 76
6. Towns with More Than 2,500 People, 1850 / 96
7. Railroads, 1880 / 156
8. Interurban Lines, with Dates of Abandonment / 159
9. Distribution of Party Strength after the Civil War / 217

Figures

1. Illiteracy and School Enrollment / 112
2. Per Capita Personal Income / 277

Tables

1. Components of Population Change, 1800–1860 / 59
2. Party Preference by Denomination / 214
3. Structure of Earnings / 279
4. Richest and Poorest Indiana Counties, 1982 / 287

Introduction

There have been no revolutions in the history of Indiana. Each generation has sometimes thought it was situated in the midst of radical, even revolutionary change: the pioneer generation that cleared the forests to plant their particular form of civilization; the late nineteenth century generation that struggled with rapid industrialization; those Indianans in the early twentieth century whose experience ranged from Progressive reform to the Ku Klux Klan; and the generation of the mid-twentieth century that witnessed the growth of government power and homogenization of culture and community. These and other changes have brought hope and bewilderment, pride and sorrow, but no great turning point, no watershed, no revolution. Change in Indiana has been evolutionary rather than revolutionary.

The people of Indiana have tended to navigate in the middle of the American mainstream, drifting if anywhere a little closer to the more secure edge of the river. Moderation has been the Indiana way, a moderation firmly anchored in respect for tradition, in appreciation of the achievements of the generations that preceded, particularly of the pioneer generation. Among the revolutions that have not occurred in Indiana is a generational revolt.

Moderation and evolutionary change have not precluded conflict and variation among Hoosiers. There have always been significant differences: between the southern and northern regions of the state, between rural and urban, between Gary and Indianapolis, and between Protestant and Catholic, black and white, Democrat and Republican, working class and capitalist. And the state has produced such different representatives as sex researcher Alfred Kinsey and right-wing politician William Jenner, writers Theodore Dreiser and James Whitcomb Riley, and the builders of the utopian communal settlement at New Harmony and of the family log cabin of Thomas Lincoln.

Hoosiers have never been all alike. Yet there has been a dominant Indiana way—a tradition of individual freedom and responsibility, of intense interest in politics, of wariness of government, particularly when it is located at a distance or is preparing to tax, of attachment to small-town and rural values of community identification and pride, of friendliness and neighborliness. These are American traditions, too, but nowhere are they more firmly rooted and more fully respected. Theirs is the most American of states, Indianans have often claimed. And if other states or regions do not share these traditions it is they who are atypical, not Indiana.

The nature of Indiana's past gives special relevance to its history, for it is a past never dead. Indiana's past and present urge the necessity of appreciating the traditions of moderation, of evolutionary rather than revolutionary change, of broad continuity in the issues, problems, and values that have been at the center of the state's history for more than a century and a half. This book is an introduction to that understanding.

This is not a reference book, however. I have imposed an organizational and interpretive foundation and framework on the content of Indiana history that leads to emphasis on certain subjects and omission of others. Particularly have I tried to show the significance of Indiana's traditions, of the continuity of the state's history even as change occurred. I have tried to place major subjects in the broadest contexts, attempting to keep the reader engaged in the long view of Indiana's past rather than tarrying in the detailed, often fascinating, but sometimes disembodied facts or arcane events of the state's history. Nor have I devoted much space to praise or condemnation. State history has often been provincially laudatory. This book is written with appreciation for the regional, national, and international contexts of Indiana's history and with the suspicion that Hoosiers are neither better nor worse than other residents of the globe. At times, as in treatment of race or education, I have been critical of the dominant Indiana tendencies. Such criticism derives from a respect for Indiana's better traditions and from an occasional assenting nod to the poet's rhetorical question: "Ain't God good to Indiana?" I will not plead the personal non-involvement I might have if I were writing about four-teenth-century China, but I have tried to see the whole of Indiana in contexts other than praise or condemnation. And I have tried to give Indiana's history the serious treatment it deserves, often sacrificing romantic stories and colorful vignettes for analysis.

The book is organized in four parts, chronologically arranged. In each part there are topically organized chapters, usually dealing in turn with economic, social, and political subject matter. Although each chapter is capable of standing alone, a fuller appreciation will derive from reading other chapters in a particular part as well as following the specific subject in the other chronological parts. There are very few cross-references in the text, but a detailed index will help the reader to follow a specific interest. The fullest understanding, how-ever, will come from reading the entire book.

Readers intent on moving beyond this book, particularly in search of more detail and different interpretations and approaches, will find the Guide to Further Reading and the notes most helpful. Rather than full and copious documentation, I have used notes sparingly and primarily to provide guidance for further reading. I have been more generous in citing recently published books and articles, particularly those published since the relevant volumes of the multivolume *History of Indiana*.

The four volumes published thus far in *The History of Indiana* series were indispensable to this study and to any serious study of Indiana's past. Cited in full in the Guide to Further Reading, these volumes were written by John D. Barnhart and Dorothy L. Riker, Emma Lou Thornbrough, Clifton J. Phillips, and James H. Madison. Two other books deserve special mention here because they also were signifi-cantly more important to this book than the notes indicate. R. Carlyle Buley's *The Old Northwest: Pioneer Period, 1815–1840* (2 volumes, In-dianapolis, 1950) very much influenced my treatment of that period. And John D. Barnhart's and Donald F. Carmony's *Indiana: From Fron-tier to Industrial Commonwealth* (4 volumes, New York, 1954) first in-troduced me and my generation of historians to serious treatment of the state's history. It remains useful for many of the topics it treats. I have sometimes disagreed with these fellow historians about choice of subject and interpretation, but in many more instances I have followed trails they have blazed. In the first history of the state, published in 1843, John B. Dillon lamented the need for "laborious investigation of confused traditions, contradictory narratives, and questionable records."[1] The work of several generations of historians since Dillon has made Indiana history a rich field of study—open, accessible, and fully challenging.

Many friends, colleagues, and strangers have contributed to this book. For ten years the history of Indiana has been my primary responsibility as teacher, editor, and author at Indiana University. I am grateful to the university for providing an environment in which I have been able to work productively and enjoyably. In the classroom, I have learned as I have taught the history of Indiana, often prompted by the questions and interests of my students. As editor of the *Indiana Magazine of History* I have benefited from the work of authors, editorial referees, and the magazine staff, especially Associate Editor Lorna Lutes Sylvester. And as scholar I have had the support of history department colleagues and of fine university librarians. In addition, the university's Research and Graduate Development Office supported a preliminary gathering of census data, ably done by Thomas Rodgers. Some of these data are included in Appendix A. And the university granted me a sabbatical leave in the fall of 1984 that freed me from teaching and other responsibilities. Support from the Ball Brothers Foundation to mark the Bicentennial of the United States constitution contributed to preparation of my lecture, delivered at Indiana University and Butler University in 1985, on Indiana's place in the federal system: some of the research for that lecture is incorporated into this book. I must note also that drafts of several chapters were written while I was teaching American history at the University of Kent, Canterbury, England. My British colleagues and students knew nothing about Indiana, but in helping distance me from the state they aided me to better understand it.

Several friends deserve special thanks: Ralph D. Gray and L. C. Rudolph read the entire manuscript and made many useful sugges-

---

1. John B. Dillon, *The History of Indiana from Its Earliest Explorations by Europeans, to the Close of the Territorial Government in 1816* (Indianapolis, 1843), iv.

tions and corrections. I benefited too from the comments of an anonymous university press reader. I am also grateful to Jack New, who helped me understand recent Indiana politics, and to Morton Marcus, who contributed to my understanding of the recent Indiana economy. Bobbi Diehl expertly edited the manuscript—and remained a friend. Many people helped gather illustrations: I am especially appreciative of the aid provided by Eileen Fry, Delores Lahrman, Donald L. Maxwell, Cheryl Munson, Timothy E. Peterson, and Saundra Taylor. My largest debts are always to my wife, Jeanne, whose principled refusal to be my research assistant or typist helps make her so important to me. The dedication to my children is a father's meager thanks.

To all who helped, I am grateful. For the errors that remain I am responsible.

PART I

Before There Was a State

Peoples and Empires before the Americans

When Indiana became a state in 1816, it was a state and a people subject to a dominant American political and cultural influence. But the American hegemony that prevailed in 1816 had not formed on a blank slate. English, French, and other European influences were present earlier. So too were those of various Indian tribes. These peoples and empires before the Americans played a significant part in shaping the early history of Indiana.

Prehistory and Prehistoric Peoples

Long before the French, English, and other Europeans reached that part of North America that became Indiana there lived there peoples of varying cultures commonly referred to as native Americans or Indians. There are no written records of these prehistoric peoples, and scholars know nothing about them as individuals and little about specific events of their lives. But by relying on evidence from physical artifacts (particularly projectile points), burial remains, and man-made changes in the natural landscape archaeologists have been able to portray the broad features of prehistoric native American cultures and to suggest patterns of cultural change and continuity over thousands of years, as long ago as 11,000 B.C.[1]

One way of studying Indiana's prehistoric peoples is to approach the centuries prior to about 1600 A.D. in terms of four cultural traditions, each occurring within a broadly distinctive chronological period: the Paleo-Indian Tradition, the Archaic Tradition, the Woodland Tradition, and the Mississippian Tradition.

The Paleo-Indian Tradition (to about 8000 B.C.) is the earliest and most ambiguous of the four cultural traditions. In parts of North America there is evidence that in the waning years of the Ice Age men hunted for food, using spears to kill now-extinct animals like bison, mammoth, and mastodon. Thus far, direct evidence for this kind of big game hunting in Indiana is not conclusive. Archaeologists have found in Indiana evidence of human life in this period in the form of fluted points—man-made projectile points with grooves or flutes on both sides of the blade, once attached to a spear.

The Archaic Tradition (8000 B.C. to 1000 B.C.) covers a prehistoric period in which the harsh conditions of the Ice Age gave way to climate, trees, and plants similar to those encountered by the first European explorers. Human life changed too, as people adapted to environmental change. Archaeologists have found for this period more efficient tools, evidence of some trade over wide geographical areas, and artifacts associated with ceremonial burials. Evidence of success in finding reliable food sources exists in the numerous mussel shell mounds in southwestern Indiana. Clues like these shell mounds are indications that people were by then living in groups and adapting their culture to local conditions.

The Woodland Tradition (1000 B.C. to A.D. 900) includes a continuation of reliance on hunting, fishing, and gathering, but also the beginnings of some plant cultivation, particularly maize. Change is most apparent in the appearance of fire-hardened pottery containers, representing a new achievement in human endeavor. Woodland peoples made ceramic pots, with different clays, shapes, and decorations, all of which enable archaeologists to sort out prehistoric cultures and establish time periods. The Woodland period also brought complex burial rituals, including the construction of burial mounds, such as those still evident at Mounds State Park near Anderson. There, the largest earthwork structure is six feet in height and 360 feet in diameter, and once included several burials, pottery, and other artifacts. Large complexes such as this suggest concentration and cooperation of peoples beyond the small family group.

The Mississippian Tradition (A.D. 900 to A.D. 1600) is the last and most complex of the four prehistoric traditions. It includes intensive cultivation of maize, beans, squash, and tobacco, permanently located settlements of several hundred people, and community structures and institutions that served political and religious functions. The most impressive of such sites in Indiana is Angel Mounds, near Evansville on the Ohio River. The Angel Mounds site included a large log stockade, a mound measuring 650 by 300 by 44 feet, and several smaller mounds, which probably served community functions. The village also contained about two hundred houses constructed of wood posts and cane mats covered with daub. The residents skillfully crafted pottery, tools, and items of personal adornment. Angel Mounds was the most complex Mississippian village, but there were many others in the lower Wabash and Ohio river valleys. For reasons not known, these people left Indiana about A.D. 1600 and were not observed by European explorers or settlers.[2]

Archaeologists and historians have not been able to connect the prehistoric Indians who lived in Indiana before 1600 with the historic Indians, those observed and met by white Europeans and American colonists. Indeed, the major historic Indians, the Miamis and the Potawatomis, did not settle in Indiana until the late seventeenth or early eighteenth centuries. Efforts to determine relationships between the pottery, tools, and other artifacts of prehistoric and historic Indians have not been successful, in part because by 1700 European-made items rapidly replaced or altered Indian artifacts.

If we do not know about individuals at all and only generally about

The Temple Mound (Mound F) at Angel Mounds (State Memorial), showing the excavated wall posts and wall trenches of one building stage. (Indiana Historical Society and Glenn A. Black Laboratory of Archaeology,
Indiana University)

any specific time period before 1600, it is nevertheless evident that
rich and varied cultures existed in the part of North America that
became Indiana and that these cultures changed through the centuries. And work continues as archaeologists dig for the artifacts and
the intellectual methods and concepts that may enable us to know
more about these very first people.[3]

The Land

The European explorers who in the seventeenth century crossed what would become Indiana found a land little changed by thousands of years of human habitation, though not a virgin land in the purest sense; prehistoric Indians had lived in ways that left few apparent effects on the natural landscape and environment. Indeed, the explorers and early white settlers found their lives in Indiana shaped less by the prehistoric people who had preceded them than by the land itself. That land and natural environment would continue to play a role in the lives of all who followed.[4]

The most important feature of the land for the history of Indiana is that it is not uniform but rather varies considerably in natural features (see Map 1). The primary difference is between the southern one-third and northern two-thirds of the state. Southern Indiana is hill country, the consequence of being relatively less affected by the glaciers that in the northern two-thirds of the state left behind a much flatter terrain and richer soil. The soil of much of southern Indiana is of comparatively poor quality, the terrain rough and uneven, although the southeastern and particularly the southwestern corners contain flatter lands and richer soils than the unglaciated triangle extending southward from Monroe County to the Ohio River. Although the hill country of southern Indiana was attractive to the first settlers, it became increasingly less so in the nineteenth century as the land proved less suited to commercial agriculture and to the construction of railroads. Nor, with the exception of coal in the southwestern section and limestone in Lawrence and Monroe counties, are there significant mineral resources to compensate for the inferior quality of soil and terrain.

The glaciers that served southern Indiana so poorly left behind in central Indiana deep, fertile soil and generally level terrain. By the late nineteenth century this area would constitute some of the most productive farmland on the face of the earth. The northernmost part of the state also includes much fertile soil but is not as flat and contains such areas as the Kankakee Valley that were marshy and unsuited to Indian or pioneer agriculture.

As important as terrain and soil to the history of Indiana are the

MAP 1.
Physiographic Regions

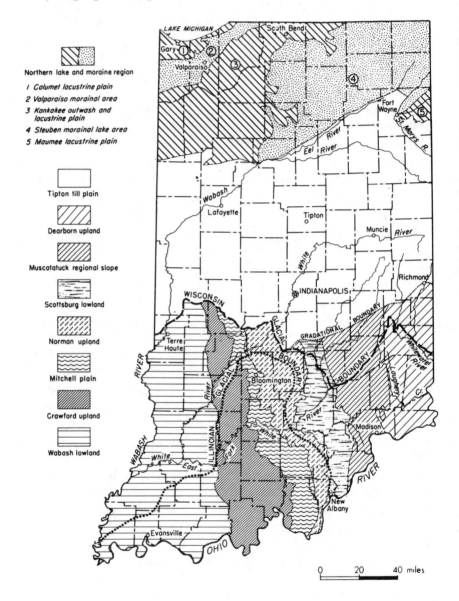

Northern lake and moraine region

1 Calumet lacustrine plain
2 Valparaiso morainal area
3 Kankakee outwash and
   lacustrine plain
4 Steuben morainal lake area
5 Maumee lacustrine plain

Tipton till plain

Dearborn upland

Muscatatuck regional slope

Scottsburg lowland

Norman upland

Mitchell plain

Crawford upland

Wabash lowland

SOURCE: Robert C. Kingsbury, *An Atlas of Indiana* (Bloomington, 1970), 14

rivers and lakes formed after the glaciers receded. Here too there is variation within the state. The first European explorers and traders came via Lake Michigan and paddled and portaged the streams and rivers, particularly the St. Joseph of Lake Michigan, the Kankakee, the Maumee, and the Wabash. The Maumee-Wabash route was the most important, connecting Lake Erie and northern Indiana with the Ohio River and from there to the Mississippi River. The headwaters of the Maumee, formed by the joining of the St. Mary's and the St. Joseph of the Maumee, was the most strategic location in the region and served in turn as the site of an Indian village, a French trading post, an American fort, and the city of Fort Wayne. This location provided access to Lake Erie and with a portage overland to the Wabash River.

The people of southern Indiana were served by the lower Wabash and its tributaries, particularly the White River, and by the Ohio River, which became a major migration route to Indiana. Until the mid-nineteenth century most Indian and white settlements were made along these rivers and the streams that flowed into them.

Indiana's soil, terrain, and rivers have been important determinants of the way people have lived. So too has been climate. The climate allows for a variety of endeavors and is particularly suited for agriculture. Hot summer days and nights, long months between killing frosts, and generally adequate and dependable rainfall during the growing season have helped shape the agricultural development of the state, particularly the emphasis on growing corn, which preceded the Europeans and continues to the present.

The natural environment—the soil, terrain, rivers, and climate—played a large role in Indiana's history. It helped shape the nature and direction of settlement, the distribution of population, the choices of economic activity, and some of the variations of people within the state. So too has the natural environment been affected by people, for in using it to their individual benefit they have changed and sometimes abused the land, water, and air. Eroded and depleted soil and polluted rivers and streams constitute evidence of a different kind of people in the four centuries since prehistoric peoples left the region.

These new people—Europeans, Americans, Hoosiers—made use of the land in different ways, and, while constrained and shaped by the land, also brought with them and developed further ways to live that allowed for considerable freedom and choice in their individual and community lives. The land shaped them, but they also shaped the land and their society. In the end, not nature but people made Indiana's history.

Contests for Empire

Through the seventeenth and eighteenth centuries the land that was to become Indiana was the scene of intense conflict and dramatic change among peoples of very different cultures. The first peoples, the native Americans, were themselves diverse and changing, before and after they came into contact with Europeans, particularly the French explorers, traders, and missionaries. Trade relationships and alliances between the French and Indians, though sometimes volatile, constituted one of the dominant features of the century prior to French expulsion from North America in 1763. A second major theme, one that became increasingly important in the eighteenth century, was the growing population size and economic and military strength of the English and American colonists. Huddled near the Atlantic coast in the seventeenth century, the Anglo-Americans began in the eighteenth century to venture across the Appalachian Mountain barrier, first to challenge French ties to the various Indian tribes and then to challenge the very right of the Indians themselves to occupy and use the land. These conflicts brought bloodshed and triumph, destruction and wealth, humiliation and pride as war and conquest joined cultural and economic influences to change the way all peoples lived.[5]

The people there first and in largest numbers in the seventeenth and early eighteenth centuries were the Indians. Many Indian tribes lived in the area that became Indiana, but the most important were the Miamis and the Potawatomis. In the early eighteenth century, after the Iroquois military power in the region had declined, Miamis and Potawatomis migrated eastward to settle near the Wabash, Maumee, and Miami rivers, generally avoiding the unglaciated region between the Ohio and White rivers. The Potawatomis concentrated north of the Wabash and along Lake Michigan. The Wea band of Miamis located their villages on the middle Wabash, between the Tippecanoe and Vermillion rivers, while the Piankeshaw band of Miamis settled on the lower Wabash. The Detroit band moved to the head of the Maumee River, and at that location, which they called Kekionga (and Americans would rename Fort Wayne), they built the most important Miami village. Kekionga was the meeting ground of the Miami tribal council, and it was one of the most significant strategic locations in the trans-Appalachian West, a major portage on the best route between Lake Erie and the Gulf of Mexico.

The Miamis and Potawatomis lived in scattered villages and engaged in extensive agriculture, raising melons, squash, pumpkins, beans, and, most important, corn. Corn was a staple of their diet, and both tribes engaged in some trade of corn to the French and to other tribes. They also gathered berries, nuts, and roots; collected maple sugar; hunted deer, bison, bear, and small game; and caught a variety of fish in nearby streams and lakes. They made their clothing of animal skins, mostly deer, prepared with a skill white settlers on the frontier were seldom able to match. They built houses of poles covered with bark or mats woven from cattails. Their daily life adjusted to the rhythm of the seasons, with times of planting and harvest, of abundance and scarcity, of winter hunts and summer games, of war and peace. And they lived in extended families, often with several generations forming a single unit and with several families gathered in a clan. Work and most aspects of life included sexual divisions in which men hunted, trapped, traded, and fought, while women tended the fields, cooked, made clothing, and cared for the children. Young boys and girls quickly learned their different sex roles through play and daily chores, with special attention to the role of warrior for boys. Religion included elaborate rituals, belief in life after death, and a world full of good and evil spirits. The tribes engaged in a variety of social activities and games, including lacrosse, which the Potawatomis played with great skill. Harvest festivals and other occasions were celebrated with games, dance, and music. Political life in both tribes was decentralized, with the authority of village chiefs dependent more on their personal influence than formal position. Potawatomi leadership was especially unstructured; in times of war a prominent chief often led several villages, but it was seldom the case that one chief could legitimately speak for all Potawatomis. The Miamis had a more structured leadership system which included a principal chief and a grand council of village, band, and clan chiefs who met at Kekionga. No leader possessed authority over all Indians in the region; for white traders and treaty negotiators it was often unclear which Indian leader possessed relevant authority.[6]

French contact with Miamis, Potawatomis, and other native Americans brought rapid adjustment and change. Although they resisted some European ways and struggled to retain their cultural and political independence, most Indians quickly adopted the superior elements of European technology and material goods. Iron and brass tools and weapons, woven cloth, and decorative items were far more desirable than items made of stone, clay, wood, and skin. After 1700 guns, knives, kettles, axes, hoes, traps, colored clothing, and alcohol became increasingly important to Indians. Their dependence on these items required them to devote large attention to the requirements of trade and particularly to trapping and transporting the furs which Europeans so eagerly sought. For the Potawatomis and Miamis this fur trade was largely with the French and evolved from an economic relationship to a diplomatic alliance. The relationship had broader consequences as well: the French constituted an indirect threat to tribal unity, in the form of an extratribal authority; a direct threat to Indian religious beliefs in the form of French Catholic missionaries; and the actuality of Indian population decline as the consequence of European disease, particularly smallpox. Potawatomi and Miami culture adjusted and changed as the people came into increased contact with the French and other Europeans.[7]

New France took root at Quebec in 1608 and soon flourished as French explorers, missionaries, and traders traversed the land from the Great Lakes to the Mississippi River to the Gulf of Mexico. Robert Cavelier de La Salle entered Indiana in 1679, though unknown Frenchmen may have preceded him. By the early eighteenth century the French had developed important trade and diplomatic relationships with the Miamis, Potawatomis, and other Indians of the region.

French policy generally was based on mutual economic advantage and on cooperation and persuasion rather than command or coercion of Indian allies. The French fur trade constituted the economic foundation of the empire and did not directly challenge Indian occupation and use of the land. The French did not turn their trading posts and forts into large settlements, and their population in North America remained small (about 75,000 in 1763, compared to 1,250,000 people in the English colonies). And French traders, particularly the *coureurs de bois*, the "woods runners" who sought pelts in the interior of the continent, skillfully learned Indian ways and often married Indian women. Thus French presence, though it certainly changed Indian culture, was generally not abrasive or harsh and was usually welcomed by the Indians, unlike the American presence of the late eighteenth and early nineteenth centuries.[8]

The French policy of harmony and cooperation did not mean an absence of conflict, however. There were conflicts between Indian tribes in which the French became engaged and which they attempted to use to their advantage. But most important, there was the new threat from the East as Anglo-American traders began in the early 1700s to cross the Appalachian Mountains and to challenge French domination of the fur trade. To meet this challenge the French in the decade and a half after 1715 built three palisaded forts along the strategic Wabash-Maumee route: Ouiatanon, near present-day Lafayette; Fort Miamis, at the village of Kekionga; and Post Vincennes, on the lower Wabash (see Map 2). These posts represented France's easternmost line of defense and were designed to provide military protection for traders and their Indian allies and thereby to ensure continued French domination of the fur trade. The first two forts, on the upper Wabash, were under the authority of French Canada, while the last built, Vincennes, was the outpost of France's Louisiana colony.

The bloodiest early conflicts associated with any of these Wabash-Maumee posts came in the raids against the Chickasaw in the 1730s, particularly the expedition of 1736, sometimes labeled "Indiana's first war." The Chickasaw were a fierce warrior tribe of the South who did not bend to French influence but allied themselves with the British. Chickasaw warriors carried this animosity as far north as the Wabash villages. The French mounted several expeditions of Miamis, Potawatomis, and other Indians against the Chickasaw. The disastrous expedition of 1736 enlisted the young Sieur de Vincennes, founder and commandant of Post Vincennes, and many of his men, joined by Indian allies from the Wabash Valley. The Chickasaw routed the invaders. Among those taken prisoner was Vincennes, who was tortured

"A Summer Evening in Vincennes" (A. L. Mason, *The Romance and Tragedy of Pioneer Life* [Cincinnati, 1884], 147)

MAP 2.

Forts and Settlements in the 1750s

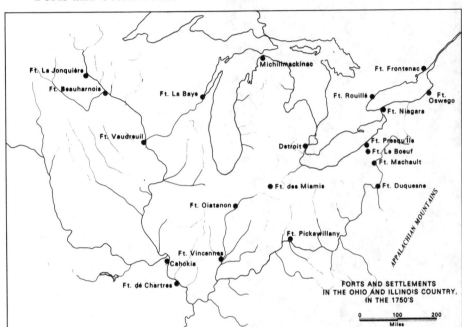

SOURCE: George A. Rawlyk, "The 'Rising French Empire' in the Ohio Valley and Old Northwest," in John B. Elliott, ed., *Contest for Empire, 1500–1775: Proceedings of an Indiana American Revolution Bicentennial Symposium* (Indianapolis, 1975), 43

and burned at the stake. Post Vincennes was decimated by this defeat, since not only the commandant but most of the garrison and many other men were lost.

The Chickasaw threat from the South was soon overshadowed by the Anglo-American threat from the East. By the 1740s Pennsylvania traders were presenting serious competition to French domination of the fur trade west of the Appalachian Mountains. The leading Pennsylvania trader, George Croghan, sent his men through the Ohio Valley and as far west as the Wabash. Partly because of the nascent English industrial revolution and superior British sea power the Pennsylvania traders could offer goods that were better, cheaper, and more abundant than French goods. The Indians knew bargains in trade and welcomed this new competition. Indeed, in 1747 Piankeshaw Chief

La Demoiselle decided to move closer to the Pennsylvania traders and left the Kekionga area to establish the new village of Pickawillany, near present-day Piqua, Ohio. There Croghan and others erected and maintained a fortified trading post. Other Miami bands soon moved to Pickawillany, which by 1750 threatened to replace Kekionga as the most important Miami village. Reflecting this shift, La Demoiselle became known as "Old Britain" and "Great King of the Miamis," although he was not in fact the principal chief of the tribe.

The new situation that developed in the 1740s in the remote Ohio Country was part of a much broader and more important conflict—the struggle between Britain and France for empire in North America and for hegemony elsewhere in the western world. The two nations were often at war in the period between 1689 and 1763, and while North America was never central to their conflict it became increasingly important as a source of friction and eventually as a bloody battleground. The friendship and trade between the Pennsylvania traders and La Demoiselle and other Miamis at Pickawillany was one such friction point, for the French quickly realized that their profitable fur trade, their Indian alliances, and their Wabash-Maumee route between Canada and Louisiana were in serious jeopardy. To secure these foundations of empire the French decided to eliminate the specific threat of Pickawillany and move their effective eastern boundary from the Wabash-Maumee line to the Allegheny and upper Ohio rivers. A French expedition attempted just that in 1749 but was too weak to do more than bury lead plates on riverbanks asserting possession of the Ohio Country for the King of France. In 1752, however, another expedition, led by Charles-Michel Mouet, Sieur de Langlade, mounted a successful surprise attack on Pickawillany. The French and their Indian allies killed Chief La Demoiselle and boiled and ate his body. Then they forced the Pennsylvania traders across the mountains and pushed the Miamis back to their original villages. France then moved to consolidate control of the Ohio Country, culminating in the erection in 1754 of Fort Duquesne at the forks of the Ohio River. This aggressive move by France sparked a British countermove, beginning with General Edward Braddock's foolish and disastrous campaign in western Pennsylvania in 1755, by which time Britain and France were well on the way to a major war, known in Europe as the Seven Years War and in America as the French and Indian War.

France achieved initial success in the struggle, aided by Potawatomi warriors who terrorized frontier settlements in western Pennsylvania, Virginia, and New York. The Miamis, weakened by smallpox and by the dissension reflected in the rise and fall of Pickawillany, played a much smaller military role, though they professed renewed French allegiance and partook again of French trade. British victories in the late 1750s and the peace treaty signed at Paris in 1763 removed France from North America, diminishing French trade and ending the empire and the Indian alliances that had so shaped the lives of peoples in the Wabash-Maumee valleys.[9]

The British Empire in the West, 1763–1776

The English victory in the French and Indian War left them in control of North America east of the Mississippi River but soon facing serious challenges from American colonists and Indians. To meet these challenges as they applied in the West and to secure the benefits of empire generally the British embarked on a zig-zag course designed to provide central regulation of Indian trade; restrain white invasion of Indian territory; and encourage orderly disposal of unsettled land. It was a course that could not succeed, as it not only failed to attain the goals of empire but contributed also to the loss of the American colonies.

The first challenge came from the Indians in the form of Pontiac's Rebellion of 1763. British military victories over the French and Indians included the capture of Detroit in 1760 and the occupation of Forts Miamis, Ouiatanon, and other former French posts in the West. To Miamis, Potawatomis, and other native Americans the new empire compared most unfavorably with the French empire they had known for a century. The British traders and military officers seemed less respectful of Indian customs and more inclined to think only of immediate profit and gain. Sir Jeffrey Amherst, commander of British forces in America, attempted to restrict the former French practice of giving presents and liquor to friendly Indians. Like other British authorities he showed a superciliousness and disdain toward Indians, an attitude based on very little knowledge of them. Amherst later went so far as to suggest the possibility of sending smallpox-infected blankets to Indians as a way to reduce their threat to British control.

Indians were well aware of English attitudes. Led by Ottawa Chief Pontiac in 1763, several tribes, including the Miamis and Potawatomis, joined in a general rebellion against the British. They laid siege to Detroit and captured Forts Miamis, Ouiatanon, and others. Pontiac's Rebellion was one of the most significant attempts at Indian unity in the West. It succeeded spectacularly but only for a short while. British military strength and news of the treaty signed at Paris in 1763, with a consequent end to hope of French aid, discouraged Pontiac's followers. And, as in other later attempts at Indian unity, no tribe proved willing to jeopardize its independence by a subordinate position in an Indian alliance.

Although the Indians could not dislodge the British from the West, Indian military strength and trade potential remained important after 1763 and contributed to shaping the momentous British western policy laid down in late 1763. The Proclamation of 1763 was a British attempt to curry Indian favor by prohibiting American colonists from settling beyond the Appalachian Mountains. The territory west of this proclamation line was reserved for Indians and licensed fur traders, to the dismay and anger of American land speculators and settlers eager to move west now that the French were defeated. The Proclamation of 1763 made no provision for French settlements, such as that at Vincennes.

British trade in the trans-Appalachian West never provided the profits anticipated, in part because many Indians continued to prefer dealing with French traders, now based west of the Mississippi. On the Wabash, British trade suffered because the financially pressed empire never succeeded in fully establishing trading posts and garrisons there, leaving the Indians free of British influence and susceptible to French traders.

Nor did the proclamation line of 1763 succeed in keeping land speculators and settlers east of the mountains. In the 1760s they surged into western Pennsylvania. In the 1770s they followed the trail of Daniel Boone and other "long hunters" into the Kentucky bluegrass region. This American pressure from the East had not yet directly affected the Wabash tribes, but they had heard sad tales told by Indians who had been displaced by American expansion. Their opportunity to stem this westward movement would come from the ever-widening split between the rulers of the British empire and the American colonies.[10]

The American Nation and the West, 1776–1800

During the last quarter of the eighteenth century the pace of change quickened in the area that became Indiana. The British strengthened and then lost their empire, a loss to which Indiana's most celebrated hero, George Rogers Clark, contributed. But American control of the territory northwest of the Ohio River brought major problems for the new nation—problems of Indian-white conflict, of land disposition, and of government structure and control.[1]

The American Revolution in the West, 1776–1783

The fighting that began at Lexington-Concord in 1775 and the eventual Declaration of Independence from Britain in July, 1776, did not have immediate cause or consequence in the territory west of the Appalachians. American grievances against the mother country did include western issues, however, particularly the Proclamation of 1763 and the Quebec Act of 1774. The latter act further discouraged American westward expansion by incorporating the territory north of the Ohio River into the Province of Quebec and allowing for protection of Indians and of Catholicism by exclusion of Americans. But British exclusions of Americans from the West were only a small part of a much broader conspiracy, so Americans came to believe—a conspiracy in which the mother country had set out to deny colonials their rights and freedoms. As the movement for freedom and independence evolved into full-scale war the West became increasingly important to each side as a place to strike at the other.[2]

The War for Independence in the West was largely a war for control of the Indians in the region. Neither the British nor Americans were able to place and supply large numbers of troops there or mount a major campaign. Guerrilla tactics predominated as each side attempted quick, surprise attacks. In such warfare the Indians were central, as American and British leaders well knew.

The British made the most effective use of the Indians, often convincing them that it was the American rebels who would take Indian land if not stopped. The primary British base in the West was Detroit, commanded by Lieutenant Governor Henry Hamilton, an unusually skilled and astute Indian negotiator. In 1777, Hamilton received orders to use the Indians to full advantage. He did just that. In June he convened a gathering of tribes, including Miamis and Potawatomis, and urged them to take up the hatchet. In war paint and Indian dress Hamilton himself sang the war song. Most important, he provided the Indians with large amounts of food, guns, knives, and other supplies. Thus began in 1777 a pattern of British-supported Indian raids across the Ohio River, directed particularly at white settlements in Kentucky. The war cries of the "year of the three sevens," the "bloody year," were long remembered on the frontier as British-supplied scalping knives and guns brought death and threatened the very existence of white settlement west of the mountains. Although Hamilton had urged his Indian allies not to harm women and children and to return prisoners alive, the conditions of frontier warfare were often those of total war, affecting all people regardless of age, sex, or race. Not only Indians but white frontiersmen too often considered the death of enemy women and children legitimate methods of war. Whites as well as Indians engaged in the practice of scalping and committed atrocities of savage proportions. To the American frontiersmen the real culprits were Hamilton and his fellow redcoats. Hamilton became the most hated British figure, known to all as the "hairbuyer general," the redcoat who paid bounties to Indians for white scalps. (There is no conclusive evidence of such bounty payments, though Hamilton did accept scalps from his Indian allies.) Hatred, fear, atrocity, and bloodshed thus mixed in large quantities in 1777, setting a pattern that would continue long after the war was over.[3]

As the Americans in Kentucky huddled in their forts in 1777 one of them, a twenty-five-year-old surveyor and major in the militia, decided that the best defense from Indian attack was a daring offense. George Rogers Clark's aggressive self-confidence and audacious military strategy would make him the American hero of the war in the West.[4]

Kentucky was a county of Virginia in 1777, and in October of that year the tall, red-headed Clark set out to present his plan of offense to the Virginia governor, Patrick Henry. Clark convinced Governor Henry and his advisers, including Thomas Jefferson, that the defense of Kentucky could be achieved by taking the old French villages located at strategic points on the Mississippi and Wabash rivers. Though Clark's motives and goals remain uncertain, it appears that his ultimate objective was to outflank the British and move up the Wabash and take Detroit, thereby bringing an end to the British-incited Indian raids. It is likely too that Clark and his Virginia and Kentucky associates were also interested in securing for themselves land claims in the West, so that individual self-interest mixed with bold self-defense and admirable patriotism.

In the spring of 1778, with the backing of the Virginia government, Clark and about 175 men set off down the Ohio. Resting and drilling at the Falls of the Ohio (near present-day Louisville), they then proceeded as far down river as the mouth of the Tennessee and then struck overland across the Illinois Country. On July 4 they reached their destination, the French village of Kaskaskia on the Mississippi River. With no resistance they took captive the British agent there and won oaths of allegiance from the French inhabitants in Kaskaskia and also in Cahokia, sixty miles to the north. Clark also sent Captain Leonard Helm to Vincennes, where the British had built a fort (Fort Sackville) and then had abandoned it. The French inhabitants there also took the oath of allegiance to Virginia. Perhaps most important, Clark skillfully convinced the Indians near all three towns that he and his "long knives" were the most powerful force in the West.

News of Clark's invasion of the Illinois Country reached Lieutenant Governor Hamilton at Detroit in August, 1778, spurring him to counterattack. With a force of British redcoats, French militia, and Indians, Hamilton set off for the Maumee-Wabash route. At Kekionga he won several hundred Indians to his cause as war belts passed and as Hamilton joined in singing the war songs. After a difficult crossing of the portage, Hamilton and his forty boats moved down the Wabash, attracting additional support from tribes in the area and reaching Vincennes in mid-December, 1778. At the sight of Hamilton's force the French militia guarding the fort deserted, leaving Captain Helm no practical course but surrender. Once more Fort Sackville was in British hands, and once more the inhabitants, who Hamilton reported numbered 621, took an oath of allegiance to Britain. In one of Vincennes's first reform campaigns, Hamilton immediately destroyed two billiard tables and confiscated all liquor, "the source," he wrote, "of immorality & dissipation."[5] More important, he set about rebuilding and strengthening the fort, intending to remain there until spring when he planned to march on Clark at Kaskaskia. And, not expecting to fight for several months, he allowed many of his Indian and French allies to return to their homes.

On learning of Hamilton's success at Fort Sackville, Clark boldly decided that the only chance of victory was a midwinter surprise attack. He wrote Virginia Governor Henry: "we must Either Quit the Cuntrey or attack Mr. Hamilton. . . . Great Things have been affected by a few Men well Conducted."[6] On February 6, 1779, Clark left Kaskaskia with about 170 men, half of them French volunteers. Unseasonably warm weather had melted snow and ice which combined with cold rain to flood rivers and lowlands, so that the men waded through water, sometimes to their waists, over much of the 180-mile journey. The last few miles, where the Wabash and smaller rivers had flooded their banks, were the most difficult, especially because the men were exhausted and their food supplies nearly gone. Clark pushed them forward with skillful discipline and encouragement. They took Hamilton by surprise. He refused immediate surrender, but as the Americans' deadly fire began to have effect and as he realized that his French militia would not continue to fight he agreed to meet with Clark in front of the fort. Clark demanded unconditional surrender and at first threatened to treat the "hairbuyer general" as a murderer. To further intimidate his opponents Clark ordered four pro-British Indians brought to the gates of the fort where his men savagely tomahawked and scalped them. Hamilton surrendered, and the Americans' flag was raised over the fort, which Clark now named Fort Patrick Henry.

Clark had boldly stymied Hamilton's potentially successful plan to solidify British control of the West and to build a British fire in the rear of the American military effort east of the mountains. His victory at Vincennes in 1779 served also to convince the Indian tribes along the Wabash that their best interests were in a pro-American or neutral stance in the conflict between Britain and America, a position Clark strongly encouraged by threat of punishment, by assurances that he had no wish to take their lands, and by very one-sided accounts of the nature of the American conflict with Britain. His was the major American victory in the West, a military feat that testified to the courage and skill of Clark and his frontier army.

With the defeat of Hamilton at Vincennes, Clark hoped to march on Detroit and eliminate completely the British and Indian threat in the West. But his men and supplies were exhausted and replacements unobtainable. The Detroit campaign had to be postponed. Indeed, American efforts to mount an attack on Detroit met failure after failure in the next few years, giving the British time to recoup and regain their position with the Indians in the upper Wabash and Ohio country.

While Clark met frustration and delay, a Frenchman took matters into his own hands. Augustin de la Balme joined the American cause with the Franco-American alliance of 1778. In 1780 he mounted an expedition against Detroit. Enlisting French inhabitants and Indians in Kaskaskia and Vincennes, some of whom were unhappy with American rule, La Balme moved up the Wabash in October, 1780. He attacked and destroyed Kekionga, but the Miamis regrouped and soon routed the French invaders, killing most of them, including La

"The Capture of Fort Sackville," by Frederick C. Yohn. (Indiana Historical Bureau)

Balme. This battle brought to the forefront Little Turtle, the most important Miami war chief and a leader who would play a major role on the frontier for the next thirty years.

La Balme's disastrous failure in 1780 did not deter Clark. In 1781 he set out at last on a campaign to take Detroit, beginning from Fort Pitt at the forks of the Ohio and moving down river. A part of his forces, a hundred or more Pennsylvanians commanded by Colonel Archibald Lochry, had delayed their departure and followed several days behind Clark. On August 24, 1781, Lochry and his men landed near present-day Aurora, Indiana, preparing to eat and rest. The brilliant Iroquois Chief Joseph Brant, far from his base in New York, had learned of the expedition and was waiting. His war party attacked and killed a third of the Pennsylvanians and captured the rest. Lochry's defeat was a major blow to Clark's hopes, which diminished further when the Virginia legislature withdrew support for the expedition. Lacking supplies and men, Clark was forced from an offensive to defensive strategy, taking his position at the fort he built in the new town of Louisville. Gloomy and disheartened, he lamented: "my chain appears to have run out."[7]

The years from 1779 to 1782 were not happy ones for Clark and many other Americans in the West. British strength grew, and many Indians returned to the British fold, taking up British-supplied hatchets to carry bloody raids across the Ohio. The war in the West became a military stalemate, neither side able to defeat or dislodge the other. To the east of the mountains, however, the long war ended with George Washington's victory at Yorktown in late 1781, preparing the way for a negotiated peace.

Of the many questions facing the peacemakers who met in Paris, one of the most important was location of the boundaries of the United States. In gaining British agreement to an American boundary at the Mississippi River rather than the Ohio, Maumee-Wabash, or some other point to the east, the American negotiators won a major victory. Historians have long debated the causes of this victory and particularly the role of Clark's campaign of 1778–1779 in achieving it.[8] There is no doubt that many diplomatic considerations influenced the final form of the treaty signed in 1783. Certainly also Clark's admirers have often overstated the effect of his campaigns on the Paris negotiators. But the general American pressure in the West, including that of Clark, was a major factor. Americans themselves had begun to see the potential of the West and to act on it. By 1780 there were between 10,000 and 20,000 settlers in Kentucky, putting down roots, laying claims for themselves and their new nation, and proving by their presence that they were determined not only to stay but to grow in numbers and expand geographically. Clark's march to Kaskaskia and Vincennes was the most important statement of this American pressure and its claims for the future.

The American Revolution and the Treaty of 1783 brought the new land to the new nation, but only in the eyes of the Americans. The British after 1783 found immediate and complete surrender of their northwest posts impossible. The French inhabitants remained skeptical of American willingness to tolerate French culture. And most important, the Indians regarded the Treaty of 1783 as inconsequential. They were not parties to it and did not believe that the land was any different than it had always been—theirs to hunt and to farm. The land had never belonged to the French or to the English, and they saw no reason why the Americans should conclude it belonged to them. But in fact the Miamis, Potawatomis, and other Indians would soon learn that the American people, their culture, and their government were different from their white predecessors. The years after 1783 would be marked by less accommodation and more conflict as the new nation and new empire asserted full and ever expanding claim to the land.

The New Nation and the Northwest Territory, 1783–1800

Three major problems faced the new nation and its people as they looked to the West, to the land they called the Northwest Territory, bounded by the Appalachian Mountains, the Ohio and Mississippi rivers, and the Great Lakes. For land-hungry pioneers the West's attractions were irresistible, yet the dangers and obstacles to settlement were immense. The most immediate challenge was the Indian insistence that the land belonged to them and that there should be no white settlement north of the Ohio. In this insistence the Indians received considerable support from the British, who although they had surrendered the territory in 1783 continued to occupy their forts at Detroit and elsewhere. A second problem inhibiting white settlement in the Northwest was the need to develop a means of orderly and democratic transfer of the land from the federal government to individual settlers. And finally, there was the problem of providing a system of government for the people of the frontier, a government that would be responsive to their needs and also fit into the evolving federal system. Each of these three problems deterred white settlement of the Northwest Territory. Each had to be solved before there would be large numbers of Americans living on the land that became Indiana.

The Indians, land sales, and frontier government presented challenges which the new government of the United States met only imperfectly. During this period the American people created and adjusted their system of national government, first in the Articles of Confederation, in force from 1781 to 1789, and then in the constitution of 1787, which led to the evolution of a stronger central government under President George Washington and his successors. As the people and their leaders struggled to build a national government they struggled also with these three problems of the Northwest Territory. The national government played a major role in opening the northwest frontier to settlement. And, while pioneer families and their descendants would often emphasize the degree to which they themselves had worked out their own futures, it is apparent that the national government was an essential force in shaping that future. Because it was a government generally responsive to the people, that federal role reflected increasingly, though never completely, the hopes and ambitions of the growing West.

The first and most difficult obstacle to white settlement was Indian resistance. Most Indian leaders and their people did not share Anglo-American concepts of land ownership. Land was not owned by individuals but rather was used in common to supply the necessities of daily life where that life existed. White settlement represented to Indians a threat not only to their land but to their way of life. To protect that way of life, Indians resisted.

To white settlers the land belonged to the American nation, as indicated in the Treaty of 1783. Indians were deemed savages who had fought with the redcoats and had never used the land in ways that God and nature ordained, that is, in ways Americans thought best. (In fact, Indian agriculture was often more extensive and sophisticated than that of early white settlers.) To most frontiersmen the only solution was Indian removal, either through purchase of Indian land and movement of Indians further westward or through killing off those who resisted. Land which the Indians would not voluntarily surrender must be taken by superior military force.

Kentucky continued to be the major destination of settlers after the Revolution; the American population there increased from 20,000 to more than 70,000 between 1783 and 1790. And as settlers streamed into Kentucky a small number began also in the 1780s to settle on the north side of the Ohio River. By the mid-1780s some four hundred Americans had settled in Vincennes, causing friction and conflict with the French population there and with the Indians of the lower Wabash. To the east, on the northern bank of the Ohio, was Clarksville, the first American town to be laid out in the Northwest (1784). Opposite Louisville, the town was part of a grant to George Rogers Clark and his men for their service during the Revolutionary War, a grant that was located in the present Indiana counties of Scott, Floyd, and Clark. Clarksville remained very small and relatively unimportant, however, with a population of only forty people in 1793. Further up river settlements on the north bank at Marietta and Cincinnati grew larger and constituted important footholds. The Indian response to these and other signs of white expansion took form in raids into Kentucky as well as on the north side of the Ohio as the tribes of the Northwest, particularly the Miamis, determined to hold the line at the river. The settlers not only protected themselves as best they could but demanded protection from the American government.

In defending settlers and preparing the way for their numbers to increase north of the Ohio, American leaders knew, as French, British, and Indians had known too, the strategic importance of the Maumee-Wabash route. Near Vincennes, the Wabash tribes showed signs of serious opposition to white settlement. In response George Rogers Clark led an expedition of Kentucky militia to Vincennes in 1786, followed by an American expedition led by General Josiah Harmar in 1787. Neither removed the Indian threat. Harmar decided to build at Vincennes a new military post, named Fort Knox. Commanded for the next five years by John Francis Hamtramck, Fort Knox provided only partial control of the lower Wabash tribes, whose war parties continued sporadic raids against white settlements.

To the north was the even more strategically important portage between the Wabash and Maumee, the council meeting ground of the Miamis, known to them as Kekionga and to the Americans as Miamistown. Here the increasingly important Miami tribe led in forming a combination of tribes in the northwest, often known as the Miami Confederacy. This Miami base would soon be the objective of several American military expeditions.

The first was led by General Josiah Harmar in late 1790 and succeeded in destroying several villages from which the Miamis had fled. But Harmar's men were poorly trained and supplied, and in meeting the Indian warriors, led by Miami Chief Little Turtle, they were badly beaten, losing 183 men. At the same time, in a planned two-pronged attack Major Hamtramck had moved from Fort Knox up the Wabash against the Weas, Potawatomis, and Kickapoos. He narrowly avoided disaster and beat a retreat back to Vincennes. This American defeat in 1790 showed Indians the vulnerability of the white forces and stimulated further resistance from Miami, Potawatomi, Shawnee, and Delaware Indians.

To redeem the defeat of 1790 Congress in 1791 authorized another expedition to the Maumee-Wabash portage, this one led by Arthur St. Clair, governor of the Northwest Territory. As with Harmar, most of St. Clair's men were volunteers and militia, poorly trained and supplied. St. Clair himself was in poor health, so afflicted by gout that he had to be carried in a litter. On the East Fork of the Wabash the old general met Little Turtle and more than 1,000 warriors, many supplied by British-Canadian traders. The battle turned to a rout and the Americans fled, leaving behind 647 dead comrades. The Indians lost about 150 warriors in perhaps the greatest Indian victory ever won over United States forces.

The repulsion of the Harmar and St. Clair invasions left the Indians more united and more determined than ever to hold the line at the Ohio River. In this stance they were encouraged by the British. Lord Dorchester, governor of Quebec, told them in early 1794 that they would have British support, and he added to other posts on American soil by building Fort Miamis on the Maumee River.

The tide turned quickly, however. In 1794 General Anthony Wayne led a third large expedition against the Indians. Unlike his predecessors, "Mad Anthony" carefully trained his 3,500 men and skillfully organized the attack. Meeting the Indians in a grove of storm-felled trees near the Maumee, Wayne won a decisive victory at the Battle of Fallen Timbers. To maintain military strength Wayne built several forts: the one at the Maumee-Wabash portage was named after the victorious general himself— "the chief who never sleeps," as Little Turtle called him. The Battle of Fallen Timbers led in 1795 to the Treaty of Greenville in which the defeated tribes promised to bury the hatchet and ceded to the United States the territory that now includes the southern two-thirds of Ohio and a narrow strip of south-eastern Indiana. The Indians also signed over the Wabash-Maumee portage, Ouiatanon, Vincennes, and Clark's Grant. In return for these lands the United States presented the Indians with goods valued at $20,000 and promised annual payments thereafter of $1,000 each to the Wyandots, Delawares, Shawnees, Miamis, Ottawas, Chippewas, and Potawatomis and $500 each to the Kickapoos, Weas, Eel River Miamis, Piankashaws, and Kaskaskias. No longer was the Ohio River their boundary. By this time also the British had agreed to evacuate their posts on American soil, deserting, as they had at the Battle of Fallen Timbers, their Indian allies.[9]

The Indians of the Northwest were not yet completely defeated: Indian raids would remain a threat on the frontier until 1815. But the Battle of Fallen Timbers and the Treaty of Greenville were major turning points. After 1795 the potential for strong, united Indian resistance to American force was greatly diminished, and the Indian barrier to settlement north of the Ohio was significantly lowered. Thousands of pioneers moved down the now peaceful Ohio and into the rich country north of the river.

While attempting to remove the Indian threat in the post-Revolutionary period the American government also attempted to create a system and method for sale of the millions of acres of land in the Northwest Territory. Although some Americans were quite willing and eager to settle and build homes without any legal title to the land, these "squatters" were relatively few in number. Only the promise of orderly, legal means of obtaining title to the land would open the way for large migration and permanent settlement.

After the knotty problem of western land claims by several of the original thirteen states was worked out in the early 1780s by transferring title to the national government, that government set about formulating a land policy. Potential western settlers wanted a policy that allowed for easy and cheap purchase of land, but many easterners argued that potential depopulation of their region and the need to build the government's depleted treasury necessitated high land prices. There was disagreement also over the best method of survey and sale.

A major step toward solving the problem of land sales was taken with passage of the Ordinance of 1785, which provided for rational

Fort Wayne in 1812. (Indiana Historical Society)

and orderly survey and sale. The land was to be surveyed in rectangular fashion, with north-south lines at six-mile intervals and east-
west lines at six-mile intervals. The resulting six-mile squares were
designated townships. Each township was divided into thirty-six one-
mile squares or sections, consisting of 640 acres. The sections were
numbered, from one through thirty-six, with the receipts from sale
of section sixteen set aside to support public education. The method
of surveying the land established in the Ordinance of 1785 was simple,
efficient, and rational, representing an enlightened approach to public
policy. The rectangular survey would spread a checkerboard pattern
across the Northwest Territory and later beyond the Mississippi, guaranteeing settlers clear and accurate title to their land.[10]

But the Ordinance of 1785 did not meet the immediate needs of
settlers. It required purchase of a minimum of 640 acres, at no less
than $1 an acre, later raised to $2. Moreover, the land was to be sold
at public auctions held in the East. This conservative and restrictive
policy encouraged land speculation and prevented many prospective
settlers from buying government land since few had the large amount
of cash required. Some settled the land without purchasing it, becoming squatters. They and many others raised voices of protest to which
Congress finally responded in the Land Act of 1800. This legislation
reduced the minimum amount of land to be purchased to a half sec-

tion of 320 acres, opened several land offices in the West near settlement, and allowed for sale on credit, with only one-fourth down payment. The Land Act of 1800 was the beginning of a general liberalization of land policy, allowing for ever more easy purchase by settlers. It represented the increasingly large voice of westerners in national government policy, and it led directly to a flood of western migration in the new century.

For orderly settlement to proceed the new nation also had to devise a system of government for the territory west of the mountains. The alternatives ranged from complete self-governance, even independence, to a new American colonial system in which the original thirteen states would function as the mother country. Within this broad spectrum of possibilities Americans worked out a pragmatic and evolutionary policy, one that began with considerable power lodged in the federal capital but allowed for gradual assumption of power by westerners themselves. During this process of change, westerners made increasingly strident calls for local democracy, laying the foundations for an attachment to government close to home and locally controlled—an attachment that would prevail in Indiana into the twentieth century.

The Northwest Ordinance of 1787 laid the basis for government in the West. The Ordinance established first a single government for all the territory northwest of the Ohio but provided for eventual division into not fewer than three nor more than five smaller territories. The territories themselves would pass through two stages. In the first stage a governor, secretary, and three judges, all appointed by the central government, would constitute the territorial government. The second stage was reached when the free adult males numbered 5,000. Those adult males owning at least fifty acres of land could then elect the lower house of a territorial legislature. The upper house or legislative council was less democratically chosen. The governor, still appointed, had absolute veto power over legislative action. The territorial legislature also chose a delegate to Congress, who spoke on their behalf but could not vote. Finally, the Northwest Ordinance stipulated that when 60,000 inhabitants resided in a territory it might petition for statehood and admission to the union on an equal basis with the original thirteen states.

The Northwest Ordinance was clearly not democratic. It denied local self-governance on the assumption that the frontier was too sparsely populated and too financially weak to provide effective, orderly government. And yet it contained the guarantee of increasingly democratic government and eventual statehood as the population grew. The West would not be forever subservient to the East; nor would its residents be second-class citizens. Here the Ordinance was especially encouraging, for it included a promise that from the beginning settlers would have freedom of religion, the right of trial by jury, and other rights of free Americans. Moreover, the Ordinance encouraged education and, in a controversial provision, prohibited slavery. It was, all in all, one of the nation's finest achievements of policy, and it greatly stimulated the westward movement.

In actually applying the Northwest Ordinance of 1787, Americans involved themselves in controversy and conflict. The appointed governor, Arthur St. Clair, assumed office in 1788 and soon became very unpopular on the frontier. His condescending manner and arbitrary rule recalled to westerners images of royal governors before the Revolution. Government below the territorial level only slightly alleviated such resentment. Knox County, organized at Vincennes in 1790 and extending beyond the boundaries of present-day Indiana, had several local officials, but all were appointed by the governor. The governor and territorial judges also made the laws pertaining to the local area, including prohibition of gambling and sale of liquor to the Indians in the Vincennes region.

Vociferous calls for more democracy and a growing population forced Governor St. Clair in 1798 to proclaim advance to the second or semirepresentative stage of territorial government. This change also brought the Northwest Territory a voice but not a vote in Congress. The first delegate to the nation's capital was William Henry Harrison, who played such an important role in the Land Act of 1800 that it was sometimes referred to as the Harrison Act. Harrison supported also the very strong western sentiment favoring division of the Northwest Territory and rapid movement to statehood. In 1800 Congress approved division into two territorial governments. The eastern division became in 1803 the new state of Ohio. The western division became in July, 1800, the Indiana Territory, extending from the border with Ohio all the way to the Mississippi River and north to the Canadian border.

From the end of the War for Independence in 1783 to the creation of the Indiana Territory in 1800 the national government had responded to the three major obstacles to settlement northwest of the Ohio River—Indians, land policy, and territorial government. The record was mixed. From the perspective of the western settler the successes included most notably the large reduction of the Indian threat, an achievement that clearly minimized issues of Indian rights and justice and maximized the rationale of military force. For westerners, the achievements of the federal government also included an efficient land policy, stated in the Ordinance of 1785, and gradual movement toward a more democratic land policy, indicated in the Land Act of 1800. And finally the West could look to the Northwest Ordinance as promising the rights of free Americans and a system of government that allowed for increased democracy and local control. In all three areas westerners charged that the national government and the East responded too slowly and too incompletely, thereby sowing seeds of sectional tension that often threatened to bloom into serious rift and division. But by 1800 the land northwest of the Ohio was well on the way to becoming a full part of the American nation, and its frontier people were already becoming in their own minds the most American of Americans.

Indiana Territory and Statehood, 1800–1816

The creation of Indiana Territory in 1800 did not bring immediate solutions to any of the problems facing westerners, but it did allow them to play an expanding role in responding to these problems. The challenges represented by hostile Indians, survey and sale of the land, and frontier desire for self-government continued to represent barriers to settlement even though the national government prior to 1800 had made considerable gains in each area. The government in Washington would remain an essential force in each of these three areas after 1800, but at the same time westerners would take more responsibility themselves for choosing and directing their own futures. By 1816 they had eliminated entirely the threat of Indian resistance, prepared the way for rapid settlement of most land in Indiana, and achieved statehood.

The Indiana Territory in 1800 extended westward to the Mississippi River and from the Ohio River to the southern boundary of Canada. The territory's white population in 1800 numbered 5,641, of whom nearly half lived in Clark's Grant on the Ohio River and in the Vincennes area on the Wabash. Vincennes was the territorial capital, the site of the first newspaper (Elihu Stout's *Indiana Gazette*, 1804), and the home of a sizable French population, described often by Americans as hospitable, easygoing, and even lazy. But Vincennes's dominant position was soon threatened as settlement and towns developed along the Ohio River and in the Whitewater Valley of southeastern Indiana. By 1810 when Indiana Territory had been considerably reduced in area by the splitting off and creation of Michigan (1805) and Illinois (1809) territories, Indiana had 24,520 residents. Reflecting the reduced size of the territory and the increased population growth in southeastern Indiana, the territorial capital was moved from Vincennes to Corydon in 1813. Few Americans had yet ventured to the central and northern portions of the territory, clinging instead to an arc of settlement along the Whitewater, Ohio, and lower Wabash rivers. The primary reason for this crescent-shaped toehold was Indian hostility to white expansion.[1]

Treaties and Conflicts with Indians

Major responsibility for dealing with Indian resistance was lodged with the governor of Indiana Territory. From 1800 to 1812 William Henry Harrison held this office. A veteran of Indian warfare, including the campaign that culminated in the Battle of Fallen Timbers in 1794, Governor Harrison adopted an Indian policy devoted to aggressive land acquisition. In this expansionist policy Harrison had enthusiastic encouragement from President Thomas Jefferson, who hoped the Indians could be taught to give up hunting and settle the land, farming it as whites did. Becoming "civilized," the Indians would have need for much less land, allowing room for white settlement. The only alternative, according to Jefferson, Harrison, and others, was expulsion westward.

Between 1803 and 1809 Harrison negotiated land cession treaties with various Indian tribes, including the Delawares, Shawnees, Pot-

William Henry Harrison, governor of Indiana Territory,
1800–1812. (Lilly Library, Indiana University)

awatomis, and Miamis (see Map 3). Most of the treaties were signed
at Vincennes or Fort Wayne. The Harrison treaties secured from the
Indians the southern third of Indiana and nearly all of Illinois, opening millions of acres of land to white settlement. Harrison's success
resulted partly from his persistence, skill, and ruthlessness as treaty
negotiator and from his ability to intimidate Indians with the military
invincibility of the "long knives," stimulated by military parades and
by treating chiefs with visits to the nation's capital. Harrison's land
cession treaties resulted also from the fact that many Indians did not
fully understand or share American concepts of land ownership and
transfer of title to land. Tribal claims to land were often uncertain
and overlapping. Harrison was able to take advantage of disagreement
and conflict among tribes and also within tribes, using more pliant
chiefs as wedges to divide and conquer piecemeal in his series of
treaties. Indian leaders were also persuaded to negotiate by promises
of annuity payments in goods and money, and by calculated use of

MAP 3.
Indian Treaties

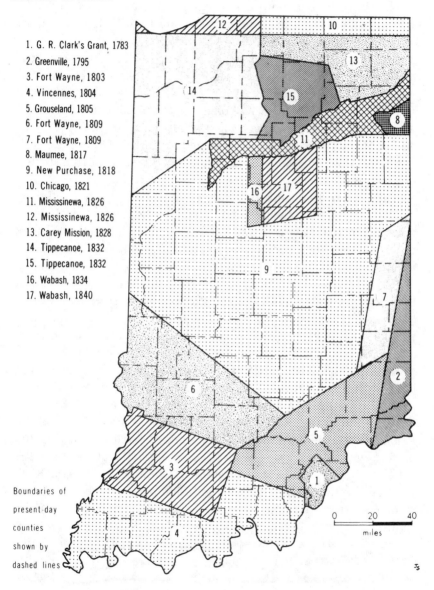

1. G. R. Clark's Grant, 1783
2. Greenville, 1795
3. Fort Wayne, 1803
4. Vincennes, 1804
5. Grouseland, 1805
6. Fort Wayne, 1809
7. Fort Wayne, 1809
8. Maumee, 1817
9. New Purchase, 1818
10. Chicago, 1821
11. Mississinewa, 1826
12. Mississinewa, 1826
13. Carey Mission, 1828
14. Tippecanoe, 1832
15. Tippecanoe, 1832
16. Wabash, 1834
17. Wabash, 1840

Boundaries of present-day counties shown by dashed lines

0   20   40
miles

SOURCE: Robert C. Kingsbury, *An Atlas of Indiana* (Bloomington, 1970), 7

liquor and presents (though Harrison had in 1802 issued a proclamation forbidding the sale of alcohol to Indians).

The Harrison treaties were both cause and result of a disintegrating
Indian culture. With hunting and trapping less and less productive
as animal populations declined and with increased dependence on
annuity payments and white goods (including liquor), Indian control
of their traditional culture waned. The Miamis, perhaps the most
important tribe in Indiana, no longer enjoyed leadership or direction
of the various bands from Kekionga. Miami Chief Little Turtle was
determined to avoid war, as he had promised at Greenville in 1795.
As the Miamis warrior society weakened and tribal cohesiveness shattered, the Miamis became lethargic and dependent, a blurred shadow
of their recent past.

While Harrison negotiated land cession treaties he and Jefferson
determined also to "civilize" and assimilate the "savage" Indian. In
response to requests from Little Turtle and other chiefs, Jefferson
ordered plows, hoes, and livestock sent to the Miamis and Potawatomis
in hope of encouraging white methods of farming and abandonment
of the hunter-warrior culture. Several religious groups also joined this
philanthropic program to "civilize" the Indian, focusing their efforts
on removing liquor and encouraging settled agriculture, while also
promoting Christianity among the heathen. Moravian missionaries
attempted to teach new farming techniques to Delawares on the White
River as early as 1801. Eastern Quakers took a very strong interest in
the Indians of the Fort Wayne area, responding to appeals for help
from Little Turtle. In 1804 three Quakers visited Fort Wayne. One
of them, Philip Dennis, remained to establish a model farm on the
Wabash where he encouraged Miamis and Potawatomis to join him
in working the land. Few did, and Dennis left at the end of the year.
Another Quaker effort at civilization was headed by William Kirk,
who came to the Wabash in 1806, and soon received encouragement
and money from President Jefferson. Kirk became involved in various
controversies with Indians and whites at Fort Wayne, however, and
left in mid-1807. These and other attempts at civilization programs
ended in failure, perhaps doomed from the outset by the vastly different cultures of Indian and white. Such failure encouraged white
assumptions that the only solution was to push Indians westward beyond the Mississippi.

In treaty negotiations and civilization programs leaders of both sides often depended on intermediaries who had ties to both Indian and white society. These men spoke English and Indian languages and acted as interpreters, but they also served as go-betweens in broader diplomatic, economic, and military contexts. Many were offspring of French and Indian marriages and able to thrive as traders or as Indian leaders. One such man was Jean Baptiste Richardville, a nephew of Little Turtle, who became increasingly influential among the Miamis. Some American traders also established important relationships. A few took Indian wives, including John and William Conner, who became important traders, guides, and interpreters.[2] Perhaps the most important of all intermediaries was William Wells, who became, in the frontier term, a "white Indian."

Wells was born in 1770, and at the age of nine moved with his family to Kentucky. In 1784 he was captured by a party of Miamis. For the next eight years he lived as a Miami warrior, joining in raids on white settlements, participating in the defeat of St. Clair in 1791, and marrying a daughter of Little Turtle. His white family eventually found him and convinced him to return to Kentucky, but after a few days he chose to return to his Indian life and family. In 1792, however, Wells returned again to Kentucky, searching for his Indian wife and mother who had been captured by a Kentucky expedition. This time Wells decided to stay and to give up Indian life. He soon became an interpreter and scout for General Wayne. He settled at Fort Wayne, serving as interpreter and Indian agent and eventually assuming major responsibility for distributing annuity payments and promoting civilizing programs. Wells and Harrison had been friends since Wayne's campaign, but as Harrison's treaties touched ever closer to the Miami heartland Wells began to oppose the governor's expansionist policy, much to Harrison's regret. Wells also became involved in bitter conflict with John Johnston, the government official at Fort Wayne responsible for directing the Indian trade.

Until his death Wells was involved in controversy, as he attempted a balancing act between his hopes that the Miamis could unite under Little Turtle and retain their land and his attachments to white civilization. Neither whites nor Indians fully trusted Wells, though he was very useful to both. His life ended in 1812, when he attempted to lead the small, besieged civilian and military garrison from Fort

"Death of Captain Wm. Wells," by Will Vawter. (Indiana Historical Society)

Dearborn (at present-day Chicago) to safety at Fort Wayne. A large party of Potawatomis overwhelmed and killed most of the whites. Anticipating the attack, Wells died that day dressed and painted as a Miami warrior, a white Indian to the end.[3]

Intermediaries such as William Wells could do little to smooth the jagged conflict between white and Indian culture. Above all, white determination to own and settle the land allowed no basis for long-term compromise. Indiana's white population grew as federal land sales began at offices in Vincennes in 1807 and Jeffersonville in 1808. The peace that prevailed since 1795 became increasingly fragile. By 1806 many Indians had become hostile and alienated as the consequence of conflicts over annuity payments, resentment over the liquor traffic they knew was rapidly debilitating their people, and outrage at the steady march of Harrison's land cession treaties and settlers' log cabins. In such a desperate and volatile situation a heroic figure often emerges to lead. In this instance there were two men and two messages, related and powerful.

Tenskwatawa, the Shawnee Prophet, began in 1806 to preach a doctrine of Indian renewal and cultural purity based on abstention from liquor and from all ways of the white man, the destroyer of Indian culture. The Prophet's religious and cultural evangelism received support and extension from his brother, Tecumseh, one of the most heroic of all Indian leaders. While the Prophet preached, Tecumseh set about uniting the tribes of the Northwest, preparing for the first united and effective Indian resistance since the early 1790s. By the summer of 1808 warriors from the Potawatomis and other tribes were flocking to Prophetstown, the new village near the junction of the Tippecanoe and Wabash rivers. Only the Miamis showed little enthusiasm. Little Turtle and other Miami chiefs determined to honor the treaties and did not share Tecumseh's message that the land belonged in common to all Indians—a message that threatened the Miamis' sole control of vast lands of the upper Wabash region.[4]

Despite Miami resistance Tecumseh and the Prophet attracted enough support to rekindle old fears of the tomahawk and scalping knife on the Indiana frontier and at the capital in Vincennes. Settlers built blockhouses for defense, and the militia, composed of all ablebodied men between the ages of eighteen and forty-five, sprang to life. As with the generation before, it was not the Indians alone the settlers feared but also the British across the border in Canada. As relations between the two nations worsened many Westerners believed the British would again supply and encourage Indian raids on the frontier.

In this crisis the two most powerful men in the West met at Vincennes in August, 1810. Tecumseh and Harrison had last talked at the Treaty of Greenville. The governor had developed great respect for Tecumseh's abilities. He was, Harrison conceded, "the efficient man—the Moses of the family . . . a bold, active, sensible man daring in the extreme and capable of any undertaking." At their council in a grove of trees near Harrison's home, Tecumseh complained angrily about the most recent land cessions at the Fort Wayne Treaty of 1809, by which Harrison had obtained nearly 3 million acres of Indian land. Such treaties were not valid, Tecumseh argued, because the land belonged to all Indians, not just a few tribes. The difficult meeting ended with no resolution, and young warriors soon were passing war belts. The following spring, in 1811, signs of Indian hostility intensified, prompting a warning from Harrison to Tecumseh:

> this is the third year that all the white people in this country have been alarmed at your proceedings, you threaten us with war, you invite all the tribes to the north and west of you to join against us. . . . I am myself of the long knife fire; as soon as they hear my voice, you will see them pouring forth their swarms of hunting-shirt men, as numerous as the musquitoes on the shores of the Wabash. . . .

Tecumseh was not intimidated but agreed to another council with Harrison, this one equally unproductive. Afterward Tecumseh set off for the South, seeking Indian allies there. Harrison was convinced that war was imminent, regarding Tecumseh as "one of those uncommon genuises, which spring up occasionally to produce revolutions and overturn the established order of things." The governor decided to strike while Tecumseh was away and before any such overturning.[5]

In the fall of 1811 Harrison gathered a military force composed of United States infantrymen, Kentucky volunteer companies, and Indiana militia, numbering about 1,000 men. Reflecting his apprenticeship under General Wayne, Harrison planned carefully and built and secured bases en route, including a new fort near present-day Terre Haute, named Fort Harrison. Moving up the Wabash, the army reached Prophetstown on November 6. The next morning before daylight the Indians attacked, confident that the Prophet's magic had made them invincible to bullets. Two hours of fierce fighting concluded with Indian withdrawal. Harrison claimed victory, though the Battle of Tippecanoe was far from the decisive Indian defeat he had hoped for. Moreover, the Americans suffered large casualties, with almost one-fifth of Harrison's men dead or wounded.

The spring of 1812 showed that the Battle of Tippecanoe had not broken Indian resistance. Raids on frontier settlements resumed, but with the critical difference that Britain and the United States were soon at war. Though the War of 1812 had many causes, western resentment against the Indians and belief that the British in Upper Canada had stirred up and armed Indian warriors played an important role. Once war was declared the majority of Indians did indeed join the British side, the major exception being the Miamis, most of whom chose to remain neutral.

The war went badly in 1812. Westerners had expected an easy conquest of Canada. Instead the British quickly captured Detroit, while Potawatomis took Fort Dearborn, killing most of the whites there, including William Wells. Indian raiding parties struck far into southern Indiana, killing in September, 1812, twenty-four men, women, and children at the settlement of Pigeon Roost in present Scott County. Settlers elsewhere fled to their blockhouses and across the Ohio. And Fort Harrison and Fort Wayne came under attack and siege. The commander at Fort Wayne, Captain James Rhea, showed cowardice and ineptitude, exacerbated by the kind of alcoholism whites usually ascribed to Indians.

In this crisis Kentucky came to the aid of Indiana. A relief force of 5,000 Kentucky volunteers gathered, soon joined by Harrison, who secured a commission as major general in the Kentucky militia and eventually became commander of the Northwestern Army. This army lifted the siege of Fort Wayne and, joined by Indiana militia, launched a scorched-earth expedition against Indian villages, some of them neutral, burning the towns and destroying the crops of Miamis, Potawatomis, and other tribes. By the summer of 1813 it was clear that the Indians were thoroughly defeated. The final blow came in October, when Harrison met Tecumseh and the British redcoats at the Battle of the Thames, north of Lake Erie. Tecumseh died on the battlefield. American victory there brought peace to the West and destroyed the last confederacy of Indian resistance. And the peace treaty that concluded the War of 1812 in late 1814 resolved long-standing tensions with the British, ending decades of fear of British presence behind Indian scalping knives.

For the Indians the era of military resistance was over. Many retreated westward. For those who remained the bleak future belonged not to warriors but to leaders such as Richardville who could adjust to white ways, live under the annuity payment system, and assent to ever-shrinking Indian "reservation" lands. Perhaps cruelest of all was the fate of the Miamis, most of whom, even after the death of Little Turtle and of William Wells in 1812, determined to remain neutral in the conflict between the long knives and redcoats and to resist the

allure of Tecumseh. Neutrality was not one of the options granted
by Americans, however. Not only were many of their villages destroyed, but in 1818 at the Treaty of St. Mary's, or the New Purchase
Treaty, the Miamis gave up most of their tribal lands, covering the
central third of Indiana.[6]

For white settlers in Indiana the War of 1812 brought an end to
Indian wars, led to opening up of vast new territory in central Indiana,
sparked a rush of self-confident nationalism, and helped prepare the
way for statehood. Not until much later would many of them or their
descendants pause to raise questions of justice and equity in the long
and bloody struggle which deprived the Indians of their land and
their way of life.

Government and Politics in Indiana Territory, 1800–1810

Negotiating land cession treaties and eliminating the threat of Indian resistance to white expansion were the most immediate tasks
confronting Harrison and the government of Indiana Territory. But
of equal long-term importance was the challenge of creating a work-
able government within the basic framework established by the Northwest Ordinance of 1787. This challenge led to considerable conflict
as the people of Indiana Territory pushed their government in more
democratic directions, culminating with statehood in 1816.

At the center of the political conflict from 1800 to 1812 was William
Henry Harrison, a Virginia-born gentleman who was just twenty-
seven years of age when President John Adams appointed him
territorial governor. Harrison avoided much of the arbitrary high-
handedness that had made Governor St. Clair so unpopular in the
Northwest Territory, but he never enjoyed the full and unqualified
support of all the people. The Northwest Ordinance denied self-government to the territories, and Governor Harrison bore the brunt of
criticism from those frontiersmen who demanded more autonomy.
He often acceded to such demands but seldom as rapidly or as completely as his critics wished. And he attracted to his side in these
struggles more conservative supporters distrustful of the arguments
for self-government, often labeled by their opponents as "Virginia
aristocrats."

The first target of Harrison's frontier critics was the non-representative stage of government in which the territorial governor and judges ruled alone. After some pressure Harrison agreed in 1804 to allow a vote on the issue of moving to the second or representative stage of government. The majority vote favored this change and led to the election in early 1805 of nine delegates to the new Indiana House of Representatives. The House prepared a list of ten nominees for the Legislative Council or upper house from which President Thomas Jefferson and Harrison appointed the five members. The way was thus opened for the first session of the Indiana General Assembly in the summer of 1805. Harrison still possessed an absolute veto over legislative bills, an increasingly galling power to the Indiana House and to his critics outside the legislature. Anti-Harrison leaders soon pushed to expand representative government by successfully petitioning Congress to allow for election rather than appointment of both the Legislative Council and the territory's delegate to Congress. And they convinced Congress in 1808 to extend the right to vote, previously limited to white males who owned fifty acres of land, to include also owners of town lots valued at one hundred dollars or more. The new political climate was vividly evident in the campaign for delegate to Congress in 1809. Jonathan Jennings, a twenty-five-year-old recent migrant from western Pennsylvania, defeated Governor Harrison's choice, Thomas Randolph, and became the rallying point for the anti-Harrison faction for the next several years. The 1810 General Assembly continued the process of suffrage extension by petitioning Congress to remove all property qualifications. Congress responded in 1811 by granting the vote to all free adult white taxpaying males who had resided one year in the territory.

The 1810 General Assembly also began the process of moving the territorial capital from Vincennes to Corydon. This too was a strike at Harrison and his supporters, for they were concentrated geographically in the Vincennes area. The southeastern part of the territory, particularly the Whitewater Valley, was increasingly opposed to the governor and his allies, and as this area grew in population so too did the anti-Harrison sentiment.

Another and related ingredient in territorial politics was the issue of slavery. Slavery had existed among the French at Vincennes as early as the mid-eighteenth century, and, despite the prohibition of

MAP 4.
Map of Indiana Drawn in 1817, with
Lake Michigan Incorrectly Located

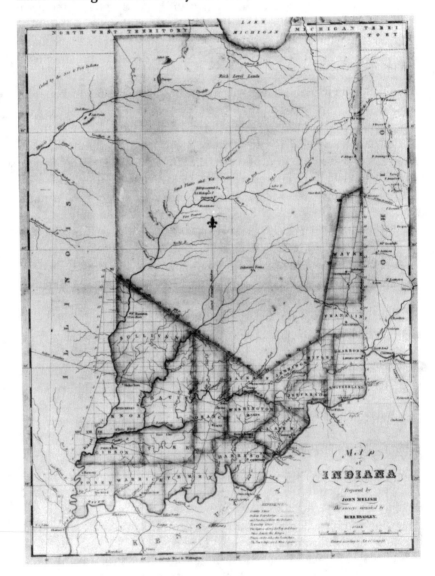

SOURCE: Lilly Library, Indiana University

slavery in the Northwest Ordinance, it continued with considerable support during the territorial period. In 1802 Harrison called a territorial convention to consider a resolution repealing the portion of the Northwest Ordinance prohibiting slavery. The convention voted to petition Congress for repeal, arguing that legalization of slavery would attract more settlers to Indiana. Congress did not grant the petition, but Governor Harrison and the territorial judges nonetheless permitted slavery under various guises. The first General Assembly, in 1805, passed an act allowing slaves to be brought into the territory and held for very long indentures, often beyond their life expectancy, a brazen and successful flouting of the antislavery terms of the Northwest Ordinance. Many prominent citizens of Indiana, including Harrison, owned slaves. The exact number of slaves in Indiana is impossible to know, in part because of efforts to disguise the fact of slavery, but the census of 1810 listed 237 slaves and 393 free blacks concentrated in the Vincennes area. It is likely that many of the free blacks were in fact slaves.[7]

The proslavery tenor of territorial government began to receive challenge by the middle of the decade in antislavery meetings and petitions to Congress. In 1810 the General Assembly repealed the 1805 indenture law, though repeal did not affect pre-1810 indentures and slavery continued to exist. It should be noted that many of the people opposed to slavery also were opposed to allowing free blacks to settle in Indiana, but their efforts to bar blacks from the territory were unsuccessful.

The opposition to slavery melded with other political currents. The antislavery strength was strongest in southeastern Indiana, especially among Quakers who had moved from North Carolina to the Whitewater Valley. Opposition to slavery thus had regional and political dimensions. Territorial politics often took the form of an antislavery, anti-Harrison, prodemocratic, and southeastern faction, increasingly centered around Jonathan Jennings, opposing a proslavery, less democratic, Vincennes-based faction allied to Harrison. While issues were significant in this development, it was also apparent that some of the maneuvering and conflict had as its objective personal office-seeking and political spoils. Moreover, not all political developments can be explained by this simple, twofold division: differences between the two factions were not always clear, the factions themselves were not solidly formed, and they did not behave as formal political parties. Nonetheless, by 1810 the initiative in territorial government had passed from the governor to the legislature, constituting a major step toward self-government and democracy on the frontier. The next step was statehood.

Statehood and the Constitution of 1816

The Indiana House petitioned Congress for statehood and admission to the Union in 1811, but the War of 1812 caused such military and financial distraction that the movement for statehood lapsed. It resumed in 1815, first with a count of Indiana's population, which totaled 63,897, more than the 60,000 required by the Northwest Ordinance. In 1815 the legislature petitioned again for statehood.

The movement for statehood aroused opposition. Perhaps the most important and valid objection was that the territory could not yet afford statehood. From 1804 to 1816, average annual territorial expenditures were approximately $10,000, two-thirds of which derived from the federal government. Not only would statehood end this federal support but additional expenses would be necessary to conduct state government, thus causing increased taxes. Some argued for delaying statehood until Indiana was more populated and economically mature. Governor Thomas Posey, whom President James Madison had appointed in 1813, made these arguments, for example, claiming that there was in Indiana "a very great scarcity of talents, or men of such information as are necessary to fill the respective Stations, & offices of government."[8]

Proponents of statehood thought differently, motivated in part by hopes of filling office themselves, replacing Posey and the Harrison faction that still dominated territorial offices. With Jennings emerging as their leader, the pro-statehood group pushed their cause as the cause of democracy, arguing that the people were eager and able to elect their own officials and to have voting representatives in the national government. Now was the time, they argued, to fulfill the promise of the Northwest Ordinance. Congress responded favorably, passing on April 19, 1816, an Enabling Act that provided for election of delegates to a convention. If the delegates so agreed, that convention could form a constitution. Thirty-four of the forty-three delegates so agreed, and the convention, meeting at Corydon, proceeded to write a constitution.[9]

The membership of the state constitutional convention of 1816 was composed largely of men from south of the Ohio River. All but nine of the forty-three delegates had lived below the Mason-Dixon line prior to moving to Indiana, including twenty-seven whose previous residence was Kentucky. In their geographical origins they doubtless were roughly reflective of Indiana's 1816 population as a whole. Most delegates had some experience in government; most had some legal training; and most knew first-hand the rigors of frontier life. Five had been with Harrison at Tippecanoe.

In the summer heat and humidity of Corydon, meeting sometimes in the shade of a large elm tree, these forty-three men prepared the state's constitution. They were wise enough to study other state constitutions and to draw especially on those of Ohio and Kentucky, states closest in circumstance and geography to Indiana. Constitution-making was not a process of mechanical cutting and pasting, however, for the delegates were by no means agreed on which portions of which state constitutions would best serve the interests of their new state. While their differences and disagreements took many forms, there was evident a majority faction, drawn from the pro-statehood, anti-Harrison group led by Jennings and geographically based in southeastern Indiana. This Jennings group succeeded in electing their leader as president of the convention and generally in having their way. Their opposition was even less cohesive, but was composed largely of men from western Indiana, friends of former Governor Harrison, and opponents of statehood. One of them, John Badollet of Vincennes, described the Jennings faction as "empty bablers, democratic to madness, having incessantly the *people* in their mouths and their dear selves in their eyes. . . ."[10]

The constitution that emerged from the discussion and debate of 1816 reflected the more democratic sentiments of the Jennings faction and of frontier Indiana generally. The constitution opened with a preamble and bill of rights, stating such enlightenment and revolutionary-era concepts as "all men are born equally free and independent," and "all power is inherent in the people." Hoosiers were promised freedom of worship, of the press, and of speech and the right to

Capitol at Corydon, 1815–1825. (Indiana Historical Society)

bear arms and to assemble peaceably. The convention adopted the American system of checks and balances and divided the powers of government among legislative, executive, and judicial branches. Reflecting their recent struggles to expand representative power, the delegates made the legislature the dominant branch, able to override the governor's veto by a simple majority vote. They set the governor's term at only three years and prohibited him from holding office longer than six years in any nine-year period. Members of the House of Representatives were to be chosen annually, reflecting a desire for close popular control. The state senators were to serve three-year terms. The judiciary power was vested in a Supreme Court and circuit courts, with inferior courts to be created by the General Assembly.

The constitution granted the vote to all white male citizens twenty-one and older who had resided in the state one year. There was no property qualification, but the tradition of not allowing blacks and women to vote was continued. All males between the ages of eighteen and forty-five were required to enroll in the militia—"Negroes, Mulattoes and Indians excepted," as were conscientious objectors, though the latter had to pay a fee in lieu of service.

One of the most progressive and creative provisions of the constitution was the promise that the General Assembly would provide for "a general system of education, ascending in a regular gradation, from township schools to a state university, wherein tuition shall be gratis, and equally open to all." In addition to free public education, the constitution provided also that the General Assembly would formulate a penal code "founded on the principles of reformation, and not of vindictive Justice" and provide asylums for the aged, infirm, and misfortunate. These noble sentiments for education, criminal justice, and social welfare all contained the provision that the legislature would act "as soon as circumstances will permit." With this loophole allowing delay, the state government accomplished very little in these areas prior to 1850.

Mindful of the conflict over slavery during the territorial days, the delegates at Corydon took up the issue of slavery and the status of blacks. The constitution stated that "There shall be neither slavery nor involuntary servitude in this state. . . . " But then another loophole opened in the provision, "Nor shall any indenture of any negro or mulatto *hereafter made* [italics added], and executed out of the bounds of this state be of any validity within the state." The "hereafter made" wording left unclear the effect on already existing indentures. In the antislavery southeastern section people generally assumed slavery of any sort no longer legally existed. In the more proslavery western counties most slaveowners continued to hold their slaves, arguing that the constitution was not retroactive. Nearly all of the 190 slaves reported in the 1820 census were living in the western part of the state. In the early 1820s, however, the Indiana Supreme Court handed down several decisions that made slavery and involuntary servitude illegal even in indentures made prior to 1816. Although there were still at least a few slaves in the state as late as the 1830s, there was no doubt that slavery was illegal in Indiana. A convention composed largely of men from the South had eradicated the South's peculiar institution from Indiana soil.

The delegates signed the new constitution on June 29, 1816. It took effect immediately. Elections in August produced the state's first General Assembly, which met in November, and the first governor, Jonathan Jennings, who easily defeated Thomas Posey by a vote of 5,211 to 3,934. On December 11, 1816, President Madison signed the congressional resolution admitting Indiana to the Union. The nineteenth state existed. It was now up to Hoosiers to shape its future.

PART II

Pioneer Indiana, 1816–1850

iv

On the Indiana Frontier

Nothing in American history is more important than the movement of peoples westward—westward across the Atlantic Ocean to the North American continent, westward across that continent to the Pacific Ocean. Indiana's history is part of that larger history, so intensely shaped by it as to constitute a dominant factor in understanding what it meant and means to be a Hoosier.

Despite the best efforts of several generations of historians, the nature of the westward movement and its causes and consequences remain unclear and imprecise. Some have credited the frontier as the source of all that was distinctive and good in America—equality, individualism, democracy, a belief in hard work. On close study such large generalities fall victim to countless exceptions and contradictions. And yet the near-certainty remains that in ways fundamental and innumerable if not precisely understood the westward movement and the frontier experience shaped Americans and Hoosiers as did no other phenomenon or process.

Perhaps the most important feature of the frontier in Indiana was the degree to which it was a success. There was failure to be sure— many individual failures that produced hardship and defeat. But for most pioneers it was a frontier of success and abundance. There was no starving time in Indiana: the land was rich, the forests bountiful, and the pioneer knew how to reap and profit. They came, most of them, looking for a fresh start, a better material life. Most achieved it. With good reason pioneer Hoosiers developed a strong sense of optimism, a conviction that progress was natural, a confidence that this was the best that America offered. Near the end of their lives many would look back on their decision to move to the Indiana frontier as proof of God's blessing and as guarantee that their lives and those of their children were better as a consequence.[1]

Migration and Settlement Patterns

They came across the mountains, down the rivers, and over the western trails and roads to the new state of Indiana. Thousands of men, women, and children made the journey in the years following the War of 1812, for that war ended Indian resistance and opened new lands for settlement. It seemed, one newcomer wrote, as though all America was "breaking up and moving westward."[2] Indiana's population increased substantially in these years, the great bulk of the increase due to migration (see Table 1).

The westward movement varied considerably in terms of settler origin, route of travel, destination, and timing of the move. The resulting patterns of migration and settlement had immensely important consequences for Indiana's history. Three major streams of migration can be identified. The smallest in size was that from the New England states. Considerably larger was the stream from the Mid-Atlantic states, principally New York and Pennsylvania. Largest of all was the population movement from the southern states. These three streams

Table 1

Components of Population Change,
1800–1860[a]

Decade	Beginning Population	Natural Increase	Net Migration	End Population	Migration Rate[b]
1800–1810	5,641	2,421	16,458	24,520	291.76%
1810–1820	24,520	10,977	111,681	147,178	455.47
1820–1830	147,178	71,723	124,130	343,031	84.34
1830–1840	343,031	155,691	187,144	685,866	54.56
1840–1850	685,866	293,470	9,080	988,416	1.32
1850–1860	988,416	402,161	− 40,149	1,350,428	− 4.06

[a]Decennial results are not strictly comparable owing to boundary changes.
[b]Net migration divided by beginning population.

SOURCE: Richard K. Vedder and Lowell E. Gallaway, "Migration and the Old Northwest," David C. Klingaman and Richard K. Vedder, eds., *Essays in Nineteenth Century Economic History: The Old Northwest* (Athens, Ohio, 1975), 163.

tended to settle in a pattern that reflected their geographic origins, with southerners most heavily congregated in the southern part of the state, Mid-Atlantic peoples in the central part, and New Englanders in the northern part. There were many individual exceptions to these generalizations, of course (some Yankee families did settle in southern Indiana, for example), but the general streams of migration and settlement constituted a pattern of fundamental significance in Indiana history.[3]

The earliest settlers came primarily from the upland South—from western Virginia and North Carolina and from eastern Tennessee and Kentucky. Many of these upland southerners had family and cultural roots in southeastern Pennsylvania. During the eighteenth century Scotch-Irish and German Pennsylvanians moved southward into the Great Valley of western Virginia. The end of the Revolutionary War allowed them to trickle across the Appalachians, particularly at the Cumberland Gap, and to make the first permanent settlements in Tennessee and the Kentucky Bluegrass region. Some began to venture across the Ohio River in the first decade of the nineteenth century, but it was the War of 1812 that opened the gate and allowed this westward and northward migration to surge across the Ohio and into southern Indiana.

Indiana's southern population was thus not from the tidewater, slave-owning, plantation South. These were people who worked their own family farms, people with years and often generations of experience in making a living on the frontier. One such pioneer was Thomas Lincoln. Born in Virgina, he moved to the Kentucky frontier in the 1780s, where his son Abraham was born in 1809. The family moved several times in Kentucky, but in the fall of 1816, when Abe was seven years old, they crossed the Ohio into Indiana, settling on Little Pigeon Creek in present-day Spencer County. Thomas Lincoln was attracted to Indiana by the rich land and the security of the systematic federal land survey, as stipulated in the Land Ordinance of 1785, and by the absence of slavery. Like many on the Indiana frontier, Tom Lincoln fit the Jeffersonian image of sturdy, yeomen farmers attached firmly to their individual freedom, to their particular notions of equality and democracy, and to their desire for a better material life.

In the first decades of the nineteenth century upland southerners crossed the Appalachians and moved to Indiana on horseback, in wagons, and on foot. Mid-Atlantic pioneers used these means of transportation and also had the advantage of the best highway to the new state—the Ohio River. From Pittsburgh and other points they set off down river in boats of all kinds, no longer after 1815 fearing attack from the northern or Indian side of the Ohio. Some also traveled overland through Ohio, following the roughly marked traces to Cincinnati and into Indiana or later through Columbus on the route that would become the National Road.

Because of the geographic origins of the first settlers, the nature of early migration routes, and the timing of settlement Indiana was settled from the south to the north. Southern Indiana was settled first as pioneers ferried across the Ohio from Kentucky or ended their long down-river journey at one of the small towns on the Indiana side. From there they set off on trails and traces into the interior. Most important was the Buffalo Trace crossing the state from the Falls of the Ohio opposite Louisville to the Wabash at Vincennes.

Central Indiana was sparsely settled at the time of statehood because of greater difficulty of access and because of Indian presence and claims to the land. The New Purchase Treaty of 1818 opened central Indiana to white settlement, and gradual improvements in transportation enabled thousands of newcomers to settle the rich lands of the Wabash Country in the 1820s.

The northern region of the state was settled last, in the 1830s and 1840s, as it was both the final refuge of Indian tribes and the least accessible part of Indiana. The Maumee-Wabash route to northern Indiana, which had served Indians and traders so well, was too difficult for many families moving west. Population growth may also have been retarded by the fact that speculators bought large tracts of land in parts of the area, especially in the northwestern prairie counties. Wet and swampy land around Fort Wayne and in the Kankakee region to the northwest created formidable barriers to migration and settlement. With Indian removal and improved transportation in the 1830s pioneers began to farm fertile lands in the St. Joseph Valley, the Door Prairie, and other areas of the north. Many joined pioneer booster and agriculturist Solon Robinson in predicting that "The north of Indiana will most certainly become the garden spot of the state."[4]

Each of the three major settlement groups brought with them a distinctive culture, elements of which persisted for generations, down even to the present. Southern Indiana was the most distinctive: upland South patterns of word usage and pronunciation, religion, place names, food, amusement, and methods of constructing barns, houses, and corn cribs were firmly implanted in southern Indiana by 1820 and remained into the late twentieth century. Northern Indiana did not show such a ubiquitous New England cultural heritage, but elements of it were there by the mid-nineteenth century. Fruit trees and clocks, dairying and haymaking, a preference for cider rather than whiskey—these and many other factors were a sign of Yankee presence. Much will be made in the chapters that follow of the conflict between Yankee and southerner in Indiana: it is an essential part of understanding the history of the state. Perhaps as interesting and important is the mixture of cultures in Indiana. Central Indiana was especially important in this regard, for there upland South, Mid-Atlantic, and New England cultures mingled and amalgamated, causing each to change and creating a distinctive culture, one that was neither northern nor southern but rather western and Hoosier.[5]

Indiana's pioneer population thus consisted of peoples drawn from

throughout the United States but in significantly different proportions. The 1850 census showed that of Indiana's American-born residents who had migrated to the state, 2.7 percent had come from the
New England states, 19.9 percent from the Mid-Atlantic states, 31.4
percent from Ohio, and 44.0 percent from the southern states. Indiana's southern-born population was larger in both absolute and
relative size than that of any other state in the Old Northwest, a
characteristic which, among others, would lead to claims that Indiana
was the most southern of northern states. Yet Indiana was not in fact
a southern state: it did not sanction slavery, nor was there any doubt
on which side it would fight in 1861. Neither northern nor southern,
it was western, and it was Hoosier.

Land and the Frontier Family Home

Making a home on the Indiana frontier was a job that required
particular kinds of knowledge, skills, tools, cooperation, and hard
work. Only those pioneers possessing such attributes would find this
to be a frontier of abundance and success. Even then forces of nature
and chance could bring hardship or failure.

The first challenge facing the pioneer in Indiana was locating a site
and obtaining the land for a home. The decision of exactly where to
settle resulted from a combination of accurate information and understanding and inaccurate hearsay and misunderstanding. Both
kinds of advice were found in the travel books that began to appear
after the War of 1812. Most were very positive in boasting the advantages of the frontier. John Scott's *Indiana Gazetteer*, published in 1826,
not only assured potential newcomers that "No soil produces a greater
abundance than that of Indiana" but also provided optimistic, detailed, and sometimes inaccurate descriptions of the counties, towns,
and natural features of the state.[6] Likely more important than travel
books were word of mouth and written descriptions from relatives
and friends who had preceded the westward moving emigrant. They
told about the availability, richness, and price of land, the quality of
timber and water, the access to rivers and streams, and the prevalence
of fever and milk sickness. Many of the early arriving pioneers from

the upland South found the hilly, unglaciated sections of southern Indiana most like the area they had left in soil, terrain, and vegetation, but there was wide variety in the criteria influencing choice of land and sharp individual differences even within the same family.

Although some pioneers simply squatted on land they found desirable, most understood also the wisdom of obtaining clear title to the land. Federal policy had made land ownership increasingly easy, for it was based since the Land Ordinance of 1785 on the assumption that economic democracy was important to political democracy, that both had some relationship to ready access to the public domain. Under political pressure from the West, Congress reduced the price of land, lowered the minimum acreage of land necessary to purchase, and opened district land offices close to the place of settlement. The first land sales at offices in Indiana occurred at Vincennes in 1807 and at Jeffersonville in 1808. The great migration following the War of 1812 brought a rush of eager purchasers, giving reality to the popular phrase "doing a land office business." The Vincennes office sold 286,558 acres in 1817, leading the nation in sales. With the opening of central Indiana by the New Purchase Treaty of 1818 Congress created land offices in Terre Haute and Brookville, later moved to Crawfordsville and Indianapolis. During the 1820s Indiana's land offices sold nearly two million acres, most of it in the central portion of the state. In the 1830s the busiest office was at Fort Wayne, selling acreage in the northern third of the state. The Fort Wayne office, which had disposed of only 18,836 acres in the 1820s, sold 1,294,357 acres in the boom year of 1836 alone. Relatively easy access to cheap but productive land was fundamental to the rapid settlement of frontier Indiana.[7]

Also fundamental to settlement was the pioneer family. The movement west was a family enterprise. Hardly anyone pioneered alone. Individual men or groups of men sometimes went ahead to select a site and construct a shelter, clear some land, and plant a crop. But these trailblazers were soon followed by the women and children, so that the sex ratio of men to women on the frontier was only slightly unbalanced and for only a short period of early settlement. The basic unit, often from the first plunge into the wilderness, was the nuclear family—husband, wife, and minor children.

The frontier family was youthful and large. Younger men and women were more likely to seek a start in the West, often soon after the wedding ceremony. And pioneer women married younger and, partly as a consequence, had more children than did women who remained in the East. It was not unusual for a frontier woman to begin bearing children at the age of eighteen and to have a child every other year until her mid-forties. The number of children and their spacing were determined less by contraception, which was seldom practiced, than by biological constraints of pregnancy, breast-feeding, and finally menopause. It is likely that as a consequence the birth rate in Indiana in the 1810s ranked among the highest in the world. Though high infant mortality reduced the total number of children in the population, there was hardly a dwelling on the frontier that did not include children, often as many as five or more. As the land became more densely settled and as towns and commerce developed the fertility rate declined and the population lost some of its youthful cast. But for the early frontier period large and youthful families were the norm. These families constituted the basic economic and social unit of pioneer Indiana.[8]

An immediate requirement of the frontier family was shelter. The first home was often an open-faced lean-to, quickly and easily constructed. A fire at the open end, which usually faced south, provided only slight comfort. It was in such a crude structure that the family of Tom Lincoln spent their first winter on the Indiana frontier. As soon as possible, but usually not until some crops had been planted, the family set about building a log cabin, the home that became the ubiquitous reality and symbolic expression of the frontier.[9] Logs, often of tulip poplar and about a foot in diameter, were cut to proper size and notched at the ends so that corners would be level and secure. Neighbors often helped to raise the cabin walls, joining in labor that included also opportunities to visit and play. On one wall a door was cut and sometimes but not always a window, on another wall a fireplace and chimney were built. Spaces between the logs were chinked with clay, mud, and small pieces of wood. The roof was of clapboards, the floor of dirt, often packed with clay and a sand covering. These early log cabins were constructed hastily with few tools and no nails, yet they served well the fundamental need for shelter. Later, as time and inclination allowed, the round-log cabin would be modified with the

Log cabin and settler in southern Indiana, sketched by Basil Hall, 1828. (Lilly Library, Indiana University)

addition of a wooden floor, a loft, or more rooms. Hewn-log houses became increasingly more desirable and possible. With the logs squared to form straight walls, these more sophisticated homes had wooden floors, several windows, and two or more rooms; and they required a large variety of tools to build, including axes, hatchets, saws, hammers, nails, and planes, not all of which were readily available on the early frontier. Only near the end of the pioneer period did houses of sawed lumber or brick appear in large numbers.[10]

The inside of the pioneer home was sparsely furnished. The father made all the furniture, including beds, three-legged stools, tables, perhaps a corner cupboard. Most utensils were also made of wood or of gourds, but each family had some iron cookware, including the three-legged spider skillet to fry meat and a larger skillet to make corn pone. These cooking irons plus a few knives and some bedclothes constituted the essential household items brought to the frontier by nearly all pioneers. Pewter dishes, reflector ovens, slat-back chairs, and clocks were luxuries often acquired only later.

With the minimum amount of time and effort spent building and furnishing the first home, the pioneer family concentrated its attention on producing food.

Food, Clothing, and Health

No one starved, but obtaining food was the major focus of life for the pioneer family. Not only their physical well-being but the content and rhythm of their days and years depended on the manner and means by which they put food on the table.

Much of that food in the early years of pioneering was wild game. A rifle was an essential tool brought to the frontier, and all men could and did use it as a part of their work-day chores. The simple single shot long rifle proved an adequate tool on the early frontier partly because wild game was so plentiful. Travel accounts and pioneer reminiscences are filled with descriptions of herds of deer too large to be counted, flocks of wild turkeys that numbered in the hundreds, and wild pigeons that darkened the sky. Deer was the primary objective of the hunter, and venison hams were commonplace in the family diet. Wild turkeys were the tastiest of frontier meats, squirrel perhaps the most common. No unusual skill was required to kill these and other animals, though the scarcity of powder and lead put a premium on marksmanship. The family hound dogs were useful companions in bringing game into the hunter's sights. Fish were also abundant and catching them required little skill or patience: almost any kind of bait or method would produce quick results.

Many of the wild animals began to disappear from Indiana with increasing density of human population, clearing of wooded land, and intense hunting. The buffalo were the first to go, even before there were many pioneers' cabins north of the Ohio. Bear and deer soon became scarce too. Pigeons were still sold by the bushel in the Indianapolis market as late as the 1840s, but the passenger pigeon would soon be gone from the state and eventually entirely extinct. Growing scarcity of wild animals demanded more skill, patience, and improved weapons, but by that time game was no longer the primary item in the diet, and hunting was becoming a sport to amuse men rather than put essential food on the table. Only gradually did state government begin to regulate hunting through licenses and closed seasons.

Wild game dominated the diet of the early pioneer, but from the forests the family could also gather other foods and add variety. Nuts, berries, and grapes were plentiful in season. Some fruits grew wild, including the pawpaw, persimmon, and crab apple. Children became especially adept at locating and gathering these wild foods. Many of the berries and fruits were much tastier when sweetened, and the forest provided the necessary ingredient. The honey bee was an emigrant from the East who usually moved in advance of humans. Locating a bee tree was one of the challenging but genuine pleasures of pioneer life, for one tree could provide many pounds of honey as well as beeswax. Sweetening also came from the hard maple tree in the form of "sugar molasses" and maple sugar, but sugar making required equipment and time that was not available until after the first years of settlement.

Food from the forest was critical in surviving the first few years on the Indiana frontier. Culturally, however, the pioneer was not a hunter or gatherer but a farmer, and from the beginning the family set to work to obtain food from the soil in a regular and controlled manner. The pioneer farmer's first task was not to plant but to chop. Nearly everywhere on the early Indiana frontier trees covered the land. The abundant virgin timber provided many items necessary for family life, including shelter, tools, utensils, and fuel for heating and cooking. Indeed, so essential were trees to the material culture that emigrants were reluctant to settle on Indiana's treeless prairies.

But trees were also an obstacle that farmers had to remove. Clearing land was the hardest and most time-consuming job facing the settler. His tool was the woodsman's ax, a tool as important on the frontier as the rifle. With it alone he felled trees from three to as much as ten feet in diameter, though the larger trees were often girdled by removing the bark the whole way around, causing them to die. Girdled trees could be burned later or left to fall. Meanwhile, with the leaves dead and the sunshine let in a crop could be quickly planted in the deadening. Some of the cleared timber was used for buildings and fuel, some split into rails for fences. Virginia or snake rail fences required large quantities of wood, and their snakelike zigzag wasted land: but both land and wood were abundant, and these efficient fences were relatively easy to build. Clearing the land produced much more timber than could be used for fences, buildings, or fuel, however. The pioneer cut trees into movable sizes and rolled them onto piles to burn. This logrolling was often a group activity that brought neighborly sport and socializing to a difficult task. Burning wood and brush made smoke omnipresent on the frontier and as much a sign of progress as the outpouring of industrial chimneys would be to the next generation.

Once cleared, the land had to be broken. Farmers from the upland South favored a jumping shovel plow, pulled by a horse or two, which would cut through small roots but jump over large ones. Yankees tended to use a heavier, cast iron plow, pulled by oxen, which would cut through even a four-inch oak root. On prairies where there were no trees thickly rooted grass required special sod plows and new techniques of plowing. Whatever the method, the soil had to be scratched and turned by a plow, the clumps and clods broken up with a harrow. It was then ready to plant.

The first crop planted was invariably corn. Corn was the base of pioneer agriculture, as it was for the Indians and as it would remain for generations of Hoosier farmers down to the present. Upland southerners were especially attached to the crop, but throughout the state corn was king. It was a good choice. Corn grew easily in the Indiana soil and climate, even when planted among trees and stumps in a deadening. It produced perhaps double the food per acre of any other grain and quickly became the staple item in the diet of humans and animals. Pioneer women pounded and grated corn into meal, which they boiled to make mush and baked to make johnny cake and corn pone (baked "hard enough," Baynard Rush Hall wrote, "to do execution from cannon").[11] With the outer shell removed they made the grain into hominy for boiling or frying. Corn was also the basis for whiskey, which according to one disapproving traveler in Indiana was "drunk like water . . . " even though it "smells somewhat like bed-bugs."[12] Whether in liquid or solid form, corn was usually on the table whenever an Indiana family sat down to a meal.

The corn not consumed by the family was fed to the livestock. Pioneer families brought with them or soon acquired a milk cow and some chickens. But most important, they raised hogs, though modern pig farmers would hardly recognize the pioneer variety. Commonly known as razorbacks or landsharks, they were long-legged and wiry, fleet afoot, able to protect themselves and to forage for their own food

in the woods, where they subsisted on mast and roots. A
prior to slaughter the farmer penned them up to fatten o
butchering usually occurred just before Christmas, with the first cou.
weather, and was often a cooperative task shared by neighbors. Pioneers wasted no part of the animal. Families savored fresh meat in
the weeks following butchering, a time when many men regained the
weight lost during the harvest. But most of the pork they preserved
with salt and smoked. Throughout the year a day seldom passed that
a pioneer family did not eat pork.

Pork, wild game, and corn constituted the basic diet of pioneer
Hoosiers, and the first years on the frontier were devoted largely to
providing these foods. But the family also began as soon as possible
to introduce variety and additional nutrition from a vegetable garden.
The garden was the responsibility of the woman, aided by the children. She planted cabbage, beans, peas, potatoes, onions, cucumbers,
pumpkins, lettuce, turnips, peppers, and other common vegetables.
The beans were especially important as they were often the only supplement to the pork and cornmeal during late winter and early spring.
In an herb garden near the cabin she grew sage, thyme, mustard,
tansy, and other seasonings to perk up a bland diet. Later she planted
also a few flowers—hollyhocks, marigolds, wild roses, and verbenas.
Most families brought some seeds with them when they moved west;
and each season they carefully collected and preserved choice seeds
for the next planting. Winter visits often included seed swapping
among pioneer women and exchange of advice on when and how to
plant.

As important as putting out a flourishing vegetable patch was preserving the harvest for use out of season. Women dried much of the
food: they strung beans, red peppers, and strips of pumpkin to hang
inside the cabin. They made jellies and preserves, pickled cucumbers,
and turned cabbage to kraut. Potatoes and turnips they buried ("holed
up") to keep into winter.

Providing food was the major occupation of most pioneer families.
They did it with increasing success, as they spent less time hunting
and gathering and more time farming. There were often desirable
foods they did without in the early years, such as sugar, coffee, apples,
and salt, and their culinary culture was limited to boiling and frying—
long and hard "till the pieces curled at the edges, and the taste of one

kind of flesh could not be distinguished from another...."[13] Although at least one traveler among Hoosiers was moved to plead, "Deliver me from their cookery,"[14] many an aged pioneer, especially if from the upland South, went to the grave convinced that there was no better meal on earth than a piece of salt pork, boiled beans, and cornbread. Whatever later judgments of taste, few successes on the Indiana frontier were more important than the achievement of producing food in large quantity and with increasing variety and nutritional content. Indeed, many among the first generation of pioneers soon produced more than they could consume. That abundance would be fundamental in transforming pioneer Indiana.

Frontier families also made their own clothing. The most common material in the first years was deerskin, which pioneers fashioned as did Indians into moccasins, shirts, and breeches. Soon after settlement they planted flax, which provided a long fiber that women spun on a wheel into thread and loomed into linen cloth. Eventually sheep provided wool that was carded and spun into yarn. Wool yarn and linen thread were often woven together to produce linsey-woolsey, a hard-wearing, coarse cloth used to make much of the family clothing. Mothers and daughters spent many hours creating the hum of the spinning wheel, the rattle and click of the home loom (though less common), and the flash of knitting and sewing needles necessary to keep a large and growing family in clothing. They also worked to make bedclothes, especially quilts and coverlets (perhaps the most sophisticated and beautiful of pioneer handicrafts), which would dress up the bed standing so conspicuously in a corner of the cabin. And if there was a cow or two, women and children did the milking, churned the butter, and, if they were New Englanders, made the cheese. In this household manufacturing, so important to the pioneer economy, women had major responsibility.

While women worked with thread, fabric, and food preparation men spent indoor time with leather and wood. Sitting in front of the fireplace they fashioned wooden utensils, tools, and furniture, ranging from forks to shovels to corner cupboards. And they worked leather into harnesses, boots, and shoes. Often they used the same last for right and left shoes, one reason why many pioneers went barefoot in warmer weather. Men's indoor chores were not as extensive as women's so that in winter months they often had greater leisure—it was time to whittle, drink corn liquor, hunt with neighbors, or just sit and stare into the fire. Work varied with the season for both sexes, but less so for women, whose work more likely was never done.

One constant in the life of the pioneer family was the threat of ill-health. There is considerable evidence to contradict the image of the pioneer as hardy and robust. Fevers of various kinds were the most common lament, particularly the ague, a malarial disease that brought debilitating fever and chills. In uncleared and swampy areas fevers could kill off dozens of individuals and leave whole families unable to work for weeks. Epidemic diseases also brought death, particularly the dreaded cholera that struck terror in Indiana in 1833 and 1849. Some diseases were seasonal, such as the milk sickness that killed Nancy Lincoln and hundreds of other pioneers. Families also knew the dangers of accidental injury: broken bones from a horseback mishap, deep cuts from a misjudged ax swing, and burns from the open fireplace were realities of life, particularly for less experienced and younger pioneers.[15]

The first line of response to accident and illness was the pioneer woman. The sources of her home remedies varied greatly: some derived from Indian medicine; some from popular home medical books; most passed from mother to daughter as folk medicine. From roots and herbs, she prepared such home remedies as sassafras tea and Jimson-leaf salve. Many pioneer families also relied on a variety of charms: a spider worn around the neck would cure ague; the water in which nine eggs had been boiled would end infertility; a toad would draw out the poison of a rattlesnake bite; an onion in the pocket would prevent snakebite. Superstitious charms and spells may not have been efficacious, but they probably did less harm than the patent medicines advertised and sold as cures for every known disease. Not only did they siphon off family cash, but such patent medicines often contained arsenic, alcohol, or opium.

The pioneer family was so largely dependent on home remedies because physicians were expensive and often ineffective. Scientific understanding of disease and treatment was very limited. Medical training was usually no more than an apprenticeship served with an older doctor. The Indiana Medical College at LaPorte organized in 1841, but the training was sadly deficient. There was considerable disagreement in pioneer Indiana about methods of treatment. State efforts to examine and license physicians began with the first legislature in 1816 but were of slight consequence. The formation of the Indiana State Medical Society in 1849 was a step toward professionalization, but the variety of therapies and their uncertain results continued to handicap the practice of medicine. Most physicians practiced bloodletting, sometimes with leeches, sometimes with a "scarificator," which cut the skin and then allowed the blood to collect in small glass cups. Following a good bleeding, many doctors prescribed a harsh drug. Powerful laxatives were most popular, especially calomel, which, unknown to its users, caused mercury poisoning. Many pioneer physicians also performed surgery despite the handicaps of inadequate instruments and no anesthesia. Under these conditions it is not surprising that doctors usually were called only as a last resort. In sickness as in health, the pioneer family often relied on its own members and on neighbors rather than specialized or formalized aid.

The people who arrived first in a new area usually set the patterns that dominated and endured. Even though larger numbers of later arrivals might have brought different values and cultural styles and even though those of the first generation might have become outmoded and no longer relevant, they endured. The patterns of pioneer life in Indiana did endure, down even to the present. The attachment to family, the belief in progress through hard work, the significance of farming as an economic activity and a way of life, the contrasting but merging streams of upland South, Mid-Atlantic, and Yankee cultures—these and other features of early pioneer Indiana remained long after the frontier was no more.

But there was change too. Hoosiers would look back on their frontier history with a romantic glow, emphasizing the valor and sacrifice of the pioneer generation and celebrating their achievement in settling a wilderness. What was too often ignored in later celebrations was that most newcomers to Indiana acted out of no sense of uncommon valor or grand purpose. Their objectives were simpler and more straightforward—to create a slightly better life than the one that seemed possible in Virginia or Pennsylvania or Kentucky. And their methods were not heroic but quite commonsensical. They did what they had to do in that time and that place to create a better life. Mostly they performed hard but repetitive and simple chores, such as girdling a tree or spinning flax, again and again as generations before them had done in the East. Their own feelings about such chores and about pioneer life generally were not romantic, not even accepting. For the pioneers' most important reaction to their frontier condition was not to preserve it but to attempt to change it, to move as soon as possible beyond log cabin, ax, and spinning wheel. The "purest patriotism," a Martin County Fourth of July orator proclaimed in 1821, was to "convert the gloomy woods into fields waving with luxuriant harvests. . . ."[16] The pioneers' achievement in doing that was perhaps more important than their initial plunge into the wilderness.

v

The Evolving
Pioneer Economy

Nearly all pioneers possessed the skills and the resources to survive; most wanted to live at a level above mere survival, however, to flourish economically. The key to moving beyond subsistence was specialization. Pioneers had to concentrate their energies on those economic activities in which they had a comparative economic advantage—those they could do better—and give up to others those activities others could do better. For most pioneer farmers in Indiana this meant concentrating on growing a surplus of corn and hogs and, at the same time, gradually abandoning the variety of household manufacturing that had provided their basic necessities. With their profits from the sale of corn and hogs they could purchase such goods as clothing, soap, furniture, and even new cast-iron stoves from local artisans or from local merchants supplied by distant manufacturers. In this way farmers moved from subsistence to commercial agriculture and became part of the larger regional and national economy. They became specialists, like the artisans, manufacturers, and merchants.

The transition to commercial agriculture required more than simply the desire of farmers to specialize and grow a surplus of corn and hogs. It required the development of manufacturing and mercantile facilities. And it required the development of means to bring together mercantile, manufacturing, and agricultural production. Farmers had to be able to reach markets in which to sell large quantities of corn and hogs; merchants and manufacturers had to be able to deliver goods and services to Indiana farmers at reasonable prices. Transportation was critical in this evolving pioneer economy.

Rivers and Roads

Isolated farmers were subsistence farmers. Breaking down that isolation was the single most important public goal in the period between statehood and the Civil War. No subject generated as much interest as possible ways to improve transportation to and from the farms and villages of pioneer Indiana (see Map 5). So strong was this need that many Hoosiers—despite their Jeffersonian sentiments favoring individual responsibility and limited government—came to believe that state and federal governments had major responsibilities to promote the general welfare through public investment in transportation.[1]

The first generation of settlers depended primarily on primitive roads and uncertain rivers. The natural routes that brought pioneer families to Indiana were suited also for trade, but not ideally so. Blocking movement of goods eastward, especially bulk goods such as corn and pork, were the Appalachian Mountains and the generally southwestward flow of the rivers and streams. As a consequence, Indiana products did not reach markets in Philadelphia or New York by moving eastward. Rather, early trade from Indiana flowed southward and in a counterclockwise, roundabout direction via the Ohio and Mississippi river system to New Orleans and then via sailing vessel to the Atlantic seaports. Only gradually with new and improved transportation facilities in the 1830s and later would Indiana's trade orientation shift toward eastern and northern routes. Development of such routes

MAP 5.

Early Routes of Transportation

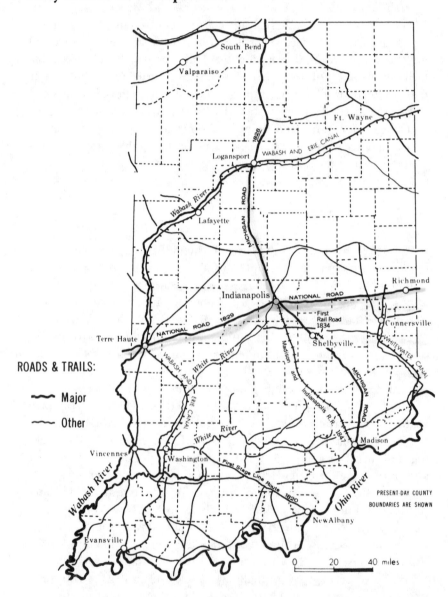

ROADS & TRAILS:

〰 Major

— Other

SOURCE: Robert C. Kingsbury, *An Atlas of Indiana* (Bloomington, 1970), 74

was essential to the growth of northern Indiana. Southern Indiana remained strongly tied to the Ohio-Mississippi river trade up to the Civil War.

Indiana's first farms and towns were nearly all located on a river— the Ohio, Wabash, Whitewater, and White rivers and the many streams and creeks that flowed into them. Rivers were the first and most important outlet for farmers wishing to sell a surplus in a distant market. The means of moving that surplus over water was usually the flatboat, a rectangular wooden box simply designed and cheaply built to carry large quantities downstream on the current. Constructed by a farmer or group of farmers or by a local merchant, the flatboat was loaded with corn, flour, pork, and other agricultural goods and launched on the spring floods toward New Orleans. The crew often included local farmboys experiencing their first glimpse of the world beyond the family clearing. Such was the case for Abraham Lincoln, who in 1828, at the age of nineteen, made the flatboat journey from Little Pigeon Creek to New Orleans, a three-month trip that earned him $24 and introduced him to American commerce and southern slavery. On reaching New Orleans flatboat crews sold their goods, often in a market glutted with hundreds of other cargoes from the frontier. The flatboat was broken up for the lumber and sold, and the crew after seeing the bawdy sights of New Orleans set off for home. In the early years many walked back to Indiana. This flatboat trade was Indiana's primary tie to a national market economy until the mid-nineteenth century.

Flatboats were one-way craft. Early up-river navigation was the task of keelboats, narrow vessels pointed at both ends. With poles and sometimes ropes, muscular crews laboriously moved keelboats up- stream. Because of the labor and time (averaging six miles a day) only goods of low bulk and weight and/or very high value were transported to Indiana in keelboats. Coffee, molasses, salt, and sugar were the most important items moved up river from New Orleans.

The most significant change in river transportation came from the nineteenth century's most revolutionary technology—steam. Steam- boats appeared in large numbers on western waters after the War of 1812. Advances in design enabled them to travel on shallow water— some said even on a heavy dew—and at increasingly faster speeds. Most important, they traveled easily up river, making the journey

Flatboats and steamboat on the
Ohio River. (Indiana Historical
Society)

from New Orleans to Indiana in eight days by the 1830s, and they brought a steady decrease in both up and down-river freight rates. With the steamboat, Ohio River towns like Madison entered periods of rapid growth. Steamboats also traveled the Wabash, reaching Terre Haute in 1823 and Lafayette three years later. Navigating the shallow White River proved impractical: only one steamboat got as far north as Indianapolis (in 1831) and it got stuck on a sandbar. The town's poor river access was a serious disappointment to its boosters and a major handicap to its economic development before 1850. On the Great Lakes steamboat navigation was well underway by the 1820s and provided significant improvements in access to and from northern Indiana. Michigan City, after receiving federal aid to improve its harbor and after construction of the Michigan Road, became a major outlet for northern Indiana produce. There was also some steamboat traffic on the St. Joseph River connecting South Bend with Lake Michigan.

Even the steamboat did not solve all the difficulties of river transportation. Low water in summer and ice in winter often made transportation impossible. Routes were fixed by nature and did not reach all parts of the state. Obstructions in the river and the alarming tendency of boilers to explode made steamboats liable to sink in an age when few people could swim. There were some government efforts to remedy these problems. The state in 1820 prohibited obstruction of navigable rivers (as with mill dams) by declaring them public highways. In 1837 the legislature passed a safety inspection law, titled "An Act to prevent disasters on Steam Boats," though it does not seem to have been enforced. And the federal government began in the 1820s to remove river obstructions and improve navigation on the Ohio and Mississippi.

Travel by land was more prosaic but increasingly more important as population moved northward and away from navigable rivers. Many roads followed animal and Indian trails, as did the Buffalo Trace from New Albany to Vincennes. Some were routes hacked out by military expeditions against the Indians. Statehood brought larger government interest in road construction. The Enabling Act of 1816 provided that Indiana would receive three percent of the proceeds from the sale of public lands within its borders to be applied to transportation. With this three-percent fund as the source of revenue Indiana embarked on an attempt to develop a state highway system. The General Assembly in 1821 provided for the construction of two dozen state roads, many reaching to the new location for the state capital at Indianapolis. The 1821 legislation was democratic and localist since it was intended to provide roads to serve many if not all citizens in the state and since construction was locally supervised. But dispersing the effort over the state rather than concentrating limited resources on a few main roads meant that the quality of construction and maintenance was exceedingly poor. Here, as would happen again and again in matters of public policy, Hoosiers preferred a local, decentralized, democratically oriented strategy rather than a more efficient centralized, coordinated plan. The 1821 act only suggested a highway network; a true state highway system did not develop in Indiana until after World War I.

The state did undertake construction of one major highway, the Michigan Road, which brought improved north-south land transport. The growth of northern Indiana and the location of the new state capital argued for a road connecting Lake Michigan with Indianapolis and the Ohio River. Urged by Governor James B. Ray, the Potawatomi Indians in 1826 gave up a strip of land north of the Wabash and added additional parcels of land to sell for revenue to construct the road. Governor Ray correctly anticipated that this "project of national and state aggrandizement" would sever the Indian land, stimulate white settlement, and "weaken the attachment of the Potawatomi to his country," leading to Potawatomi removal a dozen years later.[2] There was much controversy in locating termini for the road, but the harbor at Michigan City proved the choice for the northern end and the rapidly growing town of Madison for the southern. The road was opened the full distance by 1836, and the towns thorough which it ran benefited considerably, including South Bend, Logansport, Indianapolis, Greensburg, and Versailles.

One other major road also served Indiana. The National Road was a federal project, begun in 1811 from Cumberland, Maryland, to the West. Slowly moving westward, the road reached Wheeling, Virginia, in 1818 and then moved on through Columbus, Ohio, crossing Indiana in the 1830s. Connecting Richmond, Indianapolis, Terre Haute, and many smaller towns, the National Road provided important local transportation and became the main land route to and from the East.

Many of the early state roads were little more than partially cleared trails; none benefited from stone or gravel surfaces. Even the National and Michigan roads were often in poor condition, with stumps still standing. During the rainy spring and fall seasons they were often impassable. Baynard Rush Hall's journey on horseback from the Ohio River to Bloomington took him through "the most ill-looking, dark-coloured morasses, enlivened by streams of purer mud crossing at right angles." The traveler's goal was to find mud that had "at least some bottom."[3] As late as 1848 an Indianapolis writer humorously informed his La Porte correspondent that "The roads are not now *navigable* and this [letter] may be long in reaching you."[4] Both land and river transport were seasonal but in opposite order: dry summers and frozen winters favored land but not river movement while wet springs and falls were ideal for river navigation but not for roads.

Canals and the System of 1836

The limitations of road and river transportation caused Indiana's growing population to demand new forms of access to the outside world. The success of New York's Erie Canal, completed in 1825, sparked a canal boom in the Old Northwest. In Indiana largest attention focused on connecting Lake Erie with the Ohio River, along the Wabash trade route. But with canals as with roads there were intense regional rivalries and jealousies that urged canals for all major areas of the state. State government eventually responded to this pressure.

Indiana's first serious effort at canal construction was the Wabash and Erie Canal. The federal government provided crucial aid in 1827, when Congress authorized a half-million-acre land grant to enable Indiana to finance construction. After some delay, work began in the Fort Wayne area in 1832. Soon more than a thousand laborers, many of them Irish immigrants, were moving dirt with pick and shovel, while more skilled artisans built locks, culverts, and aqueducts under the guidance of the hard-working chief engineer, Jesse L. Williams. Fort Wayne's Fourth of July celebration in 1835 marked the opening of the canal between that town and Huntington and spurred a new intensity of canal mania throughout the state. Indeed, as with roads, each region of the state wanted a canal to ensure economic progress: notions of democracy and equality added to political logrolling to provide something for everyone.

The Mammoth Internal Improvements Act of 1836 was perhaps the most daring and most important piece of legislation passed in the history of the state. It provided for three major canal projects: extension of the Wabash and Erie Canal from Lafayette to Terre Haute; construction of the Whitewater Canal in the populous southeastern portion of the state, linking the National Road with the Ohio River; and construction of the Central Canal, running from the Wabash and Erie near Peru to Indianapolis and southward to Evansville. In addition, the system of 1836 promised a macadamized road from New Albany to Vincennes, removal of obstructions on the Wabash River, survey of a land route from Jeffersonville to Crawfordsville, and, most forward-looking of all, construction of a railroad from Madison to Lafayette via Indianapolis. To finance these enterprises, the legislature authorized an appropriation of $10,000,000 to be borrowed at five percent. A six-man Internal Improvements Board was to supervise the system.

After unprecedented public celebrations, state officials began to sell Indiana canal and internal improvement bonds in the money markets of New York, and Jesse Williams and his associates initiated planning, surveying, and construction in Indiana. Never had the state seen such a broad, concerted, systematic effort to effect change, to move Indiana rapidly from its pioneer condition of isolation.

More abruptly than it had begun, work stopped on nearly all projects. The immediate cause was a financial panic and severe depression that began in 1839. None of the several projects in the system of 1836 was completed. Canal workers had finished ninety miles on the Wabash and Erie, thirty miles on the Whitewater, and nine on the Central. Twenty-eight miles of the Madison and Indianapolis Railroad were complete and forty-one miles of macadamized road from New Albany were in place. An additional 300 miles of partly dug or graded projects did little to brighten the bleak picture. Even worse, the state was insolvent.

By 1841 embarrassed officials admitted that Indiana could not pay even the interest on its internal improvements debt, much less the principal. A London newspaper doubtless spoke for the many Amer-

ican as well as British investors in Indiana bonds when it denounced
the state as "the land of promise for all the knavery and thievery of
the known world."[5] With delinquent interest increasing by half a million dollars a year, unhappy New York and London creditors appointed a lawyer, Charles Butler, to negotiate repayment. Not until
1847 did Butler and the legislature reach a compromise agreement.
The Butler Bill provided that Indiana would be responsible for payment of half its internal improvement debt, which by then amounted
to $11,065,000. The other half would be assumed by the bondholders,
who would receive stock in the Wabash and Erie Canal in return. The
bondholders promised to complete the canal to Evansville, a risk made
more palatable by a large grant of land from the federal government.[6]

The series of events that began with the Mammoth Internal Improvements Act of 1836 and ended with the Butler Bill of 1847 are
often and misleadingly labeled the internal improvements debacle.
The 1836 legislation, one writer has argued, "was conceived in madness and nourished by delusion . . . in a lunatic climate."[7] Such a harsh
interpretation requires similar negative assessment of those presum-
ably otherwise sane and sensible investors in New York and Europe
who gave monetary support to the system of 1836. Surely there were
failures: construction of canals and other improvements was more
costly and more technically difficult than naive and enthusiastic proponents assumed; mismanagement and outright fraud marred the
program; above all, there was the debt. The state eventually paid half
of it, as promised in 1847, but no more. The creditors who had accepted Wabash and Erie Canal stock in return for the other half lost
heavily. Indiana's reputation suffered a blow that stung long after the
wooden canal boats and locks had rotted.

But the system of 1836 was not a complete debacle, and the men
who approved it were not lunatics. In some ways, in fact, their inten-
tions are understandable, their actions rational, their achievements
notable. Their most successful endeavor was the Wabash and Erie
Canal. It carried large quantities of freight and passengers in the
1840s and 1850s. When finally completed to Evansville in 1853 it
covered a distance of 468 miles, making it the longest canal in the
country. The southern section was often inoperable and never attracted much traffic. But the section above Terre Haute opened for
northern Indiana a new and important gateway for shipping agri-

culture products to northeastern markets. Corn shipments reaching Lake Erie from the Wabash and Maumee valleys totaled 2.8 million bushels by 1851. As northern Indiana farmers found new outlets for their produce, population increased and warehouses, hotels, mills, factories, and towns sprang to life along the canal line. Fort Wayne, Peru, Logansport, Delphi, and Lafayette owed much of their growth to the Wabash and Erie Canal. The Whitewater Canal, completed in 1846 and operated by a private company, was not as successful, but it too contributed to the profits of farmers in the region and to the development of towns such as Connersville, Brookville, and Lawrenceburg. Neither of these canals was profitable to investors, and both were plagued by low water, floods, and deteriorating banks and rotting locks, but they did contribute to the economic growth of the region they served.[8]

Part of the threat to canals by 1850 was the development of the railroad. The Madison and Indianapolis, provided for in the system of 1836, was turned over to private enterprise and completed to Indianapolis in 1847. Other, eventually more important, east-west railroads soon began to challenge canal transportation in speed, dependability, and flexibility. By the late 1850s the iron rail and steam engine had proven superior to the horse-drawn canal boat. But the victory ought not negate the important developmental role of canals in the three decades before the Civil War.

Exclusive focus on the financial failure of canals and the system of 1836 obscures two other important meanings: the Mammoth Internal Improvements Act symbolized both the optimism and the democracy of the age. The generation that appropriated ten million dollars to revolutionize transportation at a time when the state's annual revenues averaged less than $75,000 took a risk. They lost, and looked foolish in the end, but only in the end. At the outset one must appreciate the forward-looking optimism, the belief in progress, the intense desire to lift Indiana out of the mud and leave behind the isolation of pioneer life. So intense was this need, so hopeful was this generation that they eagerly and nearly unanimously committed the state to the system of 1836. Indeed, in a curious irony of history this venturesome pioneer generation contributed to the reluctance of succeeding generations to take similar risks, to use state government, as they had, to pursue the general welfare. Revulsion with the system of 1836 was a direct cause of the provision in the Indiana constitution of 1851 that to this day restricts the state from going into debt.[9] Even more important, this revulsion contributed generally to shaping a more conservative outlook in Indiana, a reluctance to venture actively into the public arena, a tendency of Hoosiers to prefer limited state government. Whether this is in fact the proper lesson to be learned from the system of 1836 is open to debate, but it is the lesson generations of Indianans have chosen to learn.

The system of 1836 is important also because it was a democratic system, perhaps excessively so. It promised internal improvements for nearly every nook and cranny in the state, though there were some politicians disappointed that their constituents did not receive more attention. A few cautious individuals argued for concentrating limited resources on selected major improvements, completing those first, and then moving on to construct others. But the logrolling, localist democracy of Indiana politics knocked aside such arguments for concentration and classification. Simultaneous construction thus began on many dispersed segments: when it was halted the state was left with bits and pieces of "scatteration," rather than any single completed project.

Pioneer democracy and optimism combined with the bad timing and luck of national depression to create a system of internal improvements that did not meet expectations. The system of 1836 may have been unrealistic, naive, and foolish, as many have suggested. It might be more fruitful, however, to understand it as a major window into the pioneer generation's hopes and beliefs not only about the very important subject of transportation but about the relationship of people to their government and their society. That optimistic generation wanted change and believed that improved transportation was critical in providing it, so critical that they were willing to call on their government to promote change. Rather than fearing government, they used it to promote their democratic version of the general welfare.

Merchants, Bankers, and Manufacturers

Improvements in transportation helped make possible a growth in the number of Hoosiers who did not earn their living by work on a farm. Merchants, bankers, and manufacturers became increasingly important in the evolving pioneer economy, especially in providing the means whereby the agricultural surplus reached distant consumers and whereby Indiana farmers gained access to goods produced off their own farms.

Merchants were the most important businessmen in pioneer Indiana. They bought goods from wholesalers in New Orleans, Cincinnati, and the East, particularly Philadelphia and New York, arranged for their shipment to Indiana, and offered them on credit to customers in the surrounding countryside. The first merchants were general merchants, who, as one pioneer later remembered, sold "everything from a log-chain to a cambric needle, from a grubing-hoe to a silk shawl, from a sack of coffee to a barrel of whiskey."[10] Often they bartered agricultural products in return for store goods, and thereby became responsible for the transport and sale of Indiana pork, corn, wheat, and a variety of other items to distant markets. These merchants were thus essential middlemen, performing a variety of services necessary to move Indiana beyond self-sufficient agriculture.

More than anyone else merchants began to connect the frontier with the more settled regions of the nation. They traveled personally to East Coast markets, and returned with letters, newspapers, and new ideas as well as goods. They lobbied for transportation improvements and other forms of economic progress. Leading Fort Wayne merchants, such as Allen Hamilton and Samuel Hanna, actively pushed the building of the Wabash and Erie Canal, for example. Not surprisingly, merchants often became social and political leaders in their communities, and a few became wealthy as well as influential.

Many pioneer merchants also provided banking and other financial services. They usually offered their goods on credit and sometimes kept safe a neighbor's savings or acted as a financial agent on eastern buying trips. And, with the short supply of ready cash and credit on the frontier, they were usually among the leaders in arguing for an expanded money supply and the creation of formal banks. As with transportation development, merchants joined many other pioneers to assert that government had a responsibility to contribute to the public welfare by providing banking services.

In 1814 the Indiana territorial legislature chartered two banks—

one at Vincennes and the other at Madison. The Vincennes bank became in 1817 the first State Bank of Indiana, eventually with branches at Brookville, Corydon, and Vevay. This ambitious, state-owned institution came to an unhappy end in 1821, brought about by the panic of 1819 and by dishonesty, favoritism, and other unwise policies of its directors. The demise of the first State Bank left many Hoosiers with sour feelings about banks and with little access to banking facilities. In the late 1820s and early 1830s the branches of the Bank of the United States in Cincinnati and Louisville provided most of the paper currency circulating in the state. Demand for additional banking services combined with President Andrew Jackson's successful attack on the Bank of the United States to convince the state legislature in 1834 to charter the second State Bank of Indiana.

The new state institution had ten branches, located in Lawrenceburg, Madison, New Albany, Evansville, Vincennes, Bedford, Terre Haute, Indianapolis, Richmond, and Lafayette. As settlement increased in the north in the mid-1830s new branch banks were opened at Fort Wayne and South Bend. The decentralized branch system allowed considerable local independence. And the branches were generally well-managed, usually by the local mercantile elite. The institution attracted capital from the East, and it provided currency and credit that contributed to economic development, particularly in supporting trade. Like the internal improvements system of 1836 the second State Bank of Indiana reflected the pioneer eagerness for change and for access to the outside world, an eagerness so large as to bring about state government initiative to contribute to material prosperity and the public good.

The second State Bank was better managed than the first bank, although it too had considerable difficulty. The panics of 1837 and 1839 resulted in the bank's suspension of specie payments and some loss of confidence in banks generally. The second State Bank also became a partisan political issue. Although begun with considerable bipartisan support, the bank later drew vehement criticism from Jacksonian Democrats: in the late 1830s and early 1840s some hard-money Democrats professed objection to all banks; others charged that Whigs dominated the State Bank (a charge with considerable validity); and many Democrats and some Whigs asserted that the branch officers and directors had played favorites in making loans to merchants and

The Evolving Pioneer Economy

land speculators during the boom times of the 1830s, loan
hard-pressed debtors could not repay in the depression of the c.
1840s. These criticisms sparked some changes in personnel and policies in the early 1840s, particularly in the Indianapolis Branch, so that
from the mid-1840s until the bank charter expired in 1859 the institution provoked little direct criticism and successfully went about the
business of contributing to economic development by providing a relatively stable currency and a useful source of credit.[11]

Indiana merchants and bankers focused much of their economic
energy on facilitating and profiting from the export of agriculture
surplus to eastern and southern markets. But many also became interested in manufacturing. Indeed, there was a strong general sentiment in pioneer Indiana that argued for the necessity of fostering
a manufacturing capability if the state was to become more than a
colonial dependency of the East and if its people were to move significantly beyond a subsistence economy. Promoters of manufacturing
vigorously proclaimed the benefits of industrialization: the increasing
abundance of farm and forest could be processed into products suited
for transportation to and profitable sale in distant markets; and Indiana manufacturers could produce goods that the state's farmers had
to purchase from eastern markets, make themselves, or do without.

Pioneer manufacturing had several general characteristics. Most
early manufacturing enterprises were based on agriculture or natural
resources. Most were locally financed, owned, and operated, often by
men who were merchants. Most had small workforces, often consisting
only of the proprietor, perhaps with a young helper. Many operated
irregularly, often according to the changing seasons.

Perhaps the most important of pioneer manufactures was the mill
to grind corn and wheat. The earliest mills were operated by hand
or horse power, but water was a better source of power to turn large
mill stones. As farmers cleared and planted, a grist mill usually appeared on a nearby creek or stream. The mill owner dammed the
stream to create a mill race, sometimes causing conflict with flatboat-
men. Water power turned the wooden wheel, which was connected
by a series of wooden cogs and gears to the mill stone. The miller
poured the grain between the upper, turning stone and the lower,
stationary stone, which ground it to corn meal or flour. A portion of
the grain, usually one-sixth, went to the miller as his toll; the re-

mainder belonged to the farmer. Water-powered grist mills were important in enabling farmers to feed their own families and to convert large quantities of their surplus grain to a form in which it could be most profitably sold. The traffic to mills often led to the location of a country store, post office, and blacksmith shop near the mill site. Since most mills served a small hinterland, ideally no farther than a one-day round trip by horse or wagon, they dotted the countryside, and they tended to remain small, locally owned enterprises. Unfortunate farmers not within striking distance of a mill were condemned to little more than self-sufficient agriculture.

Other artisans and businessmen also began to serve farmers. A blacksmith provided tools and made repairs farmers could not make themselves: his strong arms cut and hammered out chains, hoes, horseshoes, nails, wagon wheels, and, if especially skilled, rifles and axes. A neighborhood tannery produced leather for harnesses and shoes, usually more efficiently than the home manufacturer. And skilled shoemakers began to provide footware more comfortable than that made in the family log cabin. A distillery converted corn to whiskey, either to be enjoyed or profited from. And a saw mill, often located with a grain mill, provided lumber to replace hand-hewn logs and to supply the craftsmen who began to produce furniture, wagons, and other wooden items for use on Indiana farms and for export to distant markets.[12]

Especially important to Indiana farmers seeking distant markets was the development of pork packing. Often a local merchant added this seasonal activity to the variety of functions he performed, since such men had access to the necessary working capital and business skills. Most early pork packing was done along rivers. By the mid-1840s Madison had emerged as the premier Indiana packing center and the third largest in the Midwest. Wabash River towns also began to pack pork, especially Lafayette and Terre Haute. By 1845 Jacob D. Early's Terre Haute plant was able to process 10,000 hogs annually. Pork packing also developed in Indianapolis in the 1840s, when the Mansur family came to dominate the industry. To these towns in late fall and early winter farmers drove their hogs, usually on foot, sometimes over such long distances as to reduce the weight and profit of the animal. Converting corn to hogs and driving hogs to market was nonetheless more likely to produce profit for many farmers than attempting to transport the more bulky corn crop over Indiana's roads and waterways. The advent of rail transport greatly encouraged hog production and concentrated packing in a few towns. Madison's packing business increased in the 1840s as its railroad moved northward but then declined with the advent of better rail service to other towns. Indianapolis became a major center as its rail network developed in the late 1840s and 1850s. These and other Indiana pork packing towns had to fight stiff competition from Cincinnati and later Chicago, a struggle in which Indianapolis eventually emerged as the strongest Indiana competitor.[13]

Pork packing, grain milling, and other pioneer enterprises were relatively small, seasonal, and erratic operations. Technology and machinery were simple. Capital invested was small. Profits often were slight too, and business failure and turnover in ownership were common. Some Indiana entrepreneurs and investors attempted to build manufacturing enterprises that moved beyond this pioneer stage. One particularly important avenue of change was steam power.

To many boosters steam power was the route to factories and cities. Steam could provide steady, cheap power in large quantities, compared to water, which was limited by seasons of drought and freezing. And steam engines could concentrate much larger amounts of power at one location, enabling operation of large manufacturing enterprises and concentration of manufacturing in one particular location. Madison, Indianapolis, and Fort Wayne all boasted of steam-powered mills in the 1830s. In towns along major transportation routes, especially those with access to Indiana's southwestern coal fields, steam power spread rapidly in the 1840s and 1850s.[14]

One of the most concerted and determined endeavors toward stimulating a takeoff in manufacturing was the Indianapolis Steam Mill Company. The company was chartered by the state legislature in 1828 and was financed and organized by businessmen of the town, led by Nicholas McCarty, one of the leading merchants and land speculators. The company wagoned overland from Cincinnati heavy boilers and engines to provide steam power for a grist mill, saw mill, and wool-carding mill, all housed in a new three-story building. With constant power running this multipurpose factory, McCarty and his associates hoped "to drive foreign flour &c. from our markets." For a brief time the company did just that, but by 1835 its engines were idle. The

Indianapolis Steam Mill Company became one of the largest business failures in Indianapolis's history, the victim of inadequate transportation facilities, insufficient demand for its products, and the miscalculations of energetic, forward-looking businessmen who prematurely plunged into steam power and factory production.[15]

A dozen years after the failure of the Indianapolis Steam Mill Company another similarly venturesome enterprise formed in Perry County. At Cannelton, on the banks of the Ohio, Hamilton Smith, a wealthy Louisville lawyer, determined to build a steam-powered cotton factory. The venture was consciously modeled on the New England textile mills, except that instead of relying on uncertain water power it would be driven by steam engines fueled by coal from nearby beds. Incorporated in 1847 as the Cannelton Cotton Mill Company, Smith and his associates succeeded in building a four-story mill, the largest textile factory west of the Alleghenies. They intended also to build a model mill town by providing workers with a school, church, company-owned housing, and other inducements to proper moral behavior, basing their vision on what they assumed to be the model example of the world-famous mills at Lowell, Massachusetts. The Cannelton Cotton Mill would bring modern New England manufacturing and piety to Indiana and the West. But technological miscalculations, difficulties of transportation, and inadequate investment capital brought the company's collapse in 1851. The mill later resumed textile production under new ownership, but the grand vision of rapid industrialization and paternal benevolence was dashed.[16]

The energetic drive behind the Cannelton Cotton Mill and the Indianapolis Steam Mill was indicative of the hunger for rapid industrialization that would enable Hoosiers to be less dependent on distant producers. Both enterprises were ahead of their time. Multistory factories built with large capital investments, powered by steam, humming with machinery, tended by many workers—these would be the industrial future not the present of pioneer Indiana. Before 1850 much production was done in the home by the family for family consumption. Small, individually owned and operated shops and mills constituted the core of the industrializing economy. By providing a means of turning agricultural surplus to profit for farmer and manufacturer they spurred the gradual development of commercial agriculture and manufacturing. In industrialization, as elsewhere in In-

Cannelton Cotton Mill. (Lilly Library, Indiana University)

diana's history, not revolution but evolution was the main road to change.

Town Building

Towns were an essential part of frontier development. In the years before 1850 they became increasingly important in economic, social, and political life, providing essential services to the rural and agricultural majority of Indiana's population. The function, location, and growth (or decline) of towns reflected broad features and changes in the evolving pioneer economy.

The fundamental factor in town location and growth in the early nineteenth century was transportation. Nearly all pioneer towns were located on rivers. Most important in the first decades of the century were towns on the Whitewater, Ohio, and lower Wabash—towns serving the early crescent-shaped settlement pattern: Richmond, Brookville, Lawrenceburg, Madison, Jeffersonville, New Albany, Evansville, Vincennes, and Terre Haute, among others. As settlers filled in the crescent and moved northward, new towns appeared, from Salem, Paoli, Bedford, Bloomington, and Greencastle by 1820 to Crawfordsville, Indianapolis, and Lafayette in the mid-1820s. Further north, during the 1820s and 1830s, Logansport, Fort Wayne, and South Bend began to evolve from Indian trading posts to all-purpose service centers for pioneer newcomers.

Fort Wayne in particular experienced spectacular growth in the 1830s: its population increased from fewer than 300 people in 1830 to about 1,500 by the end of the decade. Here as in other rapidly growing towns transportation was critical, initially with the Wabash River and, more importantly, with the attractions of the canal. Entrepreneurs, merchants, investors, workingmen, lawyers, and boosters of all sorts flocked to Fort Wayne, attracted by the canal's promise of economic prosperity. With some misgiving, a Presbyterian missionary to the West wrote from the Summit City in 1832: "the general inquiry is, how shall I make my fortune? Some are for taking contracts, some for speculating in land, and others for establishing groceries & *selling whiskey.*"[17]

Most newcomers did not make fortunes, in Fort Wayne or elsewhere, but some did. The first town fortunes were accumulated in combinations of land speculation, mercantile trade, and banking, sometimes with a dash of legal work as well. Allen Hamilton in Fort Wayne, James F. D. Lanier in Madison, and Calvin Fletcher in Indianapolis combined these sorts of activities to ride the crest of material prosperity in their respective towns, often at a rapid pace. In 1835 Fletcher's birthday prompted him to look backward and to note in his diary: "the past seems a dream, a delusion. I have witnessed a total wilderness converted into a flourishing city. . . ."[18] Fletcher was only thirty-seven years of age at the time, Indianapolis only a decade and a half old, its population numbered about 1,700 people; and there was in the future a great deal more change to come and, for Fletcher, considerably more money to be made.

While most towns were primarily economic centers, many also provided political and governmental services. Military posts, Indian agencies, land offices, and post offices brought federal money and jobs. Designation as a county seat also produced economic returns to town builders and residents. Conflict over location of county seats produced some of the bitterest disputes in the pioneer period, since winning or losing often meant the difference between growth and stagnation. The most successful government town was Indianapolis. The state capital moved there from Corydon in 1825, primarily because of its central location. The town owed much of its early growth to the governmental offices, associated businesses, and transportation routes that developed as a consequence.

There were failed towns too: towns that never existed beyond the dreams of promoters, towns that lost in the struggle to be a county seat, towns that were bypassed by a new transportation route, such as the National Road or the Madison and Indianapolis Railroad; towns that were decimated by disease such as Hindostan on the White River in Martin County; towns that suffered intense trade competition from nearby settlements. Failed or stagnant towns were testimony to the fragility of urban development, to the complex of factors, including luck, that could turn a wilderness into a city or leave an urban builder's dreams unfulfilled.

As important as towns were to pioneer Indiana, they did not dominate the state. No village grew to overshadow the countryside. No Indiana city the size and importance of Cincinnati, Louisville, or St. Louis emerged—a factor which may have slowed the state's economic growth. By 1840 Indiana had only three cities of more than 2,500 people—Madison, New Albany, and Indianapolis. Rapid urban growth in the 1840s left eight cities of this size by 1850, and thus sufficient to be labeled urban by the census bureau (see Map 6). Even the very largest cities in 1850—New Albany, Indianapolis, and Madison—had just over 8,000 people and were still small towns in most essential ways. There was little need for their newspapers, for example, to report local news, since nearly everyone was known to everyone else and most communication was face to face. A few town ordinances had been passed to regulate some forms of undesirable behavior (such as violations of the Sabbath) or provide a few urban services (such as wooden sidewalks), but there was little need or desire for exercising community control through formal governmental agencies. And while boosters puffed their big-city amenities of large dry goods stores, banks, hotels, and factories, these and other activities depended primarily on providing goods and services to the town's agricul-

MAP 6.

Towns with More Than 2,500 People, 1850

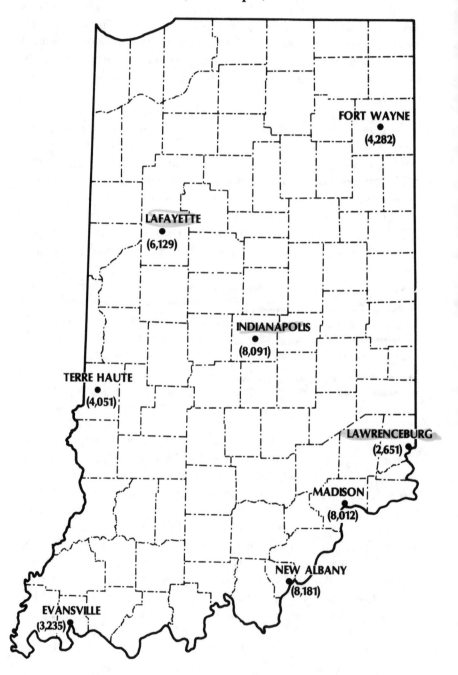

tural hinterland.[19] Urban dwellers themselves moved easily between farm and town, for the lines between rural and urban life were vaguely formed. Many people classified by the census bureau in 1850 as urban dwellers raised hogs and chickens; and many farmers had knowledge of and sometimes investments in railroads, banks, and town lots. Town and country were more thoroughly integrated than they would be later, and the farm countryside more dominant.

The domination of agriculture should not obscure significant non-agricultural features of the pioneer economy. The evolving economy included significant growth in transportation, manufacturing, commerce, and town building. The growing importance of the non-agricultural sector of the economy was not testimony to the decline of agriculture, however, but rather to the increasing specialization and sophistication of farming and, by 1850, to an expanding economy that was evolving beyond the pioneer stage of development.

Pioneer Community Life

The image of the individual pioneer confronting the inhospitable wilderness is a false one. Not only did nearly all pioneers settle as families, but they also built social relationships beyond the family. They brought with them a knowledge of community institutions and a desire for social ties and social order, and they expanded and developed these ways of living together to create a society that shared fundamental values and beliefs and that gave individuals a sense of living among others and even a responsibility for others. Of all the social and community institutions that flourished on the frontier none was more important than evangelical Protestantism.

The Protestant Frontier

Evangelical Protestantism was above all a religious phenomenon, a way of expressing and living within a relationship of the individual to God. But Protestantism was more than narrow religious belief: it helped define the individual's place in and responsibilities to this world and particularly to the immediate community. Indeed, religion helped create communities by bringing people together for common purposes. As such, evangelical Protestantism came to exert profound influence in shaping social, cultural, and political institutions and beliefs.

Not all pioneers were Protestants. Catholicism had an earlier start. A Jesuit priest was resident in Vincennes by 1749, but growing Anglo-American influence led to a decline in Catholic strength in the late eighteenth century. By the 1830s, however, there were signs of renewal. The new diocese of Vincennes was created in 1834, headed by Bishop Simon Bruté. At the same time the missionary priest Stephen Badin was organizing Catholics in the Fort Wayne area. These and other efforts were greatly aided by the immigration of Irish and German Catholics, many attracted by jobs on the Wabash and Erie Canal. Irish and German immigration was a primary source of Catholic strength by 1850 and also had the effect of bringing about an eventual decline of French influence in the church. The Catholic presence in Indiana was still relatively small, however, with only sixty-three churches reported in the 1850 census. There were also by mid-century Jewish families scattered in the larger towns of Indiana: they organized synagogues in Fort Wayne and Lafayette in the late 1840s and in Evansville, Madison, and Indianapolis in the 1850s.[1]

There were also many pioneers—doubtless a majority in the early years—who were members of no church. The presence of so many "heathens" and "infidels" sorely troubled fervent Protestants. Missionaries and neighbors gradually succeeded in winning over many of the unchurched, but every community had respectable and not so respectable citizens who had little or nothing to do with the increasingly dominant Protestant denominations. At least two well-known religious freethinkers (Robert Dale Owen and John Pettit) were elected to the Constitutional Convention of 1850.

Protestantism came in a variety of forms. The major denominations were Methodists, Baptists, and Presbyterians, which together accounted for 1,488 churches of the total 2,032 churches counted in the 1850 census.[2] But other denominations also exerted influence. The Society of Friends or Quakers were particularly strong in the Whitewater Valley, where many had migrated from North Carolina and where their antislavery beliefs had large political effect. Lutheran

churches appeared most often with German settlements, as in Fort
Wayne, which was the base for the missionary efforts of Friedrich
C. D. Wyneken to preserve and expand traditional German Lutheran
doctrine and practice. German-Americans, particularly from Pennsylvania, also brought United Brethren churches to Indiana. And in
the 1820s and 1830s a movement to create a simple, independent
Christianity led Brethren, Baptists, and others to form a new denomination known as the Christian Church or Disciples of Christ, which
eventually would grow to major strength.[3]

The proliferation of denominations and the variety of beliefs meant
that no single church achieved hegemony. Indeed, variety often meant
competition and conflict. Protestants vented anti-Catholic spleen;
there were outbursts of anti-Semitism; and, most of all, there was
jealousy and bickering among Protestants as they debated the meaning
of the Scriptures, sought new members, and built new churches. None
emerged supreme in these struggles, thereby ensuring a modicum of
religious pluralism and a freedom of worship that had been formally
promised in the constitution of 1816.

Within the broader framework of religious pluralism and freedom,
however, there developed a dominant form of evangelical Protestantism, carried to Indiana largely by the Methodists, Baptists, and
Presbyterians. The Methodists and Baptists arrived first in largest
numbers and exerted a major influence that persists to the present.
Their place of origin was that of the first settlers—the upland South
of western Virginia and North Carolina and the frontiers of Tennessee and Kentucky. Their religion reflected their origins.

Methodist belief and practice were particularly suited to the Indiana
frontier. The emphasis on renewal and God's grace appealed to pioneers intent on future progress. Simple, direct preaching conveyed
this message by focusing directly on fundamental issues of life rather
than abstract theology. And this preaching occurred within an atmosphere that was open, personal, and democratic.[4]

The frontier Methodist church was a people's church. Nowhere was
this more obvious than in the figure of the Methodist circuit rider.
Alone and on horseback, his saddlebag filled with a Bible, the Methodist *Discipline*, and a hymnbook, he traveled hundreds of miles to
preach and minister to pioneers scattered over his circuit. Efficiently
and effectively he brought the church to the people. Usually possessed

Frontier circuit rider. (Indiana Historical Society)

of frontier wisdom and practicality rather than a theology degree, the circuit rider was a welcome figure who understood the hardships of pioneer life and the joys of a new cleared field, a fatted hog, or a newborn baby. His arrival attracted nearby settlers to a log cabin, where in front of the fireplace he preached and prayed. His sermons, one pioneer recalled, "struck out right and left, and rained blows on the heads of devils and bad men like fire and brimstone on Gemorrah."[5] The circuit rider also led hymn singing, which he did by "lining out" the hymns, reading aloud each line after which his audience, without hymnbooks and many without the ability to read, would sing it. The first Methodist circuits were in the river valleys of southern Indiana and usually took their names from those of the rivers. As population increased new circuits were added and expanded northward. As villages and towns grew, "stationed" preachers and formal meetinghouses began to replace circuit riders and meetings in settlers' cabins. But the personal warmth and direct appeal represented by the Methodist circuit rider remained influential.

Another important and popular feature of Methodism was the

camp meeting. Open-air camp meetings developed on the American frontier at the beginning of the century, notably in the great Cane Ridge meeting in Kentucky in 1801. Early Hoosiers brought the camp meeting with them. Usually held in the summer, the camp meeting would draw folks from miles around to a special clearing with wooden benches and a speaker's platform. Several days of preaching, hymn singing, and praying produced strong emotional release that took form in tears and groans, jumping and shouting, wrestling with the devil, and conversion experiences. This revivalistic fervor provided an important source of energy for Methodism, though by the middle of the century meetings were less frequent and more sedate. Camp meetings were also social events, often the most exciting social events of the year. For many families the meeting was as close as they ever came to a vacation, a chance to get away from daily chores and to visit. Men talked politics and crops. Young people used the occasion to make friends, sometimes to sneak off by twos into the dark woods to be away from parental eyes.

Baptists also used the camp meeting to win new followers and hold those already in the fold. Like most early Methodists, Indiana Baptists were largely from Kentucky and the upland South. And they were even closer to the people in having a less formal church structure than Methodists and a greater suspicion of educated and paid clergy. Instead of using circuit riders Baptists usually relied on part-time, unpaid preachers. Many pioneer Baptist ministers were farmers with a simple talent for preaching: they put down the plow to take up the Bible for a Sunday sermon or weekday prayer meeting. One newcomer described the kind of preacher that appealed to Indiana Baptists and other pioneers: "They want a man that can preach in the house or out of the house, on a stump or on a barrel, in a cabin or in a barn. One who if the people cannot hear him can speak a little louder and if that will not answer, who can hollow—who must and will be heard. One who can sit on a stool and lie on the chaff or in a log cabin without chinking and his wife if he has one must partake the same spirit."[6]

Presbyterian ministers were different, and so was their church. Henry Ward Beecher came to Lawrenceburg in 1837 as minister of the town's First Presbyterian Church. Born in 1813 in Connecticut and graduated from Amherst College in 1834, Beecher prepared for

the ministry by means of three years of study at Lane Theolog
Seminary in Cincinnati, where his famous father, Lyman Beecher,
was president. The large Beecher family were talented, well-educated,
and articulate, and they were committed Presbyterians and Yankees.
The southern Indiana river town of Lawrenceburg was not suited to
Henry Ward Beecher. He was shocked by the failure to keep the
Sabbath: people visited, read novels, and conversed on street corners
rather than dedicating the day to worship and quiet study. He was
distressed at the necessity of lining out hymns because his church had
no hymnbooks. And he was dismayed by the pioneer preference for
sermons that appeared to come from divine inspiration rather than
study and preparation. Beecher did attempt to adjust his educated
Yankee ways to the sentiments of his congregation. He copied his
carefully prepared sermons onto sheets of paper he could hide in his
Bible and keep out of sight of his congregation. He developed a knack
for "loafing" in stores and on the riverbank with townsmen. But he
never succeeded in hiding from the community his own New England
prejudices and even less so those of his wife, Eunice, who, much to
the consternation of Lawrenceburg women, followed the Yankee habit
of serving every meal on a tablecloth. And he never succeeded in
gathering large numbers of new members, while the Methodists won
converts by the dozens. This defeat was all the more galling because
Beecher held a not uncommon prejudice that pictured Methodists as
salt-of-the-earth Christians but socially inferior to Presbyterians.[7]

Henry Ward Beecher's ministry in Lawrenceburg reflected many
of the difficulties confronting Presbyterians in pioneer Indiana. Eastern Presbyterians, often through the American Home Missionary Society, sent full time, paid ministers to the West—preachers who were
formally educated and thoroughly prepared to offer written exposi-
tions of complex theology. Their New England and Mid-Atlantic ac-
cents, manners, and education set the Presbyterian preachers apart
from most early settlers. This was particularly the case in Indiana,
where they experienced more difficulty and resistance than in any
other state of the Northwest. They were outsiders, welcomed by some,
particularly those settlers with Yankee backgrounds, but distrusted
and spurned by many more, particularly those with ties to the upland
South. A Presbyterian clergyman, writing from southern Indiana in
1833, shrewdly noted: "One devoted, intelligent Baptist Missionary

could do more to save the west than a dozen presbyterians, other things being equal. They could unlock bolts that we must file off. They could turn the current that now sets so strong against even enlightened effort to promote an intelligent piety;—while we must stem it until it spends its force."[8]

And yet Presbyterianism in Indiana is not the story of failure. The church grew more slowly than Methodists or Baptists, yet it did grow, and it did exert an influence far in excess of its numbers. Presbyterians were persistent and determined. Through the American Home Missionary Society and other eastern organizations they paid the salaries of many Presbyterian ministers, including Henry Ward Beecher and more than three hundred other missionaries to Indiana.[9] Among the most successful of them was Isaac Reed, who founded more churches in Indiana than any other eastern missionary. Like his colleagues Reed was appalled by the theological laxness, social disorder, and cultural backwardness of the West, but he endured its tribulations and energetically sought to improve it through schools as well as churches, bending at times but never surrendering. Reed and other Yankee missionaries were certainly guilty of meddlesome cultural chauvinism and an aggressive provincialism of their own, but they did inject a different and often positive strain into Indiana's dominant culture and brought about significant modifications.[10] If they failed to build a Hoosier Zion, their effort was an important contribution to the mixture and blending of peoples and ideas that would help create a distinctive Hoosier culture, one that was neither Yankee nor Southern.

Morality, Social Order, and Reform

Churches were signs of progress to pioneers, as important to some as grist mills or canals. To many Hoosiers, particularly evangelical Protestants, churches were essential not only in the relationship between man and God but between man and man. Methodist, Baptist, and Presbyterian churches intended to be civilizing agencies of morality and social order.

Pioneer churches regulated individual behavior in ways more important than law courts or police agencies. Not only did ministers engage in exhortations to morality and proper behavior, but congregations directly disciplined members they found wanting. The records of pioneer Indiana congregations are filled with charges of specific sins such as dancing and fiddlin', whiskey drinking, unseemly language, bearing an illegitimate child, gambling, and fighting. And there are simple general charges such as leading a "disorderly life" and "immoral and unchristian conduct." Members found guilty as charged could be dismissed from membership, especially if unrepentant.

Many Protestant churches also engaged in more public, community-oriented endeavors to uplift morals and encourage social order, especially in the growing towns. (An important exception was the anti-mission Baptists, who opposed such reform efforts.) One of the best examples of community reform took place at the Second Presbyterian Church in Indianapolis, where in 1839 Henry Ward Beecher became the minister after his unhappy sojourn in Lawrenceburg. Beecher (though not his wife) was happier and more successful in the capital city, where he developed a reputation as an effective, even brilliant preacher. One of his most notable achievements was a series of lectures he delivered in the winter of 1843–44, later published under the title *Seven Lectures to Young Men*. Beecher attacked the selfish materialism and "scheming speculations of the last ten years," expressing fears that the West was like "a city sacked by an army, in which each man seizes what opportunity allows. . . ." He urged the necessity of thrift, honesty, and hard work. Above all, he warned the young men of Indianapolis of the temptations of horse racing, gambling, alcohol, indolence, prostitution, and the theater (which "epitomizes every degree of corruption"). And he urged the churches to take responsibility for rooting out evil in public places as well as in individual souls.[11]

Protestant concern for individual morality in fact often spilled over into attempts to regulate community behavior. Violations of the Sabbath by non-members as well as members caused concern and led to legal prohibitions of all manner of public activity on the Lord's Day. An Indianapolis ordinance of 1837 provided a one-dollar fine on conviction for "Any person who shall on the Sabbath day play at cricket, bandy, town ball, corner ball, or any other game of ball. . . ."[12] Such sentiment was sufficiently widespread to produce a state Sabbath law in 1855.

Even more important was Protestant initiative in the temperance movement. Many pioneers saw nothing wrong with alcohol consumption and freely indulged in spirits distilled from corn. Store-keepers often kept a barrel and cup ready to warm a customer for a sale, and militia drills, elections, weddings, and Fourth of July celebrations were occasions for drinking and drunkenness. Even some early Methodist circuit riders found a sip of whiskey an aid in their travels. Indianapolis merchants and innkeepers in 1827 imported over two hundred barrels of whiskey to satisfy the thirst of a town of fewer than 1,500 people. By the 1830s, however, the prevailing wetness was under attack by church leaders, joined by many community leaders. Temperance societies formed in Logansport, Indianapolis, Fort Wayne, Charlestown, and elsewhere. Some of the reformers advocated total abstinence, others only moderation; some urged legal prohibition, others only moral persuasion. Some towns passed laws requiring licenses in order to sell liquor, and many prohibited its sale entirely on Sundays. By the late 1830s Indianapolis reformers were boasting of sober Fourth of July celebrations, though some of Fort Wayne's leading citizens, including directors of the branch bank and members of the local temperance society, were carried home drunk on election day in 1836.

Temperance reformers who advocated legal remedies focused their political effort on the General Assembly. In 1847 they succeeded in convincing the legislature to pass a local option bill that enabled voters in a township to prohibit sales of alcohol. Temperance thus became a part of the political debate, a cause of conflict and controversy that persisted into the twentieth century. From the beginning the debate was not between the religious and the irreligous, however. Many Christians opposed temperance and especially the attempt at legal restrictions on behavior. Baptists and Roman Catholics were especially likely to argue that temperance legislation was a dangerous union of church and state and a meddlesome threat to individual liberty. Yankee Presbyterians, like Henry Ward Beecher, were most likely to argue the necessity of joining government to the crusade against alcohol, a crusade that would eventually attract a large majority of Hoosiers.

The tendency for evangelical Protestantism to push for social reform was displayed also in the antislavery movement. Efforts to establish slavery in Indiana Territory had been defeated by opponents of the institution, and strong antislavery animus persisted thereafter. Yankee Presbyterians were particularly outspoken opponents of the institution, though the issue did cause division within the church. Many pioneers from the South also denounced slavery. Foremost among them were the Friends, who became the most vociferous antislavery group, but other whites from the upland South also attacked slavery. Throughout the state there were few defenders of the institution; most Indianans regarded slavery as a violation of the laws of God and man.

But few whites in pioneer Indiana believed in the equality of the races or made efforts to improve the unfortunate lot of many black Americans, slave or free. Some did aid escaped slaves fleeing on the underground railroad; several of its routes ran through Indiana. The Quaker humanitarian Levi Coffin was one of the most active "conductors" on the line. Many other Quakers were unusually kind to free black newcomers, with the result that black settlement was largest in the heavily Quaker counties of Wayne, Randolph, and Henry. Perhaps the most widespread public response to blacks and slavery was more ambiguous, represented by formation of the Indiana Colonization Society in 1829. The objective of this organization was to help blacks migrate to the African republic of Liberia. Colonizers professed to act out of humane motives, and many doubtless did, but many also acted from racial antipathy and a desire to remove blacks from the state and the nation. Churches and individuals debated the morality and wisdom of colonization, with many supporting it as the best means of ridding the state of an undesirable population. More militant antislavery advocates condemned colonization and gradually joined in support of the organized antislavery movement. Dozens of local antislavery societies formed in the late 1830s, usually supported by church groups. But militant, radical antislavery remained weaker in Indiana than perhaps in any other northern state.

Overshadowing feeble antislavery activity was strong race prejudice. The state legislature reflected popular antipathy to blacks when in 1818 it prohibited blacks from testifying in court. In the same year the General Assembly prohibited marriages of black and white individuals. An 1831 law required black newcomers to post a bond of five hundred dollars as security against becoming public charges. Most important, the constitutions of 1816 and 1851 prohibited blacks from voting. Outbreaks of mob violence against blacks occurred in several towns, sometimes directed against long-time residents, sometimes against newcomers or blacks preceived to be agitators. Such was the case when the noted black abolitionist Frederick Douglass was egged and vilified while speaking in Richmond and later in Pendleton.[13]

It is likely that Protestant institutions and beliefs played a leading role in stimulating efforts both to ameliorate the difficult conditions blacks faced in Indiana and in leading the campaign against slavery to the South. But it is important also to note the very limited extent of these activities in pioneer Indiana. And it is important to note that even the denominations most sympathetic to antislavery—Friends and Presbyterians—did not recruit large numbers of blacks to their memberships. The largest number of black church members by far were Methodists, but largely separate Methodists, for Indiana blacks increasingly joined the African Methodist Episcopal Church. By the early 1850s this separate church had 1,387 members, while black membership in the regular Methodist church had declined to fewer than 200. Segregation of the races in the churches was but a reflection of the dominant tendency toward white racial antipathy and prejudice, a negative sentiment that was to grow in Indiana after 1850.

Pioneer Education

Abraham Lincoln's growing up years in pioneer Indiana, from the age of seven to twenty-one, included less than twelve months of formal schooling. Such meager schooling was not unusual; nor, as Lincoln's life so nobly testifies, was formal education the sum and substance of the individual's preparation for adulthood. Pioneer education must be understood broadly to include socialization and learning outside the schoolroom, all the more so because learning inside the classroom was so limited.

As in so many other aspects of pioneer life, the family was central to education. Children learned from parents to hunt and build shelter, plant and harvest, spin and cook. And they sometimes learned from parents how to write their name, read, and do simple sums. Such skills were further developed in worship. Sermons, hymns, and Scripture introduced young people to words and ideas that became, as in Lincoln's case, permanent parts of their vocabulary and thought. Particularly important in this regard was the Sunday school.

Page from Abraham Lincoln's sumbook, about 1824. (Lilly Library, Indiana University)

Sunday schools appeared in Indiana in the 1810s. By 1829 there were one hundred Sunday schools in the state. Organized by clergymen and by lay men and women, they brought both Christianity and education to the frontier. For not only did the early Sunday schools teach Bible verses, hymns, and moral principles, but they also taught spelling and reading, in many cases offering the only opportunities for instruction outside the home and the only time a child held a book other than the family Bible.[14]

Many of Indiana's first schools were also organized and led by religiously motivated individuals who were convinced that illiteracy, immorality, and heathenism were all tools of the devil. Preachers and their wives supplemented meager incomes by teaching, and congregations kept youth on the proper denominational path by sponsoring schools. By the 1840s Fort Wayne had Lutheran, Catholic, Methodist, and Presbyterian schools. All Indiana's early colleges had close ties to one of the major denominations. Presbyterians were responsible for the founding of Hanover in 1827 and influential in Wabash's beginnings in 1832. The state university, founded in Bloomington in 1820, also had close ties to the Presbyterian Church. Methodists founded Indiana Asbury (later DePauw) in 1837, Baptists Franklin College in 1834, Catholics the University of Notre Dame in 1844, and Friends Earlham in 1847. These and other institutions often did not offer a full university curriculum, and they all struggled with financial and other handicaps, but they represented outposts of learning in the West that often provided leadership in various reform activities, particularly in the long struggle to create public schools.[15]

While Protestant churches played a major role, government also professed responsibility for education. The Land Ordinance of 1785 and the Northwest Ordinance of 1787 committed the federal government to public education, notably in the 1785 provision that the sixteenth section of land in each township should be set aside to support schools. And in the most forward looking and inclusive commitment to education up to that time, Indiana's constitution of 1816 promised that the state would create—"as soon as circumstances permit"—"a general system of education, ascending in a regular gradation, from township schools to state university, wherein tuition shall be gratis, and equally open to all." Not only did circumstances not permit such a progressive system in pioneer Indiana, but the state failed to build even the rudiments of a true public school system.

It is difficult to generalize about education in Indiana prior to 1850 because there was no statewide public school system—no uniformity, no systematic record keeping, no central financing or direction.[16] Instead, there was great variation that depended on local sentiments and resources. Where common schools existed in Indiana prior to 1850 they were locally created, financed, and controlled. Nowhere were they entirely free and equally open to all. Local governments sometimes donated a building and supported education with some public moneys, most importantly the revenue from sale of section sixteen in each township, as promised in the Ordinance of 1785. But most schools had to charge tuition in order to function. There was no state or local tax levied to support schools.

Such common schools as existed varied greatly in the education they provided. Most had very short terms, usually fewer than three months. Children attended haphazardly depending on distance, weather, home chores, and family means to pay the tuition. What pupils learned was equally haphazard, with emphasis on spelling, reading, and ciphering and with some attention to geography and history, usually tinged with moral instruction. Some teachers were well educated and dedicated; many were neither. There were no teacher training institutions in Indiana, and very low and uncertain pay often meant that teaching was a job undertaken by a young man while preparing for a more serious occupation. Books were rare and expensive; the teacher's library often consisted only of the Bible, a speller, and a reader.

Less than one-quarter of the Indiana children between five and fifteen attended school in 1840, according to the federal census. The census listed 48,189 children in common schools and 2,946 in academies or grammar schools. Some of these secondary educational institutions were entirely private; others (county seminaries) benefited from some public support but also charged tuition. Though more than half a dozen colleges existed by 1850, total enrollment at that date was only 337. Education at the state university in Bloomington was neither free nor readily available: there were only five professors in 1850 and seventy-seven students. Its purposes, though uncertain, centered on a classical curriculum of ancient philosophies and languages, unsuited, according to many critics, to the conditions and needs of the West. Its president from 1829 to 1851, Andrew Wylie, had little understanding of or interest in the state's common people and only a narrow vision of the possibilities of a public university.[17]

The consequences of limited schooling in Indiana were partly indicated in the federal census of 1840. Among the questions asked by census takers was whether the respondent could read and write. Such a large percentage of adult Hoosiers answered in the negative (14.3% compared to a national average of 11.6%) that Indiana ranked eighteenth in literacy among the twenty-eight states of the Union, lower than all other northern states and four southern states (see

FIGURE 1.

Illiteracy and School Enrollment in Twenty-Eight States, 1840

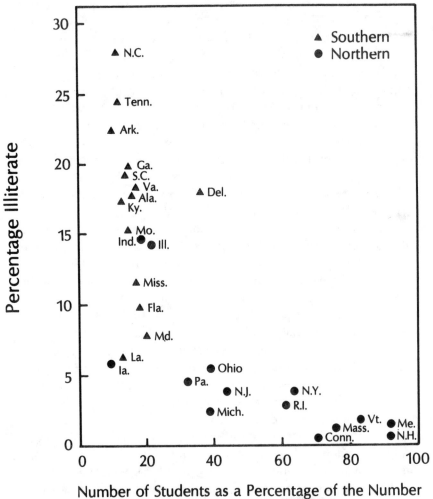

Number of Students as a Percentage of the Number of White Children 5 to 15.

SOURCE: Lee Soltow and Edward Stevens, *The Rise of Literacy and the Common School in the United States: A Socioeconomic Analysis to 1870* (Chicago, 1981), 161

Figure 1). In 1850 the state's ranking dropped to a dismal twenty-third: more than 17% of the state's adult white population and 45% of its black population were counted illiterate. Indiana's high illiteracy rate derived in part from the backwardness of education in the upland South, from which many of its illiterate citizens had come. Not surprisingly, counties in southern Indiana, where upland South settlement was largest, tended to have the highest illiteracy. But it was also a powerful indication of the state's general failure to fulfill the promise made in the constitution of 1816.

During the 1840s an energetic campaign to create a true system of public education began. Although many people contributed to school reform, its primary exponent was Caleb Mills. A graduate of Dartmouth College and Andover Theological Seminary, Mills was one of those New England Presbyterian missionaries determined to bring religion and education to the West. He arrived in Crawfordsville in 1833 to head a Presbyterian school that later became Wabash College. A decade later he emerged as the most eloquent advocate of a state system of public education. Beginning in 1846 Mills presented for public discussion a series of six lengthy and elaborately argued messages, signed only as "One of the People." They are without doubt the most important documents ever prepared on the subject of education in Indiana. Making much of the fact that one seventh of the adult population could not read or write, Mills listed the causes of Indiana's backwardness: "want of competent teachers, suitable school books, a proper degree of interest in the community on the subject, adequate funds, and the method of procuring such funds." He especially argued the necessity of a state and township school tax, for "There is but one way to secure good schools, and that is to pay for them." Moreover, Mills asserted, a tax would ensure large popular interest in education.[18]

Others made similar arguments in a series of school conventions, the first held in Indianapolis in 1847. These activities pressured the General Assembly to submit to a statewide referendum the question of whether to enact taxes sufficient to provide at least three months of free, common-school education for all children. Mills and his fellow reformers actively crusaded for a positive vote. In the referendum, held in 1848, 78,523 Hoosiers cast ballots in favor of free common schools, 61,887 against. It was not a very commanding victory, but the reformers made the most of it. They secured from the General Assembly passage of a common school law intending to provide a general system of tax-supported education. But this 1849 school act contained the loophole that a majority vote in each county must approve the law for it to take effect in that county. Again the reformers pushed their cause forward, and again they achieved a victory of limited proportions: sixty-one counties voted for the law and twenty-nine rejected it. (The total popular vote was 79,079 in favor and 63,312 opposed to the free school law.) This local option and the mixed response to it vitiated the effort to establish a uniform common school system. The constitution of 1851 and the School Law of 1852 would push forward the cause, but not until after the Civil War would Indiana finally create a permanent and true common school system.

Reluctance to create and support a uniform system of public schooling derived from many sources. Perhaps fundamental was a pioneer sense that education was a luxury that could not be indulged until after material security was obtained. Corn and pork, canals and railroads, and frame houses and store-bought shoes were more important than schools. For many pioneers taxes replaced Indians as the threat most endangering their God-given right to take from the land what was theirs. Related to this pioneer order of priority was a sense that formal education was impractical and unsuited to everyday life in the West, as indeed some of it was. Reformers argued the necessity of schooling to guarantee the functioning of democratic government, orderly community life, and religious understanding. Such claims doubtless had effect, but many Hoosiers remained suspicious. Many particularly rejected the reformers' assertions that equality and democracy required schools freely open to all. Some pioneers preferred schools affiliated with their particular religious denomination, while others feared public schools would provide an entryway for another denomination to receive public moneys. Some asserted that education was a private matter, best left to the family to provide as it thought proper and as private resources allowed. Some wealthier pioneers did not wish to send their children to free schools, which often had the stigma of pauper schools, nor did they feel obliged to provide for the education of all children. Some poorer citizens objected to having their meager incomes taxed in order to educate the children of those better off. Many Hoosiers expressed opposition to state government influence in education, arguing that local communities—townships above all—should have exclusive responsibility for schools. State education was a radical step on the road to government centralization, the loss of local control, and ultimately, they feared, the denial of individual liberty.

Arguments for and against public education came from all denominations, classes, ethnic groups, and sections of the state. But support was noticeably strong among Protestant, especially Presbyterian, Yankees: men like Caleb Mills, Henry Ward Beecher, and Calvin Fletcher actively led the campaign for public schools. Opposition was strong among those settlers from the upland South who were most numerous in southern Indiana. The vote on the 1848 common school referendum showed that of the thirty-one counties where the majority opposed free common schools twenty-two were in the southern half of the state. The largest majorities in favor were in the northernmost counties. Here were clear signs of a lag in public education in southern Indiana that would persist with ever more important consequences down to the twentieth century.

Reluctance to support public education was one of the most enduring and unfortunate legacies of Hoosier pioneers. Arguments that had made sense on the frontier continued to be repeated as the frontier receded and as society changed. The meager schooling Abraham Lincoln received was increasingly inadequate to prepare future Presidents and storekeepers, shop foremen, and farmers too. Pioneers optimistically looked toward change and progress yet paradoxically did not see clearly the significance of education in that new future. Nor, regrettably, did many of their children and grandchildren.

The New Harmony Communities

Pioneers brought with them and created a variety of community institutions and practices that formed bonds of belief and culture so that the individual did not need to combat the uncivilized wilderness alone. Churches, schools, towns, and political organizations brought people together, even as they sometimes separated them. There were also more intense community experiences in Indiana in the joining together of like-minded peoples in common purpose. Some of the

Quaker group migration and settlement in Wayne and adjacent counties provides such an example. Another religious group, the Shakers, formed a tight-knit community on Busseron Creek north of Vincennes. And black families joined together in the Lyles settlement in Gibson County and the Roberts settlement in Hamilton County. The most important examples of like-minded people creating communities in Indiana were the two utopian groups that settled at New Harmony.

The first settlement at New Harmony, in the southwestern corner of the state, was that of the Harmonists or Rappites. Led by the charismatic George Rapp, they had left Germany in 1803 and lived in Pennsylvania before moving to the wilderness of Indiana in 1814. The Harmonists were possessed of a religious conviction that they were God's chosen people, that the second coming of Christ was imminent, and that they should direct their lives to preparation for that millennium. In consequence, they abandoned private property for communal property and renounced sexual relations for celibacy. On the Indiana frontier this group of German Americans, numbering about a thousand, hoped to find the freedom denied them in Europe to practice their religion and their communal way of life.[19]

The Harmonists' religious vision did not preclude attention to everyday life. They were practical and hard-working, as befit their cultural roots. And they were organized and directed with meticulous and powerful attention by Father Rapp. Soon Harmonists turned their 20,000 acres of land into the most successful economic enterprise in Indiana. Rather than subsist on a meager diet of corn and hogs they grew a variety of crops and livestock, including prized merino sheep, planted vineyards and fruit trees, and produced a large surplus for sale beyond the community. They also developed a sizable manufacturing capacity, including a grist mill and cotton and woolen mill, products of which they sold to outsiders, and laid out and built an attractive town with 180 buildings, many of brick. Their economy was balanced and nearly self-sufficient, and it was very profitable. Religious commitment and hard work did not produce a dull or monastic life. The communitarians woke each morning to the sound of French horns, and they enjoyed singing and a town band. Much attention was directed to education: there was a school open to all children, a library, and a printing press.

And yet Indiana was not all the Harmonists hoped it would be. The climate was too extreme, the markets for their goods too distant, their neighbors too unfriendly. Resentment of the Harmonists' concentrated economic and political power and suspicion of their way of life caused animosity and even an instance of violence. In 1824 Father Rapp and his followers left Indiana to build a new community near Pittsburgh. Their Indiana property they sold for $150,000 to Robert Owen, a wealthy Scottish textile mill owner.

The Owenites were the second utopian community to settle in New Harmony. Unlike their predecessors they were exclusively interested in this world, in establishing in Indiana a model community that would prepare the way for a new moral order. Robert Owen believed that traditional family structure, religion, and private property were impediments to achieving a more just and equal society. Hundreds of Europeans and Americans joined him at New Harmony in rejecting these traditions and optimistically planning to build an environment that would uplift the individual and change the human condition. Private property was to be abolished; all were to be equal, including woman (but not "persons of color"); extensive and sustained education was provided for children and adults. All would contribute as they were able to the life of the community; all would receive an equal share of its material and cultural rewards.[20]

Robert Owen's grandiose vision never came to full bloom. The community was an economic failure. Some of the members were neither much interested in nor capable of physical labor, and there was an insufficiency of managerial planning and organization. Personal and ideological disputes of all kinds sapped energy and efficiency. In 1827, two years after the experiment on the Wabash began, Robert Owen returned to Scotland.

In important ways the Owenite community was not a failure, however. It attracted brilliant individuals who brought ideas and made contributions most unusual in pioneer Indiana. Many came with Owen on the keelboat *Philanthropist*, which quickly became known as the "Boatload of Knowledge." Among them were William Maclure, whose research and publications at New Harmony contributed to his reputation as the father of American geology, and Thomas Say, sometimes called the father of American zoology. The Owenites, particularly Maclure and Joseph Neef, also made important contributions to education by moving away from textbook memorization and re-

citation and toward encouraging the understanding of concepts and ideas and integrating everyday life experiences into daily instruction.[21] Maclure also promoted libraries, with special concern for workingmen's libraries. At his death in 1840 he left $80,000 to support 144 such libraries in Indiana.

Another legacy of the community was the Owen children. Four sons and a daughter of Robert Owen remained in Indiana. All made significant contributions to the state's development. Robert Dale Owen was perhaps most important. He served in the General Assembly and the Constitutional Convention of 1851, where he played an influential role in the cause of free public schools. Robert Dale Owen also drew on the New Harmony interest in equality and his association with women's rights reformer Frances Wright to argue the case for women's property rights. And he wrote one of the earliest American treatises advocating birth control.[22]

The religious utopia of George Rapp and the secular utopia of Robert Owen both failed to achieve their ultimate goals, yet they left behind ideas and concrete models of different ways of creating community institutions and ordering life. It is impossible to assess their full influence, but it is likely they provided a useful if spicy seasoning to the intensely practical and conventional culture of pioneer Indiana. Certainly it will always intrigue to contemplate the contrast between the two New Harmony communities and the more typical frontier community on Little Pigeon Creek a few miles away in which Abe Lincoln was growing to manhood.

Preceding pages:
New Harmony on the Wabash. (Indiana Historical Society)

vii

Pioneer Government and Politics

Pioneers did not plunge into the wilderness to escape government. Indeed, they took with them an attachment to a republican form of government and a conviction that government had responsibilities for promoting the general welfare. While they often depended primarily and proudly on their own hard work, pioneers expected government to contribute to the general welfare by helping citizens acquire and preserve private property and by creating and maintaining a degree of social order. Indianans did not always agree on exactly how government should go about achieving those ends. That disagreement would boil forth in political debate and eventually in a party system that was among the nation's most combative.

؛uisition and Indian Removal

William Darby's *Emigrant's Guide to the Western and Southwestern States and Territories*, published in New York in 1818, extolled the richness of Indiana's soil. But, Darby noted, "Near two-thirds of its territorial surface is yet in the hands of the Indians, a temporary evil, that a short time will remedy."[1] Hoosiers demanded a quick solution to this "temporary evil." They insisted that their government first aggressively acquire title to Indian lands and then remove Indians entirely from the rich soil. After 1815 the several Indian tribes proved less and less able to resist these twin remedies. The Battle of Tippecanoe and the War of 1812 left Tecumseh's vision of an Indian confederation shattered and the military strength of the tribes remaining in Indiana nearly inconsequential. The last federal troops were withdrawn from Fort Wayne in 1819, and the local militias soon became more important for social and political purposes than defense. There was one last fear of Indian attack with the Black Hawk War of 1832. That episode enabled glory-seeking Indiana militiamen to march off in search of the enemy, only to have the pioneers of Illinois annihilate Black Hawk's pathetically weak band of Sacs and Foxes long before it threatened Indiana.[2] Increasingly, in fact, it was Indians who required protection from whites. The massacre at Fall Creek proved the most vivid evidence of this need.

On March 22, 1824, five white men brutally and without provocation killed nine Indian men, women, and children camped along Fall Creek. It was not the first application of the frontier maxim that the only good Indian was a dead Indian. It was perhaps, however, the first time in the history of the United States that the law worked with full recognition of Indian humanity. One of the murderers escaped, but the other four were captured and tried in Madison County Circuit Court, which, because no courthouse had yet been constructed, met in a settler's log cabin. Although many pioneers hoped for justice in order to discourage Indian retaliation, many doubted a white man would ever be punished severely for killing an Indian. The federal government was determined to see justice done, however. Federal Indian agent John Johnston, acting with the support of the War Department, used federal funds to construct a jail, to hire men to guard the prisoners, and to engage James Noble, Indiana's popular United States senator, to lead the prosecution's case. Aided by this support from Washington, four white men were convicted of murder and sentenced to death. On the bank of Fall Creek, before a large crowd that included relatives of the murdered Indians, three were hanged. Eighteen-year-old John Bridge, Jr., who had plunged a hunting knife into at least one Indian, was pardoned at the last minute because of his youth.[3]

The massacre at Fall Creek produced a vivid and unusual demonstration of government attention to justice for Indians. More representative and important were the less successful efforts of the government to regulate Indian-white trade. Aggressive American traders, including Samuel Hanna, Allen Hamilton, and George W. and William G. Ewing, pushed aside the French in the Maumee-Wabash region. This new breed of merchants found it lucrative to provide Indians with cloth, weapons, blankets, salt, tobacco, and other goods, usually at inflated prices. More disreputable traders also supplied large quantities of alcohol despite regulations against it. In return, the traders took furs and the monetary annuities the Indians received from the federal government in payment for their lands. As land cessions continued these annuity payments grew larger and became more important in shaping Indian-trader relations. Several of the leading families of northern Indiana built their fortunes on this trade.[4]

The federal government was responsible for licensing traders and protecting Indians from unfair trade, but many merchants were shrewd and versatile in developing ways to reap very high profits from their Indian customers. These sophisticated businessmen became politically influential in shaping national Indian policy and its local implementation. Some cooperative Indian leaders joined in mutual pursuit of wealth with little regard for their people. The federal employee who was to oversee this sometimes sordid business was the local Indian agent. From 1823 until 1831 he was John Tipton. A veteran of the Battle of Tippecanoe and a frontiersman without formal education who wrote with difficulty, the rugged and dynamic Tipton became one of Indiana's most influential politicians. Tipton endeavored to serve his Indian clients and showed some sympathy for their problems, but like most pioneers he believed in the inevitability of

Indian removal. And Tipton also was careful to secure his own personal fortune, particularly through land speculation. In 1828 he moved the Indian agency from Fort Wayne to Logansport, where he had made large land purchases that soon produced handsome profits. Tipton also attended to his political reputation by carefully dispensing patronage and favors from the Indian agency. In 1831 he was elected to the United States Senate, where he continued to be closely attentive to Indian affairs.[5]

The Indians possessed two attractions for whites: cash from the federal annuity payments and land. The Wabash traders who eagerly supped at the annuity trough wished the tribes to remain in Indiana. But they were soon outnumbered by land speculators and settlers who were more interested in Indian removal as the necessary step to land acquisition. The shrewdest traders, of course, played both sides of the street and were also land speculators.

Removal was the logical consequence of the land cession treaties that territorial governor William Henry Harrison had so skillfully forced. After the War of 1812 these treaty negotiations resumed. In the St. Mary's or New Purchase Treaty of 1818 several Indian tribes ceded the central portion of the state, and the Delawares agreed to removal west of the Mississippi. The trader William Conner, who had made a fortune and found his first wife among the Delawares, aided in effecting their removal. His Delaware wife and children accompanied the tribe west. Conner remained at the family home on White River, took a white woman as his second wife, and concentrated on trade, land dealings, and town building in the new pioneer society of Hamilton County.[6]

The two major tribes remaining in Indiana were the Miamis and the Potawatomis, confined to northern Indiana. Pressure for additional land cession and removal increased as white population expanded northward and as the internal improvements fever rose. In 1826, in return for large quantities of food, alcohol, and gifts and the promise of enlarged annuity payments, the Miamis and Potawatomis ceded land that allowed construction of the Michigan Road and the Wabash and Erie Canal. These corridors of pioneer economic power were mortal wounds to the tribes. The major political blow came in 1830 with the federal Indian Removal Act, which gave the president authority to push Indians westward. President Andrew Jackson, a true man of the frontier, actively sought removal, and Hoosier politicians eagerly joined. The General Assembly petitioned Congress to enact the program in Indiana, as did Senator Tipton. The excitement of the Black Hawk War in 1832 added popular support. All argued that removal was in the best interests of the Indians: it would preserve them from the degrading effects of white culture, particularly whiskey, while allowing them time and opportunity to adopt the positive features of that superior culture. The major barrier to removal was Indian reluctance to leave their homelands. But in treaties of attrition in the late 1820s and 1830s the tribes surrendered tract after tract of land. They received in return larger annuity payments, which went to pay debts owed the traders, but they found themselves ever closer to white settlers who in ever larger numbers called in ever growing voices for removal.

The Potawatomis were the first of the two major tribes to leave. Plans for removal were in place in 1838, but some Potawatomis resisted. Led by Menominee, they claimed that they had not agreed to removal. With Senator Tipton and the aggressive Indian trader George Ewing as organizers, an armed militia company forcefully rounded up Menominee and his reluctant band. Under armed guard some eight hundred Potawatomis were soon on their way to Kansas. Carelessness in organizing the march brought sickness and hardship and contributed to the death of forty-two Indians, most of them children. This sad episode came to be known as the "Trail of Death."[7]

The Miamis held out a short while longer. But the once proud tribe had dwindled in numbers and cohesion, and its wily and increasingly selfish leader, Chief Jean Baptiste Richardville, finally agreed to surrender the remaining lands and accept removal. Along with several other Miami chiefs, Richardville received individual reserves of land and money, and he and his family were allowed to remain in their home near Fort Wayne (furnished with draperies and carpets from Paris). Among other Indian families permitted to remain in Indiana was that of Frances Slocum, who at the age of five had been captured in Pennsylvania during the Revolutionary War and eventually became the contented wife of a Miami war chief. Her "discovery" in 1837 was widely heralded, especially after she refused to return to white society. For less fortunate Miamis, removal was required. By the treaty of 1840, prepared by Fort Wayne trader Allen Hamilton, the Miamis agreed to emigrate to Kansas. Continued Indian reluctance to move and traders' greed for further access to annuities delayed departure until 1846. The Wabash traders, including the Ewings, not only profited handsomely in settlement of debts but also in arranging the removal. Those who profited most, however, were the settlers who surged onto lands vacated by the Indians.[8]

The removal of the Miamis, Potawatomis, and other Indians was to many pioneers an inevitable and happy sign of progress, of subduing nature and bringing civilization to the wilderness. The Indians had not assimilated into the pioneer culture: they had refused to become successful yeoman farmers or steady craftsmen; they had failed fully to accept Christianity (especially the Protestant version), education, or other marks of the dominant culture, despite the efforts of civilizers and missionaries such as the Baptist minister Isaac McCoy. Consequently, Hugh McCulloch remarked, they were "doomed to pass away with the game." Yet McCulloch, a Fort Wayne resident closely familiar with traders, agents, politicians, and Indians, concluded that "there is cause for national humiliation in the fact that their disappearance has been hastened by the vices, the cupidity, the injustice, the inhumanity of a people claiming to be Christians."[9]

Government and the General Welfare

Pioneers depended on government to acquire land from Indians and eventually to remove them entirely. Settlers also expected government to sell public land on favorable terms and in an orderly manner. They expected ownership of that land to be recorded in county courthouses and upheld in courts of law. Many also came to believe that government had responsibilities to develop the frontier economically by constructing roads and canals, providing banking services, and chartering corporations. And they insisted that government protect their lives and property. Some even argued that government must ensure the moral and social order of community life and provide for dependent peoples.

While Hoosiers had many expectations of government they preferred a government that was simple and democratic. And they preferred government that was located close to the people. The federal government continued to be important to them, but it was always government at a distance and consequently government to be distrusted. With statehood, Hoosiers enjoyed full representation in Washington and less dependency on decisions made in the federal capital. Like other westerners, Indiana senators and congressmen generally argued for more federal aid to develop the region economically. Willing to receive the bounties of Washington, Hoosiers were increasingly jealous in guarding their state and local government prerogatives.

State government, perhaps best symbolized by the Greek Revival statehouse built in the early 1830s, grew in importance and power during the pioneer period. The constitution of 1816 had created a structure in which the General Assembly was the most powerful branch. Meeting annually, this citizen legislature was close to the people and had few constitutional restraints on expressing its will. Its functions were broad and varied, ranging from laying out roads to licensing ferries, electing United States senators, and granting divorces.[10]

One of the General Assembly's most important functions was creating new counties. As population increased and settlers moved northward, the legislature authorized new counties, redrew the boundaries of existing counties, and selected the locations of county seats. These decisions caused considerable controversy and much politicking. County government itself was of large significance, and the courthouse became a center of local political and civil life. Officers included a sheriff—the major law enforcement official in pioneer Indiana—a coroner, circuit court clerk, recorder, and three county commissioners whose large responsibilities included county roads and taxes. The county commissioners also were empowered to create townships in their county. The township governments became more powerful in the nineteenth century as they assumed functions in road maintenance, public education, and poor relief. Even more than county government, township officials could claim to represent the popular will because they lived as close neighbors among the people who elected them.[11]

Notions of the frontier as a lawless and violent place where brute force and barbarous morality prevailed seldom applied in Indiana. Pioneers feared such possibilities, however, and were careful to ensure

31199 W H BASS PHOTO CO.

The second Indiana statehouse,
1835–1877, draped in mourning
for the death of Abraham Lincoln.
(W. H. Bass Photo Company)

that law came west with the spinning wheel, rifle, and ax. Indiana's early legal system combined attention to stability and order with a desire for popular democracy. It included a state supreme court and several circuit courts that increased in number with population. Elected justices of the peace in townships had responsibility for petty crimes and civil cases involving less than $50 and were the primary source of legal redress for most citizens. The elected county sheriff and the township constable were the primary law enforcement officials. Although there was considerable work for the sizable lawyer population, particularly in matters relating to land, there was little serious crime. A detailed study of crime in Marion County concludes that this particular frontier was remarkably peaceful. Per capita property crimes and crimes against persons actually decreased in the 1830s and 1840s despite urban growth and change (though there was increasingly more sensational attention to crime in the newspapers). Only criminal prosecutions for violations of moral order—especially gambling and liquor violations—increased significantly in these decades, perhaps reflecting more anxiety about moral order than actual increases in immorality. Such anxiety contributed to periodic vigilante campaigns in which the town's leading citizens drove away gamblers, prostitutes, and other undesirables.[12]

There was enough serious crime to create a need for prison facilities, however. The state prison at Jeffersonville opened in 1821. It was conducted under a profit-oriented leasing system in which the highest bidder was allowed to run the prison: he fed and clothed the prisoners and hired them out or employed them in prison industries, keeping for himself the profits. After a visit to the Jeffersonville state prison the noted reformer Dorothea Dix reported in 1846 that "the lodging cells are worse beyond all comparison than any cells I ever saw allotted to human creatures."[13] Counties also maintained jails for prisoners awaiting trial or those convicted of lesser offenses. Conditions varied considerably.

Reluctance to spend public money applied not only to prisoners but also to aiding dependent people. Individuals who were poor or mentally or physically handicapped had very few sources of public aid. Such care as most dependent people received was provided by the family or neighbors. But government did give some aid. The county poor farm was the most important welfare institution, providing care for the elderly, for dependent children, and for a variety of others unable to live unattended. Township trustees also had responsibility to provide relief for the poor. State government expanded its role when in the 1840s the General Assembly created a school for deaf and dumb children, another for the blind, and a hospital for the insane. These state and local institutions did constitute evidence of humanitarian sentiment and recognition of government responsibility for the general welfare. But the resulting commitments were circumscribed by reluctance to increase taxes and a distrust of large government involvement in activities many Indianans believed were best left to individual and private responsibility.

Pioneer Politics

Politics changed substantially in the period from 1816 to 1850, but as in other areas it was change that was gradual and evolutionary rather than revolutionary. Patterns developed in the territorial period persisted with statehood. But with population growth and economic development there arose new expectations of government. And there developed also new methods of conducting government and politics. Many derived from forces located outside the state.

Territorial politics had been characterized by personal loyalties and sectional jealousies, most evident in the tendency of the southwestern section of the territory to remain loyal to William Henry Harrison and his associates and of the southeastern section to follow the lead of Jonathan Jennings. The first decade of statehood saw a continuation of this personal loyalty and sectional rivalry, though the latter diminished considerably as a consequence of the increased strength of the eastern section.

Three men provided the dominant political leadership in this period of personal politics. Jonathan Jennings, a Charlestown resident who represented the territory in Congress from 1809 on, was elected the state's first governor. After the two consecutive terms allowed by the state constitution, the popular Jennings was elected to Congress, where he served from 1822 to 1831. William Hendricks, from Madison, exchanged places with Jennings in 1822, leaving Congress for the governor's office, and then represented Indiana in the United

States Senate from 1825 to 1837. James Noble of Brookville was a United States senator from 1816 to his death in 1831. This Hoosier triumvirate may have functioned as an informal alliance. They devoted special attention to ensuring that federal patronage did not go to outsiders but to deserving Indianans, especially those friendly to them. Jennings, Hendricks, and Noble did not constitute a political party, however: they had no formal organization, no articulated program, no group of devoted party workers that set them apart from other political men. What they did have was a personal popularity that was sufficient to elect and reelect them to state and national office.[14]

An important feature of the personal politics that characterized the first decade of statehood was the aversion to political parties. Like the nation's founding fathers, this first generation of state politicians believed that parties were inimical to republican government: parties divided and caused strife; they encouraged individual self-aggrandizement and petty foolishness. Regretting the conflict and factionalism of the late territorial period, this first generation of state leaders identified with a republican ideology that abhorred parties and expected instead broad popular agreement on issues and a virtuous leadership dedicated to acting on that agreement. It was necessary as a consequence that politicians not appear to seek office, that they appear instead to serve only because called on by the people. Outright political campaigning was subdued, and on occasion nonexistent, as when Hendricks ran unopposed for the governor's office in 1822. Candidates appeared at logrollings, militia gatherings, and camp meetings; took a swing with the ax, a shot with the rifle, or a swig from the whiskey jug; and then said a few words, trying always to be a man of the people among friends. The voters, for their part, vigorously debated candidates and issues. Soon after settling in Marion County from New England, Calvin Fletcher wrote his brother: "The people here . . . are bold & independent in their sentiments as to public men or measures. The most ignorant man here knows who governs him & who administers justice." Indiana was not like New England, Fletcher noted, where "the government are becoming arresticratical & the common people put all credence in great men."[15]

Vigorous popular debate, stump speaking, and campaigning as one of the common folks remained important ingredients in Indiana politics down to the twentieth century, but the pioneer aversion to political parties gradually withered away. Beginning in the mid-1820s rising party loyalty began to challenge personal loyalty as a prime engine in political contests.[16]

Political parties were not home-grown institutions in Indiana but rather were imported from the national arena. The most important cause of the rise of party politics in the state was the presidential election. Beginning with the bitterly fought contest of 1824, Hoosiers, like other Americans, began to show more interest in the presidential election, and that election began to intrude into state and local politics. The field of four presidential candidates eventually dwindled to two— John Quincy Adams of Massachusetts and Andrew Jackson of Tennessee. Jackson and his supporters were the cause of fundamental change. Old Hickory's image as the rugged frontiersman, the independent, self-made man, and the hero of the Battle of New Orleans breathed new life into presidential politics by attracting large and intense popular support. So strong was this attraction that in Indiana, as elsewhere, supporters began to organize and to campaign more systematically and professionally in order to get him elected. They began to create political machinery, initially devoted to the man but increasingly devoted to the organization, the party.

The shift from personal to party politics was not immediate. The Indiana Jacksonian organization in 1824 was feeble, the attempt at a party convention poorly attended, the turnout in the November presidential election far lower than in the August state elections. Jackson carried Indiana decisively, but he lost the White House to Adams— the consequence, his supporters charged, of a "corrupt bargain" between Adams and Henry Clay. That result and continued popular attachment to the Hero encouraged Jacksonians to intensify their efforts. In late 1827 they organized county Jackson meetings, and on January 8, 1828, the anniversary of the Battle of New Orleans, they held a state meeting. As a consequence, more voters turned out for the 1828 presidential balloting than for the gubernatorial elections. And they gave Jackson a landslide victory in Indiana that helped propel him to the White House.

By 1828 presidential politics was intruding on state and local politics as candidates for other offices began to identify with either Jackson or the Adams-Clay team and their organizations, soon known respectively as the Democratic party and the National Republican or, after 1834, the Whig party. Voters in turn began to consider this party identification in selecting candidates for state and local offices, and some voters began to think of themselves as affiliated with a particular political organization. This identification was not complete or uniform. James B. Ray professed independence of party and won reelection to the governor's office in 1828 on the basis of his personal popularity. William Hendricks maintained a cautious, nonpartisan style that kept him in the Senate until his defeat in 1836. But these men were the last of a generation. The new generation insistently forced the question: are you a Democrat or a Whig?

Accompanying the rise of this new party system were other associated changes in Indiana politics. Political patronage became more important, particularly in the form of federal jobs. These included postmaster appointments, federal judicial positions, land office jobs (the most lucrative federal appointments), and contracts to newspapers to publish federal laws. Such jobs were important in the era of personal politics, as John Tipton's successful rise from justice of the peace to United States senator dramatized, but the emergence of parties led to more deliberate use of patronage as a systematic political tool. In particular, Jackson's victory in 1828 produced wholesale housecleaning in Indiana: all but three of the twenty-four major federal officers who had served under Adams were replaced by men loyal to the Jacksonian organization. All the leading Jackson men in Indiana received federal appointments. This turnover in office was more thoroughgoing in Indiana than in most other states. Jacksonians justified it as democratic rotation of office; opponents called it a spoils system. Both parties would use it to encourage loyal workers and bind their organizations together. Patronage, often ruthlessly applied, became an accepted part of politics, with a longer and more durable history in Indiana than in nearly any other state.

Another important feature of politics that accompanied the rise of parties was the growing importance of newspapers as political organs. Indiana newspaper publishing began in Vincennes in 1804 with the *Indiana Gazette*. Prior to statehood papers were established at Madison, Brookville, Lexington, Vevay, and Corydon, with the number increasing after 1816, generally following the movement of settlers. By 1840 there were more than seventy Indiana newspapers. They contained advertisements, fiction, poetry, agricultural advice, and news reprinted from other papers. Since nearly all were rural and small town weeklies there was very little local information, with the important exception of articles and editorials promoting the economic prospects of the town and surrounding area. The primary content was political news, including passionate editorials, commentary, speeches, and letters from readers. As parties developed newspapers became firmly tied to one or the other, and any town claiming respectability had both a Democratic and Whig paper. The two Indianapolis papers were especially important because they had close access to state government. The Indianapolis *Indiana Sentinel* presented the Democratic truth; the Indianapolis *Indiana Journal* offered the Whig gospel. Neither made a pretense of nonpartisanship. Both filled their editorials with vitriolic and often personal attacks on opposing party leaders and editors. Jacob P. and George A. Chapman, editors of the *Sentinel*, were particularly talented in denouncing Whig scoundrels. They and their colleagues kept readers informed, loyal, and intensely interested in party politics. Widely read, passed from reader to reader, discussed and debated, pioneer newspapers were critically essential in making politics and parties meaningful and important to Hoosiers.[17]

Also important in generating political interest and party loyalty were new styles of political campaigning. The subdued and informal style of the era of personal politics waned as campaigns took on more hoopla and organization. Jacksonians led the way in developing the new style, with the Whigs slower to organize campaigns to rally voters. By the late 1830s, however, Whigs had mastered the new techniques and were prepared for the most exciting election in pioneer Indiana.

The Whig candidate in 1840 was William Henry Harrison, former governor of Indiana Territory. Party organizers vigorously presented voters with images of Harrison as the hero of the Battle of Tippecanoe and as a simple man of the frontier who had given unselfish service to the territory and the nation. Shouting "Tippecanoe and Tyler too," they ignored Harrison's family origins among the Virginia gentry, his ties to the "aristocratic" faction in territorial politics, and his undistinguished record in public life after 1815. Rather, pictured in front of a log cabin with a jug of cider, "Old Tip" became the embodiment of simple republican virtue, the man who stood above partisan strife and who represented the purer age of politics before parties. The Harrison log cabin campaign of 1840 represented a shrewd attempt to appeal to lingering antiparty sentiment and to a romantic longing for a frontier that was rapidly passing. And it was well organized and conducted to take these images and messages to all voters. Parades, barbecues, floats, Tippecanoe clubs, log-cabin raisings, and special campaign newspapers culminated in a mammoth rally at the Tippecanoe battleground. It was nearly impossible not to take sides or remain uninvolved. There was considerable irony and buncombe in the log cabin campaign: it looked backward in a period of rapid change; it presented a most uncommon man as one of the people; and it appealed to antiparty sentiment while in fact endeavoring to strengthen the attachment of voters to the Whig party. Most important, it worked. Harrison defeated Martin Van Buren in the state and nation. Never again would Whigs or any other major party patiently and quietly wait for the voters to discover their attributes.[18]

By the time of the log cabin campaign partisanship was a fact of political life. Candidates for state offices ran on a party ticket, and the General Assembly organized and often voted along party lines. Even many local elections featured candidates identified with one or the other presidential aspirant. There was little room for an independent or no-party persuasion. Moreover, Hoosiers had come to believe that parties were important and that politics was fun. The Indiana propensity to politic developed on the frontier and intensified with the rise of parties. Politics became entertainment—sometimes informative and even intellectual in form, sometimes mere diversion and sport.

The rise of two major parties led to a strategy of appealing to the broadest possible number of voters, a strategy that often urged minimal discussion of issues and even deliberate obfuscation of a candidate's position. Harrison's reluctance to commit himself led Democrats to label him "General Mum," but both parties sought a majority vote by treading carefully so as not to offend voters and by concentrating on emotional images of the kind associated with log cabins, military heroes, and other campaign hoopla. The result, critics charged, was a deliberate and unfortunate failure of the parties and of government to confront the important issues of public life. Henry Ward Beecher lamented in 1845 that Indiana government was "distracted in council by almost equally balanced parties, more vigilant, (it has seemed to us), of each other, than of schools, mechanic arts, agriculture, and the actual commonwealth."[19]

Although there was much validity then and ever after to Beecher's criticism, issues were important in Indiana politics and did affect the rise and changing fortunes of the two parties. Hoosiers generally wanted their state and federal governments to aid in improving transportation, removing Indians, and enabling settlers to acquire land easily and cheaply. On these and other issues there was a general consensus in the 1820s which partly broke down in the 1830s. Andrew Jackson's policies, particularly his opposition to certain federal internal improvements and to the Bank of the United States, forced many Hoosiers to take positions and divide along party lines. In the early 1830s most voters supported Jacksonian candidates. Old Hickory's popularity and the growing Democratic party loyalty caused many voters to continue to back the president despite their apparent unhappiness with his failure to support improvements on the Wabash River and the National Road. Jackson's Whig opponents argued that the president's opposition to federal internal improvements was depriving the West of its future prospects. Whigs increasingly proclaimed their support of internal improvements and also their belief in some form of government banking system. There was considerable bipartisan support for the state internal improvements program in the system of 1836 and for the creation of the state bank in 1834, but Whigs claimed these popular measures as theirs. And Whigs benefited also from the large popularity of Harrison, a candidate whom the Democrats could not match after the retirement of Jackson in 1837. So dispirited were the Democrats that they failed to run a gubernatorial candidate in 1837.

The 1840s brought the Democrats to power in Indiana and helped define more clearly the party's position. Aided by the continuing economic depression and the failure of the state internal improvements system, Democrats charged Whigs with mismanagement and corruption. They asserted that Whigs were the party of the aristocracy, of merchants and bankers who used government for their own private ends. Professing to be instead the party of the common man, Democrats argued for private construction of transportation projects, more separation of the state from banking, and low taxes and strict economy in government. In putting forth these arguments Democrats struck chords that would remain at the center of the party's appeal down to the 1930s. Building on the traditions of Jefferson, Indiana Democrats emphasized the primacy of individual liberty and urged a limited government close to the people. Whigs were more likely to support greater government efforts to secure economic growth and development and were less fearful of an active government, whether in pushing forward internal improvements, supporting public education, regulating alcohol consumption, or restricting the expansion of slavery.[20]

Differences over political issues and principles increased in the period from 1816 to 1850, yet remained fluid and imprecise. Not all Whigs agreed on issues or ideology, any more than did all Democrats. Both parties were troubled by factional conflict. There was considerable overlap between the two parties and even in the 1840s much agreement. Yet the party patterns formed in the pioneer period were important and durable. Most indicative of this was the continuity of voting, for although some voters shifted parties from election to election there was a sizable core of voters who remained firmly attached to the same party. This partisan loyalty became an increasingly important part of Indiana politics. One of its most immediate consequences was to introduce a new geographic pattern into election results. The Democratic party's appeal was most consistent in southern Indiana, particularly in the triangle that had its apex in Martinsville and its base on the Ohio between Madison and Evansville. This hilly, unglaciated region was the bedrock of Democratic strength from 1824 down to the twentieth century. Whigs had more support in central and northern Indiana, though there was considerable Democratic strength there too. This sectional pattern of party loyalty would be further hardened in the 1850s and 1860s as would also the political machinery and techniques developed in the pioneer era.

The Constitutional Convention of 1850–1851

The constitution of 1816 had served the pioneer generation well. Yet there developed in the 1840s a sentiment that it needed revising. Partly this urge reflected the fashion of the time, for most states and all those of the Old Northwest engaged in constitutional rewriting in the late 1840s and early 1850s. It was, many felt, a necessary part of an age of progress and reform. There were also more specific concerns that led to the movement for a new constitution. Many Indianans concluded that the General Assembly did not function as efficiently as it might. Legislators were awash each session in hundreds of bills pertaining to individual and local matters. Moreover, they met every year—a concession to popular democracy, to be sure, but an expensive and, many concluded, unnecessary cost of government. And there was also the matter of the unhappy memories from the system of 1836, in which the legislature had approved programs and expenditures that in the late 1840s appeared foolish. In response to these concerns the people of the state approved in 1840 the call for a constitutional convention.[21]

Indiana voters elected 150 delegates to the constitutional convention of 1850–1851. Not surprisingly in an agrarian state, 42 percent were farmers, but a quarter were lawyers and 12 percent physicians, with a sprinkling from many other occupations and professions. Reflecting the timing and origins of settlement, only thirteen of the 150 delegates were native Hoosiers; seventy-four were born in the South; fifty-seven in northern states other than Indiana; and only six in foreign countries. Perhaps the most important characteristic of the delegates was their party identification. Reflecting the strength of the Democratic party, two-thirds were Democrats and one-third Whigs. And they functioned often as partisans, beginning with a squabble at the outset of the convention over who would receive the contract to print the finished document.

The constitution that emerged from four months of debate did not radically alter the form or function of state government. The delegates responded to discontent with the General Assembly by establish biennial sessions of sixty-one days and by severely restricting special-interest and local legislation. And the new document prohibited the state from incurring debt. It stated a stronger commitment to establishing common schools and granted the vote to immigrants if they stated their intention to become citizens and had been resident in the country a year and in the state six months. This liberal extension of the vote to non-citizens was due largely to expectations of the Democratic majority that Irish and German-Ameicans were most likely to vote for their party's candidates. The delegates were not at all liberal with suffrage for women or blacks: both remained disenfranchised. A movement led by Robert Dale Owen to extend women's rights to own property was defeated. And blacks received a special battering of racism in Article XIII, which prohibited them from settling in the state.

The new constitution was not a perfect document. Some, like historian Logan Esarey, concluded it "suffers in comparision with the one it displaced." But it retained many of the best features of the 1816 constitution, including an expanded bill of rights placed at the outset. And it continued a basic framework that enabled Indianans to govern themselves largely as they wished. It would often be amended and subjected to changing interpretations. There were calls too for a new constitution, especially during the Progressive era, but the basic document continues as the foundation of government in Indiana and as one of the oldest of state constitutions.[22]

The Pioneer Legacy

The goal of pioneers was to leave pioneering behind. No event signaled their success in reaching that goal; no date marked the end of the pioneer era. Here as throughout the history of Indiana change was gradual and evolutionary rather than rapid and revolutionary. Nor was change uniform throughout the state. In some places and for some families pioneer conditions persisted into the Civil War years and beyond, as in the hills of Brown County and some other parts of southern Indiana.

Yet across much of the state there were signs by mid-century that the pioneer era was passing. Most land was sold, and much of it cleared. The frontier was to the west, in Iowa, Kansas, and Nebraska. In the 1850s, for the first time in Indiana's history, more native-born Americans moved from the state than to it. Farmers began to talk about Berkshire hogs and mechanical reapers. Their sons began to talk about the possibilities of making a living off the farm. Young women, though they often did not talk about it, began to consider the wisdom of having fewer children. City dwellers began to see a need for uniform time and a town clock, a regular police force, an opera house, sidewalks, and public health ordinances. Ordinary folk began to wear store-bought pants and dresses and even underwear. Richer folk, eager to display their prosperity and good taste, moved into large and imposing homes. The architect Francis Costigan built for Madison banker James F. D. Lanier in 1844 a Greek Revival mansion with a beautiful spiral staircase and a two-story portico overlooking the Ohio.[23] In New Albany Angelina Collins published in 1851 Indiana's first cookbook: it contained recipes for corn dodgers, corn pone, and venison, cooked before an open fireplace, but also for oysters, bon-bons, and lemon punch.[24]

There were signs also that Hoosiers by mid-century were aware that the pioneer era was waning. Some even began nostalgically to lament its passing. George Winter's paintings of Potawatomi Indians were appealing because so few people had seen an Indian; fewer still had ever feared a war party.[25] An Indianapolis newspaper editor expressed both regret and pride that Pogue's Run, where once the "Indian maid mirrored in its wave," was now "tinged with the filth of a growing city."[26] A few years later an old settlers association formed in the capital city, composed of those who had arrived there before 1825: sixty pioneers attended the first meeting, and "a great many ancedotes were told."[27] John B. Dillon began more formally to record the history of the state. The first edition of his *History of Indiana*, published in 1843, recorded the advancement of "freedom and civilization" and prepared the way for a romantic glorification of a waning age.[28]

Change and consciousness of change did not mean an end to the pioneer heritage. Patterns, beliefs, and values that developed in the pioneer era persisted long after the mid-nineteenth century. Their experiences on the frontier taught pioneers the importance of Jeffersonian individualism and republican liberty. They believed fervently in individual rights and freedoms, especially when threatened by government at a distance or even, if they happened to be Baptists, by Presbyterians close at home.

Pioneers did not wish to live in isolation or in absolute freedom, however. They lived, first of all, in family units, not because of sentimental attachments to the family but because the family met most efficiently their fundamental social, economic, and emotional needs. Most of them lived also as farmers, not primarily because they believed that farmers were God's chosen people—though many would have

eagerly approved that notion—but because farming was the most obvious and sensible way to make a living for a people with abundant
land but limited capital and labor. And as farmers they eagerly sought
ways to connect their output to distant markets and to become part
of the growing national economy. Pioneers also sought social community off the farm and away from the family. For many this meant
membership in a church, attendance at a corn husking or logrolling,
or just visiting neighbors. Pioneers also sought material progress.
They were not aggressive innovators, but they did want change that
would improve the material conditions of their lives. They were willing
even to enlist government in this effort. Though opposed to paying
taxes for public schools and reluctant to be taxed even for much-
needed transportation improvements, they did have high expectations
of their government. Generally confident that voters could readily
influence public policy, pioneers expected their government to contribute to the general welfare, especially the general economic welfare.
And they participated in heated political debate about the nature of
that welfare and joined in the partisan politicking that ensued.

These features of pioneer life did not pass away. Indianans into
the twentieth century would express attachments to individual freedom, to traditional family life, to farm and rural values, to various
forms of face-to-face community, to progress, especially of a material
kind, and to intense partisan politics. Many such values of the pioneer
culture continued to make sense. Others needed to be modified, for
changing conditions sometimes rendered foolish a continued attachment to pioneer notions. Sometimes, in fact, pioneer roots held even
when the tree was dead, when the conditions that made earlier sentiments practical and sensible no longer prevailed. This was the case,
for example, in the pioneer parsimony with which later generations
of Hoosiers continued to support public education. For those wishing
to bring change after 1850 there was often the hold of the pioneer
generation, the hold of a past never entirely dead. Not conservatives
themselves, their success as pioneers helped make Indiana a conservative state, its people usually most comfortable with traditional beliefs
and methods. It was an ironic legacy from a generation that itself so
intently wished for change.

PART III

Indiana in Transition, 1850–1920

viii

Making a Living, 1850–1920

By 1850 Indiana was moving beyond the pioneer stage of development. Isolated log cabins were rapidly giving way to frame and brick houses, and small lean-tos and stock pens to large barns. Villages and towns were bustling with commercial activity and with the occasional clank of a manufacturing enterprise. In town and countryside the sound of the railroad locomotive could be heard with increasing frequency. Yet Indiana at mid-century was still a rural and agricultural state: only 4.5 percent of the population lived in towns of more than 2,500 inhabitants, and nearly everyone, including women and children, was engaged directly or indirectly in the agricultural economy. The rapid rate of population growth in the frontier era had begun to decline: the 1850 census was the first to show less than a doubling of population in the preceding ten years. The 1850 census also showed southern Indiana losing the population dominance it had enjoyed in the frontier period as new farms and towns spread over the central and northern sections of the state, which by 1850 had 58 percent of the state's population compared to 42 percent in the southern third of the state.

In the years after 1850 Indiana moved far from its pioneer origins. The Civil War helped create a new political environment with a distinctive party system and patterns of electoral behavior that would persist for decades. Factories, cities, and railroads brought new kinds of work and living arrangments and created new social and political conditions. Blacks from the American South and immigrants from Europe began to challenge the racial and ethnic homogeneity of some Indiana towns and cities, though the state as a whole remained very largely composed of white, native-born inhabitants. The urban, industrial age of the late nineteenth century demanded a more educated citizenry, and Indiana gradually evolved a system of public education. Change was the order of the day, sometimes rapid, bewildering, even painful change. And yet Hoosiers clung tenaciously to pioneer verities and especially to the rural agrarian outlook that had formed in the early nineteenth century. By the beginning of the twentieth century Indiana was often cited as the most typical of American states, perhaps because Hoosiers in this age of transition generally resisted radical change and were able usually to balance moderate change with due attention to the continuities of life and culture.

It was in the changing ways in which they made their living that Hoosiers first became aware of the fading of pioneer life and the emergence of a new and sometimes confusing world. Economic change accompanied social, political, and cultural change and often functioned as the prime mover in transition from a pioneer, rural, agrarian society to a modern, urban, industrial one. Certainly Hoosiers of the late nineteenth and early twentieth centuries stood in awe and sometimes in fear of the economic changes around them. And when they spoke of progress, as they were often wont to do, it was usually progress of an economic sort. Here was the American Dream, one most Hoosiers fully shared in belief if not always in fact.

There is no doubt of the reality of progress, at least of a certain economic kind. Census report after census report showed upward movement in nearly all economic indicators. More bushels of corn, miles of railroad track, and tons of iron and steel were evidence of economic growth most pleasing and most consequential in improving material well-being. It was not just the fact of more production of material goods that was important, however, but also the changing nature of production. New methods of cultivating corn, organizing railroads, or manufacturing steel profoundly affected many workers and the communities in which they lived. The changing economy placed a particularly high premium on large scale, systematic organization of production and on increasingly complex and expensive technology. Some Hoosiers began to fear that the threat to individuals in choosing and directing their own manner of making a living was spurring a fundamental revolution, a tide of change that might carry away the positive as well as the less attractive features of their pioneer heritage. But such fears seemed less important than the predominant faith in a steady progress and fundamental stability, even a smugness that theirs was the best society on earth: "Ain't God good to Indiana?" the poet William Herschell asked in 1919, doubtless provoking a strong if not unanimous chorus of assent.[1]

Life on the Farm

Agriculture continued to be as it had from the beginning the most important way in which Hoosiers earned their living. Farming and rural life remained dominant in shaping much of the social, cultural, and political features of Indiana's history as well as in providing the base for economic well-being. Even the products of field and farm remained much the same. Corn and hogs continued to receive primary attention, and Indiana remained among the top five states producing both throughout the years 1850–1920. And yet while agriculture endured and flourished it was not fully constant in its form or in its relationship to other aspects of life. The number of farmers in Indiana continued to increase up to the eve of World War I, but the percentage of the male work force engaged in farming declined from 66 percent in 1850 to 59 percent in 1890 to 31 percent in 1920. Manufacturing, transportation, trade, and urban service jobs had replaced farming as the dominant way of making a living.

The nature of farming and rural life also changed. While there

An Indiana contribution to increased agricultural productivity.
(Lilly Library, Indiana University)

were still farm families in 1920 whose manner of work and living differed little from that of their grandparents in 1850 or their great-grandparents in 1820, pioneer methods of agriculture gradually gave way on most late nineteenth century farms. Vast expanses of forest and the wild game sheltered there disappeared as farmers cleared, drained, plowed, and pastured livestock on increasing numbers of acres. Improved farmland expanded from five million acres in 1850 to more than sixteen million acres by 1900, by which time nearly all the economically productive agricultural land was in use. The last large tracts opened were the swamp lands in northern Indiana, where 8,200 miles of tile and 17,500 miles of drainage ditches were in place by 1919. Pioneer practices such as logrollings, plowing around tree stumps, and planting small plots had given way to farming large tracts of land where the furrows ran in long straight lines, broken only by narrow country roads. And on this land, particularly in central and northern Indiana, farmers began to alter the ways in which they planted, cultivated, and harvested. They acquired new machinery in efforts to decrease the amount of labor and increase the amount of total crop for the farm and for each acre on the farm. They replaced wooden plows with iron and steel plows, particularly James Oliver's chilled-iron plow. By 1880 Oliver's South Bend factory was the world's largest plow manufacturer. Mowers, reapers, seed drills, and steam threshing machines appeared in increasing numbers to destroy forever pioneer methods of farming. And with the new machinery came more horses, replacing human power with animal power in many basic tasks and enabling one man to farm more and more acres. While such changes could be observed throughout Indiana, they were especially prevalent in central and northern Indiana. Poor soil, hilly terrain, and perhaps a stronger attachment to traditional ways caused many farmers in southern Indiana to lag behind their counterparts elsewhere, making the region an ever more distinctive part of the state.

The shift from pioneer to more mechanized farming required farmers to abandon practices of their parents and grandparents and learn new ways. Crop rotation, fertilizer, new breeds of livestock, and keeping farm accounts required different ways of thinking. Much of the new skill and knowledge was communicated directly to farmers through county fairs and agricultural societies. The exhibits and awards for the best of the new agriculture were most impressive at the annual state fair, first held in 1852. Farmers also learned from the growing agricultural press, the most influential of which was the *Indiana Farmer*, established in 1866. In reaching readers the farm magazines benefited from the expansion of public education after the Civil War and from rural free mail delivery begun at the turn of the century. Farmers also learned from membership in agricultural associations, such as the Indiana Corn Growers Association, founded in 1900, and the Patrons of Husbandry, more generally known as the Grange, which appeared in Indiana in 1869. The Grange served important social and political as well as informational purposes for many farmers.

The most sophisticated agricultural knowledge came from Purdue University, founded by the state in 1874 with the aid of a federal land grant. Purdue scientists experimented with new methods of farming, published bulletins reporting their findings and those of other researchers, and worked with farm organizations and the federal government in various agricultural programs. Purdue faculty not only taught in West Lafayette classrooms but also took their message through the state to farmers' institutes and other local meetings. Ag-

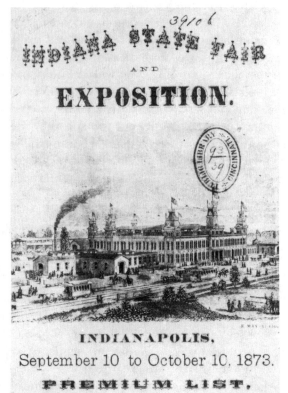

Annual focal point of agricultural change.
(Lilly Library, Indiana University)

riculture extension work in the early twentieth century included spon-
sorship of corn trains, which took the Purdue "gospel" to crowds
gathered at railroad stations throughout Indiana. And the university
cooperated closely in development of the county agent as a full-time
resident adviser to local farmers. The General Assembly began financial support of county agents in 1913, greatly boosted by federal
money after 1914. By 1918 eighty-three counties had agents advising
farmers in all manner of agricultural problems and standing as local
representatives of Purdue and of the state and federal government's
growing commitment to scientific agriculture. A vast and formal net-

work of information and sophisticated help had replaced the pioneer farmer's reliance only on himself, his family, and perhaps a few neighbors.

The self-sufficient, independent farmer of pioneer Indiana had evolved in other ways too by World War I. He was increasingly part of a complex national, even international, economic system, dependent on railroad agents, elevator operators, bankers, agricultural implement manufacturers, and market conditions hundreds and thousands of miles from his home. Often farmers feared themselves dependent on and even victims of forces far beyond their power to affect or even to understand. The terrible economic depressions from 1873 to 1878 and again from 1893 to 1896 exacerbated this anxiety as did the general price decline of the late nineteenth century. The economic grievances of farmers, many of whom were debtors in a deflationary economy, stimulated organized bursts of political action in the Greenback and Grange movements of the 1870s and the Populist protests of the 1890s, as noted below. The advent of higher farm prices and general prosperity in the decade and a half before World War I greatly alleviated such anxieties and deflated the trend toward political organization by farmers. Indeed, in the widespread turn-of-the century propensity to seek order and well-being through association and organization Indiana farmers lagged behind many other elements of the population, holding to pioneer notions of individualism and self-help long after many workers, businessmen, and professionals had abandoned such visions. Only after World War I did many farmers become fully aware of the necessity to organize and cooperate economically and politically in order to survive in a rapidly changing world.

As farming evolved in the years from 1850 to 1920 so too did life on the family farm, though only slowly. Rural isolation continued to be both celebrated and deplored—celebrated as protection from the evils of urban, industrial society but deplored as barrier to the cultural and material amenities of city life. Many farm families sought to overcome their isolation by finding ways to enjoy the best of urban society while remaining on the farm. As noted below, new forms of transportation—the railroad, the interurban, and later the automobile—combined with the rapid spread of telephone lines to narrow distances for social visiting, Saturday shopping, or school and church attendance. Many farm families sought country road improvements for their farm wagons, for the rural free mail delivery, and later for their automobiles. By 1920 nearly half (46 percent) of Indiana farm families had an automobile, often one of Henry Ford's Model Ts. And farmers eagerly installed telephone lines so that by 1920 66 percent of Indiana farm homes had telephones.

These changes in transportation and communication were especially welcomed by farm women. They threw spinning wheels, butter churns, and soap kettles into attics or on trash piles as mass-produced consumer goods arrived in Main Street stores and, from the new mail order firms such as Sears, Roebuck, at farmhouse doors. New and more readily accessible women's clubs, church groups, and farm institutes provided rural women with social and cultural opportunities beyond the farm kitchen and garden, ranging from discussion of English literature to suffrage and the temperance movement. Young people too found new social and cultural opportunities. The expansion of rural schools, the development of boys' and girls' clubs for agricultural education and of church youth groups for religious education—all helped alleviate the isolation so burdensome to rural adolescents.

And yet the responses of many youth provided the best evidence of the slowness of change and the degree to which farm life lagged behind urban life. Young people voted with their feet and their satchels; thousands of them left the family farm for jobs and homes in towns and cities. So large did this rural to urban migration become that by the turn of the century the issue was a major subject of discussion and of worry for parents and for rural farm groups. Such concern only increased when the 1910 census showed that for the first time in Indiana's history the numbers of rural Hoosiers had actually declined, while the urban population continued to grow and in 1920 surpassed the rural population in size.

The sense that agriculture and rural life were threatened, best illustrated by the cityward migration of the young, grew alongside material progress, exemplified by the spread of machinery and scientific farming. This bifocal vision of progress and peril produced contradictory rural images—images of the rustic hayseed hopelessly attached to old-fashioned ways and of the progressive, hardworking, efficient farmer; images of backward, provincial Hoosiers stubbornly attached

to outmoded pioneer traditions and of the honest, independent yeomen, deeply rooted on the family farm and living in close-knit families
and friendly rural communities. Those who criticized Indiana's slowness to change blamed farmers; those who boasted of the state's stability praised them.

The Railroad Age

In few areas was change so rapid and so visible as in transportation.
In one lifetime pioneer modes of transport faded to near oblivion as
radically new forms altered the direction, speed, and nature of transportation. At the center was the railroad, which touched nearly every
aspect of life in Indiana. Changes included also the development of
interurban railroads, the improvements of surface roads, and, near
the end of the period, the advent of the automobile.

In the face of transportation improvements pioneer modes passed,
and with them their handicaps of seasonality, limited and inflexible
routes, and slow speed. Canals made a modest revival after the return
of general prosperity in the late 1840s. The Wabash and Erie Canal
carried considerable traffic above Terre Haute in the early 1850s, but
railroad competition soon cut deeply into its business and forced abandonment in 1874. Indiana's once-thriving Ohio River ports lost much
of their river trade, and pioneer hopes of large scale navigation on
the White and Wabash rivers receded. Several attempts to improve
the two badly obstructed rivers came to naught.

Improvements in road transportation were slightly more successful.
A plank road craze swept Indiana in the early 1850s, based on the
assumption that private companies could make profits by laying a
cheap timber floor on a dirt roadbed, charging a toll for the faster,
smoother, dust-free travel. Nearly 400 miles of plank roads were constructed in 1850, but the enthusiasm soon passed: the wooden roads
quickly deteriorated, and tolls generated insufficient revenue.[2] More
prosaic gravel and macadamized roads provided most of the improved
road mileage, much of which was privately constructed toll roads,
including parts of the old National Road. By the 1890s, however, local
governments had assumed a larger part in road construction and
maintenance. County and township governments used powers of as-

sessment and taxation and the corvée, whereby all able-bodied males between twenty-one and fifty had to work at road repairs for up to four days a year. But primitive road-building techniques and fears of high taxes left most Indiana roads in a sorry state, while the jealously guarded tradition of local control and the absence of coordination or financial help from the state rendered impossible the development of a true highway system. Public clamor for such a system developed with the popularity of the bicycle, the advent of rural free mail delivery, and the growing numbers of automobiles. The ensuing good roads movement attracted increased support, particularly from promoters such as Carl G. Fisher, an Indianapolis auto parts manufacturer who did much to popularize automobiles by inaugurating the Indianapolis 500–mile race in 1911. But not until after the federal government in 1916 offered financial support to the states for rural post roads did Indiana establish a state Highway Commission and create a highway fund. This beginning led eventually to a centrally planned and financed state highway system that opened the way for the automobile's omnipresence after 1920.

Nothing was as important to Indiana's transportation in the period 1850 to 1920 as the railroad. Nothing else so symbolized progress to late nineteenth century Hoosiers, or did so much actually to alter the way they lived. Indiana's first railroad was the Madison and Indianapolis, completed from the Ohio River to the capital city in 1847. Its location is indicative of two primary determinants of railroad development at mid-century: first, early railroads like the Madison and Indianapolis were feeder lines intended to supplement rather than supersede river transportation; and, secondly, a major destination of many was Indianapolis, a magnet drawing lines to or through the center of the state and thus promoting the development of a hub with iron spokes. With the pioneering example of the Madison and Indianapolis, other railroad companies began a boom of construction in the early 1850s. The longest of these pioneer railroads was the New Albany and Salem (later known as the Monon), a 288-mile route connecting the Ohio River with Lake Michigan. By the time of its completion in 1854 eighteen railroad companies had laid over 1,400 miles of track in Indiana. Most of these companies were short-line railroads of fewer than 100 miles and were organized and financed by residents and local governments along the routes, only later attracting eastern

investment. They were home-grown enterprises, with locally prominent businessmen, farmers, and politicians taking leading roles and
with local newspapers extravagantly boosting the prospects of the railroad and the towns through which it would pass. All were motivated
by the lure of profit and progress, though Hoosiers, at least in Indianapolis, seemed more moderate and realistic in their promotional
extravagance than their urban counterparts in Chicago or Cincinnati.[3]

Many of the railroads of the early 1850s soon became parts of regional and eventually national networks, as the short lines were purchased and combined to form larger companies and as the great trunk
lines from the East moved westward through Indiana, many to connect with Chicago. Central and northern Indiana benefited more from
this expansion of the railroad network than did southern Indiana, as
Map 7 shows. The two largest systems, both concentrated in central
and northern Indiana, were the Pennsylvania and the New York Central, which by 1920 operated approximately 3,450 of the 7,812 miles
of track in the state.

The advent of big business in late nineteenth century railroading
caused considerable turmoil in Indiana. Companies like the Pennsylvania and New York Central were unprecedented in size and power—
power that sometimes led to abuse. Critics complained that railroad
rates were often unfair and discriminatory, particularly because
higher rates were charged for local hauls than for through or long
hauls. Farmers with only one line serving them complained bitterly
of unfair monopoly rates. To these concerns was added the fact of
eastern control, or, as one critic expressed it, control by "combinations
foreign to our State, whose local interests and business sympathies are
elsewhere than in Indiana." The rise of big business meant, the *Indianapolis Journal* charged in early 1873, that "the transportation of
our people is at the mercy of men who never see us, who know nothing
of us, and care nothing for us."[4] Here indeed was one of the best
examples of the outside world playing an ever larger part in Indiana's
development, for decisions made in Philadelphia at the main office
of the Pennsylvania Railroad did help shape the futures of Terre
Haute, Indianapolis, Richmond, and much of the state. Because of
the railroads these communities and the state itself were less and less
like islands separated from the rest of the nation and the world.

Hoosiers did not submit to railroad power without a fight. Just as

MAP 7.
Railroads, 1880

1. Anderson, Lebanon, St. Louis
2. Baltimore, Ohio, & Chicago
3. Bedford, Springville, Owensburg,
   & Bloomfield
4. Chicago & Block Coal
5. Chicago, Cincinnati, & Louisville
6. Chicago & Eastern Illinois
7. Chicago & Grand Trunk
8. Cincinnati, Hamilton, & Indianapolis
9. Cincinnati, Lafayette, & Chicago
10. Cincinnati, Richmond, & Ft. Wayne
11. Cincinnati, Rockport, & South-
    western
12. Cincinnati, Wabash, & Michigan
13. Cleveland, Columbus, Cincinnati,
    & Indianapolis
14. Columbus, Chicago, & Indiana
    Central
15. Eel River
16. Evansville & Terre Haute
17. Evansville, Terre Haute, & Chicago
18. Fairland, Franklin, & Martinsville
19. Ft. Wayne, Jackson, & Saginaw
20. Ft. Wayne, Muncie, & Cincinnati
21. Frankfort & Kokomo
22. Grand Rapids & Indiana
23. Indiana Block Coal
24. Indiana, Bloomington, & Western
25. Indianapolis, Cincinnati &
    Lafayette
26. Indianapolis, Decatur, &
    Springfield, Ill.
27. Indianapolis, Delphi, & Chicago
28. Indianapolis, Peru, & Chicago
29. Indianapolis & St. Louis
30. Indianapolis & Vincennes
31. Jeffersonville, Madison, &
    Indianapolis
32. Lake Erie, Evansville, & South-
    western
33. Lake Shore & Michigan Southern
34. Lake Erie & Western
35. Louisville, New Albany, & Chicago
36. Louisville, New Albany, & St.
    Louis
37. Logansport, Crawfordsville, &
    Southwestern
38. Michigan Central
39. Michigan City & Indianapolis
40. Ohio & Mississippi
41. Pittsburgh, Ft. Wayne,
    & Chicago
42. Terre Haute &
    Indianapolis
43. Terre Haute &
    Southeastern
44. Toledo, Delphos, &
    Burlington
45. Wabash, St. Louis &
    Pacific
46. Whitewater

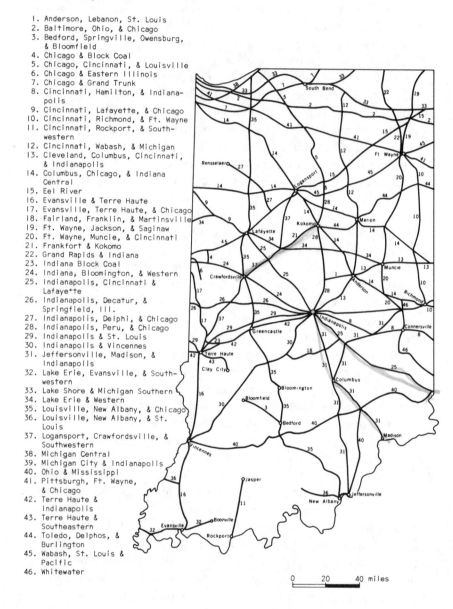

Source: Robert C. Kingsbury, *An Atlas of Indiana* (Bloomington, 1970), 76

in frontier times, they turned to their governments for aid. Beginning in the 1860s legislators in the General Assembly argued that the state must fix rates and must ensure that existing rates were uniform and fair. The depression beginning in 1873 intensified these demands, particularly from farmers and often through the Grange, which led the midwestern campaign for railroad regulation. Although several other states adopted so-called Granger laws to regulate rates and although the Indiana legislature debated the issue often during the 1870s, no legislation passed. The Democrat-controlled legislature of 1879 did petition Congress for federal regulation of railroads, despite the party's traditional concern over centralization of power in Washington. The federal government responded with the Interstate Commerce Act of 1887, a major landmark in federal regulation. Discontent with railroads persisted, however, and led in 1905 to establishment of the Indiana Railroad Commission with power to alter intrastate rates found to be unfair. In 1913 this Progressive-era body evolved into the Indiana Public Service Commission, empowered to regulate public utilities as well as transportation.

The intense debates over railroad abuse and government regulation ought not obscure the more fundamental significance of railroads in Indiana. They were essential to the changes in agriculture after 1850, the growth of industry, and the evolution of villages and towns to cities. Railroads made it possible, for example, to move more hogs to the Indianapolis stockyards, more glass jars from the Muncie factories, and more customers and goods to the Main Street retail stores. The greater quantity and variety of economic activity made possible by railroads contributed to economic growth and to improved material well-being for most Hoosiers, changing forever the ways they worked and lived and connecting them economically and socially with each other and the rest of the nation. Nothing destroyed pioneer life so thoroughly as the railroad; nothing more deserved recognition as the symbol of late nineteenth century progress and change.

There was another form of rail transportation, not so dramatic as the steam locomotive with its long line of freight or passenger cars, but of considerable significance nonetheless. The interurbans consisted of electric-powered cars designed primarily for short distance passenger transport. The first lines opened in the 1890s, as electric street railways extended to the countryside and nearby towns. By 1900

Interurban service in central Indiana. (Indiana State Library)

there were 678 miles of electric lines in Indiana and by 1914 1,825 miles, ranking the state second only to Ohio. As Map 8 shows, Indianapolis soon emerged as the hub of Indiana's interurban system; thirteen lines and nearly 400 trains daily served the city by 1910. Most stopped at the Indianapolis Traction Terminal, opened in 1904 and covering nine tracks. Though they played a major role in improving transportation, interurbans began to decline after World War I. The lines were plagued by accidents, the worst being a head-on collision in Wells County that killed forty-two people in 1910. And they suffered competition from railroads and—especially after World War I—from automobiles, trucks, and buses. The Great Depression dealt the final blow to a once thriving interurban system.[5]

Industrialization and the Rise of Big Business

Accompanying changes in transportation and agriculture were changes in manufacturing. Manufacturing in 1850 was still close to

MAP 8.
Interurban Lines, with Dates of Abandonment

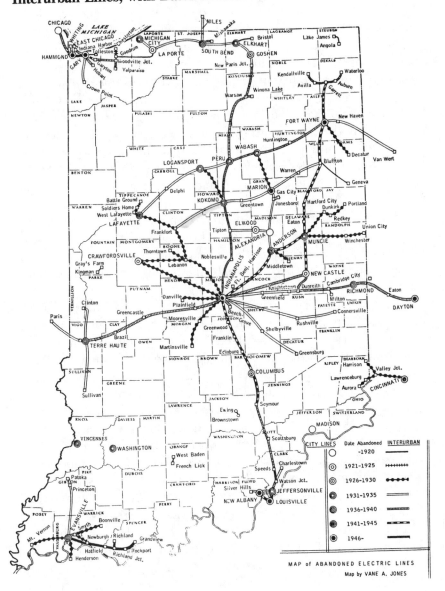

MAP of ABANDONED ELECTRIC LINES
Map by VANE A. JONES

SOURCE: James H. Madison, *Indiana through Tradition and Change, 1920–1945*
(Indianapolis, 1982), 197

its pioneer origins. Much production was still done by the family in
the home: home spinning and weaving, soap making, butchering,
food processing, and furniture making continued to make household
manufacturing a substantial part of Indiana's economy. Manufacturing outside the home in 1850 also remained close to the pioneer pattern. Manufacturing establishments were small and individually
owned, averaging only four employees per establishment. They were
simple in organization and equipment, composed primarily of craftsmen working with hand tools and aided by little or no machine power.
And they tended to concentrate in river towns, particularly Madison,
New Albany, and Jeffersonville. Most manufacturing in 1850 was
closely tied to nearby agriculture and natural resources, processing
grain, pork, and timber for consumer use. Many were seasonal in
operation.

The most important and typical of manufacturing establishments
of the mid-nineteenth century were flour and grist mills. Processing
wheat and corn from and for the nearby countryside, these mills were
locally owned and dotted the landscape throughout the state, numbering nearly 1,000 in 1850. Milling of grain was the leading industry
in Indiana, measured by value of product, until near the end of the
century. Nearly all Indiana's other important manufactured products
at mid-century were closely related to natural resources, particularly
timber, and to agriculture, including pork packing, liquor distilling,
lumber, carriages, wagons, furniture, and agricultural implements.

By 1920 the leading manufactured products were quite different.
Although processing of meat and grain remained important, joined
in the late nineteenth century by canned vegetables, agricultural products were less significant in Indiana manufacturing than new industries, sometimes called heavy industries, producing iron and steel,
glass, electrical machinery, railroad cars, and automobiles. But it was
not only the products that changed; the very nature of manufacturing
underwent dramatic transformation. New technology replaced simple
hand tools, and machines made of metal rather than wood became
awesome in complexity, power, exactness, and speed. Hand power
and water power gave way to steam power and after 1900 to electrical
power and the internal combustion engine. In east-central Indiana
the discovery of seemingly unlimited supplies of natural gas in the
1880s attracted new factories that made glass, tinplate, and strawboard
in booming towns of Muncie, Anderson, Kokomo, Elwood, Marion

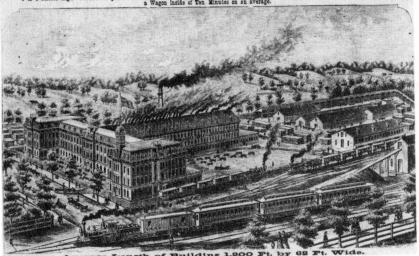

STUDEBAKER BROS., New Wagon Works, South Bend, Ind., the largest in the World
3 to 6 Stories High—Ground occupied for manufacturing purposes 13½ acres—Seasoned Stock on hand for 30,000 Wagons—Capacity to make a Wagon inside of Ten Minutes on an average.

Average Length of Building 1,200 Ft. by 62 Ft. Wide.

Industrial progress and pride in South Bend, 1873. (Lilly Library, Indiana University)

and Gas City. Due partly to foolish waste, the natural gas supply had nearly disappeared by the first decade of the twentieth century, but the industrial base of many Indiana gas belt towns allowed continued manufacturing development.

With changes in technology and motive power came changes in the size and organization of manufacturing establishments. Particularly after 1890 a decreasing number of factories and companies produced an ever increasing proportion of Indiana's manufactured products. This industrial combination and concentration meant that by 1919 Indiana's 302 largest manufacturing companies—each accounting for more than $1,000,000 worth of product and together representing only 4 percent of the total number of manufacturing establishments in the state—employed 58 percent of the state's wage earners and produced 72 percent of the state's value of manufactured product. Big business had come to Indiana, producing for regional, national, and even international markets and bringing mass production methods, large skilled and unskilled workforces, and an increasingly important managerial class. Locally owned and oriented small mills and shops and individual craftsmen remained, but they played diminished roles in the economy. Many of these big businesses included multi-plant production, with branch plants scattered in several cities, states, and even countries. Their names indicated their scope: United States Steel, American Can Company, International Harvester, and American Car and Foundry.

Some Indiana-based companies were part of this rise of big business, including Ball Brothers, the largest producer of glass jars in the nation by 1900, and Eli Lilly and Company, makers of pharmaceuticals. But increasingly Indiana's manufacturing development was affected by decisions made in New York, Detroit, or Chicago, by men whose field of knowledge and operation was no longer limited to a single town or state, whose loyalty and commitment transcended local place. In this shift Indiana may have lost important sources of state and local leadership and a degree of community self-determination. A decline in local independence and pride of place may have been part of the price paid for the rise of big business and may have been as important as the political cries of monopoly and trust that echoed through the era's political debates.

Industrialization and the rise of big business also included far-reaching regional shifts. Industry concentrated in a few urban centers, and it moved northward. The country villages and river towns of southern Indiana declined in relative manufacturing importance, excepting only Evansville, to be replaced by booming gas belt towns and by the northern manufacturing cities of Fort Wayne and South Bend. Especially important was the rise of Indianapolis as the state's leading manufacturing center, a transformation begun with the advent of railroads in the 1850s. Meat packing, foundries, machine shops, and flour mills joined later by pharmaceutic and automobile companies made the city the economic as well as political capital, accounting for one fifth of the state's total value of manufactured product by the early twentieth century. While Indianapolis's manufacturing growth was relatively steady and evolutionary, that of the other major manufacturing area was more rapid and disruptive. In Lake County and the Calumet region of northwest Indiana, the new industries of petroleum refining and steel production brought revolutionary change. Factories and refineries roared up on swamplands and sand dunes along Lake Michigan, most notably United States Steel's Gary Works, opened in 1909 as the largest and most efficient in the world. With the output also of the Standard Oil Refinery at Whiting, the Inland Steel mills in East Chicago, and other industries, Lake County produced more than one fourth the state's total value of manufactured product by 1919.

Concentration of manufacturing in a small number of urban centers, particularly in the central and northern parts of Indiana, and in a small number of large corporations meant increased industrial output and wealth for the state. Manufacturing replaced agriculture as the dominant economic activity, with the value added by manufacturing in 1919 nearly equal to the total value of all agricultural products and with 34 percent of workers employed in manufacturing compared to 26 percent in agriculture by 1920.

This pattern of industrialization and the rise of big business in Indiana was generally similar to that occuring in the manufacturing arc of the northeast United States and Great Lakes region. Located in this industrial arc, Indiana became a major manufacturing state, ranking eighth at the turn of the century. Yet there was an important qualification in that Indiana lagged behind its heartland neighbors in most indicators of manufacturing growth. Throughout the late nineteenth and early twentieth centuries all states of the Old Northwest, and Ohio and Illinois in particular, surpassed Indiana in per capita value added by manufacturing. The causes of this relative lag are uncertain, though it is likely that Hoosiers had a stronger attachment to agriculture and to traditional rural values, thus making the transition to manufacturing less rapid. The state's southern population origins and first settlement in southern Indiana likely played a role in the relatively slower industrialization. It must be reiterated, however, that this lag existed only in relation to the Old Northwest, since Indiana's manufacturing grew more rapidly than that of the nation as a whole, placing the state among the leading manufacturing as well as agricultural states.

Labor and the Workers' World

Industrialization brought changing conditions of work for many Hoosiers. In growing numbers they migrated from farm and village to factory and city. The movement to industrial employment included not only men but also women and children. And Indiana's growing economy also attracted black workers from the rural south and immigrants from abroad, particularly from southern and eastern Europe.

Many industrial workers enjoyed improvements in the material conditions of their lives. Many others discovered that industrial jobs brought low pay, long hours, tedious, unsafe, and demeaning work, and frequent periods of unemployment. In most occupations ten-hour days and six-day work weeks were customary, with many workers subjected to twelve-hour days and seven-day weeks. During the prolonged and bleak depressions of the 1870s and 1890s many Hoosier families struggled to survive at the meanest level of existence.

The political and industrial leadership of late nineteenth century Indiana subscribed to a philosophical blend of individual freedom, laissez-faire economics, and social Darwinism, all of which seemed to argue against government interference in relationships between labor and capital. Only very slowly and very moderately did Indiana government enter this tangled realm, lagging behind most other industrial states in passing labor and welfare legislation. The first meaningful forays dealt with child labor, as even some of the more hard-hearted opponents of government regulation found it difficult to justify the long hours and dangerous and dismal jobs thrust upon children. Child labor was common in glass manufacturing and coal mining, furniture manufacturing, vegetable canning, and retailing. The state legislature had begun to debate child labor at the close of the Civil War but enacted no effective laws until the end of the century. In 1897 the General Assembly prohibited employment of children under the age of fourteen in manufacturing and stipulated that children under sixteen could work no more than ten hours a day. This very modest beginning was enhanced by the state's first compulsory school attendance law, also enacted in 1897 and requiring children between eight and fourteen to attend school for at least twelve consecutive weeks a year. The 1897 legislation represented an important beginning that was expanded in later years but was not fully effective: a 1910 survey reported that Indiana trailed only Pennsylvania and Ohio among northern states in its high proportion of child labor, though there was a precipitous drop during the second decade of the century. Efforts to regulate the conditions of female employment were even slower. Not until 1913 did the legislature approve an investigation of working conditions for women, an investigation that focused on garment factories and retail stores, where nearly half the women working outside the home were employed. Despite the not surprising documentation of long hours and low pay and despite the proposals for moderate reform legislation for women and children, Indiana's government responded more slowly and tentatively than most industrial states, reflecting in part a continuing fear of government interference in individual lives and perhaps a belief that the negative and disruptive consequences of industrialization were not as large in Indiana as elsewhere.

While state government proved reluctant to ameliorate the harsher features of industrial employment, many workers became increasingly convinced of the necessity to develop their own labor organizations and to resort to their ultimate weapon of the strike. There had been some attempts during the 1850s and 1860s to form labor unions by shoemakers, printers, machinists, blacksmiths, and railroad employees. And after the Civil War several labor organizations joined to work for common political ends, particularly the eight-hour day. The severe depression beginning in 1873, which caused widespread unemployment and wage cuts, stimulated demands for currency reform and led workingmen's groups to join the Greenback movement in hopes of bringing about economic inflation and recovery. The depression of the 1870s also produced Indiana's first widespread and violent labor action, convincing some Hoosiers that class revolution was possible. Trouble plagued Indiana's coal mines, where on numerous occasions workers struck for higher wages. Mine owners generally responded by using strikebreakers, often black workers brought from south of the Ohio River, thereby provoking fisticuffs and some rioting. The most important labor unrest came on the railroads, particularly in the great strike of 1877. Trains came to a standstill when workers in Evansville, Terre Haute, Indianapolis, and Fort Wayne joined in a national work stoppage to protest wage reductions. Although there was some violence and a great deal of fear and anger, the strike ended a week later with no gains for the workers.[6]

The end of depression in 1879 brought renewed attempts to organize workers. Especially active were the Knights of Labor, who made great gains in the early 1880s organizing workers in all occupations, including seamstresses and housekeepers. The Knights of Labor lobbied politically for broad economic and social reform, including compulsory school attendance, abolition of prison contract labor, and creation of a state labor bureau. But the future of successful labor organization belonged to the craft union, increasingly organized in national federations, which in turn joined together in the American Federation of Labor, formed in 1886. Many of these craft unions also joined the Indiana State Federation of Labor at its formation in 1885 to speed the organization of labor and to pressure the state legislature for measures such as the 1897 child labor act. By the turn of the century Indiana was one of the stronger union states, and organized workers, particularly in the skilled trades, had begun to improve their conditions of labor. Indianapolis, with more than 7,000 union members by 1905, was headquarters for nine international unions, including the bricklayers, barbers, carpenters, teamsters, typographers, and mine workers. The United Mine Workers was the state's largest union, with nearly 19,000 members by 1907, and was able to achieve a degree of stability in Indiana mines after negotiating the first state wage agreement in 1892 and an eight-hour day agreement in 1898.

The growth of labor unions and the limited achievements of workers sparked a counteroffensive in the first two decades of the twentieth century. Businessmen and other local leaders formed citizens' alliances and employers' protective associations in several cities in order to promote the open shop, which allowed employers to hire non-union workers. This antiunion campaign was particularly strong in Indianapolis, where David M. Parry emerged as local and national leader, becoming president of the National Association of Manufacturers in 1902. Parry's work led in 1904 to the Employers' Association of Indianapolis, later known as the Associated Employers of Indianapolis, which mounted one of the nation's most effective open shop campaigns and also succeeded in 1919 in convincing the Indianapolis city council to enact an ordinance prohibiting labor picketing of any kind.

The conflicts between union and antiunion forces were significant also in the development of a socialist movement among Indiana workers. With some advocacy from German-Americans in the 1870s, socialism received its largest boost in Indiana in the early twentieth century, when the Socialist party elected local officials in the Indiana coal region and in several gas belt towns. But neither Indiana voters nor workers adopted a broad or enduring radical ideology or political strategy.[7]

The stresses of industrialization provided the potential for class conflict and radical change. There was conflict and change, to be sure, but what seems more important when viewed in the long-term perspective of the last hundred years and in the comparative perspective of upheaval elsewhere in the industrializing world is the relative moderation and equanimity with which Indianans confronted the industrial future. The transition from a rural, agrarian economy to an urban, industrial one was painful and confusing for many, yet they seemed to endure, even to flourish, with a strength no less solid than that of the pioneer generations that preceded them. Most Hoosiers had, one suspects, faith that things were getting better, that change was occurring without fundamental alterations in the traditions on which their lives were based. And if they were a little naive, a little too easily impressed by the signs of economic growth, a little shortsighted in seeing the negative consequences of change, perhaps also they were able to reconcile their past and present in a manner later generations would come to respect and even to admire.

Hoosiers Together, 1850–1920

All who lived within the state's borders were Hoosiers: 988,416 of them in 1850, increasing to 2,930,390 by 1920 (see Appendix A). From some perspectives they were remarkably similar. More so than perhaps any other state, Indiana's population was native born, white, and Protestant and lived in small towns and on farms. In particular, by 1920 nearly all Indianans were native born (95 percent) and white (97 percent). Nearly 75 percent of the church members were Protestants, with but a few thousand Jews, though a sizable minority of Catholics. And 71 percent of all Hoosiers lived in rural areas or towns of fewer than 25,000 residents. This population homogeneity was central to many aspects of the state's history, doubtless helping to reduce conflict and to make change more evolutionary rather than revolutionary or disruptive, to give Hoosiers a propensity to conserve and to cling to traditions rather than adopt radically new political, economic, or social arrangements.[1]

Indiana's population homogeneity was so significant that it is perhaps best to seek an understanding of it and of the state's social history generally by considering first the people and social issues that partly contradicted the images of sameness. The subjects of race, ethnicity, and urbanization provide such opportunities.

Black Hoosiers

There were just over 11,000 blacks in Indiana when delegates at the Constitutional Convention in 1851 decided to approve Article XIII, declaring that "No negro or mulatto shall come into or settle in the State. . . ." In debate over this measure delegates to the convention spread alarms about hordes of blacks poised to enter Indiana from the slave states. "We know," one delegate warned, "that when we are overrun with them—as we most assuredly will be unless we adopt some stringent measures to prevent it—there will be commenced a war which will end only in extermination of one race or the other." To another delegate blacks were "vermin," and to a third "impudent" creatures, worse than Indians. A few delegates spoke against Article XIII, one asserting that it was "an outrage upon all the principles of our boasted institutions. . . ."[2] The convention decided in favor of Article XIII by a 93 to 40 vote. Even more significant, this provision to bar blacks from entering the state was submitted to a separate vote of the entire Indiana electorate. The overwhelming response of 113,828 in favor and 21,873 against exclusion was even larger than the popular majority in favor of the main body of the new constitution. Only four counties showed a majority vote against Article XIII—Elkhart, LaGrange, Steuben, and Randolph. All but Randolph were in the far north of the state. The vote in southern Indiana strongly favored exclusion of blacks: 2,197 to 95 in Clark County; 1,711 to 143 in Floyd; 1,461 to 89 in Knox; 1,974 to 107 in Vigo.[3]

Although Article XIII was not generally enforced in the years after becoming part of Indiana's constitution, this expression of racial antipathy was a poignant symbol of the manner in which white Hoosiers often regarded blacks. Political, economic, and social discrimination was pervasive. The constitution of 1851 granted the vote only to white male citizens, and, so there would be no doubt, specifically stated that "No Negro or Mulatto shall have the right of suffrage." Indiana law at mid-century denied blacks the right to testify in court cases and prohibited marriages between blacks and whites. The Reconstruction era after the Civil War brought blacks legal rights of citizenship, including the vote for black men, despite strong opposition from Hoosiers. And the Indiana Supreme Court in 1866 declared Article XIII invalid. But the 1860s also saw the beginning of a large migration of blacks into Indiana from the South. Many arrived destitute, illiterate, unskilled, and unwelcomed. Especially troublesome was the particularly large exodus of North Carolina blacks in 1879, expecting to reach a new promised land in Indiana but finding instead unemployment and hardship. They came nonetheless in large numbers in the last decades of the nineteenth century, so that the state's black population increased from 11,262 in 1850 to 39,228 by 1880 and 57,505 by 1900. The rate of increase was considerably larger than that of the white population. And, rather than settling in rural areas where most blacks lived prior to the Civil War, most newcomers sought jobs and homes in Indiana's towns and cities, making the impact of this migration even more pronounced. Blacks constituted 12 percent of Evansville's population by 1900, with other Ohio River towns, including New Albany, Jeffersonville, and Madison also having relatively large black populations. The strongest magnet for black migrants to Indiana was Indianapolis. By 1900 15,931 blacks lived there, the seventh largest black community in the urban North and home of more than one fourth of the state's total black population. Indianapolis's black population doubled in the first two decades of the twentieth century, while other industrial cities in central and northern Indiana also attracted more black residents. Ohio River towns such as Evansville and Jeffersonville saw a percentage drop in black population by World War I.

One consequence of the increased black population in post–Civil War decades was to provide new occasions for expression of racial prejudice. Some small towns and rural areas, particularly in southern Indiana, developed reputations for special hostility and intimidation, causing blacks residing there to leave and discouraging potential newcomers. Washington County's anti-black reputation helped account for a decline there from 187 blacks in 1860 to 3 in 1880, while towns such as Leavenworth, Aurora, and Scottsburg effectively barred black residents. Restaurants, hotels, theaters, and barber shops often refused sevice to blacks. By the late nineteenth century such discrimination was apparently on the rise not only in southern Indiana but in northern parts of the state as well, a reflection of the Jim Crowism blossoming in the former Confederate states.

Most disheartening was the increase in violence and lynchings, especially in the late 1880s and 1890s, when outraged mobs seized prisoners from jail and hanged them, often under the approving gaze of hundreds of citizens and with only token resistance from local authorities. Many victims of lynch law were whites, such as the Reno band of train robbers lynched in 1868, but a disproportionate number were blacks. At least twenty blacks were lynched in Indiana between 1865 and 1903, most accused of murder or rape but none tried or convicted. Indiana's reputation for mob law became so well known that a southern governor used it to justify the practice in his own state. This embarrassment and the lynching in 1897 of five white men accused of petty robberies in Ripley County spurred the legislature to pass two anti-lynch laws in 1899. Governor Winfield Durbin courageously applied the full sanctions of the new laws, calling out the state militia to quell a threatened lynching and subsequent riot in Evansville in 1903. The tragic affair ended with the militia firing on the white mob. Eleven people died. Memories of the Evansville tragedy and the state government's hard stance were an apparent deterrent to mob law. Since 1903 only the Marion lynchings of 1930 have sullied Indiana's reputation in this way.

Despite the barriers and oppressions they faced, most blacks continued the struggle to earn a decent living, create stable family lives, and build cohesive community institutions. The conditions of daily life were often difficult, perhaps best but sadly illustrated by high infant mortality rates. In 1900 one in ten white male children died before reaching his first birthday; for black children the rate was one in four, bleak testimony to differences in diet, housing, and health care. Perhaps the major challenge facing black families was earning a living wage. Black men usually could find employment only as unskilled laborers—janitors, waiters, hod carriers, teamsters. A small number obtained slightly better jobs as barbers, blacksmiths, carpenters, or railway employees, but very few were employed in skilled crafts or industry. With the exception of a few black members in the United Mine Workers, the American Federation of Labor affiliates in Indiana were probably all white. Employment for black women, who often had to seek jobs outside the home to survive economically, was even more limited. Most worked in domestic service as cooks or maids, and many combined responsibilities at home with taking in other people's laundry and sewing. While white women were finding new employment as sales clerks, telephone operators, or stenographers, even these relatively low paying jobs were closed to black women.[4] Most unusual was the successful business career of Mrs. C. J. Walker. In 1910 this black woman established in Indianapolis a cosmetics company that became one of the outstanding black-owned businesses in the nation and made her a wealthy woman.

Perhaps the most serious barriers facing blacks were those to education. The slowly developing common school movement specifically excluded black pupils prior to the Civil War. Some black parents were able to provide private schooling for their children, sometimes aided by white church groups, particularly Quakers. In 1869 the legislature required school trustees to provide separate schools for black children in areas with sufficiently large black populations. And in 1877 the General Assembly required that if separate facilities were not available black children must be permitted to attend the white schools. While this legislation did lead to some integration, most Indiana communities with sizable black populations maintained segregated elementary schools, and, in southern Indiana especially, also created black high schools. Thus, while educational opportunities for black children expanded and included some racial integration, a separate and very unequal system of public education also developed that meant generally fewer educational opportunities for blacks.

Despite the very limited education and economic chances for blacks there did develop a class of business and professional men. In Indianapolis, Evansville, and elsewhere there were black barbers, restaurant owners, insurance agents, and other small proprietors who achieved middle-class status, joined by a small number of physicians, lawyers, teachers, newspaper editors, and ministers. This black middle class often assumed leadership positions and helped create and guide organizations and institutions central to the black community. Nearly everywhere black churches stood at the center of the community, with the African Methodist Episcopal Church and the Baptists most prominent. Black newspapers were nearly as important, with three in Indianapolis by the turn of the century—the *Indianapolis World*, the *Freeman*, and the *Recorder*. Black lodges and fraternal organizations also played important social roles. In nearly all cases blacks developed these organizations because they were excluded from white organizations and because they saw the need for the pride and the more tangible benefits that could result from race consciousness and cooperation.

Ethnic Hoosiers

The cultural consequences of place of birth had large impact for Indiana's history. The high proportion of southern-born Hoosiers in the early nineteenth century left an enduring legacy. And the fact of a high and increasing percentage of Indiana-born Hoosiers in the late nineteenth century (70 percent by 1880) spurred the tendency for conservation of traditions rather than radical change. But Indiana also became the home of people born outside the United States. Their numbers were much smaller than in all other states of the Old Northwest and in most other industrial states, but they were significant nonetheless.

Indiana's foreign-born population grew from 54,426 in 1850 to 141,474 by 1870. It remained near that figure until 1920, peaking at 159,663 in 1910. Throughout this period the foreign born were never more than 10 percent of the total population. But like the late nineteenth century black population, the foreign born were attracted to cities. By 1890 half lived in urban places; by 1920 over three fourths. Evansville, Indianapolis, Fort Wayne, South Bend, and the Calumet cities of Gary, Whiting, Hammond, and East Chicago all had large foreign-born populations. Industrial cities in northern Indiana were especially popular immigrant destinations.

In 1850 more than half the foreign-born population was German. German-American institutions had a large impact on Fort Wayne, Indianapolis, and Evansville and also on some rural areas such as Dubois County, where the German language was more often heard than English. As late as 1915 in Vanderburgh County, children whose

Evansville's German Day Parade, ca. 1911. Only July Fourth was more
important in the city's public celebrations before World War I. (Darrel
E. Bigham)

grandparents had emigrated before the Civil War had their church
confirmation services conducted in German: as one later recalled, "If
you weren't confirmed in German, you weren't confirmed. God didn't
listen to you in the English language."[5] German-language newspapers,
churches, schools, and social clubs helped preserve the homeland culture and ameliorate the sense of uprootedness. Irish immigrants were
second in number to Germans at mid-century but accounted for only
23 percent of Indiana's foreign-born population in 1850 and less
thereafter. Many Irish-Americans settled along routes of the Wabash
and Erie Canal and the railroads where construction jobs had first
brought them to Indiana.

The sources of immigration to Indiana, as to the rest of America,
changed greatly near the end of the century; more and more immigrants came from southern and eastern Europe and fewer from northern and western Europe. This "new" immigration reached a peak in
the decade before World War I and had major impact on South Bend

and the Calumet cities where Slavic and East European languages and customs were most visible. Indianapolis, Fort Wayne, Evansville, and the gas belt cities received very little of this new immigration.[6]

Immigrants did not generally suffer all the handicaps and barriers facing blacks in Indiana. There were efforts to attract immigrant workers to the state, including recruitment campaigns in Europe sponsored by Governors Oliver Morton and Conrad Baker in the 1860s and later by manufacturers such as James Oliver, the Studebaker brothers, and United States Steel. Immigrants were the objects of hostility and discrimination from native-born Hoosiers, however. The Know-Nothing movement of the 1850s generated anti-immigrant feeling that flared up occasionally afterwards. And the new immigrants were victims of special discrimination and prejudice, which the "Americanization" movement of the World War I years often exacerbated while attempting to strip away their "foreignness." During the war German-Americans were subjected to intimidation and pressure that led to the removal of German street and place names and the end of the German language in churches and schools.[7]

Urban and Small-Town Hoosiers

The migrations of southern blacks, European immigrants, and rural Hoosiers combined with the building of railroads and the growth of industry to bring increased size and importance to cities. Indiana's meager urban population, less than 5 percent of the total in 1850, increased to nearly 20 percent by 1880, 34 percent by 1900, and 51 percent by 1920. Some cities grew less rapidly than others, particularly those on the Ohio River that had been important in the first half of the nineteenth century. Madison's era of urban leadership peaked soon after completion of the Madison and Indianapolis Railroad in 1847, and the town subsequently lost out to communities located on major east-west trunk lines. Other Ohio River towns also declined, with the major exception of Evansville. Railroad towns in the central and northern parts of the state grew most rapidly, particularly Indianapolis, Terre Haute, Fort Wayne, and South Bend, all of which developed important industries. Industrialization also spurred population growth in the gas belt cities of Anderson, Kokomo, and Muncie and in the Calumet cities, particularly Gary, East Chicago, and Hammond.

Urban growth meant change, change that sometimes required modification of Hoosier traditions. In particular, as towns and cities grew individual responsibility seemed less suited to dealing with the complexities of large numbers of people living closely together—polluted well-water, muddy streets, crime, fire, and epidemic disease. Slowly and erratically Indiana's larger cities began to provide basic urban services, always facing resistance from Hoosiers fearful of higher taxes and jealous of their individual freedoms.

One of the first problems was fire protection—closely spaced wooden buildings made Indiana towns potential pyres. Early fire fighters were volunteer companies, which often served as fraternal and social clubs as well. During the 1850s several city governments began to purchase fire fighting equipment and soon also to organize paid fire departments. City governments also began to assume other responsibilities: for public safety by establishing police forces; for public health by attention to water and sewer facilities; and for public convenience by paving and lighting streets and chartering street railway companies. Public utilities in many Indiana cities were private rather than municipally owned and operated. As late as 1920 three fourths of Indiana's electrical plants and one half of the waterworks were private rather than municipal enterprises. And in some basic services remnants of the frontier tradition continued: outdoor toilets near wells and sewers that emptied directly into rivers and streams were testimony of the reluctance to shift from individual and private to community and governmental responsibility.

City growth also brought the phenomenon of residential clustering; urban dwellers tended increasingly to live among neighbors of their own economic class and racial or ethnic group. Poor blacks, immigrants, and native-born rural whites often congregated in dense, low quality housing near industrial sites and built there neighborhood churches, taverns, and clubs that preserved parts of the old way of life. All cities had such neighborhoods: the Patch, ethnic and black neighborhood south of the Wabash tracks in Gary; Stringtown, the Appalachian white settlement in Indianapolis; the Polish third ward in South Bend; Baptistown, home of most of Evansville's blacks; and the Indiana Avenue neighborhood in Indianapolis, where black music, religion, business, and politics flourished. Middle and upper-class whites simultaneously built large family homes farther from city centers, particularly with development of horse-drawn and later electric railways. In Indianapolis the suburban towns of Irvington and Woodruff Place developed in the 1870s to provide spacious havens from the city bustle. By 1888 a titled European visitor to the capital city noted that it possessed a wealthy upper class to whom "Negro servants, a span of horses and silver-mounted carriages are considered as necessities of life." In this society, as Booth Tarkington wrote, "all the women who wore silk or velvet knew all the other women who wore silk or velvet. . . . "[8]

By the beginning of the twentieth century, life in Indiana cities could be very unlike life on the farm and in rural Indiana generally. Differences of race, ethnicity, and class often were more visible. Social activity was more varied: literary and musical societies, men's fraternal lodges, and women's clubs grew in profusion. Palatial department stores, gaudy theaters and opera houses, fancy hotels and restaurants, playgrounds and amusement parks, large, well-equipped school buildings and libraries, paved streets and electric lights—all were visible signs of an urban life and culture more exciting and more attractive to many, though more repulsive to some.

But the differences between urban and rural Indiana were not radical, nor did cities and novel urban ways rise to quick and easy dominance of the Hoosier state. Many urban dwellers retained close ties to their rural heritage, and many workers in shops, offices, and factories continued to believe that God preferred Hoosiers behind a plow or at least in a vegetable garden. No single city stood apart or imperially lorded over the rest of the state. Indianapolis was the most likely to do so, but it remained cautious and conservative, a town, Meredith Nicholson wrote in 1904, "that became a city rather against its will." As historian Robert Barrows has shown, even though the capital city's population was more mobile than contemporaries assumed, it was in fact less transient, more settled than that of nearly any other large American city, with decadal persistence rates of about 70 percent. And Indianapolis was, in fact as well as in promotional literature, a "city of homes," with the highest percentage of single-family houses (94 percent) of any large turn-of-the-century American

Richmond; a watercolor by Lefevre Cranstone, 1859. (Lilly Library, Indiana University)

city. It and most Indiana cities remained, to use Nicholson's labels, "neighborly and cosy," even to rural visitors, rather than alien artifices set uneasily in the midst of rural Indiana.[9] Only in Gary, with its large black and immigrant population, its steel furnaces darkening the sky, and its company housing, would the rural Hoosier feel out of place. It was not until the early twentieth century that the kinds of rural-urban splits that characterized politics in Illinois or New York gradually began to appear in Indiana.

An important reason for the relatively short cultural distance from urban to rural Indiana was the existence of a midway place between big city and isolated farm. Small towns dotted the landscape and shaped much of the state's character. Neither urban or rural, they provided a small agricultural hinterland with essential economic, social, and political services: a few retail stores and a grain elevator, a high school and two or three churches, lawyers, doctors, fraternal lodges and women's clubs, and perhaps the county courthouse and weekly newspaper. They were the proverbial neighborly places where nearly everyone was known by name to nearly everyone else, where all important communication was face to face, where life could be secure and comfortable for many and stultifying and provincial for some. Small towns changed too, of course. Railroads and interurbans connected them more readily to other places, outside ideas and organizations began to threaten local autonomy and independence, and young people left for larger cities. But change came gradually before World War I, and small towns remained the preferred and actual home of many Hoosiers, perhaps the primary identification of most. James Whitcomb Riley expressed for many Indiana's small-town sentiment:

> You kin boast about yer cities, and their stiddy growth and size
> And brag about yer County-seats, and business enterprise,
> And railroad, and factories, and all sich foolery—
> But the little Town o' Tailholt is big enough for me!

Educating Hoosiers

Few aspects of Indiana life have been more important, and few have changed more significantly than public education. The ways Hoosiers have chosen to educate their children have often reflected fundamental features of the state's development. The history of education in the years 1850–1920 is partly a history of progress, of more and better education for more and more children. But it is also a history of challenges not fully met, of conflicts not fully resolved, of outdated pioneer traditions not abandoned.

The common school movement of the late 1840s, led by Wabash College Professor Caleb Mills, vigorously argued the case for tax-supported, free public schools. Pointing to Indiana's high illiteracy rate, the highest of any northern state, school reformers argued that an educated citizenry was a necessity in a democracy. These and other arguments achieved success at the Constitutional Convention of 1850–1851. Despite some beliefs that education was solely a local responsibility and many fears of school taxes, the convention approved a constitution that required the General Assembly "to provide, by law, for a general and uniform system of Common Schools, wherein tuition shall be without charge, and equally open to all."[10]

Gone was the loophole in the 1816 constitution, which had required the legislature to act only "as soon as circumstances will permit." The General Assembly in 1852 passed a school law that created for the first time a state property tax for education. The 1852 school law also gave township trustees responsibility for local schools but allowed cities and towns to establish schools separate from township schools. The 1852 law provoked confusion and opposition, however, especially over new taxes. In 1854 the Indiana Supreme Court declared the act unconstitutional, asserting that if local as well as state taxation were allowed public schools would vary in quality from place to place. Such variation would controvert the constitutional requirement of a uniform system of common schools. With this severe blow the development of public education nearly halted, and many newly opened schools closed. Not until 1867 were public school advocates able to act effectively. In that year the legislature simply passed a bill similar to the 1852 legislation, hoping that the Supreme Court would not stand in the way. Such hopes were fulfilled, and during the next two decades Indiana's common school system was at last firmly established.

Two features were most important in the system of public education that evolved after the Civil War: it was a system that in many ways grew better and better; and it was a system marked by diversity, indeed, by inequality.

Contemporaries judged educational progress by a variety of measures; on most, Indiana's schools improved greatly. Log school buildings quickly gave way to buildings of frame and brick. The average length of the school term increased from 68 days in 1866 to 136 in 1879 to 149 in 1900. Enrollment of children between the ages of five and eighteen grew from less than 50 percent in 1863 to more than 80 percent by 1880, at which figure it remained through World War I.

These and other measures of progress were less impressive, however, when compared with what was being accomplished in other midwestern states. At the end of the nineteenth century Indiana ranked sixth among ten midwestern states in average length of school term, seventh in amount of money spent on each pupil, and ninth in literacy rates among native-born whites. Moreover, such figures were statewide averages and did not reveal the great diversity among Indiana's public schools. Reflecting attachments to local democracy, Indiana's schools were decentralized and locally controlled. Most school revenue came from local taxes, leading to great disparaties, with schools in rural and southern Indiana generally having far less money to spend on each pupil. Rural children usually attended ungraded, one-room, one-teacher schools, where teachers were less experienced and lower paid, the school terms shorter (an average of 42 days shorter in 1900), attendance more irregular, and the curriculum more limited than in city schools. The backward conditions portrayed in Edward Eggleston's *Hoosier School-Master* could indeed be found in parts of rural Indiana throughout the years prior to 1920. And while some children acquired a good basic education, most learned little more than simple arithmetic and the rudiments of reading and writing. In town and city schools opportunities for broader and more thorough education were considerably larger and became even more so as most cities began after the Civil War to establish high schools.[11]

Efforts to improve Indiana's schools generally and its rural schools particularly came from the Indiana State Teachers Association, the Indiana Association of County Superintendents, and the state superintendent of public instruction. These educators often had interests and orientations that were considerably broader and more professional than those of the local community; they pressed for change through greater state centralization and control of schools, which they argued would bring greater uniformity and improve all schools. Education reformers mounted a campaign for compulsory schooling and in 1897, despite strong opposition, succeeded in convincing the General Assembly to pass a law requiring school attendance for all children between the ages of eight and fourteen, raised to sixteen in 1913. In 1905 the legislature approved a bill that allowed a small portion of the state school tax to be apportioned among local school corporations on the basis of need rather than only on a per pupil basis, thus beginning the state's effort to lift poorer rural schools closer to their urban counterparts. Education reformers directed much of their zeal to one-room country schools, which became to them the greatest symbol of backward education. They argued for the benefits of school consolidation, and in 1907 convinced the legislature to require closing of all schools that had fewer than twelve pupils. The new law required also that pupils so affected be transported to larger schools at public expense. In the period from 1890 to 1920 nearly 4,000 one-room schools were closed, and the horse-drawn hack and later gasoline-engine school bus carried growing numbers of rural children over great distances. Still, 4,800 one-room schools remained open as late as 1920 to continue as the major target of professional school reformers and as one of the major differences between rural and urban Indiana.

School consolidation, compulsory schooling, and other reforms, including statewide textbook selection, begun in 1889, and minimum salary schedules for teachers, approved in 1907, were not achieved without opposition. Many Hoosiers had a pioneer suspicion of education and a strong conviction of the democratic wisdom of local control trol. The *Terre Haute Journal* spoke for them when, in opposing compulsory schooling, it asserted that Hoosiers wanted "no minions of Federal or State power to coerce the people in the matter of education or religion."[12] This democratic zeal for decentralization and local independence had specific focus in rural Indiana in the person of the township trustee. Elected by his township neighbors, the trustee had primary responsibility for local schools, ranging from purchase of coal to hiring of teachers. Township trustees often were little acquainted with the concerns of professional educators and sometimes more engaged in local party politics and promoting their own self-interest. But they also could be and often were close representatives of their neighbors' sentiments and beliefs, standing as bulwarks of local democracy in the face of threats from outside experts and state-oriented political leaders. And though the power of the state gradually increased and that of the township trustee became more circumscribed, this local official remained through World War I as the single most important decision maker for Indiana schools. The trend toward centralization and uniformity thus did not overshadow continuing diversity, particularly evident in the differences between rural schools and city schools.

One of the major problems facing township trustees and professional educators was recruitment of well-trained teachers. Teachers were very poorly paid, particularly in rural areas. Many young men took teaching jobs for a year or two as a temporary way station to a higher-paying career. Low pay, adverse conditions of work, and the Civil War reduced the number of male teachers, leading parsimonious taxpayers and school trustees to hire women at very low salaries and in increasing numbers. As early as 1852 Caleb Mills had advocated hiring female rather than male teachers because "the expenses would be materially diminished, while the character of the schools might be essentially improved."[13] Women constituted only one fifth of the teachers in 1860, more than half by 1900, and two thirds by World War I. Increasingly, Indiana children owed their education to the often dedicated and always cheap labor of women. While little was done to improve the pay of teachers, even with the minimum salary law of 1907, there were some attempts to provide better teacher training. The notion long persisted, however, that anyone could teach, especially in a country school. In 1865 the state began to require annual teacher institutes, later supplemented by monthly township institutes. The meetings and publications of the Indiana State Teachers' Association, organized in 1854, also served an educational purpose for teachers. Opening of the State Normal School at Terre Haute in 1870 and of several private normal schools, such as Central Normal College at Danville in 1876, provided new opportunities for better prepared teachers. Still, although the state increased its influence over teacher preparation and licensing, township trustees and county superintendents remained the primary gatekeepers for entry into the profession, and teachers, especially in rural schools, remained poorly paid and haphazardly prepared.

Professional educators also endeavored to change the school curriculum, adding new courses and modifying instructional goals. The expansion of high schools at the end of the century offered special opportunities; the number of high school students increased from 35,000 in 1900 to 79,000 in 1920. The standard high school curriculum included mathematics, English, Latin or German (until the latter was banned by the legislature in the fury of World War I), history, and natural sciences. Initially high schools concentrated on preparing students for college, but by the first decade of the twentieth century they were changing to serve graduates going directly to jobs. As Fassett A. Cotton, the state superintendent of public instruction, argued in 1906, the high school was no longer an elite institution but rather "the people's college, and as such its aim is to meet the needs of the community—to prepare the children, in large measure, for their life work."[14] Following popular notions of progressive education, Superintendent Cotton and other reformers encouraged the introduction of practical and vocational schooling. Indianapolis Manual Training School opened in 1895 to become a model for industrial high schools in other Indiana cities. In Gary, city school superintendent William A. Wirt achieved national recognition by shaping the schools to the practical, everyday needs of society, particularly the industrial society so evident in the Calumet region. Wirt's Gary Plan platooned students between vocational and academic subjects and between different sections of the school building, providing efficient, practical, mass education much as the Gary Works produced steel.[15] The state legislature in 1913 responded to the trend by requiring courses in vocational education, including agricultural education in town and rural schools. And in 1917 Congress passed the Smith-Hughes Act to grant federal subsidies for vocational education. In vocational education and curriculum innovation generally city and town schools surged far ahead of most rural schools, as they did in all areas of educational change.

Change also occurred in higher education. Indiana University survived a series of crises in the 1850s and after the Civil War gradually began to grow. Particularly with the presidency of David Starr Jordan (1885–1891) the Bloomington institution became a university in fact as well as in name. Private institutions of higher education were prolific, most sponsored by a religious denomination, and many with small enrollments and precarious finances. Hanover, Wabash, Indiana Asbury (later DePauw), Franklin, Earlham, and Notre Dame represented major religious bodies at mid-century, joined later by Butler. The curriculum at all colleges and universities was classical, with emphasis on Greek and Latin, philosophy, theology, and mathematics. By the turn of the century many had moved to more elective systems that allowed for expansion of modern languages and natural sciences. State interest in more practical education expanded with the opening of the Normal School at Terre Haute in 1870 and Purdue as the land grant school at West Lafayette in 1874, where students could study civil and mechanical engineering and agriculture. The demands of the new industrial society also encouraged the founding in 1883 of Rose Polytechnic Institute in Terre Haute.

Opportunities for education of a more informal sort developed with the growth of public libraries. Some county libraries had been established in the pioneer period, along with a few private subscription libraries. But the sharp expansion of public libraries came at the end of the century. The General Assembly passed legislation in the early

1880s enabling incorporated towns and cities to levy taxes for public libraries, extended in 1899 to townships. Women's literary societies often promoted public libraries, as did the Indiana Library Association founded in 1891. The Indiana State Library and Public Library Commission provided help in creating and maintaining community libraries. Private philanthropy was especially important as at the Willard Library in Evansville and the Emeline Fairbanks Memorial Library in Terre Haute. But most significant was the philanthropy of steelmaker Andrew Carnegie. His grants of millions of dollars to Indiana communities led to 150 new library buildings between 1899 and 1920. By the latter date only five communities of over 3,000 residents were without a public library, and most libraries were Carnegie libraries. As with schools, development of libraries was generally more benefical to urban than rural Hoosiers.

Religious Hoosiers

Religion was a central part of life for many Indianans, not only in a spiritual sense but in a social and political sense as well. Churches served important functions in charity, education, entertainment, leisure activity, political action, and community life generally.

Church membership grew and denominational forms continued, perhaps increased, in importance. Most numerous were Methodists, Disciples of Christ, Baptists, Presbyterians, and Roman Catholics. The Methodists, the largest Protestant denomination in Indiana, moved away from their frontier revivalist and circuit riding origins to become a more sedate and settled church, with as much strength in towns and cities as in rural areas. The Catholics were the fastest growing church, particularly as a consequence of European immigration.

Denomination sometimes meant conflict: simple local rivalry; deeper doctrinal differences leading to splits within denominations and congregations; ethnic differences, reflected in the formation of ethnic congregations and parishes, such as the Slovene Catholic parish in the Haughville neighborhood of Indianapolis;[16] and, most significant, Protestant-Catholic tension. The nativist Know-Nothing movement of the 1850s provoked the most intense anti-Catholic expression, but conflict broke out after the Civil War on such issues as tax support for parochial schools and use of the Protestant (King James) Bible in public schools. It appears however, that Indiana anti-Catholicism at the end of the century was muted, particularly in the generally weak showing of the nativist American Protective Association in the 1890s.

Most Protestant denominations seemed less concerned with denominational rivalry than with preserving a strict observance of the Sabbath. Their efforts spurred the General Assembly in 1855 to prohibit hunting, fishing, or unnecessary work on Sundays and in 1865 to ban Sunday sale of intoxicants. Hoosiers were attracted nonetheless to expanding leisure activities, especially Sunday railroad and interurban excursions. Immigrants proved especially unwilling to observe a strict Sabbath, much to the disgust of many Protestant leaders. Protestant denominations also took public stands against the use of tobacco, dancing, card playing, and horse racing. But their most intense fury was directed toward alcohol; the Protestant churches constituted the foundation of the temperance movement, as discussed in Chapter 11. Methodists were most visible in these moral crusades, partly because of their large membership.

Other than issues of personal morality and particularly temperance and the Sabbath, Indiana churches were not active in debating public issues after the Civil War. The reforming zeal of the pre–Civil War antislavery movement did not carry over into social issues of urban, industrial society. The Social Gospel movement, which attempted to apply liberal Christian theology and ethics to contemporary social problems, was not strong in late nineteenth century Indiana. The most important exception to the generally conservative Protestant clergy was the Reverend Oscar C. McCulloch, minister of Plymouth Congregational Church in Indianapolis from 1877 to 1891. McCulloch was appalled by the city's inattention to its poor working class. His Plymouth Church was soon engaged in charitable organization, vocational programs, and working-class clubs, while from the pulpit his sermons dealt not with abstract theology but with problems of child labor, prison reform, public health, free kindergartens, and labor unions. There were other Social Gospel ministers in Indiana, but they were a small minority.[17]

Much more popular than the Social Gospel was the Sunday school, though the two sometimes did merge. Sunday schools developed in the pioneer period to provide general as well as religious education—

for many children before the Civil War the only formal education they received. Organization of the Indiana Sunday School Association in 1865 led to a flowering of the movement in the late nineteenth century. By 1898 there were 5,617 Sunday schools with over 500,000 scholars, reciting Bible verses, singing hymns, and studying uniform Sunday school lessons. For many children and adults the Sunday school conveyed not only the Christian message and ritual but also developed skills in reading and public speaking and in organization and social relationships. And the Sunday schools worked across Protestant denominational lines, more so than any other religious organization. The Sunday school movement also spurred other religious gatherings, particularly the Chautauqua. These and other summer assemblies were initially designed for study of the Bible and development of Sunday school teaching methods but later expanded to include broader educational and recreational activities. Among several Chautauqua-type meetings in Indiana, that at Winona Lake in Kosciusko County was most important, becoming the home of revivalist William S. "Billy" Sunday and gospel-song writer and performer Homer Rodeheaver.[18]

Culture and Leisure

The years between 1850 and 1920 brought Hoosiers new opportunities for cultural enrichment, popular entertainment, and leisure activity. Perhaps most apparent was the large number of best selling books by Indiana authors, which in the early twentieth century exceeded those from any other state except New York. Indiana's reputation as the home of authors was reflected in popular jokes and stories and in college textbooks, some going so far as to refer to a Hoosier school of literature. Just why Indianans were a scribbling people has not been and perhaps cannot be satisfactorily explained, despite commendable efforts by such scholars as Howard Peckham and Arthur Shumaker to do so.[19] Perhaps as important is the possibility that this Golden Age of Indiana literature provides some insights into the popular culture.

Most of the literature and poetry produced by Indiana authors in the late nineteenth and early twentieth centuries was sentimental and

Contributors to Indiana's golden age of literature: left to right, James Whitcomb Riley, George Ade, Meredith Nicholson, and Booth Tarkington. (Indiana Historical Society)

romantic, often nostalgic in its appeal to traditional rural and small-town values. Lew Wallace's *Ben Hur* (1880), Maurice Thompson's *Alice of Old Vincennes* (1900), Meredith Nicholson's *The House of a Thousand Candles* (1905), and Gene Stratton Porter's *A Girl of the Limberlost* (1909) are representative of this literature. There was little harsh realism, though Edward Eggleston's *The Hoosier School-Master* (1871) portrayed (and perhaps exaggerated) some of the crudities of the rural one-room school in southern Indiana. And there was little biting criticism or satire, though a great deal of very good popular humor came from the pens of George Ade and Kin Hubbard (the latter as creator of the cracker-barrel philosopher Abe Martin).[20] Many authors celebrated Indiana and the Midwest, intending to create a sense of regional pride. As Eggleston wrote in his preface to *The Hoosier School-Master*:

It used to be a matter of no little jealousy with us, I remember, that the manners, customs, thoughts, and feelings of New England country people filled so large a place in books, while our life, not less interesting, not less romantic, and certainly not less filled with humorous and grotesque material, had no place in literature. It was as though we were shut out of good society.[21]

By the turn of the century claims were made that Indiana literature was the most typically and truly American literature, claims supported by its wide appeal beyond Indiana.

The most popular of Indiana's Golden Age authors were the poet James Whitcomb Riley (1849–1916) and the novelist Booth Tarkington (1869–1946). Riley's poetry was sentimental and nostalgic for a rural and small-town childhood, for a past and present often seen through rose-colored lenses. Poems such as "The Old Swimmin'-Hole," "When the Frost Is on the Punkin," and "Little Orphant Annie" were memorized by generations of school children and fondly remembered to old age. More than anything else Riley's poetry created for Indiana an image of quiet rusticity and commonsense wholesomeness, an image that endured long after his death in 1916. Booth Tarkington's novels were almost as well known as Riley's poetry. They also were often set in Indiana, particularly Indianapolis. Beginning with *The Gentleman from Indiana* (1899) through his Penrod stories to his two Pulitzer prize winning novels, *The Magnificent Ambersons* (1918) and *Alice Adams* (1921), Tarkington chronicled in evocative detail the changing fortunes and styles of middle and upper-class Hoosiers against the backdrop of sometimes bewildering transformation. Though always hopeful for the best, Tarkington feared that urban, industrial growth was threatening the traditional individualism and stability he held so dear. Even his own beloved Indianapolis seemed at times alien and cold, consumed by zeal to build more factories and housing additions and covered by a pall of sooty smoke.

During their lifetimes Riley and Tarkington were the popular giants of Indiana literature. Each can still be read with pleasure and profit, if primarily to understand a time long past. But gradually their literary reputations have paled in comparison to that of Theodore Dreiser (1871–1945). Dreiser too drew on his Indiana childhood but in a grimly realistic manner to write about poverty, immorality, corruption, and sex—as he had known them in Terre Haute, Evansville, and Chicago. His first masterpiece, *Sister Carrie* (1900), shocked traditional sensibilities. Always out of step with his time and place, Dreiser left Indiana as a young man, rejecting the romantic rural and small-town images projected by most of his fellow Hoosier authors. The reluctance of Hoosiers past and present to welcome him as one of them is perhaps nearly as indicative of the nature of Indiana's dominant literature and culture as is the reception of Riley and Tarkington.

Indiana authors also achieved distinction in works of nonfiction, especially history. John Clark Ridpath became one of the most prolific and widely read historians of his generation. Charles Beard grew from a Henry County boyhood and DePauw education to influence markedly American historical scholarship, particularly with his *An Economic Interpretation of the Constitution* (1913). And there was an awakening of interest in state and local history, led by John B. Dillon and reflected in the reorganization of the Indiana Historical Society in 1886, the beginning of the *Indiana Magazine of History* in 1905, the elaborate celebration of the state's centennial in 1916, and the publication of dozens of county histories.[22]

The main current of Indiana art flowed in the same direction as literature. The most popular paintings were those of the so-called Hoosier Group, many of whom studied in Bavaria in the 1880s and returned to Indiana to paint romantic landscapes celebrating Indiana's rural beauty. The best known was Theodore C. Steele, who later settled in rural Brown County, where a flourishing artists' colony developed by World War I. Indianapolis remained the state's most important location for artists, however, particularly after opening of the museum and school of the John Herron Art Institute in 1902.

Indianapolis was also the most important center for theater, music, and other public performances. As religious objections to theater declined and as public transportation improved Hoosiers flocked to English's Opera House and other theaters in the capital city. They could see there Lawrence Barrett playing *Hamlet* (1880), Christine Nilsson singing in *Lucia di Lammermoor* (1872), and other leading artists who brought metropolitan culture to Indianapolis. Locally produced culture ranged from the Indianapolis Maennerchor, founded in 1854, to amateur productions of Gilbert and Sullivan and plays presented by the Little Theatre Society, organized in 1915. The first decades of the twentieth century brought a flowering of ragtime music, composed and published in Indianapolis and also in Fort Wayne, Hammond,

Lafayette, and other towns. Ragtime originated in Afro-American rhythms, and some of the best composers and performers were black musicians on Indiana Avenue, the main street of Indianapolis's black community. One of them, Reginald DuValle, strongly shaped the later work of Hoagy Carmichael. Indeed, by 1910 ragtime was widely performed throughout Indiana, most ubiquitously by young people on the upright parlor piano.[23] Other towns and cities besides Indianapolis also offered an increasing diversity of public culture and entertainment, both home produced and imported. By the end of the century many boasted of elaborate opera houses and theaters, which hosted classical music and drama and more popular vaudeville and variety shows. Most Indiana towns had changed greatly since the internationally famed Jenny Lind arrived in Madison in 1851 to sing in a converted pork packing house.

Hoosiers also gathered in large numbers for state and county fairs, circuses, balloon ascensions, parades, veterans' reunions, Fourth of July celebrations, summer band concerts, political rallies, and railroad excursions to places like the resort springs in French Lick and West Baden. Spectator sports like horse racing and boxing enjoyed popularity, as did baseball. Several cities joined a state baseball association in the late 1860s, with the Fort Wayne Kekiongas becoming the most successful of early teams, though strong opposition to Sunday games handicapped the sport in Indianapolis and elsewhere. College athletics also grew in popularity. Intercollegiate competition in baseball and football began in the 1880s and in basketball in the 1890s. High schools began in the 1890s to compete in football and basketball. In 1903 they formed the Indiana High School Athletic Association, with 450 member schools by 1916. With organization of the first state high school basketball tournament in 1911 that sport quickly emerged as the Hoosier favorite. The year 1911 also marked the beginning of another attraction closely identified with the state, the first run of the Indianapolis 500–mile race.

State basketball tournaments and 500–mile auto races seemed far removed from the logrollings and husking bees of pioneer Indiana, just as there appeared to be a wide distance between the one-room school and the large consolidated high school, between the noisy, homespun crowds of the pioneer Methodist camp meeting and the orderly, Sunday-dressed congregations of the new Gothic-style

churches, between the country general store and the urban department store, between the homogeneous population of the pioneer
countryside and the ethnic and racial diversity of the industrial city.
Yet these and other evidences of social change in the period from
1850 to 1920 were neither revolutionary nor all-encompassing. Social
change was usually slow enough to permit Hoosiers to adjust and often
to hold to much of their traditions. Rural and small-town Indiana
especially changed only gradually, sometimes imperceptively, and pioneer and agrarian ideals, particularly notions of individual freedom
and responsibility, continued to exert major influence on the state's
history. The result was a lag, to some a backwardness, compared to
modern, urban, industrial America. To many others, however, gradual and conservative social change meant that God was indeed good
to Indiana and that Indiana represented the best of truly American
traditions.

x

The Politics of the Civil War Era, 1850–1873

For decades they would endure: the political divisions, animosities, and ideologies formed and hardened during the debates of the 1850s and the bloody years of Civil War would pass from generation to generation of Hoosiers, largely through the agency of one of the most tightly structured two-party systems in the nation. The Democratic and Republican parties became in the 1850s the beginning and end of serious politics in Indiana, defining the issues and setting the boundaries of political debate and of government policy. And they continued into the twentieth century this nearly unchallenged dominance of state politics and government. The two major parties helped also to sustain the intense popular interest in politics that so characterized Indiana's history and set it apart from most other states.[1]

The Politics of the 1850s

The Democratic party was the oldest and strongest of Indiana's political organizations at mid-century. Formed during the presidential battles of the Jacksonian era, it dominated state government from the early 1840s to the mid-1850s. Democrats professed close attachment to individual freedom and argued for very limited government involvement in social and economic matters. They were especially fearful that a powerful national government might threaten the rights of the states and the liberties of individuals. As was often the case with majority parties, the Democrats were split into two factions, one organized around Joseph A. Wright, governor from 1849 to 1857, and the other led by Jesse D. Bright, who served in the United States Senate from 1845 to 1862. The animosity between the two men was an important source of eventual Democratic decline in the late 1850s.

Democrats in the early 1850s could afford to quarrel among themselves because organized political opposition was so weak. The Whig party, after reaching power in the late 1830s, soon declined and by the early 1850s had only a small following and no leader of Bright's or Wright's influence. In the early 1850s some former Whigs joined other political drifters to form the American or Know-Nothing party, a new party dedicated to protecting the nation from the supposed evils of foreign immigration and particularly Catholicism. Many other political activists believed that the most important issue in American politics was not foreign immigration but slavery. Asserting that none of the party organizations had taken a sufficiently strong antislavery stance, men of this persuasion soon joined in formation of a new political organization, known at its birth in 1854 as the Fusion or Peoples party and by 1858 as the Republican party.

The Republican party made its appeal not just on antislavery arguments. Party adherents tended to be temperance supporters, convinced that eradication of alcohol was the moral obligation of government. And they tended to favor an effective system of public education and more government involvement generally in the economy and society, particularly to stimulate economic growth. But the major issue on which Republicans built their party was antislavery. That issue kept forcing its way into state and national politics despite the efforts of most Democratic leaders, particularly Jesse Bright, to compromise and sweep it under the political carpet.

Inheriting the antislavery mantle of the Free Soil party of the 1840s, the Republican party of the 1850s was convinced that certain questions in the slavery debate could not be compromised. Above all, most Republicans were certain that the expansion of slavery was wrong and that Congress had the right and obligation to limit the cancerous spread of this evil institution by barring it from America's western territories—just as it had been barred from the Northwest Territory in 1787. The Democratic produced Kansas-Nebraska Act of 1854 opened the door to slavery in the new territories by advancing the doctrine of popular sovereignty—of allowing the people in the territory themselves to decide whether slavery should exist there or not. Such a notion was abhorrent to a growing number of Hoosiers. A few believed that there must be no compromise whatsoever with the hated institution and that it must be abolished immediately. The most popular of these so-called abolitionists was George Julian, who represented in Congress the heavily Quaker Whitewater Valley of eastern Indiana, where antislavery attitudes were most extreme.[2] Most Hoosiers were not radical abolitionists, however, and Indiana generally was less militantly antislavery than most northern states, reflecting the state's large southern-born population. Nonetheless, more and more Hoosiers became increasingly uneasy about the apparent growth of slavery. Many had moral and religious doubts about the institution, particularly after publication of such books as *Uncle Tom's Cabin*. Many also had less altruistic reasons for adopting emerging antislavery attitudes: they saw slavery as unfair competition to free, white labor, and they feared its potential to increase America's black population, a race many whites regarded as inferior and undesirable.

These noble and ignoble sentiments helped push people from various political persuasions, including the old Whig and Free Soil parties, the Know-Nothing party, and the Democratic party, into the new Republican party. A complex process of political realignment eventually created this new party, which, like all major parties, was thus a coalition of diverse groups. It included an evangelical reform element, committed to the abolition of slavery and also to temperance and public education. This more radical Republican faction had its strongest support in central and northern Indiana but was always a minority within the party. More moderate and conservative Republicans dominated the party: they were not particularly committed to moral reform or abolition but were increasingly concerned about slavery and fearful that the Democratic party was allowing the South to expand its peculiar institution. This Republican moderation was to be the path to victory for the new party in Indiana and the nation.

The Republican party won an impressive victory in 1854. Campaigning against the Kansas-Nebraska Act and for temperance, the new party elected the entire state ticket and won nine of eleven congressional seats. Reflecting the increasingly important sectional division within Indiana, both Democratic congressmen elected in 1854 were from the state's southernmost districts. The 1856 campaign was even more intensely fought. Democrats made strong appeals to racist sentiments, charging that Republicans were fanatical abolitionists intent on "amalgamation" of the races. Such arguments were to be a standard part of Democratic campaign tactics throughout the Civil War era, and in 1856 proved effective as the party generally carried the state. The Republicans did better in the 1858 elections but won their most impressive victory in the crisis election of 1860.

Carefully avoiding any hint of abolitionism or belief in equality of the races, Indiana Republicans professed in 1860 a moderate antislavery stance that focused on stopping the extension of slavery in the territories and on casting as wide an electoral net as possible. Deeply divided, Democrats responded with now traditional appeals to racist sentiment, branding Republicans as radical abolitionists and reaffirming popular sovereignty, states' rights, and individual freedom. Republicans won a decisive victory. Indiana cast its presidential vote for Abraham Lincoln and sent seven Republicans to Congress, with all four Democratic congressmen elected coming from the state's southern districts. Republicans also elected the state ticket, including a majority of state legislators. Within a few months after this major Republican victory in state and nation the Stars and Bars rose over Fort Sumter and the Civil War began. Newly elected and untested Republicans in Washington and Indianapolis would now have to prove that they could govern in the state's and nation's most trying crisis.

A Civil War at Home

News of Fort Sumter and the beginning of war in April 1861 sparked an initial feeling of euphoria, excitement, and even enthusiasm. After months of uncertainty, division, and bitter partisanship Hoosiers now rallied behind their political leaders, resolving, in the language of an Indianapolis meeting, "to repel all treasonable assaults . . . peaceably, if we can, forcibly, if we must."[3] Under banners of patriotism, nationalism, and the Union thousands of men flocked to Indianapolis to volunteer for military service—many more men than could be armed and supplied. And with martial music filling the air and bayonets and buttons gleaming in the sun they paraded off to war, confident of a conquering heroes' return in a few short months.

The war many thought would be short and bloodless turned out to be dishearteningly long and appallingly bloody. In the military effort Hoosiers generally acquitted themselves well. Of the slightly more than 300,000 men of military age in the state, 197,141 served, ranking Indiana second among the northern states in relative size of manpower contribution. Indiana's regiments participated in the eastern and western campaigns and served with distinction in many of the major battles, from Bull Run through Vicksburg and Gettysburg to the surrender at Appomattox. Perhaps the most celebrated Hoosier regiment was the Nineteenth Indiana, part of the venerable Iron Brigade. The Nineteenth's stature came from the valor it showed again and again, beginning with the Second Battle of Bull Run, and from the blood it shed. By war's end nearly 16 percent of the men in the Nineteenth Regiment had been killed or mortally wounded in battle, the heaviest battle losses of any Indiana regiment. The war death toll for the whole state totaled 25,028 men, 12.6 percent of those who served. Deaths from battle numbered 7,243, while 17,785 Hoosiers died of disease, a bleak commentary on sanitary and medical conditions in military camps and battlefields. Many thousands more returned home with empty sleeves or trouser legs, with debilitated bodies or minds, with memories that would never allow them or their families to forget the nation's bloodiest war.[4]

The war produced hardship also for those who remained at home. Perhaps most difficult were the challenges faced by those many families in which the husband, father, or son was off to war. In addition to suffering the emotional anxiety of separation from a loved one, women and children often were left with sole responsibility for running the family farm and often with very little monetary compensation for the lost income of the male wage earner. The suffering and valor of female heads of families in such circumstances doubtless was often equal to that of men in uniform. Women also made direct contributions to the war as nurses and as volunteer workers in local soldiers' aid societies and in the Indiana Sanitary Commission. And they raised money and collected food, clothing, books, and other items to ease the plight of Indiana soldiers. There was also female employment in important war-related industries, most notably at the state arsenal in Indianapolis.

The war that seemed so romantic and glorious at the outset gradually came to be understood for what it was—the grimmest and most difficult collective experience Americans had yet faced. As northern armies suffered defeats or bloody draws in 1861 and 1862 and as sobering casualty reports and draped coffins reached home, Hoosiers began to show dissatisfaction, to question the way the war was being conducted. Some of this questioning may have been influenced by the traditional ties of family, culture, and trade which many Hoosiers, especially those in southern Indiana, had with the South and its people. Certainly the rosy unanimity and nonpartisanship of the first few months of the war gave way to disquiet and dissent and eventually to some of the most bitterly fought political battles of Indiana's history.[5]

At the center of nearly all these homefront political struggles was Oliver P. Morton. Elected lieutenant governor in 1860, Morton soon assumed the governorship by a prearranged agreement in which the Republican legislature sent the newly elected governor, Henry S. Lane, to the United States Senate. Morton was thirty-seven years of age, a rugged, energetic, and ambitious man who in 1854 had left the Democratic party to join the new Republican party. As the secession crisis deepened he became Indiana's most effective spokesman for the preservation of the Union, by force if necessary. Morton quickly became one of the nation's most enterprising and forceful war governors, playing a crucial role in raising and supplying troops and in supporting the Lincoln administration's conduct of the war. Like Lincoln, Morton was willing and able often to use unprecedented and sometimes unconstitutional powers in quest of his goal of winning the

Oliver P. Morton, governor of Indiana, 1861–1867. (Indiana Historical Society)

war. Morton's blunt and ruthless drive earned him many enemies. Within his party he and George Julian quarreled bitterly. The two Republicans clashed in personality and over issues, with Morton unwilling to accept Julian's radical brand of Republicanism and Julian unwilling to subdue his convictions in the name of war harmony or Morton's ambitions. Very quickly Julian and his friends came to fear that Morton was using the war to build his own political machine in Indiana.[6]

But the opposition from Julian and other Republicans paled in comparison to that from Democrats. Some Democrats heeded Morton's call for an end to parties and cast their lots with his Union party, an amalgam of War Democrats and Morton Republicans. At the other end of the spectrum a small minority of Democrats opposed the war and favored an armistice and reconciliation with the South. In the middle, most Democrats supported the war as a necessary means to preserve the Union but objected vehemently to the manner in which Lincoln and Morton were leading their war governments. In particular, according to these Democrats, the Republican leaders were using the rationale of wartime necessity to expand radically the powers of government at the state and federal levels, thereby threatening the individual liberties and local self-government that were central to Democratic belief since the days of Jefferson and Jackson. Moreover, Democrats charged, in expanding government power the Republicans were expanding also the power and position of their party, intending under the subterfuge of a non-party or a Union party label to make the Democratic party one of the casualties of war. These differences of ideology and politics boiled forth in a variety of debates but in none more intensely than those concerning emancipation of slaves and the draft.[7]

From the outset Democrats expressed fear that Republican abolitionists would use the war to free the slaves, sending, the Democratic *Indianapolis Sentinel* charged, hoards of "lazy, helpless and thriftless negroes" into Indiana.[8] At a special legislative session in April 1861 both the Indiana senate and house resolved that the state's troops and taxes should never be used "in any agression upon the institution of slavery or any other constitutional right belonging to any of the states."[9] Although Julian and a minority of more radical Republicans wished to do just that, the more moderate Republican majority, led by Morton, opposed emancipation. Lincoln's Preliminary Emancipation Proclamation of September 1862 unleashed a storm of Democratic outrage and racist propaganda in Indiana and left the embarrassed Morton and other moderate Republicans to defend the president's new policy not as a humanitarian program but as a "stratagem of war."

Equally embittering to many Hoosiers was the beginning of the draft. As the romance of war waned and as the carnage demanded ever more men, volunteers were no longer sufficient to fill Indiana's troop quotas. The first conscription occurred in October 1862, with several other calls made in the next three years. Forcing men to fight was very unpopular in Indiana, and Democrats immediately made conscription a major political issue. Compulsory military service was a threat to individual freedom and represented the ways of European despotism, not American democracy. Moreover, Democrats objected to the challenge to states' rights in the increased federal rather than state control of the draft. And they attacked the "class legislation" contained in the provision that enabled a man to buy an exemption for $300 or furnish another person as a substitute. In several counties there was active draft resistance as mobs destroyed enrollment records. And in Rush County and in Sullivan County resistance led to killing of a draft official.

While conscription and emancipation were the issues most often cited by Democrats as evidence of the evils of despotic Republicanism, there were many others. Democrats charged Morton with using for partisan purposes his gubernatorial power to appoint and promote regimental and company officers, favoring Republicans over Democrats. And they attacked the Lincoln administration's increased taxes and protective tariff, designed, they charged, to make the agricultural West subservient to the manufacturing Northeast. Democrats also criticized restraints on newspapers and military arrests of civilians charged with disloyalty and tried in military courts. Only after the war was over did the United States Supreme Court, in the Milligan case, hold such violations of civil liberties unconstitutional.

The growing list of grievances against the Lincoln and Morton administrations lifted Democratic hopes for the October 1862 elections. Conscription, emancipation, and military arrests of civilians provoked a barrage of Democratic charges that Republicans were subverting the constitution, destroying individual freedom, preparing the way for equality of the races, and planning other revolutionary changes. These arguments combined with northern military reversals, particularly the Confederate invasion of Kentucky in late summer of 1862, to give the Democrats a large victory at the polls in October. They won seven of eleven congressional seats and substantial majorities in both houses of the General Assembly.

The Democrats' hard-fought victory in 1862 was but a prelude to the fanatical and bitter partisanship that followed. Democrats controlled the General Assembly, but Morton was still governor and even more determined to do all he thought necessary to defeat the military enemy south of the Ohio River and the political enemy at home. Indeed, Morton's major political stratagem increasingly was to identify the two as one, to charge that the Democratic challenge to Republican wartime leadership was tantamount to disloyalty, even treason. Wrapping himself in the American flag, Morton claimed to speak not for the Republican party but for the Union cause; those who would challenge or question the governor were aiding the enemy. They were not simply unpatriotic; they were copperheads. Nor did Morton stop there. His counteroffensive concentrated on charges that Democratic and pro-Southern sympathizers had organized secret societies, which, particularly in southern Indiana where ties to the rebels were strongest, were drilling and preparing for an attempt to seize the state arsenal, overthrow the government of Indiana, and withdraw the state from the Union, perhaps to join Illinois and Ohio in a Northwest Confederacy.

In this bitterly partisan atmosphere, perhaps the harshest in Indiana's history, the 1863 legislature took its seats. The vengeful Democratic majority devoted most of the legislative session to denouncing Morton and Lincoln. When they attempted to pass a bill that would have reduced the governor's control of the state militia the Republican legislators bolted, fleeing Indianapolis in order not to be forced to provide a legislative quorum. Their bolt forced the session to end without enacting significant legislation, including appropriation bills. Democrats assumed that Morton would have to call a special session, since without legislative appropriations there would be no money to run the government. Instead, the wily and determined governor devised a variety of extralegal and unconstitutional means to finance state government, relying on loans from friendly bankers, including former Hoosier James F. D. Lanier of New York City, and on financial help from the Lincoln administration. These moneys Morton kept in his office safe rather than with the Democratic-controlled state treasury, and he paid them out as he alone thought necessary. For two years legislative democracy was moribund in Indiana, while Morton held his ground as the last bulwark of the Union.[10]

Morton continued to justify his unprecedented use of power as a necessary wartime measure in a state honeycombed with copperheads and treasonous secret societies. The many incidents of violence that flared over the draft and at political meetings in 1863 were cited as evidence of this treasonous "fire in the rear," but Morton was unable to point to any concrete case of a serious, organized conspiracy. Indeed, the most exciting event in 1863 served primarily to contradict Morton's refrains of the copperhead threat.[11] In July 1863 the daring Confederate General John Hunt Morgan led 2,000 cavalrymen across the Ohio River into southern Indiana, the section of the state supposedly rife with copperheads. Morgan may well have intended to rely on copperhead sympathizers, perhaps to release Confederate prisoners of war in Indianapolis and capture the state arsenal. But as Morgan's cavalry swept north to Corydon and Salem and then to Vernon and Versailles, seizing horses, burning railroad bridges, and pillaging food and money, they drew not sympathy or support but scorn, resistance, and gunfire from poorly armed civilians. The dashing raid by the "thunderbolt of the Confederacy" was most significant not in a military sense but in demonstrating the overwhelming pro-Union sentiment existing even in southern Indiana.[12]

While it is nearly certain that most Indianans and most Democrats supported prosecution of the war until the South was defeated, there were indeed some venomous snakes in Indiana's political grass. In 1864, as war weariness and strong attacks from Democrats seemed likely to produce a Republican defeat in the fall election, these real copperheads showed themselves—to the great benefit of Morton and the Republican party. For two years Hoosiers had heard and read Republican accounts of secret societies plotting to take Indiana out of the war. Morton and others had regaled them first with tales of

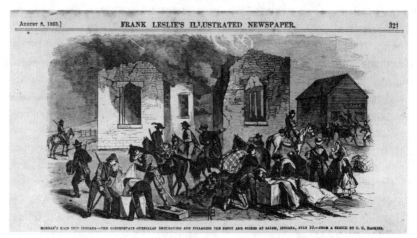

Aᴜɢᴜsᴛ 8, 1863.]   FRANK LESLIE'S ILLUSTRATED NEWSPAPER.   321

MORGAN'S RAID INTO INDIANA—THE CONFEDERATE GUERILLAS DESTROYING AND PILLAGING THE DEPOT AND STORES AT SALEM, INDIANA, JULY 10.—FROM A SKETCH BY C. C. HASKINS.

Morgan's Raiders in Salem, July 10, 1863, as sketched for *Leslie's Illustrated Newspaper*, August 8, 1863. (Indiana Historical Society)

the Knights of the Golden Circle and then of the Sons of Liberty. It was a few extremist leaders of the Sons of Liberty, with Grand Commander Harrison H. Dodd at the head, who played into Morton's hands. From spies in the organization the crafty governor learned of Dodd's plan to seize the arsenal and release Confederate prisoners at Indianapolis on August 16, 1864. When responsible Democratic leaders learned of Dodd's harebrained conspiracy they immediately forced him to abandon it, so that August 16 passed with no uprising. Only then did Morton have Dodd and others arrested, indicating that the governor himself did not think the plot very likely to succeed.

The arrest and conviction of the handful of men involved in Dodd's conspiracy became primary evidence in Morton's long running campaign to tar all Democrats with accusations of disloyalty and treason. Republican hopes also revived with Union military victories by Generals Sherman and Sheridan. Though Democrats repeated their charges that Republicans had subverted the constitution, violated civil liberties, and promoted black equality, the party of Lincoln and Morton won a major victory in 1864. Eight of the eleven congressmen elected were Republicans, as were a majority of both houses of the General Assembly. Morton was elected governor. (Even though the constitution prohibited a governor from succeeding himself Republicans claimed that Morton's election as lieutenant governor in 1860 made this in fact his first election to the office.) The Republicans and Morton especially were in the ascent, commanding a dominant position that would endure well after peace at last came in the spring of 1865.

The Civil War left many often contradictory legacies: the intense homefront divisiveness over the war, on the one hand, and the very large contribution to the military effort, on the other; the loss and suffering of men in uniform and of their families, combined with the great patriotic pride in victory achieved; the threat to constitutional government by the high-handed methods of Morton, yet also the example of a state governor providing forceful, effective, perhaps necessary wartime leadership; the intense, often appalling political partisanship, combined with the achievement of creating one of the strongest and most enduring two-party traditions in the history of American politics.

Hoosiers would gradually forget some of the more unpleasant legacies of the war and concentrate their public memories on battlefield valor and patriotic sacrifice. Veterans and the major veterans' organization, the Grand Army of the Republic, would help keep the memories of the cause for which they fought in the forefront of the public conscience, thereby strengthening collective sentiments of achievement by state and nation. But even without the annual parades and reunions, the courthouse square statues and memorials, and the flowery oratory and handsomely illustrated books, Hoosiers would never forget. The Civil War remained a part of their lives long after Appomattox, casting shadows of gloom and sunbursts of light into the twentieth century.

Reconstruction, 1865–1873

Although the fighting ended in 1865 many political issues and partisan divisions of the war continued in questions relating to the future of the former Confederate states and the future of the emancipated slaves. These immediate issues of the Reconstruction period raised broader questions regarding the proper sphere and power of the federal government and the commitment to racial equality. On such matters Hoosiers were far from agreed.

More radical Indiana Republicans, led by George Julian, insisted that the war should lead not simply to emancipation of slaves but to full legal equality for blacks. Most important was the granting of suffrage. Julian, like other Radical Republicans, also urged a harsh peace for the South, including confiscation of land and punishment, perhaps even execution, of leaders of the southern rebellion. Morton and more moderate Republicans initially resisted the Radical program but gradually moved toward acceptance, in part because they saw political advantage in playing on southern treason, which, they repeated again and again, had been aided and abetted by Democrats at home. Morton and other Republican orators thus waved incessantly the bloody shirt of war, urging Hoosiers to vote as they had shot. This vivid partisanship combined with some genuine sentiments favorable to legal equality for blacks to produce Republican support for the fifteenth amendment to the federal constitution, guaranteeing blacks the right to vote. Morton, who was elected to the United States Senate in 1867, used all his political power to secure Indiana's approval of this Radical Republican amendment in 1869. It was for Morton and many of his colleagues their last such victory.

Indiana Democrats responded to the Republican embrace of ever more radical policies with a flood of oratory, defending states' rights, attacking centralization of power in Washington and Indianapolis, and bitterly denouncing steps toward legal equality for blacks. As had their Jacksonian predecessors, Democrats also opposed such federal government involvement in the economy as Republican-sponsored tariff protection and national banking. And as in Jackson's time these arguments struck responsive chords among Hoosier traditionalists. In 1870 voters chose the first Democratic-controlled General Assembly since 1862, and in 1872 they elected a Democratic governor, Thomas A. Hendricks. A strong opponent of Radical Reconstruction as a member of the United States Senate, Hendricks became the first postwar Democrat elected to the governor's office in a northern state.[13]

The two-party balance was thus restored in Indiana more quickly and more firmly than in most northern states. The Democratic party not only survived the bloody shirt campaigns but provided a serious opposition and counterbalance to Republican policies and leadership. Late nineteenth century politics would find Hoosiers evenly divided between the two parties, firmly attached to one or the other, and intensely interested in politics. Here as in so many other ways the era of Civil War and Reconstruction would provide a critical reference point for decades of political debate and voting behavior.

xi

The Indiana Way of Politics, 1873–1920

The period from the end of the Civil War to the end of World War I was one of political as well as social and economic change. The thirty years after Appomattox was a period of hard-fought campaigns during which Indiana acquired its reputation as one of the nation's most politically vigorous states. For much of this period the two major parties were evenly balanced. Republican ascendancy at the end of the century did not diminish party rivalry, but political debates after 1900 began to ring with new calls for different responses to social and economic change.

Politics, Indiana Style, 1873–1896

Several characteristics gave Indiana's late nineteenth century politics its distinctive quality. Most obvious was the even balance between the two major parties. Nowhere else were elections more closely fought, with only a few thousand votes often spelling the difference between victory and loss and with the majority party seldom claiming more than 51 percent of the two-party vote. Most often the majority party was Republican, but Democrats were never far from victory and sometimes achieved it.[1]

The well-balanced, highly competitive two-party system in Indiana attracted large national attention, which in turn affected Indiana politics. Because the state's vote in presidential elections was always so close and could be had by winning only a few thousand extra popular votes, the national campaigns focused major effort on Hoosier voters. Indiana became one of the handful of swing states that attracted most of the national parties' strategic planning, campaign oratory, and money. The parties were also very likely to put a Hoosier on their national ticket, particularly as vice-president. Major-party vice-presidential nominees included: Schuyler Colfax (1868), William H. English (1880), Thomas A. Hendricks (1876, 1884), Charles W. Fairbanks (1904, 1916), John W. Kern (1908), and Thomas R. Marshall (1912, 1916). Benjamin Harrison was the only major-party presidential nominee (1888, 1892) and served in the White House from 1889 to 1893.[2] Hoosiers also received a large share of national patronage, including several appointments to cabinet office. Few if any of these men were distinguished politicians or statesmen: no better or worse than most of their political contemporaries elsewhere, their main advantage was their residence in a state whose voters were highly competitive and evenly divided. Indiana's presidential vote was influential also because it reflected national preferences: the Hoosier majority was on the winning side in every presidential election between 1876 and 1916.

Even balance of the vote, national attention, and frontier traditions of politicking helped make Indiana's campaigns elaborate, even raucous affairs. Parades, barbecues, rallies, and speeches were partly entertainment, but testimony also to deep political involvement. This intense campaign style reached its peak in 1888, when Indiana's own Benjamin Harrison, grandson of William Henry Harrison, was the Republican presidential nominee against the incumbent Democrat, Grover Cleveland. Orators delivered an estimated 10,000 speeches that fall in Indiana, and political leaflets, posters, and tin buttons were as abundant as pumpkins and corn shocks. "The whole state," one

The Indiana statehouse, completed in 1888. (Indiana Historical Society)

leading Democrat exclaimed, was "a blazing torchlight procession from one end to the other."[3]

The 1888 campaign was also a high point in allegations of political corruption and fraud, particularly in efforts to buy votes of so-called floaters, men who sold to the highest bidder. Near the end of the campaign the Democratic *Indianapolis Sentinel* printed a purloined letter written by William W. Dudley, treasurer of the Republican national committee, to Indiana party workers, brazenly outlining the procedure for purchasing votes: "Divide the floaters into blocks of five, and put a trusted man with necessary funds in charge of these five, and make him responsible that none get away and that all vote our ticket."[4] Democratic cries about the Dudley letter and "blocks of five" were most embarrassing to Harrison and his fellow Republicans, though they could with justice claim that Democrats also attempted to buy votes. Both parties carefully watched each other on election day. More important, calls for reform led the General Assembly in 1889 to approve the Australian system of secret voting and the use of a single, uniform ballot, replacing the private ballots provided by the party, which were already marked and easily identified as they were publicly dropped into the box. Thereafter, it was nearly impossible for anyone attempting to buy a vote to be sure that the seller actually kept up his end of the corrupt bargain. The new Indiana ballot was true to the state's political culture in that it listed candidates by party affiliation rather than by office and had a circle at the top to allow straight-ticket voting.

In addition to and partly because of the competitiveness and intensity of the campaigns Indiana politics was also characterized by extensive popular interest and participation. This was particularly evident in the very high percentages of eligible voters who actually turned out on election day to cast their ballot (see Appendix B). Nearly all of the Indiana electorate voted in late nineteenth century presidential contests. With peak turnouts close to 95 percent in 1876 and 1896, Indiana's mean turnout for the years 1860 to 1900 was 91 percent, far ahead of its nearest midwestern challengers in this important measure of citizen participation. Even in non-presidential years the turnout for congressional elections was in the mid-80 percent range. No other evidence so strongly supports popular images of the Hoosier propensity to politick. Among possible reasons for this very high turnout are the endurance of democratic pioneer traditions; the absence of significant legal barriers to voting for adult males (not until 1911 did Indiana enact a voter registration law); the highly competitive, balanced parties; and the intense loyalty most Hoosiers felt for one or the other of the two major parties.

Loyalty to party complemented high turnout and competitive, intense politics as a major characteristic of late nineteent century Indiana political life. The Indiana vote was a relatively stable and consistent vote. Nearly all Hoosiers voted year after year for the same party. And most voted a straight party ticket. Very few citizens were undecided, wavering, or independent in their party preference. A voter unhappy with a candidate or with his party's platform generally did not vote a split ticket or switch parties. Rather, he simply did not vote. The slight shifts in the two parties' strength derived generally from this fluctuation in turnout rates. And since a slight increase in turnout could mean victory, each party's campaign strategy was directed primarily toward getting its voters to the polls on election day. The hoopla of the campaign and the exertions of party workers were directed less to changing voters' minds on the issues than simply to turning out the party faithful. The intensity of partisan loyalty is demonstrated by the fact that even a fellow Hoosier at the head of the national ticket failed to alter normal voting patterns. Harrison's strenuous front porch campaign of 1888 did not increase the Republican plurality of 1886 in Indiana and brought Republicans victory in the state by only 2,300 votes of half a million cast.

Although the percentage of wavering and independent voters and non-voters was generally small, it could be very important because of the even balance of the two parties. Especially in times of social disruption or economic crisis such voters might surge to the polls and upset normal patterns. The severe depression of 1873–1878 provoked such behavior: some farmers, hard-hit by the economic crisis and perhaps less attached than other voters to one of the two major parties, responded to the third party appeals of the Grange and Greenback movement, particularly in calling for an inflationary monetary policy. Farm discontent in the 1870s did not radically or permanently alter the two-party balance, however, although it seems generally to have helped the Democrats, notably in 1876 when their gubernatorial candidate, James D. Williams, defeated the Republican newcomer, Benjamin Harrison. Williams not only voiced agrarian demands for an inflationary currency but made good use of his own farm background. His blue denim suit quickly became his campaign symbol. "Blue Jeans" Williams contrasted sharply with Harrison, whose opposition to the Greenback movement and urban, professional background enabled Democratic opponents to label him the "kid gloves candidate."[5]

The politics of the 1870s show the possibility of economic factors affecting voter behavior and raise broader questions about the general sources of party allegiance. Was choice of party identification or propensity to join a third-party movement the consequence of economic influence? Did party allegiance divide by economic class or were other influences more significant? Such questions have received considerable attention from scholars but are beset by problems of inadequate data, particularly on individual voting behavior; by the almost certain fact that voting behavior was the consequence of a multiplicity of influences, some working at cross purposes; by the possibility that voters were not always consistently rational in their choices; and by the large difficulties of drawing generalizations about thousands of individual preferences over long periods of time. Sophisticated, computer-aided analysis has eased but not overcome these challenges. Some generalizations may be ventured, but only cautiously.

It does appear that economic factors influenced party choice. Historian Melvyn Hammarberg's detailed study of voting in nine central Indiana counties in the 1870s suggests that voters of lower status occupations were more likely to be Democrats and those of higher status occupations were more likely to identify with the Republican party. A farm laborer owning no property or a factory worker, for example, were more likely to vote Democratic, partly because that party's program of monetary inflation seemed more likely to improve their economic condition. A large property-owning farmer or a dry goods merchant were more likely to vote Republican.[6]

But such findings do not lead to pure economic determinism in Indiana politics, for there is evidence of other influences on party allegiance as well. In particular, historians Richard Jensen and Paul Kleppner have argued for a strong relationship between religious denomination and partisanship. Table 2 shows this possibility as it applied to voters in Hendricks County in 1874. At the extremes, nearly all Quakers were Republicans, and nearly all Roman Catholics were Democrats, with other denominations falling between. More broadly, Kleppner and Jensen suggested, evangelical and pietistic denominations, principally Quakers, Disciples of Christ, Methodists, and Presbyterians, had religious and cultural values and traditions that squared more fully with the Republican party. Roman Catholics, Lutherans, and Regular Baptists might be grouped as liturgical denominations and were more attuned to the Democratic party. The religious messages each received could be political without using the vocabulary of politics, since church members heard sermons, studied Sunday school lessons, and read church periodicals and reports that had a more Republican or Democratic orientation. Pietistic denominations tended to be more eager to have government regulate moral behavior and thus more strongly supported antislavery causes before the Civil War and Sunday blue laws, abolition of saloons, and the temperance and prohibition movement. The Republican party was more receptive to these pietistic, moral values than the Democratic party. Liturgicals preferred that the church rather than government deal with issues

Table 2

Party Preference by Denominaton,
Hendricks County, Indiana, 1874[a]

Denomination	% GOP	%Dem.	% none/other	N
Friends (Quakers)[b]	96.4	1.2	2.4	83
Christian-Disciples of Christ [b]	73.6	23.7	2.7	291
Methodists[b c]	72.8	21.9	5.2	232
Presbyterians[d]	64.3	31.4	4.3	70
Universalists[b]	58.3	42.7	0	12
Missionary Baptists[b]	57.4	38.6	4.0	101
Miscellaneous Protestant[e]	50.0	33.3	16.7	12
No Denomination listed	47.0	48.3	4.6	699
Regular Baptists[f]	17.0	78.7	4.3	94
Roman Catholics[f]	4.2	83.3	12.5	24

[a]Liberty, Lincoln, Marion, Middle, Union, and Washington Twps.
[b]Predominantly pietistic
[c]Includes African Methodists, who were also pietistic
[d]Mostly Cumberland Presbyterians (pietistic)
[e]Mixed pietistic and liturgical
[f]Predominantly liturgical

SOURCE: Richard Jensen, *The Winning of the Midwest: Social and Political Conflict, 1888–1896* (Chicago, 1971), 60.

of morality. Moreover, liturgicals included many European immigrant members who had little or no interest in such puritanical concerns as a strict observance of the Sabbath or total abstinence. The Democratic party, with its traditions of individual freedom, was generally a more comfortable home for liturgical denominations and for immigrants. Partisan division based on religious denomination and on the broader cultural implications of denomination was often very important, causing one of the most significant lines of cleavage for many voters in late nineteenth century Indiana. But it was not the only line, nor was it always the deepest line for all voters.[7]

While late nineteenth century Hoosiers voted on the basis of religious, cultural, and economic influences, they also voted according to other and often related traditional ties to party. In particular, the party identifications forged in the political heat of the 1850s and 1860s held sway into the late nineteenth century and often passed from father to son. The Republican party constantly reminded voters that it was the party that had saved the Union in its greatest crisis, that it was the party that had taken a patriotic and moral stand, while Democrats mired themselves in vacillation, cowardice, even treason. The bloody shirt, stained in defense of the Union, became the Republican symbol, the banner they waved long after Appomattox. They would bury the bloody shirt, Harrison told a veterans rally in the 1876 campaign, only when the Democrats "purge their party of the leprosy of secession."[8] With veterans thick in their ranks and on their tickets Republicans promised to defend the cause of the Union soldier (and his government pension as well) so long as he voted as he had shot. Democrats had strong traditions too. They appealed above all to the frontier individualism and freedom so well defended by Jefferson and Jackson. They presented themselves as the party that had always resisted usurpation of the constitution and had defended the common man against the growth of centralized government power and economic monopoly. In both Democratic and Republican campaigns of the late nineteenth century these broad traditions were always used to frame discussion of specific issues such as the tariff, prohibition, or the money question.

Late nineteenth century Indiana politics becomes even more complex when considered at a local as well as state level. Counties were important political units. Each county had its own particular political environment, and the courthouse, sidewalks, and stores and office buildings around the town square often rang with political debate and conflict over local as well as state and national concerns. Counties were parts of state politics and government, especially since the county party chairman and his associates were the workhorses of party politics. Unlike the state as a whole, most counties did not divide evenly into Republican and Democratic. Map 9 shows a measure of the distribution of party strength in the years 1880–1896, based on the vote for secretary of state in the five presidential years. Eighteen counties were strongly Democratic, with the party in each averaging more than 55 percent of the two-party vote. The Republicans enjoyed similar strength in twenty-two counties. Seventeen counties were so closely contested that the leading party averaged less than 51 percent of the

Orange County courthouse, Paoli, photographed by Frank Hohenberger. (Lilly Library, Indiana University)

MAP 9.
Distribution of Party Strength after the Civil War

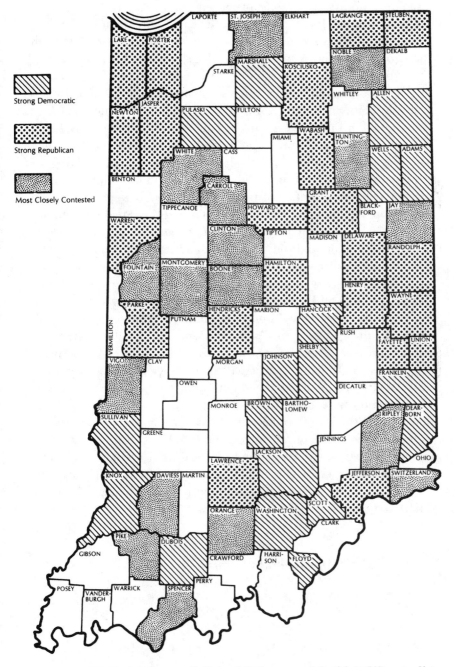

Strong Democratic

Strong Republican

Most Closely Contested

Source: Charles S. Hyneman, C. Richard Hofstetter, and Patrick F. O'Connor, *Voting in Indiana: A Century of Persistence and Change* (Bloomington, 1979), 86

two-party vote. The remaining thirty-two counties leaned either to the Democratic or Republican party. This distribution of party strength supports a commonly proposed generalization about Indiana politics. Southern Indiana remained the base of the Democratic party, with most of the strong Democratic counties located there. Most of the strong Republican counties were located in the northern half of the state. Early nineteenth century settlement patterns, with a southern-born population concentrated in southern Indiana, and Democratic strength in these counties before and during the Civil War continued to influence voters in the late nineteenth century. Areas of heavy immigrant settlement also tended to remain Democratic, such as the German-Catholic population of Dubois County. Areas of stronger New England and Mid-Atlantic migration and of heavily pietistic religious orientations tended to be strongly Republican, such as the upper Whitewater Valley and LaGrange and Steuben counties.

But these sectional tendencies were not sharp patterns. The Democratic party could and did win in many northern counties, and Republicans often elected candidates in southern Indiana. Of necessity, then, each party waged its state and national campaigns throughout the state, so that all Hoosiers breathed the invigorating air of intense two-party politics. Divided into Republicans and Democrats, they all shared in the games, symbols, and substances of politics itself. No public issue was apolitical or non-partisan, as illustrated in the party squabbles over Indiana's participation in the Columbian Exposition of 1893.[9] Indeed, politics seemed to take on a life of its own, removed if never entirely separate from specific issues, candidates, and elections, just as the act of voting was removed from simple correlations with economic, social, or religious influences. More than anything else, politics gave Indianans a common interest and bond, a distinctive culture to claim as their own, not because it was radically different but because in their view it was thoroughly within the American tradition and yet was theirs.

The Politics of Moderate Reform, 1890–1916

The end of the century did not bring a sharp change to Indiana politics. Politics continued to be intensely argued and loyalties passionately held. Yet by the 1900s there were shifts in electoral patterns and new issues, personalities, and dynamics that began to alter though not destroy main features of late nineteenth century politics. Movements of Populism and Progressivism and politicians such as Albert Beveridge and J. Frank Hanly brought winds of change to Indiana even though the main structure stood.[10]

Like many states of the American South and West, Indiana in the 1890s was the scene of renewed agrarian discontent. Coalescing into the People's or Populist party, agrarian reformers proposed sweeping changes, including government ownership of railroads and other utilities, an inflationary monetary policy through unlimited coinage of silver, government loans at low interest to hard-pressed farmers, and enhanced democracy through the initiative, referendum, and women's suffrage. The severe depression beginning in 1893 added fuel to the Populist fires, though in Indiana they were able to garner only 5 percent of the total vote in the 1894 elections. In 1896 this third party joined with the Democratic party to support William Jennings Bryan's crusade for free silver and to mount one of the most exciting presidential campaigns in American history. Although Hoosiers debated the questions of free silver intensely, even bitterly, there was in the end no doubt as to where the majority of them stood. They swept Republicans into office at national and state levels, pushed the Populist crusade onto the ash heap of history, and left the Democrats in a divided and minority position that would last a decade.

It is important to note the relative weakness of Indiana's Populist party—both as compared to the strength of the state's two major parites and to the strength of Populists in states to the south and west of Indiana. Loyalty to the two major parties remained strong in Indiana as did distrust of new or radical programs. The Populists were too far from the center of Indiana's traditions, though their movement doubtless helped prepare the way for other reform-minded Hoosiers. Populism did have another significance, for it seems to have scared enough independents and sound-money Democrats into non-voting positions or into the Republican party to give the GOP an unprecedented ascendency from 1896 to 1908, and more generally, through much of the twentieth century. This was not a radical voter shift and 1896 was not a pure realignment of voters, but the even balance of the two parties was no more.

In banishing the Populists and defeating the Democrats Indiana Republicans did not create a political consensus and harmony, even though their ascendency was accompanied by general economic prosperity. Not only was there the usual party competition, but there was also conflict within the Republican party.

Intraparty conflict was not new. During the 1880s Republicans had suffered a struggle for party control between a faction led by Benjamin Harrison and another headed by Walter Q. Gresham. The 1890s brought a new generation of Republican leaders to power, the most important of whom was Charles Warren Fairbanks. A wealthy corporation lawyer and strict Methodist, Fairbanks built a strong political organization which included part ownership of the *Indianapolis News*. In 1897 he was elected to a United States Senate seat, and in 1904 to the vice-presidency as Theodore Roosevelt's running mate. Opposing Fairbanks's leadership of the Indiana Republican party was Albert J. Beveridge, in many ways the opposite of Fairbanks. Beveridge was a charming, dynamic personality and a powerful orator, while Fairbanks was cold and aloof, the "Indiana Icicle," his detractors charged. Fairbanks was cautious about American overseas expansion, an issue highlighted by the Spanish-American War of 1898. Beveridge quickly emerged as one of the nation's most popular exponents of the new American empire, particularly with his "March of the Flag" speech advocating expansion to Cuba, Puerto Rico, and the Philippines. The speech helped propel him to a United States Senate seat in 1899. What most separated Indiana's two Republican Senators initially was simply their rival political ambitions. Gradually there developed also a profound difference on the issues of progressive reform, a difference that eventually would split the Republican party in two, with Beveridge becoming Indiana's leading progressive reformer and Fairbanks cast as the epitome of standpat conservatism.[11]

New issues flooded the political arena in the first decade and a half of the twentieth century, challenging the programs and traditions of politicians of all persuasions. Progressive reformers in both parties called for increased government response to the more negative consequences of the expanding urban industrial society. As Beveridge challenged the 1906 Republican state convention:

> We must turn to these new social and economic questions which have
> to do with the daily lives and happiness of human beings and which

press for answer; questions that involve the righteousness of American business, a juster distribution of wealth by preventing dishonest accumulation of gain; questions that look to the physical, mental, moral upbuilding of all the workers in factory and on farm throughout the entire Republic. . . . [12]

Reformers in both parties advocated child labor and workmen's compensation laws, regulation of monopolies and trusts, a state income tax, public health measures, conservation of natural resources, prohibition of the sale of alcohol, and expanded democracy through direct primary elections, direct elections of United States senators, the initiative and referendum, and women's suffrage. These progressive proposals bitterly divided Hoosiers, so much so that the Republican party itself split in half, with the progressive or insurgent wing led in Indiana by Beveridge eventually joining Theodore Roosevelt's Progressive or Bull Moose party. The Republican split played a major role in making Democrats the dominant party between 1909 and 1916, particularly causing Republican defeats in 1910 and 1912. It also ended the political career of Beveridge, though he made an unsuccessful effort at a comeback as late as 1922.

Democrats found themselves divided over issues of reform also, but they were more fortunate in finding popular leaders such as Thomas Marshall and Samuel Ralston who were able to minimize intraparty conflict with programs of cautious reform. Marshall, governor from 1909 to 1913, has been described as a "liberal with the brakes on." He favored modest progressive legislation, including some increased state regulation, and unsuccessfully sought a more modern state constitution. Ralston, Marshall's successor in the governor's office, characterized Hoosiers as "conservatively progressive," a label that would describe his governorship as well. Though allied to Democratic party boss Thomas Taggart, Ralston achieved a reputation as an independent and commonsensical governor.[13]

By 1916 Republicans had learned the bitter lesson of party division. Under the expert leadership of party chairman Will H. Hays they reunited to elect their ticket, headed by James P. Goodrich. Like Democrats Marshall and Ralston, Governor Goodrich favored moderate reform and a touch of progressive efficiency, including constitutional revision, a fairer and more efficient tax system, and a centralized highway commission. Reform plans after 1917, however, were severely limited by American entry into World War I, which turned attention to campaigns for war support and let loose a patriotic but intolerant spirit that demanded conformity and unanimity.

Moderation was the hallmark of Indiana's progressive reform. Conservative resistance among citizenry and political leadership combined with a cautious state supreme court and difficulties of amending the state constitution to defeat or postpone many of the progressive proposals, including the state income tax, women's suffrage, municipal home rule, and the initiative, referendum, and recall. Those enacted into law did not bring radical change, though measures such as the Indiana Railroad Commission (1905), Indiana Public Service Commission (1913), the revised child labor law (1911), the inheritance tax (1913), the voter registration law (1911), and direct primary elections, first conducted in 1916, brought some amelioration of undesirable conditions and a degree of moderate reform.

There were also several broad reform movements with significant implications and consequences. Worthy of further consideration are public health, public welfare, prohibition, women's suffrage, and socialism.

One of the important areas to attract reform attention was public health, an area in which Indiana was closer to the forefront of reform than perhaps any other. The Indiana General Assembly created the Indiana State Board of Health in 1881 to collect vital statistics and disseminate information about disease and sanitation. Public health matured under the leadership of Dr. John N. Hurty, secretary of the State Board of Health from 1896 to 1922. A national survey of state public health boards in 1915 by the American Medical Association ranked Indiana's program sixth in effectiveness and specifically commended Hurty's pioneering work. An energetic and skillful reformer, Hurty began campaigns of publicity and regulation to combat typhoid fever, smallpox, tuberculosis, and venereal diseases and to improve the purity of water and food in Indiana. In 1899 the legislature passed Hurty's pure food and drug law, among the first such state laws in the nation. The nationwide campaign for pure food and drugs received major impetus from two other Indiana reformers: Dr. Harvey W. Wiley, a Purdue University chemist who became chief chemist of the United States Department of Agriculture, and Senator Albert Beveridge, whose campaign for a meat inspection bill brought the issue to the political arena and helped secure passage of a federal meat inspection law in 1906 and the federal Pure Food and Drug Act in 1907. The health of Hoosiers doubtless also benefited from state licensing and regulation of physicians, nurses, dentists, and pharmacists during the Progressive era and from the expansion of regularly accredited medical education through creation of the Indiana University School of Medicine in 1908. Improved material well-being brought by an expanding economy combined with the public health movement to bring the kinds of changes most poignantly reflected in the welcome drop in infant mortality rates in the early twentieth century.

The Progressive era also brought increased attention to the plight of the poor, the insane, and other dependent individuals. Many such charitable and reform activities began at the local level and expanded on earlier voluntary programs. The Social Gospel minister Oscar C. McCulloch reorganized the Indianapolis Benevolent Society, formed in 1835, into the ambitious Indianapolis Charity Organization Society. Similar organizations appeared in other Indiana cities in the 1880s. In 1912 they joined in the Indiana State Federation of Organized Charities, bringing more systematic and professional directon to local, voluntary relief for the poor. Reformers in larger cities also founded social settlement houses, modeled on Jane Addams's famous Hull House in Chicago. Flanner House and Christamore House in Indianapolis, Stewart House in Gary, and Nebraska Center in Fort Wayne were among the more important of such attempts to ameliorate the conditions of urban poverty. Among the most effective of Indiana urban reformers was Albion Fellows Bacon of Evansville. Shocked by slum tenements in her city, Bacon began a crusade to improve housing by vigorous lobbying pressure on the General Assembly. Her campaign led to Indiana's first housing law in 1909, specifying minimum building and maintenance standards for Indianapolis and Evansville, extended in 1913 to all incorporated cities.[14]

State government's more systematic attention to public welfare began with formation of the Board of State Charities in 1889. The board sponsored conferences, published the quarterly *Indiana Bulletin of Charities and Corrections*, and supervised state prisons, hospitals, and institutions for orphans and for the blind and deaf. These state institutions retained large administrative independence, however, and despite the efforts of reformers provided opportunities also for political patronage that retarded professional development.

Of all the reform movements of late nineteenth and early twentieth century Indiana, none attracted more attention than prohibition. A state temperance society formed in 1829, but not until the 1840s and 1850s did the movement become popular. Initially relying on education and moral suasion, particularly through the churches, and closely connected at first to the antislavery movement, temperance forces began to lobby for governmental regulation of alcohol manufacture and sale. They persuaded the 1853 legislature to pass a local option law, allowing voters in a township to declare their township dry. The law was soon held unconstitutional by the Indiana Supreme Court. But the moral and political ferment that created the Republican party in 1854 also led to passage in 1855 of a statewide prohibition law. This too was declared unconstitutional. These blows and the rising tide of sectional crisis washed temperance off the political agenda. The increasing importance of German-born voters, who generally opposed temperance, also made many political leaders reluctant to take up such a divisive cause. For some pietistic and native-born Hoosiers, however, temperance and anti-immigrant sentiment were very much related and continued to be so into the twentieth century. The temperance committee of the Presbyterian Synod of Indiana reported in 1887 that "The ranks of the drinking men are constantly recruited by the influx of bibulous and intemperate foreigners," and that "The great majority of these alien immigrants . . . are addicted to the use of strong drinks, as well as steeped in ignorance and vice."[15] Anti-immigrant prejudices combined with convictions of the sinfulness of drink and fears of the social threat to stable family and community life to keep the cause alive. Protestant churches, particularly the Methodists, Baptists, Disciples of Christ, and Presbyterians, and many women's groups spread powerful arguments against drink. Formation of the Indiana branch of the Women's Christian Temperance Union in 1874 and the Indiana Anti-Saloon League in 1898 focused organized and very intense pressure on politicians. With their reliance on pietistic church members, Republicans were particularly sensitive to this grassroots moral crusade, as illustrated by the uproar caused when an unidentified person served Manhattan cocktails at an Indianapolis lawn party given by Vice-President Fairbanks and attended by President Theodore Roosevelt. So serious was the incident that the innocent but embarrassed Fairbanks was excluded from the General Methodist Episcopal Conference in 1908.

A major prohibition victory came during the governorship of Republican J. Frank Hanly, a teetotal Methodist Republican who mounted campaigns against gambling at the popular West Baden and French Lick resorts, against betting on horse races at the state fair, and against sale of cigarettes to minors. At the base of these and many other ills was liquor, Hanly argued. In 1908, just before the fall elections, he created a furor among his own party leaders by calling a special legislative session to force through a county option law, which allowed voters to ban liquor sales within their county. By late 1909 seventy of the ninety-two counties were dry. Prohibition remained controversial, however, and opposition may have contributed to Republican losses in Indiana in 1908 and 1910. In 1911 the Democratic legislative majority replaced the county option law with a more moderate township option. Prohibition forces continued their pressure, with former Governor Hanly now devoting his career to the cause and joining with Edward S. Shumaker, head of the Indiana Anti-Saloon League, as major spokesmen. World War I gave them the final boost, as anti-German prejudice, the need to conserve grain, and general patriotic sentiment led the General Assembly to adopt statewide prohibition in 1917. Two years later Indiana joined in ratifying the Eighteenth Amendment to the federal constitution, making the whole nation dry.[16]

Concurrent with the prohibition battle was the campaign for women's rights. Many women first ventured from home and family to support temperance, many others to further the cause of the Sunday school or their church denomination. Rapidly growing women's clubs also provided enrichment outside the kitchen or nursery. Literary and music societies, sewing circles, and sororities, particularly Tri-Kappa, proliferated in small towns and large cities after the Civil War. From such activities middle-class women developed skills in organization, publicity, and public speaking. Though women's groups and their members did not always support the cause of women's rights, and sometimes actively opposed it, many contributed directly or indirectly.

The struggle for women's rights was long and hard. Delegates to the Constitutional Convention of 1850–1851 rejected Robert Dale Owen's proposal to guarantee women's right to hold property and restated the tradition of limiting suffrage to men. A few women protested against their inferior legal and political status and formed in 1851 the Indiana Woman's Rights Association. And in 1859 Dr. Mary F. Thomas, a Richmond physician, became the first woman allowed to speak before the state legislature when she presented a petition for equal political rights for women. Legislators listened, some ridiculed, nothing resulted.[17] Extension of suffrage to black males after the Civil War encouraged the women's suffrage movement and led to legislative petitions and debates. Legislators responded that most women themselves did not want the vote, that God had ordained women's place in the home and church, not in politics, where women would be exposed "to the vulgar rowdyism of men on election days."[18] Rather than a suffrage bill, the legislature enacted in 1873 a new divorce law intended to protect marriage and the family by tightening Indiana's relatively easy divorce requirements. No longer would the state be a mecca for non-Hoosiers, such as the archaeologist Heinrich Schliemann, who established temporary residence to secure a quick divorce. The issue of women's rights revived again briefly in the early 1880s and then subsided, although feminists such as Helen M. Gougar, a Lafayette lawyer, May Wright Sewall, an Indianapolis educator and club woman, and Ida Husted Harper, a Terre Haute newspaper columnist, waged determined battles. The Progressive era brought a renewal of interest in women's rights, focused largely on suffrage. The Indiana Woman Suffrage Association, organized in 1869, revived in 1906, while in 1911 activists organized the Woman's Franchise League of Indiana, which soon had sixty branches. At last in 1917 the General Assembly responded favorably, but the difficulty of amending the state constitution and an adverse state supreme court decision delayed suffrage. Finally in early 1920 the state legislature ratified the Nineteenth Amendment to the federal constitution and in 1921 adopted a women's suffrage amendment to the state constitution, ratified by voters at a special election. Women had the right to vote: social and economic equality would prove even greater challenges.[19]

The struggles for women's suffrage and for prohibition were largely middle-class reform movements and generally not radical in goals or methods. Some Hoosiers argued that there were more pressing problems than alcohol or votes for women, and demanded more than the kinds of ameliorative reforms generally supported by the two major parties. The Socialist party responded to industrial growth by presenting an alternative course, a course most cogently argued in Indiana and the nation by Eugene V. Debs.

The son of immigrant parents, Debs was born in Terre Haute in 1855 and lived there all his life. He worked on the railroad and as a warehouse clerk, and he participated in labor organizations and the Democratic party. He served one term in the state legislature, but gradually became discontented with union and political moderation in the face of working-class hardship. His leadership role in the 1894 Pullman strike led to a six-month jail sentence and a national reputation. Debs supported the Populists briefly but soon became convinced of the inevitability of class struggle and of the necessity of replacing private property and greedy capitalism with humanitarian socialism, moving from moderate reform to radical revolution. Debs was not an intellectual or Marxist purist, however, but rather an idealistic crusader for social justice whose strength lay in the integrity, courage, and conviction with which he preached an often unhappy view of the status quo. He was widely respected in Terre Haute and Indiana. His incongruous friend, the poet James Whitcomb Riley, wrote:

And there's Gene Debs—a man 'at stands
And jes' holds out in his two hands
As warm a heart as ever beat
Betwixt here and the Jedgment Seat.

But respect, even love, for Debs did not mean agreement. Five times he ran for the presidency on the Socialist ticket, never winning as much as 6 percent of the Indiana vote. And although Socialists showed some voter strength in Indiana coal mining areas and in a few industrial towns, including Marion and Elwood, the party remained generally a very minor third party at both state and local levels. Harsh class conflict and radical change were not part of the political vocabulary of most Hoosiers.[20]

The day-to-day politics of late nineteenth and early twentieth century Indiana certainly seemed to Hoosier contemporaries to be marked by conflict and divisiveness. Yet viewed from broader perspectives of time and place conflict appears muted, the degree of harmony and the areas of agreement more significant than the divisions and acrimonies. Differences were there—between urban and rural, working class and middle class, immigrant and native born, Protestant and Catholic, black and white, agrarian and industrial, southern Indiana and northern Indiana, Republican and Democrat. While it is impossible to measure precisely such differences it does seem that they were not as large generally as in many other places and at other times in America. Forms and patterns familiar across American history are discernible in Indiana, but the corners are rounded off, the sharp points blunted. Populism, progressivism, and socialism appear, but they lack the intensity and strength of many other states. Politicians like Hanly and Beveridge might split their parties over issues of substance, but most of the time Indiana leaders were able to meet arguments for change with moderation of the kind shown by Governors Marshall, Ralston, and Goodrich. And nearly all of the time they never forgot the importance of politics as the politics of winning a majority vote. Tom Taggart's building of Democratic strength in Indianapolis and state politics and Will H. Hays's leadership in unifying the Republicans after the insurgent split in 1912 provide examples of the skills of political organization that abounded in Indiana. Taggart and Hays achieved such large reputations as state party chairmen and political prestidigitators that their national parties called on them to serve as national party chairmen.[21] Taggart, Hays, Marshall, Ralston, and Goodrich are most representative of Indiana politics. They were as important to Indiana as Robert La Follette was to Wisconsin, Tom Watson to Georgia, or Woodrow Wilson to New Jersey. They left smaller and rather different wakes than these contemporaries elsewhere, perhaps because Indiana's political traditions were still waters that ran deep and were not easily diverted even if storms roughed the surface.

A Golden Age?

A later generation of Hoosiers would look back on the several decades between the Civil War and World War I as Indiana's Golden Age. Through rose-tinted glasses, they remembered the excitement and entertainment of politics, the comfort and security of rural and small-town community life, the pleasures and popularity of Indiana literature, the sense of growth and progress in education and religion, the visible signs of improvement in material well-being. They took pride in moderate change and comfort in traditions preserved. They boasted that Indiana's middle-of-the-road way was the American way. When they celebrated their centennial of statehood in 1916 there were the usual reenactments of pioneer achievements, real and fancied, but there was also a flowering of the natural conservation movement that led to the establishment of one of the nation's finest state park systems. It was perhaps a typical reconciliation of past and future, of tradition and change, one that many Hoosiers greeted with pride.

PART IV

Continuity and Change since 1920

xii

The People since 1920

The social beliefs, relationships, and institutions of twentieth-century Indiana seemed increasingly uniform and homogeneous. The people of Indiana seemed ever more alike, with divisions of race, ethnicity, religion, and perhaps even class becoming less obvious. And Hoosiers seemed more like Americans everywhere. All ate the same hamburgers, read the same books, and worshipped at the same kinds of churches. Hoosiers became less distinctive in the twentieth century. But they did not disappear into an American cultural melting pot. Nor did all Hoosiers themselves share the same social values and institutions. Variety, heterogeneity, and pluralism remained important within the state and within the nation.

Many Kinds of Hoosiers

Indiana's population changed considerably in the years after 1920, with significant consequences for nearly all aspects of life. Most obvious was the growth in size, from 2,930,390 people in 1920 to 5,490,260 in 1980. This addition of two and a half million people was the consequence of a variety of factors. European immigration dropped off after World War I, but black migration from the rural South increased; the birth rate continued to decline and families became smaller, but fewer infants died and the life span increased. These factors contributed to decennial population increases in Indiana that exceeded 10 percent in every decade except the 1930s and the 1970s, when the rate dropped to 5.8 and 5.7 percent respectively. The slowing of population growth in the 1970s caused Indiana's congressional representation to drop from eleven to ten.[1]

The decline in fertility and the smaller family size that marked the end of pioneer life and the coming of industry and cities in the nineteenth century continued through the twentieth century. But during the 1930s and the 1970s there was an especially large fall off in the birth rate and during the late 1940s and 1950s an especially large increase. Aided by a growing awareness of effective birth control, Hoosier couples in the Great Depression postponed marriage and children until prosperity returned. World War II and especially the return of servicemen after 1945 brought dramatic increases in numbers of marriages and children, producing the postwar baby boom that constituted one of the most important social forces in late twentieth century life. This wave of postwar babies formed a large population bulge as they moved through the life cycle: school and then college enrollments zoomed in the 1950s and 1960s, and adults confronted a youth culture of music, dress, and sometimes rebellion, with Hoosier representatives stretching from James Dean in the 1950s to Michael Jackson in the 1980s. Their numbers were so large that they became a political voice in the 1960s, especially on the issue of the Vietnam War. The political system that some youths denigrated conceded them the vote in 1971, though a relatively small percentage chose to exercise that new right. By the 1970s and 1980s the postwar babies, now adults, were the cause of a declining fertility rate as they postponed marriage and children for careers and material comforts.

Such lifestyle choices were aided by the ready availability of new contraceptive methods and legalized abortion, although Indiana's abortion rate was considerably below the national average. And as they competed among themselves for jobs and home mortgages many of the baby boomers contributed further to the declining growth rate of the state's population by deciding that better career opportunities were to be found in the American sunbelt.

Indiana's twentieth-century population grew slightly more rapidly in cities than in rural areas. The 1920 census was the first to show that there were more urban than rural Hoosiers, just over 50 percent. During the 1920s there was a large farm-to-city migration, so that by 1930 just over 55 percent of the population lived in cities. The figure remained near that level, with an increase to 61 percent urban by 1970, then falling to 58 percent in 1980. The growth in urban population was most pronounced in central and northern Indiana, especially in the industrial cities. Only Evansville retained major city status in southern Indiana, though by 1980 Bloomington had joined the list of ten largest Indiana cities. By that time some of the once-thriving industrial towns, particularly those connected to the auto industry, were experiencing no growth or actual declines in population.

One of the most important developments affecting all Indiana cities was the decline of the central business district and the expansion of suburbs. The automobile and highway construction produced commercial strips and shopping malls on city outskirts that adversely affected downtown economies. In the late 1950s six downtown Indianapolis department stores accounted for 90 percent of department store sales in Marion County; by 1972, downtown Indianapolis stores rang up only 18 percent of Marion County department store sales. Shoppers had moved from stores on Washington Street to the new suburban malls, beginning with the Eastgate and Glendale malls in the 1950s. Across Indiana downtown movie theaters, train stations, department stores, and hotels closed, while branch banks, drive-in theaters, restaurants, auto dealerships, and outlets of national chain stores sprang up close to suburban populations. In small towns from Madison to Greencastle to Lagrange downtown merchants struggled to keep customers from the new stores on the periphery. This turning inside out of cities was most pronounced in Gary where the process was exaggerated by white flight to southern Lake County in the 1960s and 1970s. By the mid-1970s Sears and Holiday Inn had joined many local merchants in closing their downtown Gary operations. Mayor Richard Hatcher and other black leaders struggled energetically to revive the "City of the Century": by the 1980s Gary's black citizens could point with pride to individual and community achievement that counterbalanced the negative and often uninformed images of outsiders.[2]

Gary's urban challenges were larger than in most cities, but they were not unique. City leaders throughout the state in the late twentieth century struggled to encourage economic growth, provide necessary urban services, revitalize downtowns and older neighborhoods, and maintain the cultural and leisure amenities that had made cities attractive to generations of Hoosiers. The most logical response was to seek public aid, but Indiana's oft-stated opposition to government spending and outside intervention created some reluctance in the immediate postwar years to pursue state and federal dollars. Nor were state and federal government officials always as sympathetic to urban problems as many mayors and city councils wished. Many city leaders, including some Republicans, strongly opposed the property tax freeze of the Bowen administration in the 1970s, which restricted local income. Many also expressed dissatisfaction with cutbacks for federal urban programs in the 1980s. Nonetheless, most Indiana cities remained attractive places to live and work. Many, in fact, remained not far removed from the small towns that dominated life at the turn of the century. What Muncie's residents liked most about their town, a sociological study in the 1970s reported, was that "it is not a big city and is not likely to become one."[3]

Perhaps the city that changed most significantly in the mid and late twentieth century was Indianapolis. The capital city initiated in the 1960s a process of urban development that showed major results by the 1980s: interstate highways surrounded and penetrated the city; suburban development spread over Marion County and reached into contiguous counties; downtown office buildings and hotels rose to symbolize economic development; the campus of Indiana University–Purdue University expanded educational opportunities; new sports, leisure, and convention facilities, including Market Square Arena, the Hoosier Dome, and the White River State Park complex, offered the hope of wide popular appeal. The move of the Baltimore Colts profes-

sional football team to Indianapolis in 1984 seemed to many to mark
the transition from overgrown town to major city. These changes were
the work of public and private agencies. Private investors and the
business community played large roles. Particularly important was the
Lilly Endowment, which provided millions of dollars of community
development money. And, abandoning 1950s Republican opposition
to government spending, the political leadership of Mayors Richard
Lugar and William H. Hudnut, III, aggressively sought local, state,
and especially federal government assistance through low-interest
loans and tax abatements for downtown construction. Also significant
was the creation in 1970 of Unigov, a precedent-setting, consolidated
city-county governmental structure that many felt greatly boosted the
city's development. Such changes were often controversial. Many believed that Unigov—a Republican measure—intentionally reduced the
efficacy of Democratic and black votes in city politics by diluting them
with the more numerous votes of the white Republican suburbs. Other
critics noted that Unigov did not include countywide school consolidation. And some questioned the high levels of public assistance for
downtown development, asserting that more attention needed to be
paid to such less glamorous projects as housing and urban services
for poorer residents of inner city neighborhoods.[4]

An important part of the history of many cities, and some rural
areas too, was the role of immigration. Indiana never attracted as
many European immigrants as most northern industrial states. With
the xenophobic constriction of immigration to America underway by
the 1920s the state's ethnic divisions gradually diminished. The foreign-born population in 1920 was just over 5 percent of the state total;
by 1950 it had dropped to less than 3 percent. Some cities and counties
continued to display a distinctive European heritage into the late twentieth century, however. Over 10 percent of Lake County's population
was still foreign born as late as 1950, with Mexican-Americans and
southern and eastern Europeans largest in numbers.

Prejudice and pressure for assimilation from native-born Americans, so strongly expressed through the Ku Klux Klan in the years
after World War I, declined by the late twentieth century, to be replaced often by self-conscious celebrations of ethnic diversity. Ethnic
festivals, churches, clubs, stores, and food continued to be part of the
history of the Calumet region and of other Indiana communities.

Hoosiers three and even five or six generations removed from their immigrant forebears began to take pride in their special heritage. In Dubois County where nearly everyone in the nineteenth century was of German heritage, an ethnic revitalization in the 1970s brought the reinstitution of teaching German language in the high schools and a revival of folk festivals; but because twentieth-century assimilation had proceeded so fully there was some confusion among Dubois County residents about the meaning and purpose of "German" culture. German-Americans in Evansville and Vanderburgh County were also many generations removed from the fatherland by the late twentieth century: traces of the heritage remained in the importance given to family ties, religious belief, and public celebrations and in organizations such as the Germania Maennerchor. There was overwhelming evidence of assimilation there too, however. The Maennerchor for a while had a Volksfest chairman named O'Donnell; the few so-called German restaurants served more fried chicken than bratwurst; and only among the elderly in the countryside were there traces of a German accent.[5]

Just as ethnic differences declined so too did many of the religious differences that separated Hoosiers. Much of the denominational rivalry and animosity faded. In particular, the virulent anti-Catholicism that had burst forth in the Ku Klux Klan of the 1920s diminished considerably in post–World War II Indiana. John F. Kennedy's presidential campaign in 1960 stimulated a flurry of old-style Protestant bigotry, but it was the last public hurrah. Both Protestants and Catholics grew to fuller toleration of one another, even to the point of intermarriage, though religion continued to play a significant role in choice of spouse in many families and communities. Jewish Hoosiers also welcomed the growing tolerance and openness and began to focus less on remnants of anti-Semitism than on efforts to strengthen Jewish community identity.[6]

The denominational rivalry that plagued Protestant churches also faded. Mainline Protestant denominations joined in a variety of ecumenical endeavors and agencies. County and city church councils and federations provided forums for ministers to meet and cooperate. Sunday schools were particularly effective in promoting interdenominational work. And in 1943 major Protestant denominations joined to form the Indiana Council of Churches, a body that exerted considerable influence in religious and secular areas, including civil rights at home and missionary and economic development programs abroad.[7]

Despite the trend toward cooperation and toleration religion could still be contentious, and it could spill into the political culture. During the 1920s especially, the major Protestant denominations—Methodists, Baptists, Presbyterians, and Disciples of Christ—struggled mightily with the uncertainty and conflict engendered by Darwinian evolution, higher criticism of the Bible, and the modernist movement generally. And they continued to exert influence over community as well as individual morality. Protestant support for prohibition was intense during the 1920s, particularly in sponsoring the Indiana Anti-Saloon League, headed by Methodist minister Edward S. Shumaker. One of the most influential men in the state, Shumaker successfully led the "dry" campaign to pass a state prohibition act, known popularly as the Wright bone-dry law. Enacted in 1925, this measure provided severe penalties for possession of alcohol and defined possession so broadly as to include as evidence even empty bottles and kegs. The Great Depression and the victory of the "wet" Democratic party brought an end to this noble experiment in 1933, though the state continued to regulate alcohol though prohibition of Sunday sales and various licensing requirements. Early twentieth century Protestant churches continued also their efforts to limit secular activity on the Sabbath and to encourage wholesome diversions for young people on Saturday nights as well as Sundays. During the roaring twenties motion pictures, new styles of music and dance, and the freedom of the automobile were often sources of concern. Each generation of adults discovered a "youth problem": that of the 1920s declared, in a Methodist resolution, that "by agitation, education, and, if necessary, legislation, we must have clean motion pictures, decent pleasures, normal recreations. . . ."[8] Later generations would worry about rock and roll music in the 1950s, long hair in the 1960s, and "punk" styles of dress in the 1980s and, with more seriousness and continuity, about misuse of drugs and alcohol, irresponsible sexual behavior, and pornography.

As the twentieth century proceeded the mainline Protestant churches became less determined to force their particular views of morality on all citizens, and they modified their notions of what constituted immorality. By the late twentieth century even the most devout Methodist might smoke, drink a glass of chablis, and shop at the local suburban mall on a Sunday afternoon. Indeed, concern for morality and social order among mainline Protestants took its most effective form in support of the civil rights movement of the 1960s. Although their church members often lagged behind, many Protestant and Catholic clergy were in the forefront of the campaign for racial equality—a campaign that helped balance the Protestant leadership's silence or cooperation with the Ku Klux Klan forty years earlier.

As the mainline Protestant churches became more tolerant, liberal, and ecumenical, some other denominations made opposition to these tendencies a primary part of their religious program. Taking the words "fundamentalist" and "holiness" as terms of honor instead of opprobrium, they held fast to views of the Bible and to standards of social conduct they associated with the old-time religion. Some also began in the 1970s to translate their religious beliefs into political action, including support for prayer in public schools and opposition to abortion, a position in which Protestant fundamentalists joined with Roman Catholic leaders. There was much political and theological variety among fundamentalists, however, which created conflicts, schisms, and a proliferation of new congregations that attested to the continuing change and vitality of religion in Indiana.

Signs of change in twentieth-century religion were everywhere, but they should not obscure the basic continuity of belief and practice. Nearly every generation worried about a decline in religion, particularly in the 1920s and the 1960s. But neither church membership nor the patterns of denominational support changed radically, though the fundamentalist churches often grew more rapidly than the major Protestant denominations. Even so, in 1980 the largest denominations in Indiana were Catholics, Methodists, Christians, Baptists, Lutherans, and Presbyterians—the same denominations that constituted most of the church membership in the pioneer period. Most important, despite omnipresent signs of secularization, religious belief and church institutions continued to play large roles in individual and community life. In their study of Muncie in the 1920s Robert and Helen Lynd noted that newcomers to the community, which they called Middletown, were usually greeted with the question, "What church do you go to?" A massive followup study of Muncie in the 1970s found religion still thriving, with only modest changes in belief or practice. The Lynds' successors concluded that "The Reverend Rip Van Winkle, Methodist minister, awakening in Middletown after a 60-year sleep, would hardly know he had been away."[9]

Black Hoosiers and the Civil Rights "Revolution"

There was continuity also in race relations and the lives of black Hoosiers. The patterns of black migration and settlement that developed in the late nineteenth century endured through the first half of the twentieth century. Migration from the rural South to the urban, industrial North continued, with the exception of the Depression years of the 1930s. Blacks who settled in Indiana almost invariably chose the larger towns and cities, particularly Indianapolis and Gary, which by 1950 were home to nearly 60 percent of the state's black population. Industrial towns like Muncie, Anderson, South Bend, and Fort Wayne also began to attract black newcomers. Most southern Indiana towns were less attractive in offering jobs and suitable living conditions, so that black populations stabilized or actually declined in many. Rural Indiana continued to lose its black population. By 1950 95 percent of all Indiana blacks lived in urban areas.

Another pattern persisted from the late nineteenth century through the first half of the twentieth century: black Hoosiers suffered the burdens of discrimination, segregation, and second-class citizenship in every aspect of their relationship with white Hoosiers. Not only did this sad legacy endure, but there were many areas in which obstacles to black achievement and well-being increased.

With growing black populations there emerged a more intense and aggressive racism. The most dramatic vehicle was the Ku Klux Klan, which gave formal, organized voice to prejudice and hatred in the name of Christianity and Americanism. In large cities like Indianapolis the Klan in the early 1920s found especially eager recruits among whites living near expanding black neighborhoods.[10]

The passing of the Klan by the late 1920s did not significantly change race relations. Expressions of racial hatred seldom led to violence, although there was one notable exception. On a hot August night in 1930 a mob of angry whites in Marion removed from the

Grant County jail two blacks accused of murdering a white youth and assaulting his girlfriend. While thousands watched, the mob lynched the two men from a tree on the courthouse square. No one was punished for this vigilante outrage.

The Ku Klux Klan in the early 1920s and the Marion lynching of 1930 were the most vicious expressions of white prejudice. But they were phenomena of short duration. More important and more pervasive were the commonplace barriers denying blacks access to jobs, schools, homes, and public accommodations. These barriers were raised higher in the first decades of the twentieth century. Particularly important was the intensification of school segregation, best indicated in the construction of all-black high schools in Gary (Roosevelt) and Indianapolis (Crispus Attucks) in the late 1920s. Segregation in the schools continued in many southern Indiana communities, including Evansville, while in Fort Wayne, South Bend, and some other northern cities black and white students attended the same schools. A few blacks were admitted to the state's colleges and universities, but they generally were denied access to dormitories, social organizations, and athletic teams. Indiana University's 1953 national championship basketball team did not have a single black player. Limited educational opportunities and white prejudice combined to restrict severely employment opportunities for black Hoosiers. Men worked as unskilled laborers, women as domestics. There was only a small skilled and professional representation, consisting largely of teachers, barbers, ministers, and a few lawyers and doctors, nearly all serving the black community. Blacks in Indiana were also denied access to many restaurants, hotels, theaters, parks, and other public accommodations. They might enter the state parks but were not allowed to use the swimming pools. Finally, there was residential segregation, a complex process that forced blacks to live in enclaves within the larger cities. Invariably black neighborhoods had the least attractive housing and the most inadequate urban services and amenities.[11]

Many of these conditions of second-class citizenship continued into the late twentieth century, though often in less blatant form. But most changed substantially—so much so that by the 1960s many began to speak of a civil rights revolution. There is no doubt that changes in race relations were among the most significant developments of the twentieth century, but they always encompassed a blending of past traditions. Nor was the revolution as far reaching and complete as its leaders hoped.

The first signs of change came early in the twentieth century when some blacks and whites began to organize to combat racism. The National Association for the Advancement of Colored People (NAACP) was the most important result. An Indianapolis branch began working in 1912. Its primary method was to function within the legal system to bring about equality before the law. The NAACP made laudable efforts to fight school segregation and other forms of discrimination, particularly in opposing the building of Roosevelt and Crispus Attucks high schools, but it lost more battles than it won prior to World War II.

The struggle for racial equality did not receive serious attention from political leaders before World War II. But a political shift of major long term consequence did occur during the interwar years. Since Emancipation blacks had always voted Republican. The Klan's attachment to the Republican party in the early 1920s spurred a bolt by black voters to the Democratic party. Though many returned to the party of Lincoln in 1928 and 1932, by 1936 most black Hoosiers were voting Democratic, responding to the New Deal's attention to economic hardship. This voter realignment endured, and blacks became an important part of the liberal, urban coalition that was to influence Democratic politics into the late twentieth century and eventually to give them a greater voice in politics and government.[12]

World War II initiated more direct blows to discrimination, extending beyond legal challenges and party politics. A new spirit developed as some white Hoosiers and most blacks saw the moral incongruities of fighting Nazism abroad while condoning racism at home. Perhaps more compelling for many whites was the simple fact that black Hoosiers were needed in uniform and in industry in order to win the war. By 1943 there was a severe manpower shortage that forced many formerly all white factories and businesses to hire black workers. Often these new workers faced discrimination on the job, especially in gaining access to skilled positions, but important economic gains were made during the war. The significance of black participation in the war effort also sparked the first state government recognition that there was a race problem in twentieth-century Indiana. In 1941 the Indiana Defense Council joined with the Indiana

State Chamber of Commerce to prepare the Indiana Plan of Bi-Racial Cooperation, in which government, business, and labor leaders joined to improve job opportunities for blacks as part of the war effort at home. Similar objectives led to passage of the Indiana Fair Employment Practices Act in 1945, one of the first state laws to seek an end to discrimination in employment. Both were voluntary programs, however, without compulsory enforcement. They represented nonetheless a public recognition of the problem and thereby helped prepare the way for fuller responses.[13]

Many blacks feared that peace would bring a retreat from wartime gains. Although such apprehensions seemed warranted by the late 1940s, the experiences of the war years could not be erased fully. Some blacks continued to hold jobs won during the war; many remembered the possibilities opened by the war. Black veterans were especially unhappy to return to a segregated society. The NAACP pushed ever harder against Jim Crow segregation and discrimination, which continued to thrive in hotels, restaurants, theaters, parks, and schools throughout much of Indiana. A major victory came in 1949.

Local campaigns to end segregation in schools blossomed in Indianapolis and Gary in the 1940s and put pressure on the state legislature to act. The Indiana Conference of the NAACP, under the leadership of Indianapolis attorney Willard Ransom, took the lead in this lobbying effort. Joining the NAACP were the Congress of Industrial Organizations (the most sympathetic of labor groups), Protestant and Catholic church groups, the Indiana Jewish Community Relations Council, and even the conservative *Indianapolis Star*. The campaign produced what one scholar has labeled "the most significant effort at interracial cooperation in the history of the state." The result was passage of the Indiana School Desegregation Act of 1949, which required an end to segregation and discrimination in Indiana schools. The law lacked strong compulsory features, and many school officials and parents objected in principle and in practice, but peaceful compliance with the law was the general response in most communities. After nearly a century of existence legal segregation passed from the schools: Indiana was among the last northern states to root out this obnoxious weed from its school garden. The United States Supreme Court in the celebrated case of *Brown* vs. *Board of Education* gave federal support in 1954 to the position that Indiana had reached five years earlier.[14]

Peaceful school desegregation and outward quiet in the 1950s were the calm before the storm of the civil rights movement of the 1960s. Here too state action preceded federal legislation, only this time Indiana was in the vanguard of state responses. Before passage of significant federal civil rights legislation, notably the United States Civil Rights Act of 1964, the General Assembly in 1961 enacted a state civil rights law which promoted equal opportunity in employment and equal access to public accommodations. The 1963 legislature strengthened the law by giving to the newly created Indiana Civil Rights Commission power to issue enforceable cease and desist orders where it found discrimination. The 1963 law made Indiana one of the most progressive states in the Midwest in terms of state civil rights legislation. Much of the credit for this legislation went to Democratic Governor Matthew Welsh. Welsh was an outspoken advocate of civil rights, and his party, though still partly tied to a rural constituency, was increasingly dependent on the liberal, urban coalition that included black voters. But there was even more important support outside the party arena, for by the early 1960s many Hoosiers were coming at last to recognize the injustice and immorality of discrimination and segregation. The times they were a-changing, as the song of the day proclaimed, and nowhere was this more true than in attitudes toward race relations.[15]

Many civil rights advocates hoped that change would follow peaceful, legal channels and at the same time prove revolutionary in impact. Change did occur more peacefully in Indiana than in many other states. There was conflict and tension, to be sure, but little of the violence, and none of the destructive rioting that burst forth in Detroit, New York, or Los Angles. But if change was largely peaceful it was not as revolutionary as many hoped. Rather, in their struggles with civil rights during the tumultuous 1960s and 1970s Hoosiers reaffirmed their reputation for moderation.

Indiana's moderate approach was demonstrated in the 1964 primary election. Alabama segregationist George C. Wallace entered the Indiana presidential primary, hoping to appeal to the racist and states'-rights sentiments of Hoosiers. His opponent was Governor

Welsh, standing in for President Lyndon B. Johnson in a determined effort to prevent Wallace from reviving and giving credence to traditional racism. The election attracted national attention; television newsman Walter Cronkite and others came to Indiana to listen to and repeat the tales about D. C. Stephenson and the Klan and doubtless to see Hoosiers at their worst. Wallace did win votes, particularly from whites in Lake and Porter counties, both of which gave him a majority. (One ironic consequence in Lake County was black abandonment of white party leadership that led to the election of Richard Hatcher in 1967 as one of the first black mayors of an American city.) But Wallace lost the state to Welsh by a vote of 172,646 to 376,023, winning a smaller share of the vote than he had won earlier in the Wisconsin primary. It was not evidence of a revolution, but the 1964 primary indicated that Hoosiers were not what they had been forty years earlier.[16] Similar conclusions followed from the unequivocal rejection of the revived Klan in the 1960s and 1970s by all responsible leaders and its attraction to only a small minority of the meanest and most ignorant Hoosiers.

Change in laws and even attitudes in the 1960s and 1970s did not mean full equality for all black Hoosiers. Nonetheless, more blacks graduated from high school and college. And employment opportunities expanded as more blacks became policemen, politicians, and professors. More blacks also moved to middle-class suburban neighborhoods, sent their children to summer camp and college, took family vacations, and participated fully in the material prosperity of American life. The legacy of the past remained for many, however, and particularly for blacks living in inner city neighborhoods. Many schools remained segregated in fact if not in law, since school districts followed neighborhood lines. Those neighborhoods often also remained racially separate, especially as whites fled from city to suburb in Indianapolis, Gary, and elsewhere. Federal court–ordered busing of children to achieve racial balance addressed the problem of de facto segregation in the 1970s and 1980s without fully solving it and even produced in 1983 the horrible spectacle of a burning cross at a suburban Marion County high school. Nor did the large amounts of federal money to cities, especially to Mayor Hatcher's Gary in the late 1960s, bring the full benefits anticipated. Indeed, on every indicator of the quality of life black Hoosiers lagged behind whites. Perhaps most poignant and tragic was the infant mortality rate, which declined substantially in the twentieth century but which in 1980 still stood at an appalling 23.4 deaths per 1,000 births for black babies compared to 10.5 for white infants. Despite the evidence of progress and of genuine goodwill the revolution that promised equality for all Hoosiers and all Americans was still to come.

The Continuing Challenges of Public School Reform

Indiana schools have never been static institutions. Often, in fact, they have been at the center of change and conflict in the social, political, and economic history of the state. Since the time of Caleb Mills and his reform-minded colleagues of the 1840s there have been Hoosiers dissatisfied with public education. Despite the progress made in the late nineteenth century, twentieth-century critics found considerable reason to argue for change and improvement. The years since 1920 have been marked by three periods of unusually intense interest in public education: the early 1920s; the late 1950s and early 1960s; and the early 1980s. The programs of reform varied in detail, but there was large continuity in basic objectives and even in specific proposals.

One element of continuity was concern over differences in schooling in rural areas compared to cities, differences usually portrayed by reformers as a lag in rural schooling. The burst of reform activity in the early 1920s produced one of the most comprehensive studies of state education ever undertaken, with the problems of rural schools given priority. Sponsored and organized by John D. Rockefeller's General Education Board, this survey united outside experts and Hoosier school professionals in a campaign to lift rural schools to a level closer to those in town. The published report, *Public Education in Indiana*, identified and analyzed shortcomings that would dominate school politics for the first three quarters of the century. The major shortcoming of Indiana public education, according to the report, was the large number of one-room, one-teacher schools, which in 1920 were the core of Hoosier education. School reformers found these schools inadequately staffed, with teachers handicapped by low pay, no tenure, little sense of professionalism, and insufficient education

An abandoned one-room schoolhouse in Clinton County. (Indiana State
Library)

themselves. Only 7 percent of rural elementary teachers in 1921 had
a high school degree and two years of teacher training. One-room
school buildings were often dilapidated, and their outdoor toilets particularly offensive. School terms were short, generally of only 160 days
or less.[17]

Presiding over this sorry state of affairs was the township trustee.
The trustee had almost unchallenged authority to hire and fire teachers, decide on curriculum, select books, and purchase supplies. Often
he was politically ambitious. Seldom was he attuned to main currents
of professional education. More important to him and much of his
constituency, the trustee could claim that the people of the township
got what they wanted and what they could afford in their schools
because the trustee was democratically elected and because local taxes
provided almost all school revenue. Many trustees and citizens argued
that this local administration and financing represented the best of
home rule and democratic traditions in Indiana.

School reformers thought otherwise. They concentrated their scorn
and proposals for change on the rural schools generally and the township trustee specifically. Their primary goal in the 1920s became to

eliminate entirely the trustees' authority in education and to abolish
the township as the unit of administration and finance. In place of
the township the reformers proposed the county as the primary unit
of school administration and financing. A county unit bill, which com-
pelled schools to consolidate and reorganize along county lines, became one of the most controversial issues in the 1923 General Assembly. Proponents argued that it would lift up rural schools to a level
commensurate with urban schools and bring efficiency, lower costs,
and professionalism to Indiana's education system. They also hoped,
though less publicly, that the county unit would advance processes of
centralization and standardization in schooling by enabling the state
more readily to set and enforce uniform standards, particularly by
eliminating the trustee and much of the local control he represented.[18]

The 1923 county unit bill sparked large opposition. Rural Hoosiers
were not fooled about the objectives of professional, urban-oriented
educators. The editor of the *Winchester Democrat* vented the feelings
of many:

> Now comes the theorists and reformers, led by the well paid experts
> from the East and the self-appointed prophets from the state university
> and Purdue, ably re-enforced by the school book drafters and cheered
> on by the politicians with a mania for centralization. . . . The taxpayer
> has his belly full of centralized government. The trustees are partic-
> ularly precious, for they represent the last vestige of the fading right
> of the voter to have a personal hand in the management of local
> affairs.[19]

With the Indiana Farm Bureau and the township trustees leading the
opposition and with strong support from rural Democrats, the 1923
state legislature voted down the county unit bill. Similar proposals
later met similar fates. Despite continued pressure from professional
educators, Hoosiers made clear their determination to run their own
schools.[20]

By the late 1950s, however, attachments to locally financed and
administered schools seemed less persuasive. The same arguments
were made, including always the assertion that local township schools
were anchors and symbols of community, expressed most vividly in
the attachment to the basketball team. But variations in the quality of
education became ever more apparent, with city schools offering
wider curricula, more experienced and better educated teachers,

more modern school buildings, football teams, and marching bands as well. Many rural townships lagged far behind and struggled to maintain the minimum standards, even with increased state aid beginning in the 1930s. And the Russian launching of the Sputnik satellite and the general anxiety over American education reached to the most tradition-bound rural communities. After decades of debate the General Assembly passed in 1959 the School Reorganization Act, one of the most significant pieces of legislation in twentieth-century Indiana.

The purpose of the School Reorganization Act of 1959 was to consolidate the many small township schools into a few large consolidated schools, administered and financed on a countywide basis. The act established a State Commission for the Reorganization of School Corporations to oversee the process and set standards. Each new school corporation had to have a minimum of 1,000 students in average daily attendance and a tax base of at least $5,000 of adjusted assessed valuation per pupil. In response to Hoosier traditions, there was considerable leeway for local decision-making: a citizens' school reorganization committee in each county proposed the boundaries and structure of the new corporation for that county. The state commission held public hearings and approved the final proposal, after which voters in each new corporation accepted or rejected the plan. The procedures for local participation generated considerable public discussion and debate. Seldom were the glories of grass-roots democracy so proudly displayed, and seldom were its propensities for producing conflict and frustration so fully vented. The process dragged on for a decade, with some corporations quickly and easily created and others painfully, incompletely, and sometimes irrationally formed. Many covered only part of a county. By 1968, however, the number of school corporations had declined from 939 to 382, and more than 90 percent of Indiana students attended consolidated schools. Nearly everywhere the township trustee was gone from school administration, and rural one-room schools joined train stations, wooden barns, and windmills as abandoned relics of the countryside. Basketball trophies engraved with the name of a community now sat forlornly in a new school known as North Central or Eastern or some other innocuous, no-place name.[21]

Large, consolidated school corporations run by professional ad-

ministrators allowed more direction and centralization from Indianapolis. This process of increased state control had begun in the nineteenth century and continued in the twentieth. In the 1920s the state
began to set specific standards for teacher training and to require
state-issued teacher licenses. The 1927 legislature passed a teacher
tenure law. And professional educators began to exert more control
over the content of the curriculum, pushing for new courses in manual
arts, home economics, and civics in the 1920s and 1930s, sociology in
the 1960s, global studies in the 1970s, and computer proficiency in
the 1980s. Accompanying increased state control was growth in state
financing. Prior to 1933 the state provided less than 10 percent of
school revenues, with over 90 percent derived from local property
and poll taxes. The Depression forced a change, made possible by the
state gross income tax of 1933, which increased the state share of
revenue to 30 percent. The state share remained at about one third
and the local share two thirds until 1973. Then the property tax freeze
prompted an increase in state financing that reversed the proportions,
with the state contributing about two thirds and the local share at one
third by the end of the 1970s. Federal aid to education increased also,
enough to stir the anti-Washington passions of conservative politicians
like William Jenner in the 1950s, but federal support remained in the
early 1980s at less than 4 percent of all school revenues.[22]

The changes that accompanied school consolidation were among
the most momentous of the twentieth century. Almost entirely a local
responsibility at the beginning of the century, public education by the
late twentieth century was primarily the responsibility of the state
government—its most costly responsibility and its most important.
Schools at times, especially with the consolidations of the 1960s and
the flurry of standards-setting in the early 1980s, seemed more like
the branch plants of large corporations, run by distant professional
managers, who oversaw hierarchical structures and assembly line procedures designed to turn out a homogeneous product of moderate
quality in high volume and low cost. The intimate, organic relationship
between school and community became more formal and structured.
Local influence remained, of course, usually through elected school
boards and more informal community mores and pressures: certainly
not all schools in Indiana were alike in style or substance. Hoosiers
often waxed romantic over the lost world of the one-room school, but

they too often discounted its many real shortcomings and failed to appreciate the large if mixed benefits of the modern, consolidated school.

School consolidation and increased state aid and control did not eliminate variations among Indiana schools, not even the lag in poorer rural school corporations. But these problems seemed less pressing in the late twentieth century than issues relating to the quality of education offered and attained by Hoosiers generally. In many ways it appeared that Indiana was lagging behind other states. Particularly controversial was Indiana's low ranking among the states in per pupil expenditures for education. That ranking was especially low when compared to the state's per capita personal income. At issue here, in part, was the continuing traditional aversion to taxation and government expenditures, exacerbated by the property tax freeze of 1973. Not only was Indiana not spending as much on education as it could or should, many argued, but Hoosiers were not achieving the level of education that they needed to compete in the modern world and were in fact falling behind. Though ever-larger percentages of young people were graduating from high school and college the proportions of formally educated adults did not grow as rapidly as in the nation as a whole. The lag was particularly significant in regard to college graduates. By 1980 the state ranked forty-seventh in percent of population with four or more years of college. Part of the cause was doubtless a migration from the state of young, highly educated Hoosiers—a "brain drain," which was likely the consequence of less attractive career opportunities in the state. And there was also the unhappy possibility that many Indianans, like their pioneer forebears, continued to be unenthusiastic about the benefits of formal education.[23]

Although Indiana lagged generally in public education there were many examples of high achievement. Within the state there were schools, teachers, and students that were among the best in the nation. The state public universities achieved large respectability in the post–World War II years. Particularly was this true of Purdue University under the leadership of Frederick L. Hovde and Indiana University under Herman B Wells, both of which became institutions of national and international excellence. And Ball State, Indiana State, and Vincennes universities helped extend the advantages of college education to a growing percentage of Indiana youth, joined in 1985 by the

University of Southern Indiana. Although the Indiana Vocational Technical College (Ivy Tech) was not authorized until 1963 the state eventually built a good system of technical education. With the intent of planning for and coordinating this diverse system of state-supported post-secondary education the legislature in 1971 created the Indiana Commission for Higher Education.[24]

There were many educational achievements that were sources of pride, and it would be very misleading to conclude that Indiana was uniformly backward in the area of education. But it was the case that the record of achievement was not as full and extensive as it should have been.

Basketball and Other Forms of Leisure and Culture

Ever larger numbers of Hoosiers had ever more time for leisure activities. Length of the work week declined and paid vacations, nearly unknown to factory workers in the 1920s, became in the post–World War II era an ordinary part of the package of fringe benefits. And perhaps because families no longer worked together and because so many families included two working parents, more attention was paid to formal leisure and recreation. Such activities ranged from the annual auto vacation trip, which first began among middle-class families in the 1920s, to family night at the local drive-in theater in the 1950s, to family membership in an exercise club in the 1980s.

Accompanying the growing importance of leisure was a national homogenization and formal organization of leisure pursuits. Sporting, cultural, and recreational activities became more organized, often with forms and objectives similar to those of big business. Local and regional distinctions diminished as Hoosiers spent leisure time in the same ways as did the people of Maine, California, or Alabama. The homogenization and nationalization of newspapers, film, radio, and television played a large role in this process, bringing mass entertainment and information to all Americans. Local heroes gave way to Babe Ruth, Jack Dempsey, and Tom Mix, while club and church meetings, neighborly chats on the front porch, and many small-town newspapers fell before the magnetic power of the radio and later the television. By the 1970s the median television viewing time of Muncie's residents

Basketball in a Nashville alley, photographed by Frank Hohenberger.
(Lilly Library, Indiana University)

was twenty-eight hours a week, and almost all of it was national pro-
gramming. There was still state and local content in newspapers and
on radio and television, but the development of mass media in the
twentieth century doubtless isolated and distanced people from their
own immediate community while it brought the nation and the world
closer.

Trends toward formal organization and national homogenization
of leisure and culture were not omnivorous, however. Even here there
was room for pluralism and diversity and for Hoosiers to maintain
distinctive twists and turns in the ways in which they played or relaxed.
One kind of leisure activity to which Indianans remained more fervently attached than most Americans was basketball.

Basketball was well underway to its first-place rank in popularity
by the turn of the century but flowered to "Hoosier Hysteria" in the
1920s. By that time high schools were building gymnasiums that held

more spectators than there were residents in the town. Martinsville, Muncie, and Vincennes boasted gyms that packed more than five thousand spectators on the bleachers, all calling out the names of the players and shouting the team cheers in bursts of community pride and identification. High school basketball was especially important to the small towns and rural townships. Because it required relatively few players and because skills could be developed with only a ball and a hoop above a barn or garage door, every school had the chance to compete. Rather than classifying schools by enrollment as most states did, the elaborate state tournament was open to all schools, regardless of size. First played in 1911, the state tournament was the climax of each season. Everywhere from December through March Hoosiers talked about basketball: the tales and arguments most often centered on the small-town teams that emerged as the very best in the state, particularly Franklin's "Wonder Five," which won an unmatched three straight state championships in 1920, 1921, and 1922, and Milan, which upset Muncie Central in 1954. With an enrollment of 162 students and no player taller than six foot two, "tiny Milan" became the state champions after the most famous shot in Indiana basketball—Bobby Plump's fifteen-foot jumper in the last seconds. Fans not yet born in 1954 included that game and shot among their active basketball lore a quarter century later.

Basketball often seemed a fairy-tale sport with a timeless form and ritual that created shared emotions and bound individuals in a community that seemed to transcend everyday life. But it was also a sport subject to influences and changes outside the gym. School consolidation, especially the consolidations of the 1950s and 1960s, created conflict and diminished community solidarity by closing small schools and obliterating their records, uniforms, and cheers. Most of the tiny Milans disappeared. For much of the twentieth century the sport was largely the privilege only of white boys. Blacks played for a few teams before World War II but often faced barriers that limited their freedom to accompany their teammates into restaurants on trips. And the Indiana High School Athletic Association (IHSAA), which was formed in 1903 to oversee student athletics, did not allow the state's all-black high schools, including Crispus Attucks in Indianapolis and Roosevelt in Gary, to join the association or participate in the state tournament. Nor were Catholic schools allowed to participate. In 1941 these re-

strictions were at last removed, though other schools remained reluctant to schedule all-black schools. Change came with time and with
the marvelous teams assembled at Crispus Attucks, which won the
state championship in 1955 and 1956, and which featured the best
player in the history of Indiana basketball, Oscar Robertson. Girls'
basketball was played in the 1920s but did not develop fully until the
1970s. The pressure of the federal government combined with a sense
of fairness and changing attitudes about women to force schools to
expand basketball along with other athletic opportunities for girls.
The first girls' state tournament was played in 1976. The world beyond the gym also brought criticism that student athletics and particularly basketball placed too much pressure on young people and
detracted from the primacy of academic programs. Each generation
of Hoosiers debated this issue, but basketball endured as the state
sport if not religion. The popular success of the sport in universities,
from the University of Evansville to Indiana University, and the move
of a professional team to Indianapolis in 1967 only added to the
identification.[25]

Basketball was the favorite but not the only sport played and
watched in Indiana. There was hardly an American sport not represented in the state, with football doubtless second to basketball in
popularity, especially at the University of Notre Dame, where Coach
Knute Rockne began in the 1920s a tradition of fielding nationally
ranked teams. Other sports developed also, including baseball, tennis,
bicycling, and soccer. Indianapolis in the 1970s began a campaign to
become the nation's amateur sports capital, attracting several sports
organizations' headquarters to the city. But the event most commonly
identified with the capital city was the Indianapolis 500-mile race, first
run in 1911. Originally designed to promote automobiles, the race
retained a dominant commercial purpose. It offered large prize moneys and attracted 300,000 spectators, giving claim to be "the greatest
spectacle in racing." But the 500 did not affect most Hoosiers as in-
timately or completely as basketball.

Another leisure development in which Indianans took particular
pride was the state park. A fortunate combination of circumstances
led to the creation of one of the nation's best state park systems.
Progressive-era interest in natural preservation and the state centennial celebration in 1916 sparked acquisition of McCormick's Creek

THE SEASON OF WEEKEND PROBLEMS

The new state parks and family decisions, as depicted
by Charles Kuhn, 1925. (Lilly Library, Indiana
University)

and Turkey Run parks and, in 1919, led to creation of the Indiana
Department of Conservation. The prime mover in this enterprise was
Richard Lieber, a German-born Indianapolis businessman who
preached that state parks were an "antidote for our social ills caused
by industry."[26] Under Lieber's energetic direction the Department of
Conservation added other state parks in the 1920s, extending from
Clifty Falls to Pokagon, and also took responsibility for state memorials, including the Corydon state capitol, the Lanier home in Madison,
and the territorial capitol at Vincennes. Depression-era federal aid,
particularly through the Civilian Conservation Corps, added to these
outdoor facilities. An unhappy combination of circumstances, includ-

ing political patronage, combined to cause deterioration of the parks in the mid-twentieth century, but state leaders and the Department of Natural Resources in the 1970s wisely began a renewal that led once again to a state park system of which Hoosiers could be proud. The Department of Natural Resources also began to build a genuine state museum, moving it from the basement of the State House in 1967 to the renovated former Indianapolis City Hall. By the 1980s the museum was well on the way to becoming a first-class showcase for exploring Indiana history and culture.[27] The state museum, parks, and memorials were among the most important expressions of Indiana's distinctive heritage, particularly in showing in the best light notable features of pioneer life. For the sensitive visitor they helped define the meaning of being a Hoosier.

Another form of leisure and culture especially important to Indianans was literature. In the late nineteenth and early twentieth centuries the state developed an unusual reputation as the home of popular authors. This Golden Age of Literature produced works that spoke to rural, agrarian, individualistic, and romantic strains in the Indiana tradition. Some of the most important writers lived into the interwar years and beyond, most notably Booth Tarkington. But by then their work seemed to be an afterglow; the maincurrents of American literature were beginning to flow toward more realistic fiction. Theodore Dreiser was Indiana's best contributor to this new style, but his popularity in Indiana prior to mid-century was limited. The fading light of the Golden Age did not bring forth a new, dominant school or style. But Indiana continued to produce writers of large popularity and talent after World War II, ranging from Jessamyn West to Kurt Vonnegut, Jr., from Ross Lockridge, Jr., to Jean Shepherd to Dan Wakefield. These and many others often drew on Indiana settings, personalities, and attitudes as part of their work.[28] And interest in the state's writers and literary traditions continued with publication of anthologies and a major biographical project in the 1970s and 1980s.[29]

Writers of nonfiction also contributed to defining the state's character and providing reading for its citizens. Interest in prehistoric archaeology spurred Indianapolis businessman and philanthropist Eli Lilly to produce respectable publications of his own as well as supporting the field work and writing of archaeologist Glenn Black. State history matured with Logan Esarey in the early twentieth century and, after World War II, with John D. Barnhart, R. C. Buley, William E. Wilson, and Donald F. Carmony: Indiana University supported their teaching and writing and also the publication of the quarterly *Indiana Magazine of History*. Especially important in broadening and deepening knowledge of and interest in the state's past was the Indiana Historical Society, which has long been among the best state societies in the nation, and, after a major bequest from Eli Lilly in 1977, also one of the most active. The state-funded Indiana Historical Bureau, with considerably smaller financial resources, has nevertheless continued to make important contributions to understanding the state's past.[30]

Readers of nonfiction and fiction benefited from the expansion of libraries in twentieth-century Indiana. The gifts of steelmaker Andrew Carnegie enabled many Indiana towns to construct handsome library buildings, while public donations, tax support, volunteer workers, and often a dedicated professional librarian combined to provide books and services to children and adults. By 1930 almost every town of more than 2,500 people boasted a public library. Seldom funded as fully as they deserved and often outgrowing their Carnegie buildings in the post–World War II years, Indiana's libraries were nonetheless among the most valuable jewels in the state's literary and cultural treasury.

Indiana's music and art reflected main trends of the twentieth century. As with literature there was in painting a large interest in the romantic and sentimental, particularly in landscapes of rural Indiana. The influence of the "Hoosier Group" continued into the interwar years and beyond, especially as it emanated from artists in Brown County, led by Theodore C. Steele, and from the exhibits of the Hoosier Salon. More diverse forms developed in Indianapolis at the John Herron Art Institute and at the Herron Museum, opened in 1906. The museum evolved to become the Indianapolis Museum of Art and moved to beautiful new quarters in 1970. Modern architecture made tentative appearances in several Indiana cities, often in the monotonous form of the glass and steel office building. Unique was the proliferation of new styles in Columbus, where the imagination and financial support of industrialist J. Irwin Miller helped create an architectural showcase of public buildings. Columbus and many other towns also began in the 1960s and 1970s to show interest in preserving

Wes Montgomery. (*Indianapolis Recorder* Collection, Indiana Historical Society)

older buildings of historical and architectural interest. Madison was particularly successful in preserving its rich antebellum architecture. Growing state and federal government interest in historic preservation and the work of the privately supported Historic Landmarks Foundation, organized in 1960, spurred wider interest and support in an area formerly the burden and pleasure of only a few dedicated preservationists.[31]

Music in the state ranged from the flowering and fading of ragtime in the first decades of the century to the beginning in the 1930s of the Indianapolis Symphony's evolution to a major orchestra to the emergence to national excellence of Indiana University's School of Music after World War II. Jazz was especially popular as it developed in the black clubs and theaters on Indiana Avenue in Indianapolis. Black Indianapolis musicians from Noble Sissle in the 1920s to Wes Montgomery in the 1950s made significant contributions to this distinctly American music form. Even more popular, though perhaps not as innovative, was the music of Hoagy Carmichael. He and other white musicians produced music that especially appealed to the young people who in the interwar years flocked to new dance halls and pavilions, sparking a trend of youth, music, and dancing that would endure with only superficial change into the late twentieth century.[32]

Music, art, literature, and humanistic learning received important patronage through increased private and public funding in the post–World War II era. Art galleries, history museums, orchestras, and theater organizations emerged in many Indiana towns. Nearly always struggling to survive, they offered cultural opportunities that often reflected state and local themes and interests as well as introducing more cosmopolitian ideas to their communities. Important to many local endeavors were the Indiana Arts Commission and the Indiana Committee for the Humanities. These agencies combined federal financial support and guidance with state and local public and private aid to encourage wider access to arts and humanities programs.

The nationalization of culture and the changing patterns of work and play often made the countless new forms of sport, leisure, and culture seem centuries removed from pioneer logrollings and quilting bees. And yet at street festivals, town softball games, county fairs, and family reunions there were opportunities for community interaction and recreation not radically different from those enjoyed by pioneers. Even basketball seemed in many ways not so far removed from a pioneer shooting match. The pleasure of competition, the identification between audience and contestants, and the feeling of spectacle were simple but powerful in both.

The Economy since 1920

Hoosiers by 1920 had experienced fundamental economic change in agriculture, manufacturing, and other areas of the economy. The transformations underway in the late nineteenth century not only continued after 1920 but became nearly omnipresent, greatly affecting the manner in which all earned their living. But economic change was not steady, uniform, or one-directional. Some individuals and groups benefited more than others; some flourished while others merely survived. And some years were good and others less so. Above all, there was the Great Depression of the 1930s to shock Hoosiers into uncertainity about their assumptions of economic progress. And by the 1980s there were diverse signs of structural change in the state and national economy that also caused anxiety and confusion. Throughout, Hoosiers came to realize the large and expanding degree to which national and international forces shaped their economic lives. Depression and world war, federal government regulation, international trade, big business, powerful labor unions—all served as reminders that Indiana was an integral part of a nation and world that could both expand and restrict opportunity, freedom, and material well-being.[1]

Agriculture and Farm Life

Indiana had more farmers than ever at the beginning of the twentieth century, but they were a declining percentage of the workforce and would soon decrease in absolute numbers as well. The total number of Indiana farms, which had more than doubled in the last half of the nineteenth century, declined by over half in the twentieth century. By 1980 there were only 88,000 farms in the state, fewer than in 1850. Accompanying the drop in the number of farms was an increase in average farm size from 103 acres in 1920 to 193 in 1980. These fewer but larger farms produced ever-increasing quantities of crops and livestock. In terms of output certainly, twentieth-century Indiana agriculture was a story of unparalleled success, so much so that the farm problem came to be the problem of producing too much food. By the 1980s Indiana farmers were averaging corn yields of more than 100 bushels an acre, compared to less than 40 bushels before World War I. The changes in agriculture since 1920 were not immediately beneficial to all farmers, however, and included experiences and periods of hardship and conflict for most.

Fundamental change in agriculture came partly from the application of science and technology to farming. Mechanization was underway in the nineteenth century, but the twentieth century brought rapid change. Most important was the tractor, which best symbolized modern agriculture. The percentage of farms with tractors increased from 4 percent in 1920 to 22 percent in 1930 to 37 percent in 1940. By 1950 farm horses had virtually disappeared. The power and flexibility of tractors allowed development of new machinery to plant, cultivate, and harvest crops. The corn picker and grain combine were perhaps most important. They brought an end to the long, lonely days spent husking corn by hand and the more social but hot and

Demonstration of a new plow and tractor. (Indiana State Library)

dusty days of hauling wheat to the steam threshing machine.[2] The mechanical corn picker and grain combine were among a wide range of new machines that reduced the strain of physical labor and allowed farm workers to perform tasks more quickly and efficiently. Electrification, begun in the 1930s, brought further savings in machinery that milked cows, fed hogs, gathered eggs and dried corn. Less and less manpower was needed to harvest a bushel of corn, produce a hundredweight of hog, or milk a herd of cows.

Farmers also increased productivity by application of scientific agriculture and innovative methods of farming. Most dramatic was hybrid corn seed. Introduced in 1937, it quickly showed great superiority in yields and in resistance to disease and insects. Farmers also began to increase use of commercial fertilizer in order to offset deteriorating soil productivity and to allow for planting the same crop (often corn) year after year in the same fields. And they used more chemical herbicides and insecticides to increase output and reduce the need for crop cultivation: many farmers in the 1970s began to use the no-till method of planting, substituting chemicals for the task of plowing. And they adopted new breeds of livestock and new treatments for animal diseases. Indiana farmers also began to devote increased acreage to soybeans, especially after World War II. This new crop proved a highly nutritious animal food and joined corn as a big money crop in Indiana.

The scientific and technological transformations on Indiana farms derived in large part from the work of agricultural scientists and economists in government employment, especially at Purdue University. Purdue experts developed and aggressively disseminated new approaches to farming through on-campus teaching and the work of the Agricultural Experiment Station, the agriculture extension service, and the county agricultural agent program. Purdue farm expert Earl Butz could boast by mid-century that "Brainpower has replaced horsepower as the central ingredient on our farms."[3] By the 1980s agricultural research included analysis of photographs of fields taken from a satellite 450 miles above the earth. All these activities were largely dependent on state and federal government financial support.

To the pride of many and the regret of some, the successful farmer became by the late twentieth century a "book farmer" and a businessman. He spent long hours at a desk figuring farm accounts, using paper and pencil in the 1930s, an adding machine in the 1960s, and a personal computer in the 1980s. He worried about interest rates and the ever-increasing capital investment necessary to compete, which required ever-larger ties to banks. He depended on detailed and long-term weather forecasts, on oil prices set thousands of miles away from his farm, on sometimes fickle changes in consumer tastes, and on good and bad harvests in Russia and Argentina. He was part of a complex of enterprises that produced and distributed food, sometimes labeled agribusiness, and part also of the modern global economy.[4]

Indiana farmers also became a more formal and distinctive part of the political order. Farm discontent had earlier produced the short-lived Grange and Populist movements but did not lead to an enduring or effective farm organization. The formation of the Indiana Farm Bureau in 1919, with nearly 60,000 members by 1945, gave farmers a large and organized voice. The Farm Bureau formed cooperative associations that provided a variety of economic services, but its most important activity was to argue agriculture's case in state and federal government. By mid-century it was among Indiana's most powerful political organizations. A second farm organization appeared in Indiana in the mid-1950s in the National Farmers Organization. The NFO employed methods similar to those of labor organizations, including withholding products from markets, but it did not achieve the large support of the more moderate Farm Bureau.

Government became increasingly important to farmers, especially federal government. The New Deal brought a variety of programs to raise prices by limiting production, achieved by paying benefits to farmers for not growing corn or raising hogs. These federal programs continued and expanded after World War II, doubtless to the benefit of many individual farmers.

The years since 1920 included periods of serious economic hardship for many farmers. The 1920s and 1930s were economically frustrating for even the best farmers. World War II and the postwar years brought significant improvement, along with some years of low prices and bad harvests. But the changes in agriculture that brought prosperity to some forced an end to farming for many others. Most of the productive changes of twentieth-century agriculture were more likely to benefit those with large farms and those whose farms were located on the flat, fertile areas of central and northern Indiana. Small farmers and those who farmed the hilly, less fertile land of southern Indiana were less able to buy or use corn pickers in the 1930s or computers in the 1980s, or the many other components of modern agriculture. Indeed, many such farms became marginally profitable at best, kept going only because one or more members of the family had a job off the farm. Some survived by specializing in chickens, strawberries, or tobacco. Many eventually gave up and abandoned the farm for work in town. Large parts of southern Indiana were converted from farmland to state and national forests and parks, or simply abandoned. Thousands of farm people, especially those in their late teens and twenties, moved to towns and cities. This rural to urban migration reversed temporarily in the 1930s, when the Depression forced many Hoosiers back to the land, but resumed with World War II and postwar prosperity. By the 1970s there was another shift, with significant population movement underway from urban to rural Indiana, but most of these migrants were not farmers, and rural Indiana was no longer very rural.

The large farm to city migration of the first half of the twentieth century was the clearest evidence of the perceived lag in rural living conditions. It was not only low farm prices that pushed Hoosiers off farms, but also a belief that life in town was better, that rural life lagged behind urban life. Everywhere there was evidence of this lag; and increasingly, it seemed, the gap widened. Running water, indoor toilets, central heating, and electricity were standard features of town life long before they appeared on farms. On the eve of World War II, for example, when 98 percent of urban homes had electricity, only half of the state's farms did. Rural Hoosiers would later recall cooking on a wood stove, carrying water, taking Saturday night baths in the kitchen, walking the path to the two-seater behind the house, and doing the chores of spring housecleaning with only slight nostalgia and with much keener memories of the hard work.[5] In addition to the fact of hard work, there were rural schools and churches that appeared shabby and forlorn compared to their urban counterparts, while opportunities for leisure, recreation, and culture seemed to be more exciting and more abundant in cities. Young people were especially influenced by these attractions and moved to town. By 1930 34 percent of the urban population was between the ages of twenty and thirty-nine, while in rural Indiana only 24 percent of the population was in this young adult category.

Post–1945 affluence and technology narrowed the gap between farm and city as television, telephones, cars, improved roads, and consolidated schools brought many of the enticing urban features within reach of rural Indiana. Indeed, many Hoosiers concluded they could have the best of both worlds by living in the country and working in the city. By the late twentieth century conflict between rural and urban Indiana seemed less sharp and the blending and merging more as it had been in the pioneer era.

In the years since 1920 the farmer became a businessman and rural Indiana became less distinguishable from urban Indiana. The consequences of these changes may be as momentous as the closing of Indiana's frontier or the passing of the pioneer era. Late twentieth century farmers might still enjoy the thought of soil under their feet, and rural Hoosiers might proclaim the pleasures of their bucolic independence and rustic isolation, but such claims were often made while seated in an air-conditioned tractor cab or in front of a television set.

The Automobile Age

Transportation changed significantly in the years since World War I. New forms of transport increased the speed and efficiency of movement of people and goods, reshaped the landscape of town and country, and introduced new requirements in government taxation, regulation, and investment.

What the railroad was to the nineteenth century the automobile was to the twentieth. Not only did the car permanently alter ways of travel but it affected a multiplicity of social arrangements, creating a society in which automobile ownership became almost a necessity for economic and social well-being. Pioneer inventor and entrepreneur Elwood Haynes drove his first horseless carriage along the Pumpkinvine Pike near Kokomo in 1894, but only slowly did Hoosiers join him in enthusiasm for the new vehicle. In the 1920s, however, auto sales skyrocketed; by the end of that decade there was one car for every four Hoosiers. Even the depths of the Great Depression did not greatly reduce auto registrations, and annual motor fuel consumption never fell below pre-Depression levels and increased rapidly in the late 1930s. World War II brought rationing of gasoline and tires and a stop to the production of new models, but peace quickly reestablished the attachment to the car. Convenience, flexibility, and pride of ownership, which often involved a perceived rise in status, greatly increased sales in the affluent postwar decades and eventually produced many two-car families. Sunday drives and other forms of leisure combined with expanded educational and employment access to give car owners a new freedom and independence. In the 1950s and 1960s suburbs sprang up around every town and city, and huge shopping centers and long shopping strips appeared with homogeneous regularity. The car made the Indiana landscape look like all of America.

Technology that was as pervasive and inclusive as the automobile surely brought new problems and challenges. Early twentieth century Hoosiers feared the car would destroy traditional morality, bringing about an abandonment of Sabbath observance and too much freedom for young people. Some feared dangerous and wasteful joy-riding or even backseat sex—"a house of prostitution on wheels," a Muncie judge charged in the 1920s. Gradually Hoosiers began to perceive other problems as well: traffic congestion, air pollution, highway fatalities, a decline of inner city retailing and housing, and expensive road construction and maintainence—all suggesting that the automobile was a mixed blessing.[6]

Highway construction was one of the first and most important consequences of expanding automobile ownership. County and township governments had traditionally been responsible for roads, but the auto required a more systematic, professional, and centralized approach. In 1919 the General Assembly created the Indiana State Highway Commission, which assumed responsibility from local governments for a 3,200-mile network of state roads. Road paving moved rapidly forward, though never as quickly as most motorists wished. Costs of the new highway system were met by user fees, particularly a state gasoline tax begun in 1923, and by federal aid, which began in 1920 and by 1924 provided one fourth of total Highway Commission revenue. In addition, the New Deal public works programs significantly augmented highway construction and maintenance so that the Depression brought improvement rather than deterioration of Indiana's roads. A new level of federal aid began with the interstate highway program, which in 1956 designated 1,115 miles of four-lane highway for Indiana. By the mid-1970s twelve interstate highways crossed the state, providing Indianapolis with especially superior facilities. The Indiana toll road across northern Indiana was built in the 1950s. Despite this highway network some boosters of economic development argued by the 1980s that the state needed to make even larger investments in maintaining and expanding the highway system, especially in southern Indiana.

The construction and maintenance of roads for an ever increasing volume of traffic brought large challenges and considerable conflict. Spurred by the federal government, Indiana generally avoided the selfish if democratic localism of the pioneer era in order to concentrate resources on main, arterial highways. And while rural and urban legislators often quarrelled bitterly over location and funding of highways, the state assumed increased responsibility for country roads, eliminating the township government entirely and assuming some of the county govenment's functions. Here state government moved earlier and more quickly in the direction of centralization than in many other areas.

The large sums of money necessary for highway work provided

Travel near Kendallville, spring,
1920, just before the state highway
department took charge of maintenance. (Indiana State
Library)

opportunities for abuse. Political patronage thrived in the Highway Commission, from road workers through engineers to superintendents. And the use of private contractors allowed considerable opportunity for political favoritism to overshadow consistently efficient business arrangements. The highway scandal of the 1950s, which resulted in more than half a dozen convictions, was the major example of political misuse of public funds.

At the same time that the automobile and highways were increasing in importance, rail transportation was on the decline. Passenger and freight traffic began to shift to cars, trucks, and buses in the 1920s, while the Depresssion forced track abandonment and for some companies, including the Monon, bankruptcy. The Monon recovered briefly after the war but canceled passenger service in 1967 and was swallowed up in the ensuing wave of railroad mergers and consolidations, becoming part of the Louisville & Nashville system in 1971. By the 1970s passenger train travel in Indiana was very limited, and one-time architectural monuments to the passenger train, such as the Indianapolis Union Station, were abandoned shells or had become objects of "adaptive reuse." Many small towns also lost freight service; more than 1,600 miles of track were abandoned in the late 1970s and early 1980s. The state joined federal government efforts in the 1970s to rationalize these changes and to mitigate the effects of railroad decline on Indiana's economic development. Freight trains remained significant components of Indiana's transportation system in the late twentieth century, but motor trucks and the highway system were more important. In the 1980s both forms of transport were in flux as a consequence of federal government deregulation as well as cyclical changes in the economy.[7]

As the railroad declined another form of transportation essential to the nineteenth century began to revive, often along familiar patterns. With considerable government aid water transport improved significantly on the Ohio River and Lake Michigan. The St. Lawrence Seaway opened in the late 1950s, and the state constructed a new Lake Michigan port at Burns Harbor, opened in 1970, to allow improved access to the Great Lakes, the northeastern United States, and world markets. Southern Indiana benefited from improvements in Ohio River navigation as a result of federal construction of a system of locks and dams and state construction of the Southwind Maritime

Center, opened at Mt. Vernon in 1979, and the Clark Maritime Center, opened in 1985. There was even in the post–World War II years some revived interest in building a water route from Lake Erie to the Ohio, although no new Wabash and Erie Canal developed.

Air transportation began in the 1920s and was spurred by federal airmail contracts and New Deal funds for airport construction. Major trunk lines operated in Indiana by the 1930s. By the 1960s every city considered air transport an essential component in its economic well-being and struggled to maintain and expand its service.

The importance of transportation to the public interest, the difficulties of unrestrained competition among private transport companies, and rapid technological and economic change brought significant state and federal government regulation and aid in the twentieth century. The Indiana Public Service Commission was established in 1913 and had responsibility for safety, rate changes, and line abandonments for intrastate rail traffic. In 1925 the commission also assumed regulatory responsibility for buses and trucks. But state regulation of common carriers proved constitutionally and practically difficult, and the federal government soon became the dominant regulator. In the important area of automobile licensing and highway traffic control, however, the state did remain dominant. Indiana's Automobile Regulation Act of 1925 established uniform speed limits and rules of the road. In 1929 the state required a driver's license along with vehicle registration. Licensing provided new opportunities for controlling driver behavior and safety. Automobiles also permitted the expansion of political patronage through the scores of license branch offices staffed by political appointees. And formation of the Indiana State Police in 1921, with primary responsibility for highway safety, initiated a centralization of law enforcement at the state level to match the centralization of highway administration. Not until the late 1930s did the state police begin to develop efficient methods of fighting crime, spurred by the embarrassing success of John Dillinger's daring bank robberies.

Twentieth-century transportation changes moved Hoosiers far from the pioneer era with its flatboats and muddy horseback rides. Physical distance, which so limited the range and nature of economic and social activity in the early nineteenth century, often seemed nearly inconsequential by the late twentieth century. Rural Hoosiers drove to town on Saturday nights in the 1920s and to suburban shopping centers on Sunday afternoons by the 1980s. Urban Hoosiers drove to the new state parks in the 1920s, and to Yellowstone and Yosemite as well by the 1980s. Transportation changes enabled young Hoosiers to attend consolidated schools, their parents to commute as far as fifty miles daily to work, and their grandparents to travel to Florida in January—the kinds of freedom and independence unknown to pioneer forebears. And transportation further stimulated the expansion of Indiana manufacturing, with the transportation industry itself becoming a major part of the economy.

The Industrial Economy

The first half of the twentieth century brought the maturation of Indiana's industrial economy, making the state one of the nation's manufacturing leaders and a part of the American industrial heartland that was the envy of the world. By the late twentieth century, however, there were fears that Indiana's industrial strength was turning to weakness, that the state was lagging in economic development and in material well-being of its citizens. Prophecies of economic gloom and radical change in the early 1980s did not always recognize that even in recession the Indiana economy provided unparalleled material abundance for more citizens. (The percentage of Hoosier families living below the poverty level was much lower than the Midwestern and national averages, with only six states more favorably ranked in 1979.) Nor did predictions of an economic revolution seem well-founded. Rather, for Indiana's economy, as with political and social change, evolution rather than revolution seemed more likely.

The industrialization of the late nineteenth century developed to full maturity in the early twentieth century. Most important, Indiana industries became ever more successful in producing durable manufactured goods, particularly steel, auto parts, household appliances, and machinery. These products were produced in high volume in large plants by means of sophisticated technology, large workforces, and large capital investments. And they were concentrated in growing cities of central and northern Indiana, particularly Indianapolis, Fort Wayne, South Bend, and the gas belt towns of Kokomo, Muncie, and

Women at work in a modern industry: the finishing line for insulin, Eli
Lilly and Company, 1923. (Eli Lilly and Company Archives)

Anderson, and the Calumet cities of Gary, Hammond, and East Chicago. Hundreds of small machine shops and factories produced automobiles and auto parts in the early decades of the century. Early
Indiana auto manufacturers included the Marmon, Cole, Stutz, Au-
burn, Duesenberg, Haynes, and Studebaker companies. All but Studebaker failed to make the transition to high-volume, mass production
and went out of business in the 1920s and 1930s. Auto parts manufacturing remained a fundamental part of the state's economy, however, particularly at the branch plants of the Detroit companies. In
the auto industry and in other durable goods manufacturing many
Indiana factories became units of larger corporations engaged in national and worldwide production and distribution. General Motors'
Anderson factories and United States Steel's Gary Works were prominent examples of the kinds of plants and big businesses that dominated the Indiana economy in the first half of the twentieth century.[8]

Nineteenth-century-style industries that depended on processing
natural resources and agricultural products generally declined in importance. Meat packing, flour milling, woodworking, and coal and
limestone production, which were generally unable to adopt signifi-

cant technological innovations or derive economies of scale from mass production, became relatively less significant. Coal mining was a partial exception; mechanization and the advent of surface mining in the 1920s and 1930s enabled the consolidation of several large coal companies. Many other companies in these traditional industries remained small or, like Bloomington's Showers Brothers Furniture Company or South Bend's Singer plant, went out of business altogether by mid-century.

Although the Great Depression adversely affected nearly all industries and companies, World War II and postwar affluence stimulated further growth of the Hoosier economy and especially of durable goods manufacturing. Indiana factories made major contributions to war production: steel mills, oil refineries, and converted auto, home appliance, and chemical plants provided much of the metal and energy that defeated Germany and Japan. Indiana's prosperity continued with peace. Growing middle-class expectations included, for example, purchase of a large, new model automobile every other year by the 1950s and two-car families by the 1960s. Despite minor ups and downs in the business cycle and the closing of some plants, most notably the end of Studebaker in 1963, the Indiana economy appeared healthy and productive. Indiana per capita personal income, which had lagged far behind the United States average in the first three decades of the twentieth century, began to rise in the late 1930s and, for the first time, exceeded the national average through most of the 1940s and 1950s (see Figure 2). In this booming economy, many industrial workers, unlike their counterparts in the 1920s, were no longer content with a second-hand car: with rising wages they joined the middle-class procession of biannual auto trade-ins and family vacation trips, television sets, and college educations for their children. A major study of Indiana's economic potential in 1955 concluded that "The future is bright—bright perhaps beyond our feeble imagination."[9]

Affluence and abundance continued though the 1960s, but by the 1970s there were disturbing signs that the state and national economies were undergoing fundamental structural changes, changes that threatened the material well-being of many Hoosiers. Manufacturing growth slowed in the 1970s, but the major shock came in the great recession of 1979–1982, when more than a quarter million Hoosiers

FIGURE 2.

Per Capita Personal Income, Indiana and Great Lakes States as a Percentage of U.S., 1930–1980

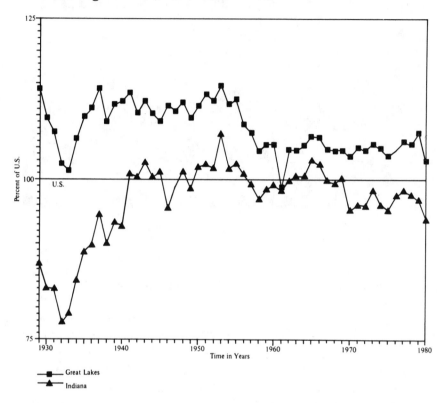

SOURCE: Morton J. Marcus, "Trends in the Heartland," *Indiana Business Review*, 56 (October, 1981), 8

lost their jobs and Indiana's unemployment rate was among the highest in the nation. Employment dropped by 25 percent in Indiana's durable goods manufactures, with the auto industry especially affected. Muncie and Anderson ranked among the nation's top ten cities in unemployment, with rates in excess of 18 percent in early 1982. Large numbers of Hoosiers left the state. Indiana's per capita personal income dropped to 7 percent below the national average in 1981, a level it had not seen since the Great Depression. The economic crisis of 1979–1982 led to agonizing reevaluations of the structure and pros-

Boom times in heavy industry: Gary Works, United States Steel, ca.
1962. (Indiana University Archives)

pects of Indiana's industrial economy and produced widespread
pessimism.[10]

Indiana's traditional strength in the manufacture of durable goods
now seemed to many a liability. By 1981 durable goods accounted for
more than 31 percent of total earnings in the state, compared to a
national average of only 17 percent (see Table 3). This heavy dependence on durable goods, which had increased in postwar Indiana
while declining nationally, had several consequences. It made the
Hoosier economy unusually sensitive to national business cycles, with
less unemployment in times of prosperity but considerably more suffering in times of economic downturns. Some observers also argued
that this concentrated manufacturing left the state overly dependent
on only a few big businesses: large manufacturing establishments em-
ploying more than 1,000 workers numbered only 93 in 1980 but accounted for 40 percent of all manufacturing jobs. Few of these companies had headquarters in the state, making Indiana a branch plant
state. "Indiana's manufacturing base," one report prepared in 1983
concluded, "has been hampered by being dominated by branch plants
and from the physical and emotional distance separating these facil-

Table 3
Structure of Earnings: Percent
of Total Earnings by Sector

	Indiana		United States	
	1958	1981	1958	1981
Farm	5.85	1.22	5.18	1.79
Agric. Services, Forestry, Fisheries	.20	.23	.34	.44
Mining	.76	.79	1.56	1.94
Construction	5.90	5.76	6.05	5.51
Manufacturing—Durables	30.53	31.37	17.41	16.89
Manufacturing—Nondurables	10.57	8.91	11.80	9.11
Transportation, Communication, and Public Utilities	7.16	7.00	7.77	7.67
Wholesale Trade	4.76	5.64	6.25	6.93
Retail Trade	11.38	9.45	11.76	9.63
Finance, Insurance, and Real Estate	4.12	4.56	5.10	6.10
Services	9.23	13.34	12.69	18.04
Federal—Civilian	2.09	2.62	4.13	3.72
Federal—Military	.74	.39	2.66	1.51
State and Local Government	6.71	8.72	7.29	10.72

SOURCE: Morton J. Marcus, "Structure and Performance of the Indiana Economy: An Overview," James A. Papke, ed., *Indiana's Revenue Structure: Major Components and Issues* (West Lafayette, 1983), 7.

ities from corporate decision-making authority."[11] More important was the possibility that durable goods manufacturing as practiced in Indiana and much of the industrial Midwest was outmoded and no longer competitive. Critics began to speak of a "Rust Belt" that was losing out to expanding manufacturing in the Sun Belt of the American South and West. Hoosiers reacted with fear and anger to such developments as General Motors' shift of some production from Anderson to the South. Even more disquieting was the increased competiton from foreign manufactuers, often able to produce steel, autos, and electronic equipment that were cheaper and better than American products.[12]

The recession of 1979–1982 increased expert and popular concern about Indiana's traditional concentration on manufacture of durable goods. Often disparagingly labeled "smokestack industries," steel, autos, and other durable goods no longer had the economic allure they enjoyed in the early twentieth century. The economic action was elsewhere, many claimed, particularly in the service industries and in so-called high-technology industries. Here Indiana lagged far behind the nation. While service industries continued to grow in importance in the state, they accounted in 1981 for only 13 percent of Indiana earnings compared to the 18 percent average for the United States. Likewise, large and rapidly growing high-technology industries were poorly represented in Indiana: there was, for example, almost no production of office and computing equipment in the state in the early 1980s. As Indiana continued its reliance on smokestack industries, many called for diversification.[13]

No one argued that moving away from Indiana's traditional dependence on manufacturing would be easy. Indeed there were fundamental obstacles to change. In part because young Hoosiers had found well-paying jobs in auto factories, steel mills, and machine shops there was less incentive to pursue a formal education. Indiana's workforce did not offer special appeal for companies seeking high-tech skills or entrepreneurial talent. Futhermore, other parts of the country and world were so far ahead of Indiana in developing their service and high-technology industries that it often seemed impossible to compete: there was little likelihood in the late twentieth century that California's Silicon Valley or Boston's Route 128 complex could be replicated in Indiana. And organized, systematic efforts to attract new and different industries to the state were slow to develop. Only with the crisis of the late 1970s and early 1980s did state government begin to respond by publicizing the advantages of the state for new business, offering help with worker training programs, loans, and tax credits, and promoting international trade. Other states were engaged in similar activities, however, and competition was intense.

The recession of 1979–1982 brought an economic soul-searching unparalleled in Indiana since the Depression of the 1930s and perhaps even since the internal improvements crisis of the 1830s. Many professed to discover fundamental, even radical change, as did the *Indianapolis Star* in the summer of 1983 when it ran a series of articles under the heading "Indiana's Economic Revolution."[14] By the mid-1980s, however, news of an economic revolution seemed exaggerated.

The auto plants were again booming, as were other manufacturers. Few were so optimistic as to assume that prosperity was permanent or that the good old days had returned, but, as one economist happily concluded in 1984, "Indiana's smokestack industries are by no means dead."[15]

Indiana's economy in the 1970s and 1980s was doubtless in a period of transition and evolution rather than revolution, a transition that was underway as early as the 1950s and was part of the national and world economies. Change did not entail a radical shift to a fully post-industrial economy, as some observers expected. Rather, substantial attachment to durable goods manufacturing would likely endure (and perhaps even made good economic sense), but Hoosiers by the 1980s were wisely learning the necessity of accommodating their economic lives to different and more intense competition from other regions of the nation and other countries of the world. They might hope to continue producing automoblies that were competitively made and priced, but they knew that such production had to include room for robots and computers. Many also were more sensitive to the need to educate children and the adult workforce for jobs beyond the assembly line or steel furnace—just as their great-grandparents had learned to work off the farm. Most important, perhaps, they were more aware of the certainty that no economic order was fixed, that late twentieth century Hoosiers had to be prepared for changes as challenging as those their pioneer forebears faced.

Government, Labor, and the Economy

Local, state, and federal government intervention in and regulation of the economy increased substantially in the twentieth century. Such government involvement was neither unprecedented in origin nor revolutionary in its consequences, however. The nineteenth-century Indiana economy, particularly that of the pioneer era, had allowed and even welcomed significant government intervention. And twentieth-century developments in this area were seldom as consequential as proponents hoped or opponents feared. Nonetheless, population growth, industrialization, urbanization, and changing interpretations of the general welfare brought arguments for new and expanding government aid and regulation of the economy.

State government often served as a mediator between business and professional interests and those of the citizen consumer by licensing or regulating a range of activities that extended from barbering and banking to medicine and utilities. Sometimes government licensing or regulation served to protect a particular group from full market competition by limiting access to a trade or profession. Often such regulation was argued in the name of preserving tradition, as with the discriminatory state tax on chain stores, which was intended in the 1930s to protect corner grocers from large supermarket chains. Utility regulation by the Indiana Public Service Commission was also used at times to meet the interests of the utility companies by providing a more stable and uniform business environment: critics often charged that the rates allowed were unreasonably high and that companies made investment and pricing decisions without due consideration of consumer welfare. Such charges combined with the issue of nuclear safety to force abandonment of construction on the Marble Hill Nuclear Plant in 1983.

Government regulation of banking was also an area in which business and consumer interests sometimes clashed. In the midst of alarming bank failures the Indiana Financial Institutions Act of 1933 increased bank regulation and brought welcome stability to a troubled sector of the economy. By the late twentieth century, however, many critics argued that Indiana banking was too stable and insufficiently competitive. Unlike most states, Indiana law long prohibited branch banking outside the county in which the bank was located and did not allow multibank holding companies. Indiana banks thus remained small, local institutions: only three Indiana banks, all located in Indianapolis, ranked among the nation's top 300 in size of deposits in the early 1980s. And Indiana banks tended to be conservative in their loan and investment practices. Some argued that in this way they best served hometown interests. Critics responded that large companies had to go out of state for adequate financial services and that Indiana's banking structure retarded economic development. After decades of debate, the 1985 General Assembly modified the law to allow cross-county branch banking and multibank holding companies.[16]

Equally controversial but prompting more widespread public debate was government responsibility for protection of the environment. Much of this burden initially fell to the Indiana State Board of Health, but in the 1960s and 1970s the federal government took on a larger role. Indiana streams and lakes were dangerously polluted by the early twentieth century, particularly by industrial waste and untreated sewage from growing towns and cities. The Indiana Stream Pollution Law of 1927 made a beginning in improving water quality, carried forward by New Deal–financed construction of sewage treatment plants. Progress thereafter was slow but significant: by the late twentieth century many Indiana streams and lakes were cleaner than they had been for nearly a century. But as traditional sources of water pollution lessened new sources began to cause concern. Particularly important was chemical pollution of streams and landfills. Indiana was one of the first states to pass legislation (1971) to limit the amount of phosphorus in detergents. The problems of other chemicals, such as PCBs in the Indiana waters of Lake Michigan and some streams in south central Indiana, proved more troublesome. Air pollution also became a serious problem. Some progress was made here too, particularly with federal pressure from the Environmental Protection Agency in the 1970s. Indiana had special difficulties with air pollution, however, due particularly to the industrial concentration in the Calumet region and to high sulfur content of the state's coal. Nearly all Indiana-produced electricity derived from coal-fired boilers, and electric utilities consumed most of the coal mined in the state. The result was a spewing forth of sulfur dioxide that, many scientists claimed, had serious adverse effects on the environment, not only in Indiana, but, in the form of "acid rain," in the Northeastern United States and Canada. The acid rain controversy presented a major challenge for regulators in the 1980s and created uncertainty about the future of Indiana's coal and utility industries. Here as elsewhere many Hoosiers feared that environmental protection meant a loss of individual freedom and a threat to economic growth. Those who believed otherwise often proved insufficiently organized to make their case effectively. The Indiana League of Women Voters was nearly alone in showing serious and sustained attention to environmental issues during the 1970s.[17]

Indiana's coal industry also was affected by regulations over changing methods of mining. Responding to increased competition, coal operators began in the 1920s and 1930s to shift from underground mining to surface mining. This permitted mechanization that cut labor costs and achieved greater efficiencies, and it contributed to the concentration of a very small number of large coal companies that came to dominate the industry. But strip mining turned a bucolic countryside into a scarred landscape of little practical value. State efforts to force coal companies to restore the land began with legislation passed in 1941, which required planting of trees and grass, but controversy over proper land restoration continued, with strengthened state legislation in 1967 and 1980 and with the federal government taking larger roles in regulation during the 1970s.

Much government involvement in the economy was intended to protect citizens and the environment, but, some critics charged, it too often retarded economic growth. In other instances, however, government specifically attempted to encourage economic growth, particularly to save or create jobs for Indianans. The New Deal programs attempted large-scale job creation in the 1930s. With similar purposes in mind, the 1980 General Assembly approved a state loan of $32 million to the financially pressed Chrysler Corporation, which had large plants in Kokomo, Indianapolis, and New Castle. And in 1984 General Motors agreed to build a large truck assembly plant near Fort Wayne after state officials pledged more than $25 million in incentives to lure the company. These arrangements were often complex and sometimes controversial, but their objectives were not significantly different from the efforts of state and local governments in the nineteenth century to attract business, create jobs, and spur growth.

Doubtless the most notable twentieth-century change in government's role in the economy was the increasing importance of the federal government. Often, as in many New Deal work programs and the loan to Chrysler, this involved cooperation with state government. Sometimes, as in the controversy over acid rain, there was considerable conflict with the federal government and with other state governments. In many cases federal regulation prompted considerable resistance from Hoosiers.

Among the most important areas of increased federal power was the growing involvement in labor-management relations. State and federal government had begun to enact protective labor legislation in the Progressive era, while craft unions that provided benefits to skilled

workers grew in strength. But the growing numbers of unskilled workers in the mass production industries remained largely unorganized.
The failure of the 1919 steel strike was an especially strong blow to
organizing efforts. The great push came in the 1930s when New Deal
legislation, particularly the Wagner Act of 1935, protected the right
of workers to organize unions and to bargain collectively. Strikes occurred in many industries and towns during the Depression decade.
Terre Haute's workers were sufficiently embittered and emboldened
to call a general strike in mid-1935, closing nearly all businesses in
the city for two days and causing Governor Paul McNutt to declare
martial law.[18] McNutt also used martial law to respond to strikes and
violence in the coal region. Although McNutt's relations with labor
were rocky, Indiana's Democratic party gradually came to realize the
wisdom of closer ties to the growing labor movement.

The most important labor activity of the 1930s occurred in manufacturing, particularly the automobile industry. The newly formed
United Auto Workers began in 1935 to seek bargaining contracts,
concentrating on General Motors. The climax came in the sit-down
strikes of 1936–1937, which occurred at several GM plants, including
the Guide Lamp plant in Anderson, where anti-union citizens and
city officials attempted unsuccessfully to intimidate striking auto workers. But the support of the Wagner Act and the new power of unskilled
workers after the formation of the Congress of Industrial Organizations (CIO) combined to win recognition for the United Auto Workers not only at General Motors but also at Studebaker, International
Harvester, and other plants in Indiana and the nation. Steel workers
also succeeded in winning recognition in the late 1930s and early
1940s. By 1939 nearly 22 percent of Indiana's nonagricultural workers
belonged to labor unions, with the newly formed CIO unions accounting for almost one-third of the union membership in the state.

Union membership continued to grow in the postwar years, so that
Indiana became one of the nation's largest union states. In 1980, when
25 percent of the national nonagricultural workforce belonged to labor unions, over 30 percent of Hoosier non–farm workers were union
members. But despite this strength labor unions were seldom secure
in Indiana. Partly this was due to a decline in relative size of their
membership, especially in the 1970s, when Indiana union membership dropped from nearly 38 percent of the nonagricultural work-

force to 30 percent. The growth of service, clerical, and government employment, with traditionally low union membership, and the relative fall-off in durable goods manufacturing accounted for much of this decline. One of the few bright spots for labor was the increase in organization among public school teachers following state legislation that in 1973 gave them the right to bargain collectively.

Labor unions in Indiana also had to contend with a citizenry and a state government that often were not sympathetic. Unions seemed to many Hoosiers to violate traditions of individual freedom. Employers, led by the Indiana State Chamber of Commerce, often aggressively fought union power in order to keep down labor costs. And conservative Republicans resented the alliance between unions and the Democratic party. These anti-union forces joined in 1957 to pass a right-to-work law, making Indiana the first northern industrial state to pass such legislation. The law was intended to prohibit unions from requiring membership as a condition of employment, although it proved less effective than its proponents had hoped. A Democratic majority in the General Assembly repealed the legislation in 1965.

The twentieth-century history of labor unions in Indiana presents a mixed record. Doubtless unions helped bring better pay and working conditions for their members and also for workers who did not join unions. But they achieved these important objectives, critics claimed, by causing unreasonably high labor costs (though not as high as in most other midwestern industrial states) and by helping create adversarial labor-management relations that handicapped the state's effort to attract new industry.[19] By the 1980s unions were hard pressed to respond to structural shifts in the Indiana economy and to win the attention of state and federal government leaders who were often only mildly sympathetic to their traditional concerns.

Changes in agriculture, transportation, manufacturing, labor, and government combined in the twentieth century to provide a better material life for nearly all Hoosiers. The Great Depression was most certainly a searing experience for the generation of the 1930s, while the recession of 1979–1982 left a later generation anxious about the present and future. But despite a growing recognition that change could bring adversity as well as progress there remained through the twentieth century a fundamental optimism. Material prosperity of a kind unimaginable to pioneers was attainable to most. Material pros-

Table 4
Richest and Poorest Indiana Counties, 1982,
as Measured by Per Capita Personal Income

Rank	County	1982 Dollars
1	Hamilton	11,750
2	Marion	11,718
3	Vanderburgh	11,488
4	Benton	10,799
5	Lake	10,657
6	Allen	10,655
7	Howard	10,646
8	Hancock	10,641
9	St. Joseph	10,573
10	Pike	10,528
92	Crawford	6,448
91	Washington	6,474
90	Switzerland	6,579
89	Owen	6,656
88	Franklin	6,874
87	Jennings	6,941
86	Lagrange	6,969
85	Orange	7,002
84	Brown	7,117
83	Starke	7,180

SOURCE: Morton J. Marcus, "County Level Personal Income During the Great Recession," *Indiana Business Review*, 59 (March-April, 1984), 22.

perity was not uniform, however. Black Hoosiers continued to suffer economic discrimination. So too did many women. And parts of southern Indiana continued to lag behind the rest of the state in per capita income and other indicators of economic growth (see Table 4). Nor was prosperity without cost. Traditional values of individual freedom and local autonomy often bent before the winds of huge multiplant, multinational manufacturing and agribusiness corporations, state and federal government regulatory agencies, powerful labor unions, and improved communication and transportation facilities. Such bending brought accommodation and adjustment but never an abrupt break with the Indiana past.

xiv

The Politics
of a State

Politics and government in Indiana after 1920 sometimes seemed to bring shadows of gloom and frightening possibilities of radical change. The Ku Klux Klan threatened the state's reputation for moderation and decency in the 1920s; Indiana's New Deal suggested the possibilities for change that might reject fundamental traditions of individual self-help and a government close to the people; and stridently conservative, right-wing Republicans after World War II seemed to signify that Indiana was out of step with urban, industrial America. In fact, however, these and other political phenomena were not as enduring, fundamental, or simple as they appeared to many contemporary observers. There were no radical discontinuities in Indiana's political history. Rather, politics and government retained strong roots in the Hoosier past; many traditions held even with modifications and occasional innovations; moderation remained the norm; decency and fair play generally prevailed; and the citizen majority usually received the kinds of government services it preferred.

The Klan and the Politics of Mediocrity: The 1920s

World War I left Hoosiers, like other Americans, with an uncertain legacy. Pride in Indiana's contribution to the war effort and veteran esprit led to formation of the American Legion with state and national headquarters in Indianapolis, and to construction with local and state tax support of the huge limestone World War Memorial in the capital city. But Hoosiers seemed as eager as Americans elsewhere to forget the war and to follow President Warren G. Harding's return to "normalcy." Unenthused about the League of Nations and making a world safe for democracy, Indianans showed little interest in reform at home. The moderate progressivism of Governors Hanly, Marshall, Ralston, and Goodrich during the first two decades of the century attracted no large audience or popular leader in the 1920s. Democrats retreated into Jeffersonian appeals for home rule and resistance to expansion of federal and state government power, warning loudly of extravagance and high taxes. Republicans made some efforts to push for public health and education, highway construction, and a new state prison, always emphasizing the businesslike efficiency of their proposals. But Republicans too called for an end to reform. Governor Warren T. McCray told the 1923 session of the General Assembly that "what the people of Indiana want is a season of government economy and a period of legislative inaction and rest."[1] That was what the legislatures of the 1920s provided.

The postwar decade brought to both major parties a stand-pat perspective and a mediocre leadership. Many one-time progressives, such as Albert Beveridge, were now as conservative as their Old Guard Republican opponents of the prewar era. The decade's leading politicians, best represented by Senator James E. Watson, seemed little concerned with social and economic problems of urban, industrial change, preferring to concentrate on the back-slapping and vote-getting of issueless campaigns and on the backstairs maneuvering of party preferment and organization. Neither the Democrats nor Republicans produced a leader capable of inspiring wide confidence or popular enthusiasm. Perhaps no other decade was so bereft of positive political leadership as the 1920s. Certainly no other decade produced leaders who so actively embarrassed Indiana. Governor McCray misused his office for personal financial gain and was eventually tried and sentenced in 1924 to ten years in the Atlanta penitentiary. His elected successor, Ed Jackson, likely should have joined McCray behind bars. In a sensational trial in 1928 the prosecution presented damning evidence that Governor Jackson had accepted bribes and received unreported money from the Ku Klux Klan, but the statute of limitations prevented his conviction. Jackson's punishments instead were abandonment by his political colleagues and the enduring stigma of a reputation as the state's most unfit governor.

In addition to conservative, stand-pat politics and mediocre and disreputable leadership, the 1920s also saw a sharp drop in voter turnout. This decline in citizen participation had many causes: the new voter registration law in 1911 and the advent of women's suffrage in 1920 doubtless had some effect. Perhaps also Hoosiers responded to the mediocrity and disreputableness of 1920s politics by turning away from participation. Others may have drifted into not voting by the confusion injected into politics by various groups and organizations intent on disrupting normal patterns and traditional ways.

Returning war veterans, newly enfranchised women voters, workers intent on building labor organizations, farmers eager to counter the postwar agricultural depression, and prohibitionists determined to keep Indiana dry—all threatened to disrupt the outward calm of 1920s politics, even to blur or erase the lines between the two major parties. These interest groups worked through formal organizations—the American Legion, the League of Women Voters, the American Federation of Labor, the Indiana Farm Bureau, and the Anti-Saloon League—to lobby state legislators and governors and to appeal directly to the electorate for their particular cause. Interest group politics, which was to become so important in the late twentieth century, emerged with sufficient force in the 1920s to frighten and confuse traditional politicians. In their response to its most important manifestation these politicians showed most clearly their failure to lead.

In some ways the Ku Klux Klan was like the League of Women Voters or the Indiana Farm Bureau. It offered a community of membership, a program of action, and a potential to engage in politics outside the structure of the two major parties. It differed from other interest groups of the 1920s in its much larger membership, its wider program of issues, and its essentially negative and wicked influence on Indiana politics, government, and society. The Klan cast a pall and left a legacy more disheartening than any other in Indiana's history. It cannot be dismissed as either an aberration or as simply the insidious appeal of a fanatical few. Nor should the Klan be seen as thoroughly dominating the state and accurately reflecting racist, violent, or provincial beliefs shared for all time by all Hoosiers. It must be understood in the context of time and place, of Indiana in the 1920s, for this was the soil that nourished the poisonous crop.

The Klan first appeared in Indiana in 1920 and by 1923 was organizing Klaverns and holding rallies and parades throughout the state. Membership by that summer probably numbered around three hundred thousand Hoosiers, making Indiana one of the nation's largest Klan strongholds. Some have attempted to dismiss the Klan as limited in its appeal only to rural Hoosiers or those with southern ties. But there is strong evidence of the Klan's success in small towns and in urban as well as rural Indiana and among all sections of the state, from Hammond to Evansville, from Richmond to Terre Haute, among farmers, factory workers, bank clerks, druggists, and ministers.

The Klan attracted such a diverse membership by means of a broad based, shotgun-like appeal, skillfully varying its message so as to—in the words of a South Bend Klansman—"sell them the thing they want."[2] There were two fundamental and universal components of the Klan's messages. Always the Klan preached patriotism—a flag-waving, Fourth of July kind of patriotism that gloried in the exceptional superiority of America and of Indiana. And the Klan preached Protestant Christianity, always with Protestant rituals and hymns used as the bright window-dressing of public meetings. Protestantism and patriotism were powerfully but simply displayed when ten thousand Klansmen assembled at the 1923 state fair to recite the Lord's Prayer and sing "America." Certainly more Protestant and likely more patriotic than most Americans, Hoosiers responded warmly to such familiar and reassuring images.

The Klan often defined its patriotism and Protestantism in a negative manner. Attacks on ideas and people that threatened flag and

Ku Klux Klan members departing a Protestant church in Knox, ca. 1923. (Indiana State Library)

Bible united patriotic Protestants in an exclusive community and provided the comfort and security of fighting together for the good cause. At the top of the list of enemies were Roman Catholics. Centuries-old tales and prejudices revived under Klan propaganda, with emphasis on a foreign-led church intent on destroying Protestantism and American democracy. The foreign-born themselves constituted a second Klan enemy, for they too threatened Protestantism and democracy. Blacks were a third enemy, though less dangerous than Catholics, except in the few cities where their segregated neighborhoods were expanding. And the enemy included all those immoral and indecent Hoosiers who put the roar into the Roaring Twenties: adulterers, gamblers, prohibition violators, corrupt politicians, and undisciplined youth.

The Indiana Klan fought these enemies largely by words rather than deeds. The Klan newspaper, the *Fiery Cross*, published in Indianapolis, burst forth with torrents of abuse and prejudice against Catholics, Jews, immigrants, and blacks, against immorality, and against presumed threats to God and country. But the Klan also used intimidation and secrecy. Masked and robed Klansmen marched to courthouse squares, burned crosses, soaped the initials "KKK" on window screens, organized boycotts of Catholic businessmen, and spread rumors and threats. There was very little actual violence and no lynching. But intimidation produced fear and silence that Indianans would sadly remember for the rest of their lives.

Some Hoosiers spoke out courageously against the Klan. Catholic and black newspapers were vigorous critics, particularly the *Indiana Catholic and Record* and the *Indianapolis Freeman*. A few other newspapers, most notably George Dale's *Muncie Post-Democrat*, also attacked the hooded order. Several Protestant ministers courageously opposed the Klan, as did a few fraternal organizations and the Indiana Bar Association. But such critics were in the minority during the Klan's peak in the years 1923–1925. Most newspapers were noncommittal or favorably disposed to the Klan; most Protestant denominational meetings meekly chose to ignore the Klan, while not a few ministers actively supported it. And, most important, political leaders generally had neither the vision nor the courage to counter effectively an organization that threatened not only ideals of human decency and toleration but also the very strength of the two major parties.

By 1924 the Klan had become a political issue, the most important issue in state politics. As one Republican regretted, "Ideas of race and religion now dominate political thought. Agencies and influences that were once powerful now are without influence. . . ."[3] The Klan backed or opposed candidates on the basis of their willingness to support it and the issues it favored, cutting across party lines and seriously dividing and disrupting both parties. Its major victory came in 1924, when the Klan-backed gubernatorial candidate, Ed Jackson, won first the Republican primary and then the general election. The legislature elected in 1924 was also composed of a Klan majority, or so most observers assumed. It appeared that the Klan dominated Indiana government.

The assumption of Klan dominance was not entirely accurate, however. Jackson's electoral victory was not of landslide proportions, and he lagged behind several other Republican candidates. The Klan legislative program for 1925, directed against parochial schools and alleged Roman Catholic influence in public schools, was a complete failure. Legislators' concern about religious freedom and about local rather than state control of education combined with internal feuding among Klansmen to bring defeat to all Klan-sponsored bills. The nonproductive 1925 session might well have been the preliminary to a more successful Klan program, as indeed many hoped, had it not been for a shocking crime committed by Indiana's leading Klansman.

D. C. Stephenson was to many the embodiment of the Indiana Klan. A powerful orator and charming personality, he possessed superior organizational and propaganda skills, leading to his appointment as Grand Dragon of the Indiana Realm in 1923. But unknown to his pious and patriotic followers, Stephenson was also an arrogant and evil man, more interested in personal power than in principle and more concerned about hedonistic pleasure than about humanity or heaven. In early 1925 Stephenson assaulted, raped, and held captive Madge Oberholtzer, a young Indianapolis woman. Distraught, Oberholtzer took poison, suffering for two days before Stephenson took her home. A month later Oberholtzer died, but not before giving testimony that led to a sensational trial and a life prison sentence for the former Grand Dragon.

Stephenson's brutality and stupidity destroyed the Klan. Indianans turned their backs on the man and the organizaton he had led. Newspaper reporters and some politicians began to press for public investigation of Klan influence. The *Indianapolis Times* won a Pulitzer Prize in 1928 for its crusade against the Klan. And, when Governor Ed Jackson refused to pardon Stephenson—the man who had stood next to him at his inaugural reception in 1925—Stephenson took revenge by providing information about the Klan's role in state politics that led to the governor's indictment and trial for bribery. Jackson was acquitted in early 1928 on a technicality, but widespread assumption of his guilt added to the growing revulsion against the Klan. As the 1920s closed, the Klan was dead.

Indiana survived its most serious political crisis since the Civil War, but with little grace and less honor. Whether Madge Oberholtzer's suffering and death were essential to the destruction of the Klan can never be known. What is known is that few Hoosiers could look with pride on their state or its leaders. And though they preferred to forget the Ku Klux Klan, most could not. That bitter memory was perhaps the saving grace of this tragedy. It may well be that the tendency to hate in the name of patriotism or Protestantism has been mitigated by memories of the searing experience of the 1920s. Certainly the revived Klan of the 1960s and 1970s—despite the attention it received from the media—was but a pale imitation of its predecessor and was soundly repudiated by the large majority of Hoosiers and by all responsible leaders. Indianans did not learn toleration in a decade or even half a century, but there was always before them the dark and negative image of the tragedy of the 1920s. This extreme experience perhaps paradoxically reinforced the tendency to moderation even in religious and racial hatred.

Liberalism, Ambition, and the New Deal: The 1930s

Perhaps never in Indiana's history have the politics of two decades been so different. The Great Depression of the 1930s ended the Republican party's position as the majority party and brought to power a Democratic party very different from its predecessor. Voters changed too: they came to expect more of government, willing to allow it greater power to respond to social and economic ills of the Depression. Despite continuing strong attachments to individualism and home rule Hoosiers watched their state government expand its powers at the expense of local government. The federal government under Franklin D. Roosevelt also grew in power, sometimes by taking responsibilities from the state. Conflict, excitement, and talk of radical change filled political debates. Beneath the surface storms, however, many of the main features of Indiana politics remained.

Standing tall at the center of the political debate of the 1930s was Paul V. McNutt. Handsome, intelligent, and ambitious, McNutt moved from the Indiana University Law School faculty and American Legion politicking into a well-organized quest for the governor's office. The Democratic landslide of 1932 brought him the office and a cooperative General Assembly, with Democrats holding 91 of 100 seats in the house and 43 of 50 seats in the senate. And all twelve federal congressmen were Democrats. No governor since Oliver P. Morton held such power or so forcefully directed state government and his party.

McNutt took office in January 1933 ready to prove, he said, "that

Democratic smiles in 1932: left to right, Frederick Van Nuys, Paul McNutt, Thomas Taggart, Jr., Reginald Sullivan, and Franklin D. Roosevelt in Indianapolis. (Indiana State Library)

government may be a great instrument of human progress."[4] His most immediate job was relief for the tens of thousands of unemployed Hoosiers. By 1933 voluntary agencies such as the Community Chest organizations and traditional government aid in the form of township poor relief had proved hopelessly inadequate to meet the demands caused by the worst Depression in American history.[5] McNutt's response took two related forms: he extended and centralized relief at the state rather than the township level, and he cooperated actively in organizing New Deal federal relief programs in Indiana. The first objective led in 1933 to passage of a state old age pension and establishment of the Governor's Commission on Unemployment Relief and in 1936 to creation of the Indiana Department of Public Welfare. McNutt thereby brought about a much increased role in relief for the state and diminished the power of locally elected township trustees. Moreover, McNutt and the new state relief agencies eagerly and effectively cooperated in setting up and administering the "alphabet soup" of New Deal agencies, from the Federal Emergency Relief Administration and the Civil Works Administration in 1933 to the Works Progress Administration and the new Social Security programs of 1935 and 1936. The result of these state and federal programs was welcome aid for unemployed, aged, and dependent Hoosiers and a significant shift from local and private administration and financing of relief to state and federal responsibility.[6]

These changes in relief engendered controversy and conflict. Republicans charged that the new relief and welfare programs encouraged waste and indolence at the expense of honest, hardworking taxpayers and that they threatened to bring "about a state of communistic or socialistic government. . . ."[7] The federal programs were an invasion of states' rights, critics asserted, and McNutt's power-hungry cooperation and centralization would destroy home rule, particularly the local control represented by the township trustees. Defenders responded that Indiana at long last was on the road to efficient, systematic, and professional care for its dependent citizens and that humanitarian responsibility and common sense justified new departures. The welfare programs set up in the 1930s were not, in fact, as radical or far reaching as many critics feared or as proponents of reform hoped, particularly because there remained considerable leeway for local community direction and responsibility. But the changes were substantial and significant not only as a short-run response to the Depression crisis but as an enduring shift in the relationship between government and citizen. And controversy over public welfare would continue into the post–World War II era.

While Governor McNutt and his fellow Democrats struggled with problems of relief they also set about to change other features of state government. Two areas were most important: taxation and government organization. Nearly everyone had long agreed that Indiana's tax system placed an unfair burden on local property taxes while allowing large amounts of intangible wealth to go untaxed. But many efforts to change the system had failed. McNutt in 1933 proposed a state gross income tax, in effect, a combination of sales and income tax. The legislature quickly passed the measure and thereby significantly reduced the property tax as a share of tax revenue while still allowing the state to maintain total revenue near its pre-Depression level. The state gross income tax of 1933 thus allowed Indiana to balance its budget and even to increase state aid to hard-pressed public schools. The measure also represented a step toward further state as opposed to local control over taxation and thus strengthened arguments for responsibility and centralization at the state rather than the local level.

Another major piece of legislation put forth by McNutt in 1933 was a plan to reorganize state government. As with income tax reform, many leaders in both parties had long recognized the degree to which the state's bureaucratic disorder had impeded efficient management. More than one hundred state departments and agencies existed in a haphazard patchwork of uncertain authority and imprecise control. McNutt's Executive Reorganization Act of 1933 placed them all in eight new departments, with responsibilities more clearly defined and control more centrally administered. Reorganization greatly strengthened the governor's power over state bureaucracy, a strengthening many observers believed essential to efficient management.

The major achievements of McNutt's administration— government reorganization, gross income tax, and new public welfare and relief programs—had one common theme: they served to strengthen the power of the governor. McNutt doubtless was motivated by liberal and progressive sentiments to bring efficiency and humanitarian reform to Indiana, objectives he pursued with more vigor and success than any other governor in the state's history. But McNutt also sought power, power that he argued was necessary to achieve such reforms in a conservative state, power his detractors argued was designed primarily to push forward McNutt's own career in general and his growing presidential ambition in particular.

Whatever his motives and objectives, McNutt's quest for power resulted in major strengthening of the office of governor and a significant increase in the incumbent's political patronage. McNutt certainly did not invent patronage—it had a long and respected history in Indiana since territorial days—but he expanded and made more systematic the operation of this feature of politics. With the Reorganization Act of 1933 state employees from top to bottom came under the governor's control, dependent for obtaining and keeping jobs on their commitment to him and the Democratic party. State policemen, hospital nurses, highway and park employees, and state librarians were or became loyal McNutt Democrats. And they were encouraged to show their support by joining the Hoosier Democratic Club, known more commonly as the "Two Percent Club," since each member was assessed that percentage of his or her pay. Though membership was voluntary in principle, it was generally assumed that no state job was secure without the two percent assessment.

Joined by the Indiana League of Women Voters and civil service reformers, Republicans vehemently denounced the Two Percent Club and McNutt's strengthened patronage machine. In 1936 McNutt allowed limited movement toward a merit system, particularly in public welfare agencies that administered federal money, but the general features of the patronage system, including the Two Percent Club, remained intact and were adopted by Republicans when they returned to power in the 1940s. Indeed, the bipartisan support for and longevity of thoroughgoing patronage in Indiana exceeded that of nearly all other states, making this one of McNutt's most enduring legacies.

The extraordinary power and dramatic reform legislation that flowed from the governor's office in the years 1933–1937 stirred up bitter resentment from most Republicans and many Democrats. The Republicans were clearly on the ropes in these years. While the Democratic share of the Indiana two-party vote had averaged only 45.1 percent in the 1920, 1922, and 1924 elections, that average share increased to 54.8 percent in the 1932, 1934, and 1936 elections. Accompanying this increase in the Democratic vote was a major shift in voting behavior. The economic and social issues of the 1930s brought new voters to the polls, increasing voter turnout to the general benefit of the Democratic party. And the Depression decade also pushed many formerly Republican or independent voters firmly into the Democratic camp. Blacks, ethnic voters, industrial workers, and urban dwellers constituted the most important pieces of this new Democratic majority. The party of McNutt and Roosevelt seemed to these voters more responsive to their circumstances in its support of public welfare, labor organization, and a government more active in improving the quality of life. The upsurge and realignment of these voters created a liberal Democratic coalition that presented to Indiana Democrats the possibility of enjoying a long-term majority.

To the regret of McNutt and other liberal Democrats the gains of the early 1930s were not permanent. A major source of trouble was intense Democratic factionalism. "The Indiana mess," as one of FDR's advisers called it, derived from ideological differences and personal rivalries, with younger, more liberal, McNutt Democrats ranged against older, more conservative, anti-McNutt Democrats. McNutt held control, even to the extent of securing the nomination and election in 1936 of his lieutenant governor, M. Clifford Townsend, as his successor. But he faced increasing challenges after leaving office in 1937. The major one came from Frederick Van Nuys.

Van Nuys was a moderate "old timer," although a Democrat never part of the McNutt circle. After his election to the Senate in 1932 he became increasingly critical of McNutt, Roosevelt, and the liberal Democratic party. By 1937 Roosevelt and McNutt agreed that Van Nuys should be "purged." Governor Townsend publicly declared from the White House steps that the Indiana Democrat would not be renominated in 1938, setting off one of the most vitriolic intraparty feuds of the twentieth century. For a time there was even talk of a Republican nomination of Van Nuys as the basis for a new bipartisan, anti-New Deal coalition. Van Nuys energetically fought for the Democratic nomination, however, to the great embarrassment of his party. Van Nuys's threat to Democratic victory and to McNutt's growing hopes for the White House eventually led McNutt and Townsend to accept Van Nuys back into the party. But by this time, to the glee of Republicans, the Democrats had washed a great deal of dirty family linen in public.[8]

Van Nuys narrowly won reelection in 1938, but the political tide was clearly shifting as Indiana Republicans began to revive. Businessman Homer E. Capehart's Cornfield Conference, held on his Daviess County farm in the summer of 1938, was a potent indication of Republican revival. Not only did they organize and campaign energetically for the fall election, but they began at last to abandon the Old Guard conservativism of the 1920s. While critical of the New Deal, many moderate and pragmatic Republicans began to accept certain of its features and assumptions, including the wisdom of some government intervention in the economy and the necessity of some federal relief programs and social security. This pragmatic and moderate shift came as popular support for the New Deal began to decline. The economic recession of 1937–1938 showed that recovery had not been achieved. Many Indiana farmers were especially bitter over New Deal agricultural policies, low farm prices, and what they regarded as wasteful, urban-oriented relief programs. Capitalizing on this discontent and on the low morale of a scared and divided Democratic party, Republicans in 1938 won their first majority in the Indiana house in ten years and elected seven of Indiana's twelve congressmen. The 1940 elections continued and confirmed the Republican revival, including a defeat of incumbent Senator Sherman Minton, a staunch McNutt New Dealer, by Raymond E. Willis, and a clear Republican majority in both houses of the General Assembly. The once popular Roosevelt narrowly lost Indiana to Wendell L. Willkie, though Willkie's claim as a native son doubtless helped him. The only bright spot for Democrats was Henry F. Schricker's narrow victory in the gubernatorial election.[9]

The Democratic majority of the early and mid-1930s thus proved fragile and fleeting. The liberal coalition that promised a major realignment of voters was insufficient to sustain party hegemony. That coalition of labor, urban, black, and ethnic voters would continue to exist and to shape significantly Indiana politics, but not with the strength and effect shown in other urban, industrial states. Rural and more conservative Democrats continued to play a major part in party affairs and to influence cautious skepticism about continuing liberal reform. No Democrat with McNutt's pragmatic liberalism, ambition, and power appeared to lead the party to victory in the 1940s and 1950s. Schricker was popular and likeable, but his appeal and interests were those of rural, small-town Indiana, and his desire and ability to effect change were limited.

But the politics of the 1930s did not end where they began. Both parties and most Indianans were not what they had been in the 1920s. Many Democrats had moved away from their century-long insistence on individual freedom, self-help, and home rule as unaltering principles and had begun to accept portions of liberal New Dealism. Many

Republicans had sloughed off much of the Old Guard conservatism of the 1920s. And Hoosiers generally had seen government at the state and federal levels actively and energetically assume new responsibilities for their social and economic welfare. These changes were not complete or radical. Continuity and ties to traditions remained and were often loudly reasserted, especially by conservative Republicans in the 1940s and 1950s. But the boundaries of political debate were no longer the same. With difficulty, but gradually, Hoosiers would come prepared to enter the new debates.

Party Politics since 1940

Political life in Indiana since 1940 is often labeled conservative. It is a valid label, but one that only hints at some important issues and themes and obscures others. A brief discussion first of the most obvious shifts occurring on the surface of Indiana politics will provide necessary background for consideration of more fundamental themes, including political parties, voting behavior, the structure and function of state government, citizen expectations of government, and the relationships between state government and the federal government.

During the 1940s and 1950s it appeared that both the active, liberal state government and the dominant Democratic party of the 1930s had been aberrations. Republican revival was well under way by 1940 and proceeded for nearly two decades, and state government officials adopted policies and outlooks of conservatism and inaction that often seemed more akin to those of the 1920s than the 1930s. Democrat Henry F. Schricker won in 1940 and again in 1948, to be sure, but the popular governor who wore the white hat did not share McNutt's liberalism or activism. Moreover, Schricker was encircled by large Republican opposition, particularly in 1941, when the Republican-dominated General Assembly attempted to strip him of many of his gubernatorial powers. Although the state supreme court, in the case of *Tucker* v. *State*, held the Republican plan unconstitutional, this legal victory did not enable Schricker to lead an active government. Republican Governors Ralph F. Gates, George N. Craig, and Harold W. Handley tinkered with various programs of state government, such as Craig's modest improvements in mental health care, but they functioned generally more like caretakers than innovative or active leaders. And they often suffered the consequences of intense intraparty feuding among Republicans. This was particularly the case in the Craig administration: most of the governor's moderately progressive program fell victim to factional feuding. [10]

Particularly consequential in the Republican revival of the 1940s and 1950s was the strength of the party's conservative wing, which was determined to repeal much of the New Deal and to fight communism at home and abroad. Such nationally popular Republicans as Wendell Willkie (despite his Indiana upbringing), Dwight Eisenhower, and Nelson Rockefeller were much too liberal for these Hoosiers. Even fellow Indiana Republican Charles Halleck was thought too pragmatically moderate. The best known of Indiana's conservative Republicans was William E. Jenner, who was elected to his first full term in the United States Senate in 1946 and soon became a nationally prominent spokesman for right-wing causes. His salty language and gift for political invective have seldom been matched in Indiana politics. Jenner strongly supported Senator Joseph McCarthy in the search for disloyal Americans they believed responsible for America's presumed weakness in its relations with the Soviet Union. His most vicious attack occurred in 1950 when he charged that popular World War II general George Marshall was a "front man for traitors" and a "living lie." Jenner set the dominant tone for Indiana politics during the 1940s and 1950s, often joined by Homer Capehart, his Indiana colleague in the senate, and supported by the Indiana Farm Bureau, the American Legion, the Indiana State Chamber of Commerce, and Eugene C. Pulliam's very conservative and influential *Indianapolis Star* and *News*. The organization of the ultra-right-wing John Birch Society in Indianapolis in 1958 seemed to confirm this tone and to promise a large national hearing.[11]

There were winds of change blowing by the beginning of the 1960s, however, recalling faintly the liberalism and activism of the 1930s. Democratic revival began in 1958, when Jenner decided not to seek reelection. Evansville Democrat Vance Hartke won his seat. Even more important was the election of Democrat Matthew E. Welsh to the governor's office in 1960. Welsh did not enjoy the legislative support that McNutt had, however, and Republicans threatened to hamstring him as they had Schricker. But Welsh proved an astute and determined politician, able, with some Republican support, to bring new energy to state government. Democratic revival continued with the upset victory of Birch Bayh over Capehart in 1962. For three terms Bayh combined a very liberal voting record in Washington with an "aw shucks" style of moderation back home in Indiana. The 1964 election proved to be the capstone of Democratic revival and the tombstone of effective right-wing Republicanism. Conservative Republicans had long argued that Indianans wanted a true conservative, one firmly committed to overturning New Deal social programs: they were overjoyed with the party ticket, headed by presidential candidate Barry Goldwater. To their great regret, Goldwater and the state Republican ticket went down to a defeat of landslide proportions: Indiana cast its vote for Democratic presidential candidate Lyndon B. Johnson (the first Democratic presidential vote since 1936), for gubernatorial candidate Roger D. Branigin, and for a large majority of seats in both houses of the General Assembly.

Liberal Democratic hopes for continuation of the programs Welsh had begun were not fulfilled. War in Vietnam sapped the energies and treasury of the national administration, and Branigin proved to be a Schricker rather than a McNutt or Welsh type of governor—a Jeffersonian Democrat not much interested in the Great Society. Moreover, in 1968 Republicans returned to power, electing Edgar D. Whitcomb, a moderately conservative governor handicapped by more than the ordinary level of intraparty feuding.

Whitcomb's two successors were Republicans and two-term governors. Otis R. Bowen was first elected in 1972 and proved to be one of the state's most astute politicians. Robert D. Orr followed him with a first victory in 1980. Joined with Indiana's two Republican Senators, Richard Lugar and Dan Quayle, Orr and Bowen represented a moderation that rejected the strident conservatism of the Jenner generation, accepted much of the New Deal liberalism as it had evolved by the late twentieth century, and attempted nonetheless to preserve some of Indiana's traditional attachments to individual freedom, self-help, and simple government.

These shifts in party sentiments and control since 1940 had important relationships to public policy and political ideology, as will be argued below. The major point to be made now is that Indiana has been a generally conservative state politically since 1940, a state in which Republicans have won more often than Democrats. But Democrats have never had to wander long or deep in the wilderness. At times they governed, and nearly always they were able to mount a serious threat to Republican electoral success. Despite Republican leanings, Indiana has been a vigorous two-party state.[12]

Vigorous partisanship has been one of the most important and enduring features of the state's history. This was true in the nineteenth century; it continued to be true in the twentieth. A *Congressional Quarterly* survey of the fifty states concluded in 1983 that "The salient feature of Indiana politics is fierce partisanship, more pronounced here than almost anywhere else in the country."[13] Hoosiers have always shown an unusually large interest in politics and have turned out to vote in larger numbers than their fellow Americans. And they have identified more intensely and loyally with one or the other of the two major parties. Electoral patterns persisted for generations; citizens voted the way their parents and grandparents did, and many regarded changing party or even voting a split ticket as an act of apostasy never to be forgiven.[14] Supporting the high turnout and intense partisan identification were vigorous parties that were more strongly organized and professionally run than their counterparts in most other states. The best evidence of this enduring, intense partisanship and party strength was patronage.

Like all the fundamental features of late twentieth century Indiana politics, patronage has a long history, extending all the way back to the territorial period. McNutt made rewarding political friends more systematic, especially with the Two Percent Club. His successors continued the process. When Governor Welsh took office in 1961 he found only about 10,000 of 20,000 state employees protected by state merit or civil service systems. He and his staff spent many long days replacing Republicans with Democrats, a standard procedure for a new administration.[15] The Highway Department and Department of Natural Resources were the largest sources of patronage job appointments. Employees all the way down to the teen-aged lifeguard at the state park pool had to be approved by the party. At times of intraparty conflict the faction of the party a job applicant had supported was also important. Patronage of a different sort often prevailed in awarding government contracts and special privileges, with highway and insurance contracts providing especially lucrative opportunities for political supporters of the party in power. A special feature of patronage was the motor vehicle license branches. Their operation and profits were the responsibility of the party occupying the governor's office, with the branches in each county managed by the party county chairman. Employees were patronage appointments, and profits were divided between the state committee and the county chairman. In a gesture of bipartisanship begun in 1977, the profits from fees for personalized license plates were split between the two parties—a feature that has tended to lessen the propensity of the party out of power to complain about the system. Through these various sources, then, the party that won in November had a guaranteed source of income and thousands of jobs and favors to use as rewards to loyal party workers.

The extent of Indiana's patronage system was nearly unparalleled in mid and late twentieth century American state politics. But there were signs by the 1970s and 1980s that the system was declining in significance and extent. Knowledgeable critics became increasingly vigorous in denouncing it as conducive to corrupt, unfair politics and inefficient government. They argued that appointments should be made primarily on the basis of job qualifications rather than party service. They asserted that state employees often felt a larger loyalty to party officials than to the state department or profession in which they worked. Many Indiana citizens also showed unhappiness with the system as they complained of inefficiencies in state parks, corruption in the highway department, and long lines in license branch offices. Such criticisms combined with pressure from the federal government to bring a gradual reduction in patronage. And United States Supreme Court decisions in 1976 and 1980 struck serious blows at the practice. By the mid-1980s it appeared that patronage was but a pale shadow of its former condition, though still more prevalent than in most states. The Indiana State Employees Association estimated that a merit system covered about 17,000 state jobs but that about 9,000 still required political clearance from the party in power.

Defenders of patronage claimed that it was a primary source of the strength of political parties in Indiana and that these parties were conducive to open, accountable, and democratic govenment. The Hoosier propensity to politick, to vote, and to debate depended, many party officials claimed, on the continued vitality of party organization.

Critics responded that parties as they functioned in Indiana had not led to good government because state and county party chairmen have been interested in politics and not government. A visiting Englishman attended the Republican state convention in 1956 and was awed by the "back slapping, free drinks, general fun." Politics, he concluded, "seems to depend largely on personalities, connections, bargaining. There are no major issues." A long-time political observer suggested in 1970 his preference for a "party system without so much reliance on patronage and a little more concern about issues rather than what faction is going to have the license bureau. . . ." Another critic charged that "state government is considered the field on which the game of politics is played . . ." and that "Too often in Indiana, politicians feel that winning is the end of the game." The result was "particular resistance to change at almost all levels."[16]

Whether for good or ill, the decline in patronage in recent decades has contributed to a weakening of party organization. The power of the parties also diminished as a consequence of efforts to open up the candidate selection process by using primary elections rather than party conventions to nominate candidates. In 1975 the General Assembly provided that the governor, lieutenant governor, and United States senator should be nominated in primaries rather than party conventions. (Nomination of the lieutenant governor was placed back in party convention by 1981 legislation.) Reformers claimed that the primary would move politics out of the smoke-filled room. Party professionals claimed that it deprived them of a fundamental reason for existence. Some also believed that the increasing importance of television gave candidates additional freedom to campaign independent of the party organization. Party politics also became less significant in the selection and work of Indiana's judges, with, many believed, consequent improvements in the state's judicial system in the 1970s.[17]

The vitality of political parties also was threatened by two major trends in late twentieth century American politics: a drop in voter turnout and a decline in party identification. In both cases the falloff was less steep in Indiana than in most other states, but it was significant nonetheless. Increasingly fewer Indiana voters identified loyally and consistently with one party. A growing number professed to belong to no party and claimed status as independent voters. A growing number also changed party from election to election and split their vote between the two parties' candidates in the same election. These trends produced particularly high instability rates in the party vote by the 1960s and 1970s.

At the same that Hoosiers showed evidence of caring less about party they also showed evidence of caring less about government and the responsibilities of citizenship. The high voter turnouts of the late nineteenth century, with rates as high as 95 percent, began to drop in the early twentieth century (see Appendix B). The New Deal brought a revival of high turnout, but the post–World War II years witnessed a large decline. The Indiana turnout for presidential elections in the 1960s and 1970s averaged below 70 percent. And there was evidence not only of a growing number of nonvoters but also of an increase in the proportion of occasional or peripheral voters so that the core of consistently participating citizenry shrunk in size. The likelihood that Hoosiers were turning off rather than turning out was reinforced by survey interviews that suggested apathy and even cynicism about Indiana politics and government.[18]

The decline in turnout, the lessening of partisan identification, and the weakening of formal political party organization in Indiana were sources of concern for those interested in democratic politics and responsive government. It is likely that these features of recent politics were causally related and that they marked the beginning of a new era in political life. Those who feared that this was change for the worse could take consolation in the fact that these declines were less precipitous in Indiana than in most other states. For Hoosiers, turnout, partisan identification, and party organization remained more as they had been even as they evolved. This particular conservatism was perhaps as important in recent Indiana political life as the ideological conservatism more often evident at the surface.

State Government since 1940

Indiana's government in the mid and late twentieth century continued to function under the constitution of 1851. In fundamental respects it was much like government in the nineteenth century. But as political parties and political issues changed, so too did government.[19]

The governor remained a comparatively weak executive in terms of formal powers. But Indiana governors by the post–World War II era could be very powerful leaders if they so chose and particularly if they had support in their party and the General Assembly. Political infighting, as occurred with Governors Craig and Whitcomb, could deprive them of leadership power.[20] But governors could always derive considerable strength from their ability to make patronage appointments. And while this source of power declined in the 1970s and 1980s the office gained new power from the constitutional amendment approved in 1972 that allowed a governor to serve two consecutive terms, so that he was no longer a lame duck on his first day in office. Both Bowen and Orr benefited from this change.

Proponents of strong executive leadership and government efficiency also argued the needs of government reorganization. McNutt's 1933 reorganization was an important beginning, but it had to be continued as agencies proliferated and functions changed. Governor Craig undertook some reorganizations, and Governor Welsh created in 1961 the Department of Administration to reorganize purchasing, personnel, and internal administrative procedures. Welsh also succeeded in obtaining legislation that gave the governor's office more power in preparing the state budget. In Welsh's view this new budgeting procedure was "the most significant action taken by any legislature since 1941."[21] The lieutenant governor also became a more important part of state government, with responsibilities by the 1970s for promoting economic development, tourism, and world trade. Indicative of the increase in executive responsibilities was the growth of the governor's staff. Nineteenth-century governors usually had, at most, one or two assistants. Governor Welsh had a dozen staff members, Governor Bowen more than twenty.

The General Assembly changed too in the years since 1940. It had always been a citizens' assembly, with its members interrupting their work in law, farming, and business to meet for a sixty-one-day session only every other year. Many argued that this non-professional, citizen legislature provided representative government at low cost and that it was especially unlikely to enact drastic or foolish changes. (The General Assembly, for example, did not get around to establishing an un-American activities committee to investigate subversives until 1957, by which time the Red Scare was waning.) Critics asserted that the General Assembly was not responsive to the needs of modern, urban, industrial society: a national survey in 1971 ranked the Indiana General Assembly fortieth among the fifty states in legislative capability and effective response to substantive issues.[22] Legislators were inadequately informed, poorly paid, overly partisan, and too closely tied to rural constituencies, critics charged. Legislative turnover was high so that continuity was minimal. And there was inadequate provision for legislative action in the long twenty-two-month period between the biennial sessions. A variety of reforms in the 1960s and 1970s addressed these concerns.

The issue of legislative reform that attracted most attention was reapportionment. The state constitution required apportionment every six years to ensure that representation was fair. That was generally done in the nineteenth century, but, following the drawing of new districts in 1921, reapportionment was conveniently ignored by a legislature in which, because of population shifts, rural voters had increasingly larger representation than urban voters. By 1960 a vote for a representative in the Indiana house from rural Vermillion County had more than four times the value of a vote from urban St. Joseph County. This imbalance doubtless contributed to legislative reluctance to confront the growing problems of cities. Republicans, who depended more than Democrats on rural votes, were especially reluctant to reapportion the legislature. The decisive push came not from within Indiana but from the United States Supreme Court, which in *Baker* v. *Carr* (1962) and later cases held that legislatures must reapportion regularly and fairly so that each member represented roughly the same number of voters. Federal pressure finally produced a reapportionment in 1965, the first since 1921, and then every ten years, following the federal census returns. The procedure was not neutral or bipartisan, however; the party in power used sophisticated computer analyses to draw district boundaries so as to create the best chance of winning the most legislative seats. But this new gerrymandering was not nearly so unfair as the four decades in which failure to reapportion had produced a silent but most extreme gerrymander.

A variety of changes in the structure and operation of the General Assembly followed reapportionment. Perhaps most important was the shift to annual sessions. Indiana voters ratified in 1970 a constitutional amendment allowing annual sessions, and the General Assembly instituted this change in 1971. Sessions in odd-numbered years would be sixty-one days; those in even-numbered years only thirty days. Accompanying this change were several salary increases for legislators, increases in the size of the professional support staff, and more use of interim study commissions. These and other changes were intended to make legislators more knowledgeable and attentive, able to function more like professional than citizen legislators.[23]

Indiana legislators also had available sources of information from the growing number of interest groups lobbying for their particular causes. Citizens and groups had always pleaded their special case in Indianapolis, but in the post–World War II decades this lobbying grew in extent and sophistication. Among the most powerful interest groups were the Indiana AFL-CIO, the Indiana State Teachers' Association, the Indiana State Chamber of Commerce, and the Indiana Farm Bureau. The first two groups tended to find more support among Democratic legislators, the latter two were better received by Republicans. These and other groups spent large sums of money to influence legislators and claimed also to be able to mobilize votes from among their memberships.[24]

One constant and troubling source of concern for legislators, governors, and voters was taxation. Hoosiers had always been reluctant to pay taxes, and any politician who dared suggest increasing taxes to provide needed services was risking political suicide. A major difficulty for Indiana officials was that because of the rapid increase in the number of school age children in the 1950s and 1960s government expenditures increased even without addition of new services. Governor Harold Handley pushed through a modest increase in the gross income tax in 1957: his bid for a United States Senate seat the following year fell before the label of "High Tax Harold."

It was apparent to most officials in state government by the early 1960s that the property tax and the gross income tax were inadequate to generate the revenue necessary to maintain government services, particularly in education. An acceptable solution was less apparent. The 1963 General Assembly, perhaps the most important session since 1933, debated the issue of tax increases and adjourned without a solution. Governor Welsh was determined to effect an increase and immediately called a special session. Considerable arm twisting, maneuvering, patience, and courage by both Republicans and Democrats eventually produced a compromise tax package that included a two percent individual and corporate adjusted gross income tax and, even more controversial, a new two percent sales tax. The most dramatic moment came during the Senate vote on the sales tax, which ended in a 24–24 tie. After a moment of tense stillness, Lieutenant Governor Richard O. Ristine broke the tie by voting aye. Ristine was a Republican working with a Democratic governor to effect a tax increase: his political career never recovered from the shadow of that courageous vote. Welsh too suffered ever after as "Sales Tax Matt," and Hoosiers began to attach plates to their cars reading "Indiana—Land of Taxes."[25]

Ten years later taxation was again the primary item on the agenda. This time Governor Bowen led a successful effort to restructure the tax system by means of a property tax relief fund that would derive from an increase in the sales tax from two to four percent and an increase in the corporate income tax. This fund would be used to lower the taxes paid by property owners. The program also provided for a freeze on local tax levies at the 1973 rates. The 1973 property tax relief program was very well received by many Hoosiers and was especially important in making Bowen one of the most popular governors in the state's history. But because it limited local government revenues Bowen's program sparked great and growing disapproval from many city mayors and school administrators unable to meet their revenue needs. The new tax program led to an increase in the state's share of school financing from about one third the total to nearly two thirds by 1980, but, proponents of the schools argued, failed to provide sufficient revenue.[26]

Taxation was also a primary item on the agenda of the 1982 special session of the General Assembly. The combination of economic recession and property tax freeze left state and local governments hard-pressed financially. Much to the regret of many Republicans, but after the November elections, the Orr administration increased the income and sales taxes. This unpopular solution did not prevent Orr's reelection in 1984, however.

Controversies over taxation were not unique to Indiana, but it may be that they were more intensely argued than elsewhere and that increases were more stridently resisted—often resisted as though the very foundations of individual freedom and economic well-being were being destroyed by high taxes. Notwithstanding the Hoosier aversion to taxation, there was in fact very little of it. Throughout the post–World War II era the state always ranked low in per capita state and local taxes—for example, forty-third in 1982.[27] The auto plates should in truth have read "Indiana—Land of Low Taxes."

For many Hoosiers there were twin devils in government in the years since 1940. One was high taxes. The other was the federal government. The federal government had played a major role in pioneer Indiana by removing Indians, surveying and selling the public lands, and boosting economic development. Hoosiers, though strongly patriotic and nationalistic, were seldom very grateful. From the outset they tended to distrust government in Washington: it was uninformed about their needs, unresponsive to their wishes, and likely to gather to itself ever larger powers. As a consequence the federal government was often to be ignored and always to be distrusted. The New Deal challenged these nineteenth-century notions by making it impossible to ignore Washington but by providing innumerable reasons to distrust its greatly augmented power.[28]

Indiana's most symbolic and widely known expression of opposition to federal power came with passage of House Concurrent Resolution Number 2 in 1947. This resolution attracted such attention for so long a period and its language conveyed the emotionalism of the argument so well that it needs to be quoted in full:

> Indiana needs no guardian and intends to have none. We Hoosiers—like the people of our sister states—were fooled for quite a spell with the magician's trick that a dollar taxed out of our pockets and sent to Washington, will be bigger when it comes back to us. We have taken a good look at said dollar. We found that it lost weight in its journey to Washington and back. The political brokerage of the bureaucrats has been deducted. We have decided that there is no such thing as "federal" aid. We know that there is no wealth to tax that is not already within the boundaries of the 48 states.
>
> So we propose henceforward to tax ourselves and take care of ourselves. We are fed up with subsidies, doles, and paternalism. We are no one's stepchild. We have grown up. We serve notice that we will resist Washington, D.C. adopting us.
>
> Be it resolved by the House of Representatives of the General Assembly of the State of Indiana, the Senate concurring: That we re-

spectfully petition and urge Indiana's Congressmen and Senators to vote to fetch our county court house and city halls back from Pennsylvania Avenue. We want government to come home.

Resolved, further, that we call upon the legislatures of our sister states and on good citizens everywhere who believe in the basic principles of Lincoln and Jefferson to join with us, and we with them to restore the American Republic and our 48 states to the foundations built by our fathers.[29]

The 1947 resolution produced no concrete response because it was only an expression of sentiment that bound no one to do anything. Yet it doubtless made an impression in Washington, where it caused embarrassment and difficulty when Indiana officials did seek federal aid. As late as 1960 the resolution was read out at a Congressional committee meeting considering an Indiana request for federal aid. Even more important, the 1947 resolution set the tone for Hoosier responses to federal aid and power for a long time thereafter.

The most significant response came in the "revolt" of 1951. Indiana Senate Bill 86 required that the names of Indianans receiving welfare payments should be made available for public inspection. The head of the Federal Security Administration warned that this bill would violate federal law and that passage would necessitate cutting off federal money to Indiana. This threat from the outside stirred up Hoosier politicians, the press, and much of the public. The Republican-dominated General Assembly thumbed its nose at Washington and passed Senate Bill 86, expressing its willingness to forego the estimated $20 million of annual federal welfare aid to defend the principles involved. Indiana was in revolt against Washington, and the defenders of freedom worked themselves into a rage over the right to inspect welfare rolls. Involved, they claimed, was the right of the states to govern themselves, the ever-enlarging and dangerous power of the federal government, the insulation from popular will of the federal bureaucracy, and the steady march of socialism in American life. The issue was compared to the struggle begun at Lexington in 1775. According to the *Indianapolis Star*:

Indiana has an opportunity to start a backfire of resistance to the usurpation of Federal power that will respread through the nation. We have an opportunity to show the nation and the Federal government that we have the ability and the right to run our own affairs. Indiana can spark a revolt against the arbitrary power of a government that

has grown arrogant, wasteful and secretive and thus endangered all
our liberties as free states and free men in the republic.[30]

The *Indianapolis Star* played a major role in explaining the issue in
these terms, joined by most other newspapers in the state and by the
Indianapolis and Fort Wayne Chambers of Commerce and other organizations. The Republican party also saw the popular appeal of the
issue and vigorously pushed it forward. Indiana's Washington representatives took up the cause. Led by Representative Charles Halleck
and Senator William Jenner, they succeeded in putting through Congress the Jenner Amendment, which allowed the states themselves to
decide on the confidentiality of welfare records. The Jenner Amendment solved the practical difficulties created by Indiana Senate Bill
86: there would be no need to make up the $20 million in federal
revenues or to cut welfare rolls.

Opponents of Senate Bill 86 and the Jenner Amendment were few,
and they had a hard case to argue. The most important opposition
came from the Democratic party. The issue was such that it became
a party measure, with Republicans favoring and Democrats opposing.
But Democratic opposition was not very convincing, largely because
many Democrats in fact approved the bill and the larger sentiments
behind it. Opposition also came from labor unions, professional welfare workers, and a small minority of Indiana newspapers. House
Democratic leader S. Hugh Dillin stated the Democratic case: "Instead
of fighting the battle of Lexington, the Republicans are more nearly
like the rebels who fired against the flag of the United States at Fort
Sumter."[31] It was a logical argument, but popular appeal and emotional sentiment were on the other side.

The 1951 revolt began because of a belief that welfare "chiselers"
were rampant and that publicizing their names would embarrass them
off the rolls. Public welfare was perhaps the most common source of
federal-state controversy. Hoosiers were particularly uneasy about
public support of dependent people, fearing that federal programs
were wasteful and often unnecessary and that recipients too often
were undeserving. Increases in federal financing and control of welfare programs, particularly in the 1960s, met strong opposition in
Indiana, even though there remained considerable room for state and
local latitude in distributing aid. As with taxes, however, the point
often ignored was the comparatively low level of welfare payments in

the state. Indiana ranked very near the bottom in total per capita welfare expenditures and in percent of the population receiving aid in the 1950s and 1960s, when debates of this sort were most intense.[32] This low ranking reflected widely held attitudes toward public welfare and the government in Washington.

The rousing defense of the freedom to inspect public welfare rolls in 1951 was the most notable instance of federal-state conflict, and it certainly put Indiana in the national spotlight for a time. But the principles of the 1951 revolt continued to be enunciated in Indiana as conflict burst forth over a wide range of issues in federal-state relations. Alabama Governor George Wallace's foray into Indiana presidential politics in 1964 attracted attention largely because of his racist politics, but it was likely that Wallace's stand on states' rights in general and welfare chiselers in particular touched equally sympathetic chords among the nearly 30 percent Democratic vote he attracted in the state.

By the 1970s and 1980s other issues often replaced welfare as a source of tension in federal-state relations, though Indiana's hard-nosed welfare director, Wayne Stanton, involved the state in controversy over federal food stamps and other programs in the 1970s. Increasingly important, however, were environmental and public health issues. As the federal government enacted new legislation in these areas, the State Board of Health was often caught between federal regulations and a reluctant legislature and an uninterested citizenry, as with the mandates of the federal Environmental Protection Agency. There was also conflict with the federal Occupational Safety and Health Administration that led in 1980 to withdrawal for a short time of federal certification of Indiana's program. And the long-standing controversy over use of Indiana's Lake Michigan shore smoldered even after the designation of the Indiana Dunes Lakeshore National Park in 1966: the compromise that permitted steel and industrial plants in the midst of a national park and a state park satisfied neither conservationists nor those favoring economic development.[33]

Despite the continued federal-state friction Indiana government officials gradually began to work more cooperatively with the federal bureaucracy. Important changes began in the Welsh administration, which not only quietly overturned the 1947 resolution against federal aid but also began actively to seek such aid. Ten years later the Bowen administration brought Republicans into closer working relationships with Washington, including staffing a four-person office in the national capital to represent the state's interests. By this time there were approximately 225 federal programs in Indiana administered through state government. Similar proliferation occurred at the local level: in Muncie in 1976 there were twenty-nine agencies of the federal government, operating more than ninety programs. State and local officials often expressed frustration and exasperation with the "feds" and their "maddening bureaucratic obstacles," but there was less ideological stubbornness and no retreat into the past of the kind that occurred in 1947 or 1951.[34] Past attitudes and practices continued their hold in part, however, for Indiana remained near the bottom in per capita federal spending, ranking forty-ninth in 1983.[35] And there were still in the 1980s many Hoosiers annoyed and angry over what they perceived to be Washington's intrusions into their state, their communities, and their lives.

In politics and government Indiana in the 1980s appeared to have changed greatly. Political parties had declined in strength, voters seemed less interested in traditional forms of politicking, state government responsibilities were considerably expanded and fed by larger sources of tax revenue, and the federal government seemed more dominant. But none of these changes was rapid or radical: all were resisted by tradition-minded Hoosiers; all were less pronounced in Indiana than in most other states; all occurred in ways that evidenced the tendency to seek moderation and to adjust the pace of change to traditions deeply embedded in the Hoosier state.

Hoosiers Past and Present

What is a Hoosier? The oft-asked question usually is directed to seeking the origin or meaning of the word itself. In this context the question has no answer. Many have tried, but no one has yet successfully explained the derivation or meaning of the word "Hoosier."[1]

The question can also be asked in the sense of inquiring about the characteristics that make Indianans distinctive. "What is a Hoosier?" is thus similar to asking "What is an American?" And answers are equally imprecise and contradictory. For every generalization there is an exception, often several. For every characteristic presented as distinctive to Indiana there are voices that will object and disagree. Yet there are a people called Hoosier and, more important, a people who call themselves Hoosier. They perceive themselves as distinctive, different from residents of California or Pennsylvania.

The image of the Hoosier that developed in the late nineteenth century was often negative, particularly outside the state. East coast savants created a robust stereotype of an illiterate rustic, a stereotype they used to contrast Hoosier with Yankee.[2] Indiana's golden age of literature in the late nineteenth and early twentieth centuries made this stereotype increasingly suspect, even among provincial Yankees. Yet as late as 1904 Meredith Nicholson was lamenting "the assumption in Eastern quarters that [the Hoosier] is a wild man of the woods. . . ."[3] It need hardly be added that the popularity of the Ku Klux Klan in the 1920s reawakened outsiders' perceptions of Indianans as provincial and narrow-minded.

Hoosiers themselves seldom shared this stereotype. Their problems were not ones of a negative self-image. Often the traits outsiders criticized Hoosiers celebrated. This was particularly true of the attachment to rural and small-town life. Increasingly in the twentieth century Indianans venerated values and lifestyles they saw as antithetical to urban, industrial America. Their state song ("On the Banks of the Wabash, Far Away") and the state poem ("God crowned her hills with beauty") celebrated wooded hillsides, the smell of new-mown hay, and moonlit rivers. Both song and poem were adopted by the legislature in the twentieth century when most Hoosiers lived in cities and worked in offices and factories. Brown County became the state's premier tourist spot in the early twentieth century, not only because of its scenery but because it represented to visitors a world that was lost and a chance to idealize a rural past of genial community and individual contentment. By the 1920s Sunday afternoon would bring as many as 5,000 automobiles to the hills of Brown County in search of Indiana's traditions.[4]

But those traditions were not to be found on Brown County's Bear Wallow Hill and certainly not in the tourist shops of Nashville. They were to be found instead in Rushville and Brookston, in Fort Wayne and Evansville, in Wayne County and Washington County—across Indiana, on farms, to be sure, but in towns and cities too. Hoosiers perceived themselves to be independent, responsible, and God-fearing Americans. They took immense pride in those who had settled and cleared the land, venerating them as embodiments of the answer to the question "What is a Hoosier?" They gloried in the material prosperity and progress that came from the land and from railroads

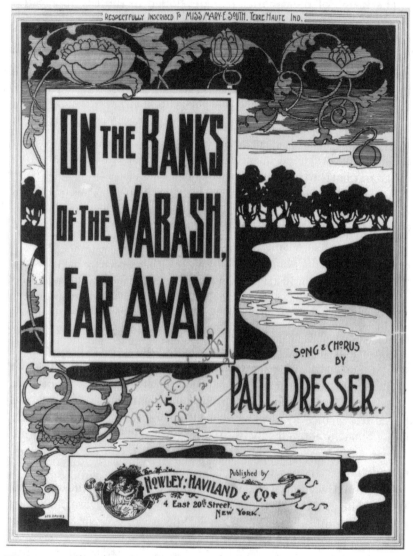

The state song. (Lilly Library)

and factories. They celebrated the broad and intense popular interest in politics as an expression of their determination to direct and control their individual and community lives. And they took pride in their security and comfort, their "sense of belonging" as one writer commented, of "being part of something permanent and substantial."[5] These traditions they would conserve.

The attachment to and celebration of tradition did not create a static society in Indiana. Every generation experienced change, sometimes welcoming the new, sometimes resisting. Hoosiers built canals, factories, railroads, city office buildings, and even slums. They consolidated their one-room schools and abandoned churches too small to support a professional minister. They strengthened the power of their state government and accepted aid, advice, and regulation from their federal government. They moved toward greater toleration for those Indianans who were not white, native-born Protestants. They came to realize the connections between their lives at home in Indiana and the lives of people and institutions over the face of the globe. They indulged themselves in all the best and worst of American popular culture. Some young Hoosiers even learned how to play soccer despite the handicap of hands and feet best suited to basketball.

These and many other changes occurred in Indiana as they did in most of America. But they often came about more gradually. Never did Hoosiers rush to the barricades to overthrow the status quo. When they sought change it was with respect for and attention to the present and past. Often they opposed the new and innovative and were able to resist; when forced to change they were always able to blend the old with the new. In Indiana there was no loud call to scuttle the past in order to enter the future.

Moderation was the Indiana way. Evolution, not revolution, was the route taken in Indiana. The state could be backward and out of step, its people close-minded and provincial. But more often Hoosiers navigated in the middle, away from the snags and shallow water, moving slowly but surely, confident that the stream flowed in the right direction, secure that they were on waters others had traveled, and hopeful that still more Hoosiers would follow over the same route.

Appendixes

A. *Indiana Population, 1800–1980*

B. *Percentage of Indiana Voting-Age Population Casting Votes, 1824–1984*

C. *Indiana Governors*

Appendix A.
Indiana Population, 1800–1980

	Total Population	White Population	Black Population	Foreign Born Population	Total Urban Population	Total Rural Population
1800						
Numbers	4,875[a]	4,577	298[b]	——	0	4,875
% of Total		93.89%	6.11%	——	0.00%	100.00%
Change	——	——	——	——	——	——
1810						
Numbers	24,520	23,890	630[c]	——	0	24,520
% of Total		97.43%	2.57%	——	0.00%	100.00%
Change	+403.14%	+421.95%	+111.40%	——	0.00%	+403.14%
1820						
Numbers	147,178	145,758	1,420[d]	——	0	147,178
% of Total		99.04%	0.96%	——	0.00%	100.00%
Change	+500.23%	+510.12%	+125.39%	——	0.00%	+500.23%
1830						
Numbers	343,031	339,399	3,632[e]	——	0	343,031
% of Total		98.94%	1.06%	——	0.00%	100.00%
Change	+133.07%	+132.85%	+155.77%	——	0.00%	+133.07%

	Total Population	White Population	Black Population	Foreign Born Population	Total Urban Population	Total Rural Population
1840						
Numbers	685,866	678,698	7,168[f]	——	10,716	675,150
% of Total		98.95%	1.05%	——	1.56%	98.54%
Change	+99.94%	+99.97%	+97.35%	——	——	+96.81%
1850						
Numbers	988,416	977,154	11,262	55,537	44,632	943,784
% of Total		98.86%	1.14%	5.61%	4.51%	95.49%
Change	+44.11%	+43.97%	+57.11%	——	+316.49%	+39.78%
1860						
Numbers	1,350,428	1,338,710[g]	11,428[h]	118,284[i]	119,398[j]	1,231,030
% of Total		99.16%	0.84%	8.75%	8.84%	91.16%
Change	+36.62%	+37.00%	+1.47%	+112.98%	+167.51%	+30.43%
1870						
Numbers	1,680,637	1,655,837	24,560	141,474	247,657	1,432,980
% of Total		98.52%[k]	1.46%	8.41%	14.73%	85.27%
Change	+24.45%	+23.68%	+114.91%	+19.60%	+107.42%	+16.40%

	Total Population	White Population	Black Population	Foreign Born Population	Total Urban Population	Total Rural Population
1880						
Numbers	1,978,301	1,938,798	39,228	144,178	388,316	1,589,985
% of Total		98.00%	1.98%	7.28%	19.62%	80.38%
Change	+17.71%	+17.08%	+59.72%	+1.91%	+56.79%	+10.95%
1890						
Numbers	2,192,404	2,146,736	45,215	146,205	590,039	1,602,365
% of Total		97.91%	2.06%	6.66%	26.91%	73.09%
Change	+10.82%	+10.72%	+15.26%	+1.40%	+51.94%	+0.77%
1900						
Numbers	2,516,462	2,458,502	57,505	142,121	862,689	1,653,775
% of Total		97.69%	2.28%	5.64%	34.28%	65.72%
Change	+14.78%	+14.52%	+27.18%	-2.79%	+46.20%	+3.20%
1910						
Numbers	2,700,876	2,639,961	60,320	159,663	1,143,835	1,557,041
% of Total		97.74%	2.23%	5.91%	42.35%	57.65%
Change	+7.32%	+7.38%	+4.89%	+12.34%	+32.58%	-5.84%

	Total Population	White Population	Black Population	Foreign Born Population	Total Urban Population	Total Rural Population
1920						
Numbers	2,930,390	2,849,071	80,810	150,868	1,482,855	1,447,535
% of Total		97.22%	2.75%	5.14%	50.60%	49.40%
Change	+8.49%	+7.92%	+33.96%	-5.50%	+29.63%	-7.03%
1930						
Numbers	3,238,503	3,116,136	111,982	135,134	1,795,892	1,442,611
% of Total		96.22%	3.45%	4.17%	55.45%	44.55%
Change	+10.51%	+9.37%	+38.57%	-10.42%	+21.11%	-0.34%
1940						
Numbers	3,427,796	3,305,323	121,916	110,992	1,887,712	1,540,084
% of Total		96.42%	3.55%	3.23%	55.07%	44.93%
Change	+5.84%	+6.07%	+8.87%	-17.86%	+5.11%	+6.75%
1950						
Numbers	3,934,224	3,758,512	174,168	100,630	2,217,468	1,716,756
% of Total		95.53%	4.42%	2.55%	56.36%	43.64%
Change	+14.77%	+13.71%	+42.85%	-9.33%	+17.46%	+11.47%
1960						
Numbers	4,662,498	4,388,554	269,275	93,202	2,650,378	2,012,120
% of Total		94.12%	5.77%	1.99%	56.84%	43.16%
Change	+18.51%	+16.76%	+54.60%	-7.38%	+19.52%	+17.20%

	Total Population	White Population	Black Population	Foreign Born Population	Total Urban Population	Total Rural Population
1970						
Numbers	5,193,669	4,820,324	357,464	83,198	3,161,812	2,031,857
% of Total		92.81%	6.88%	1.60%	60.87%	39.13%
Change	+11.39%	+9.83%	+32.75%	-10.73%	+19.29%	+0.98%
1980						
Numbers	5,490,260	5,004,567	414,732	101,802	3,181,145	2,309,115
% of Total		91.15%	7.55%	1.85%	57.94%	42.06%
Change	+5.71%	+3.82%	+16.02%	+22.36%	+0.61%	+13.64%

[a]This figure includes areas not included later in the state of Indiana. The 1870 Census gives the figure of 2,517 for what later became Indiana.
[b]Includes 135 slaves and an indeterminate number of Indians.
[c]Includes 237 slaves.
[d]Includes 190 slaves.
[e]Includes 3 slaves.
[f]Includes 3 slaves.
[g]290 Indians subtracted from the Census figure for white pop.
[h]This number includes 14 foreign born.
[i]The Census also uses 118,184.
[j]This figure includes an 1850 estimate of the Fort Wayne population, which was left out of the 1860 Census.
[k]White and black totals do not include orientals and Indians and thus will not produce a sum of 100.00%.

SUMMARY STATEMENT—The numbers in this table were derived from the published United States Census. The figures for each year were taken from the census published for that year, except for 1800, 1810, and 1820, which were taken from the 1830 census. The figures given for urban population are all given according to the old census definition. Thus, figures given in the table will not usually match those given in the urban population tables in the 1950, 1960, 1970, and 1980 censuses. Where retrospective tables in later censuses have shown a different total than that given in the earlier census year, the earlier census year figure was used.

Appendix B.
Percentage of Indiana Voting-Age Population Casting Votes, 1824–1984

1824	1828	1832	1836	1840	1844
37.1	68.7	71.9	69.2	84.4	84.7

1848	1852	1856	1860	1864	1868
78.5	80.3	88.3	89.4	82.9	92.5

1872	1876	1880	1884	1888	1892
85.3	94.6	94.4	92.2	93.3	89.0

1896	1900	1904	1908	1912	1916
95.1	92.1	89.7	89.9	77.8	81.9

1920	1924	1928	1932	1936	1940
71.0	70.7	74.9	78.9	78.7	81.1

1944	1948	1952	1956	1960	1964
71.7	67.2	75.7	73.7	76.9	71.7

1968	1972	1976	1980	1984	
69.5	60.8	60.1	57.7	59.9	

SOURCES: United States Bureau of Census, *Historical Statistics of the United States: Colonial Times to 1970* (Washington, 1975), part 1, pp. 1,071–1,072; United States Bureau of the Census, *Statistical Abstract, 1984*, p. 265; United States Bureau of the Census, *Current Population Reports*, Series P-20, No. 397 (January, 1985).

Appendix C.
Indiana Governors

Jonathon Jennings	1816–1822	
Ratliff Boon	1822	
William Hendricks	1822–1825	
James B. Ray	1825–1831	
Noah Noble	1831–1837	Whig
David Wallace	1837–1840	Whig
Samuel Bigger	1840–1843	Whig
James Whitcomb	1843–1848	Democrat
Paris C. Dunning	1848–1849	Democrat
Joseph A. Wright	1849–1857	Democrat
Ashbel P. Willard	1857–1860	Democrat
Abraham A. Hammond	1860–1861	Democrat
Henry Smith Lane	1861	Republican
Oliver P. Morton	1861–1867	Republican
Conrad Baker	1867–1873	Republican
Thomas A. Hendricks	1873–1877	Democrat
James D. Williams	1877–1880	Democrat
Isaac P. Gray	1880–1881	Democrat
Albert G. Porter	1881–1885	Republican
Isaac P. Gray	1885–1889	Democrat
Alvin P. Hovey	1889–1891	Republican
Ira Joy Chase	1891–1893	Republican
Claude Matthews	1893–1897	Democrat
James A. Mount	1897–1901	Republican
Winfield T. Durbin	1901–1905	Republican
J. Frank Hanly	1905–1909	Republican
Thomas R. Marshall	1909–1913	Democrat
Samuel M. Ralston	1913–1917	Democrat
James P. Goodrich	1917–1921	Republican
Warren T. McCray	1921–1924	Republican
Emmett Forest Branch	1924–1925	Republican
Ed Jackson	1925–1929	Republican
Harry G. Leslie	1929–1933	Republican
Paul V. McNutt	1933–1937	Democrat
M. Clifford Townsend	1937–1941	Democrat
Henry F. Schricker	1941–1945	Democrat
Ralph F. Gates	1945–1949	Republican
Henry F. Schricker	1949–1953	Democrat
George N. Craig	1953–1957	Republican

Harold W. Handley	1957–1961	Republican
Matthew E. Welsh	1961–1965	Democrat
Roger D. Branigin	1965–1969	Democrat
Edgar D. Whitcomb	1969–1973	Republican
Otis R. Bowen	1973–1980	Republican
Robert D. Orr	1981–	Republican

Notes

1: Peoples and Empires before the Americans

1. James H. Kellar, *An Introduction to the Prehistory of Indiana* (second edition, Indianapolis, 1983), provides the best overview. See also Eli Lilly, *Prehistoric Antiquities of Indiana* (Indianapolis, 1937).

2. Glenn A. Black, *Angel Site: An Archaeological, Historical, and Ethnological Study* (Indianapolis, 1967).

3. Much of this work is reported in the Indiana Historical Society's *Prehistory Research Series*. See, for example, Patrick J. Munson, ed., *Experiments and Observations on Aboriginal Wild Plant Food Utilization in Eastern North America, Prehistory Research Series*, VI (Indianapolis, 1984).

4. Alton A. Lindsey, ed., *Natural Features of Indiana* (Indianapolis, 1966), provides good essays on subjects ranging from bedrock geology to climate to birds and insects. See also Richard S. Simons, *The Rivers of Indiana* (Bloomington, 1985).

5. For more detailed treatment see John D. Barnhart and Dorothy L. Riker, *Indiana to 1816: The Colonial Period* (Indianapolis, 1971), 57–177.

6. Bert Anson, *The Miami Indians* (Norman, Okla., 1970); R. David Edmunds, *The Potawatomis: Keepers of the Fire* (Norman, Okla., 1978).

7. James A. Brown, "The Impact of the European Presence on Indian Culture," John B. Elliott, ed., *Contest for Empire, 1500–1775: Proceedings of an Indiana American Revolution Bicentennial Symposium* (Indianapolis, 1975), 6–24.

8. John Francis McDermott, "French Settlers and Settlements in the Illinois Country in the Eighteenth Century," *The French, The Indians, and George Rogers Clark in the Illinois Country: Proceedings of an Indiana American Revolution Bicentennial Symposium* (Indianapolis, 1977), 3–33; W. J. Eccles, *France in America* (New York, 1972).

9. George A. Rawlyk, "The 'Rising French Empire' in the Ohio Valley and Old Northwest: The 'Dreaded Juncture of the French Settlements in Canada with those of Louisiana'," Elliott, ed., *Contest for Empire*, 41–59.

10. Jack M. Sosin, "Britain and the Ohio Valley, 1760–1775: The Search for Alternatives in a Revolutionary Era," Elliott, ed., *Contest for Empire*, 60–76; Thomas D. Clark, "The Advance of the Anglo-American Frontier, 1700–1783," ibid., 77–95.

2: The American Nation and the West, 1776–1800

1. John D. Barnhart and Dorothy L. Riker, *Indiana to 1816: The Colonial Period* (Indianapolis, 1971), 178–313, treats the period from 1776 to 1800.

2. George M. Waller, *The American Revolution in the West* (Chicago, 1976).

3. Bernard W. Sheehan, "'The Famous Hair Buyer General': Henry Hamilton, George Rogers Clark, and the American Indian," *Indiana Magazine of History*, LXXIX (March, 1983), 1–28.

4. George M. Waller, "George Rogers Clark and the American Revolution in the West," *Indiana Magazine of History*, LXXII (March, 1976), 1–20; Robert M. Sutton, "George Rogers Clark and the Campaign in the West: The Five Major Documents," *Indiana Magazine of History*, LXXVI (December, 1980), 334–45.

5. Quoted in Barnhart and Riker, *Indiana to 1816*, 202n.

6. George Rogers Clark to Patrick Henry, February 3, 1779, James Alton James, ed., *George Rogers Clark Papers, 1771–1781* (Springfield, Ill., 1912), 99.

7. Clark to Thomas Nelson, October 1, 1781, ibid., 608.

8. Dwight L. Smith, "The Old Northwest and the Peace Negotiations," *The French, the Indians, and George Rogers Clark in the Illinois Country: Proceedings of an Indiana American Revolution Bicentennial Symposium* (Indianapolis, 1977), 92–105.

9. Paul Woehrmann, *At the Headwaters of the Maumee: A History of the Forts of Fort Wayne* (Indianapolis, 1971), 21–58; Reginald Horsman, *The Frontier in the Formative Years, 1783–1815* (New York, 1970), 21–49; Joyce G. Williams and Jill E. Farelly, *Diplomacy on the Indiana-Ohio Frontier, 1783–1791* (Bloomington, 1976).

10. George W. Geib, "The Land Ordinance of 1785: A Bicentennial Review," *Indiana Magazine of History*, LXXXI (March, 1985), 1–13. Clear and accurate titles in Indiana and the Old Northwest contrasted most favorably with the confused muddle in Kentucky and other states settled before the rectangular survey was instituted.

3: Indiana Territory and Statehood, 1800–1816

1. John D. Barnhart and Dorothy L. Riker, *Indiana to 1816: The Colonial Period* (Indianapolis, 1971), 314–463.

2. Donald Chaput, "The Family of Drouet de Richerville: Merchants, Soldiers, and Chiefs of Indiana," *Indiana Magazine of History*, LXXIV (June, 1978), 103–16; John Lauritz Larson and David G. Vanderstel, "Agent of Empire: William Conner on the Indiana Frontier, 1800–1855," *Indiana Magazine of History*, LXXX (December, 1984), 301–28.

3. Paul A. Hutton, "William Wells: Frontier Scout and Indian Agent," *Indiana Magazine of History*, LXXIV (September, 1978), 183–222.

4. R. David Edmunds, *The Shawnee Prophet* (Lincoln, Neb., 1983), 67–116; R. David Edmunds, *Tecumseh and the Quest for Indian Leadership* (Boston, 1984), 107–160.

5. William Henry Harrison to Secretary of War, August 6, 1810, Logan Esarey, ed., *Messages and Letters of William Henry Harrison*, Vol. I: *1800–1811* (Indianapolis, 1922), 456; Harrison to Tecumseh, June 24, 1811, ibid., 522–23; Harrison to Secretary of War, August 7, 1811, ibid., 549. See also Marshall Smelser, "Tecumseh, Harrison, and the War of 1812," *Indiana Magazine of History*, LXV (March, 1969), 25–44.

6. Bert Anson, *The Miami Indians* (Norman, Okla., 1970); Paul Woehrmann, *At the Headwaters of the Maumee: A History of the Forts of Fort Wayne* (Indianapolis, 1971), 105–273.

7. Emma Lou Thornbrough, *The Negro in Indiana: A Study of a Minority* (Indianapolis, 1957), 1–30.

8. Quoted in Donald F. Carmony, "Fiscal Objection to Statehood in Indiana," *Indiana Magazine of History*, XLII (December, 1946), 317.

9. Charles Kettleborough, ed., *Constitution Making in Indiana*. Vol. I: *1780–1851* (Indianapolis, 1916). The text of the Constitution of 1816 is found on pages 83–125. See also John D. Barnhart, *Valley of Democracy: The Frontier versus the Plantation in the Ohio Valley, 1775–1818* (Bloomington, 1953), 178–96.

10. Gayle Thornbrough, ed., *The Correspondence of John Badollet and Albert Gallatin, 1804–1836* (Indianapolis, 1963), 261.

4: On the Indiana Frontier

1. An excellent introduction for understanding life on the Indiana frontier is Malcolm J. Rohrbough, *The Trans-Appalachian Frontier: People, Societies, and Institutions, 1775–1850* (New York, 1978). More important for its evocative detail is R. Carlyle Buley, *The Old Northwest: Pioneer Period, 1815–1840* (2 vols., Indianapolis, 1950; repr. Bloomington, 1983). Interesting for its slightly different perspective is Geneviève D'Haucourt, *La Vie Agricole et rurale dans l'état d'Indiana à l'époque pionnière* (Paris, 1961).

2. Morris Birkbeck, *Notes on a Journey in America from the Coasts of Virginia to the Territory of Illinois* (Philadelphia, 1817), quoted in Rohrbough, *Trans-Appalachian Frontier*, 163.

3. Gregory Steven Rose, "Hoosier Origins: The Nativity of Indiana's United States–Born Population in 1850," *Indiana Magazine of History*, LXXXI (September, 1985), 201–32; Elfrieda Lang, "Southern Migration to Northern Indiana Before 1850," *Indiana Magazine of History*, L (December, 1954), 349–56; Richard K. Vedder and Lowell E. Gallaway, "Migration and the Old Northwest," in David C. Klingaman and Richard K. Vedder, eds., *Essays in Nineteenth Century Economic History: The Old Northwest* (Athens, Ohio, 1975), 159–76.

4. Herbert Anthony Kellar, ed., *Solon Robinson: Pioneer and Agriculturist* (2 vols., Indianapolis, 1936), I, 54.

5. James M. Bergquist, "Tracing the Origins of a Midwestern Culture: The Case of Central Indiana," *Indiana Magazine of History*, LXXVII (March, 1981), 1–31; Richard Lyle Power, *Planting Corn Belt Culture: The Impress of the Upland Southerner and Yankee in the Old Northwest* (Indianapolis, 1953); Henry Glassie, *Pattern in the Material Folk Culture of the Eastern United States* (Philadelphia, 1968); Robert W. Bastian, "Indiana Folk Architecture: A Lower Midwestern Index," *Pioneer America*, 9 (December, 1977), 115–36; Thomas J. Schlereth, "The New England Presence on the Midwest Landscape," *Old Northwest*, 9 (Summer, 1983) 125–42. For political consequences into the early twentieth century of this migration stream, see Philip R. VanderMeer, *The Hoosier Politician: Officeholding and Political Culture in Indiana, 1896–1920* (Urbana, Ill., 1985), 135–45.

6. John Scott, *The Indiana Gazetteer or Topographical Dictionary* (Centreville, Ind., 1826, reprint edition, Indianapolis, 1954), 40. Other contemporary descriptions are contained in Harlow Lindley, ed., *Indiana as Seen By Early Travelers* (Indianapolis, 1916).

7. Paul W. Gates, "The Nationalizing Influence of the Public Lands: Indiana," in *This Land of Ours: The Acquisition and Disposition of the Public Domain:*

Papers Presented at an Indiana American Revolution Bicentennial Symposium (Indianapolis, 1978), 103–26; Malcolm J. Rohrbough, "The Land Office Business in Indiana, 1800–1840," ibid., 39–59; Stephen F. Strausberg, *Federal Stewardship on the Frontier: The Public Domain in Indiana* (New York, 1979).

8. John Modell, "Family and Fertility on the Indiana Frontier, 1820," *American Quarterly*, 23 (1971), 615–34; James E. Davis, *Frontier America, 1800–1840: A Comparative Demographic Analysis of the Settlement Process* (Glendale, Calif., 1977).

9. Perhaps the best descriptions of pioneer living are provided in Logan Esarey, *The Indiana Home* (Bloomington, 1953).

10. Warren E. Roberts, "The Tools Used in Building Log Houses in Indiana," *Pioneer America*, 9 (July, 1977), 32–61.

11. Baynard Rush Hall, *The New Purchase or Seven and a Half Years in the Far West* (Princeton, N.J., 1916), 54–55. Hall's description of life in southern Indiana in the 1820s, originally published in 1843, is one of the best written and most interesting first-hand accounts. The 1916 edition includes the full original text and a key to identify people and places.

12. Shirley S. McCord, ed., *Travel Accounts of Indiana, 1679–1961* (Indianapolis, 1970), 134, 135.

13. Hall, *New Purchase*, 124.

14. McCord, ed., *Travel Accounts of Indiana*, 135.

15. Katherine Mandusic McDonell, *Medicine in Antebellum Indiana: Conflict, Conservatism, and Change* (Indianapolis, 1984); Madge E. Pickard and R. Carlyle Buley, *The Midwest Pioneeer: His Ills, Cures, and Doctors* (Crawfordsville, 1945).

16. William Barlow and David O. Powell, eds., "An Oration, Pronounced at Hindostan, Martin Co. (I[ndian]a) on the 45th Anniversary of American Independence," *Indiana Magazine of History*, LXXIV (June, 1978), 144.

5: The Evolving Pioneer Economy

1. A good introduction to the subject is *Transportation and the Early Nation: Papers Presented at an Indiana American Revolution Bicentennial Symposium* (Indianapolis, 1982). Particularly useful are the essays by Donald T. Zimmer, "The Ohio River: Pathway to Settlement," 61–88; and Ralph D. Gray, "The Canal Era in Indiana," 113–34.

2. Dorothy Riker and Gayle Thornbrough, eds., *Messages and Papers Relating to the Administration of James Brown Ray, Governor of Indiana, 1825–1831* (Indianapolis, 1954), 180.

3. Baynard Rush Hall, *The New Purchase or Seven and a Half Years in the Far West* (Princeton, N.J., 1916), 50.

4. J. W. Hunt to John B. Niles, December 14, 1848, John B. Niles Papers (Lilly Library, Indiana University, Bloomington).

5. *London Morning Herald*, quoted in Paul Fatout, *Indiana Canals* (West Lafayette, 1972), 160

6. John Denis Haeger, *The Investment Frontier: New York Businessmen and the Economic Development of the Old Northwest* (Albany, N. Y., 1981), 217–24.

7. Fatout, *Indiana Canals*, 76.

8. Charles R. Poinsatte, *Fort Wayne during the Canal Era, 1828–55: A Study*

of a Western Community in the Middle Period of American History (Indianapolis, 1969); A. L. Kohlmeier, *The Old Northwest as the Keystone of the Arch of American Federal Union: A Study in Commerce and Politics* (Bloomington, 1938). For a discussion of the estimated size of the contribution of canals to growth and a cost-benefit analysis see Roger L. Ransom, "Public Canal Investment and the Opening of the Old Northwest," in David C. Klingaman and Richard K. Vedder, eds., *Essays in Nineteenth Century Economic History: The Old Northwest* (Athens, Ohio, 1975), 246–68.

9. Donald F. Carmony, "Historical Background of the Restrictions Against State Debt in the Indiana Constitution of 1851," *Indiana Magazine of History*, XLVII (June, 1951), 129–42.

10. John N. B. Nowland, *Early Reminiscences of Indianapolis . . .* (Indianapolis, 1870), 155.

11. James H. Madison, "Business and Politics in Indianapolis: The Branch Bank and the Junto, 1837–1846," *Indiana Magazine of History*, LXXI (March, 1975), 1–20.

12. For a good account of one sort of artisan development see Betty Lawson Walters, *Furniture Makers of Indiana: 1793 to 1850* (Indianapolis, 1972), 11–34.

13. Donald T. Zimmer, "Madison, Indiana, 1811–1860: A Study in the Process of City Building" (Ph.D. dissertation, Indiana University, 1974), 94–97, 128–43; Margaret Walsh, *The Rise of the Midwestern Meat Packing Industry* (Lexington, Ky., 1982), 1–54.

14. Jeremy Atack and Fred Bateman, "The Development of Industrial Steam Power in the Midwest with Special Reference to Indiana," *Old Northwest*, 8 (Winter, 1982–1983), 329–37.

15. James H. Madison, "Businessmen and the Business Community in Indianapolis, 1820–1860" (Ph.D. dissertation, Indiana University, 1972), 1–35.

16. Kate Douglas Torrey, "Visions of a Western Lowell: Cannelton, Indiana, 1847–1851," *Indiana Magazine of History*, LXXIII (December, 1977), 276–304.

17. James Chute to Absalom Peters, March 12, 1832, quoted in Poinsatte, *Fort Wayne during the Canal Era*, 41, 43.

18. Gayle Thornbrough and Paula Corpuz, eds., *The Diary of Calvin Fletcher* (9 vols., Indianapolis, 1972–1983), I, 239.

19. The relatively restrained quality of Indianapolis boosterism is argued in Carl Abbott, "Indianapolis in the 1850s: Popular Economic Thought and Urban Growth," *Indiana Magazine of History*, LXXIV (December, 1978), 293–315.

6: Pioneer Community Life

1. Thomas T. McAvoy, *The Catholic Church in Indiana. 1789–1834* (New York, 1940); Judith E. Endelman, *The Jewish Community of Indianapolis: 1849 to the Present* (Bloomington, 1984), 8–13.

2. *The Seventh Census of the United States: 1850* (Washington, D.C., 1853), 799–807.

3. David B. Eller, "Hoosier Brethren and the Origins of the Restoration Movement," *Indiana Magazine of History*, LXXVI (March, 1980), 1–20; Henry

K. Shaw, *Hoosier Disciples: A Comprehensive History of the Christian Church (Disciples of Christ) in Indiana* (n.p., 1966), 45–154.

4. Elizabeth K. Nottingham, *Methodism and the Frontier: Indiana Proving Ground* (New York, 1941).

5. Logan Esarey, ed., *The Pioneers of Morgan County: Memoirs of Noah J. Major* (Indianapolis, 1915), 337–38.

6. James A. Carnahan to American Home Missionary Society, September 14, 1831, quoted in L. C. Rudolph, *Hoosier Zion: The Presbyterians in Early Indiana* (New Haven, Conn., 1963), 29. See also John F. Cady, *The Origin and Development of the Missionary Baptist Church in Indiana* (Franklin, 1942), 11–180.

7. Jane Shaffer Elsmere, *Henry Ward Beecher: The Indiana Years, 1837–1847* (Indianapolis, 1973), 3–18, 33–50, 62–75.

8. J. W. Parsons to Absalom Peters, February 20, 1833, quoted in Richard Lyle Power, *Planting Corn Belt Culture: The Impress of the Upland Southerner and Yankee in the Old Northwest* (Indianapolis, 1953), 120. An excellent study of Presbyterianism and Protestantism generally in pioneer Indiana is Rudolph, *Hoosier Zion.*

9. The very illuminating correspondence of these missionaries is abstracted and indexed in L. C. Rudolph, W. W. Wimberly, and Thomas W. Clayton, eds., *Indiana Letters: Abstracts of Letters from Missionaries on the Indiana Frontier to the American Home Missionary Society, 1824–1893* (3 vols., Ann Arbor, Mich., n.d.).

10. W. William Wimberly, III, "Missionary Reform in Indiana, 1826–1860: Education, Temperance, and Antislavery"(Ph.D. dissertation, Indiana University, 1977).

11. Henry Ward Beecher, *Seven Lectures to Young Men. . .* (Indianapolis, 1844), 44, 45, 183–84; Clifford E. Clark, Jr., "The Changing Nature of Protestantism in Mid-Nineteenth Century America: Henry Ward Beecher's *Seven Lectures to Young Men,*" *Journal of American History,* LVII (March, 1971), 832–46.

12. *Indianapolis Journal,* May 13, 1837.

13. Emma Lou Thornbrough, *The Negro in Indiana: A Study of a Minority* (Indianapolis, 1957), 55–150; Morton M. Rosenberg and Dennis V. McClurg, *The Politics of Pro-Slavery Sentiment in Indiana, 1816–1861* (Muncie, 1968).

14. Grover L. Hartman, "The Hoosier Sunday School: A Potent Religious/Cultural Force," *Indiana Magazine of History,* LXXVIII (September, 1982), 215–41.

15. Timothy L. Smith, "Uncommon Schools: Christian Colleges and Social Idealism in Midwestern America, 1820–1950," *Indiana Historical Society Lectures, 1976–1977* (Indianapolis, 1978), 3–36.

16. Nor is there an adequate published history of education in Indiana. Some useful information is contained in Richard G. Boone, *A History of Education in Indiana* (New York, 1892).

17. Thomas D. Clark, *Indiana University: Midwestern Pioneer.* Vol. I: *The Early Years* (Bloomington, 1970), 25–77.

18. Charles W. Moores, *Caleb Mills and the Indiana School System* (Indianapolis, 1905), 410, 444. Moores's uncritical biography reprints the "One of

the People" messages. See also Val Nolan, Jr., "Caleb Mills and the Indiana Free School Law," *Indiana Magazine of History*, XLIX (March, 1953), 81–90.

19. Donald E. Pitzer and Josephine M. Elliott, "New Harmony's First Utopians, 1814–1824," *Indiana Magazine of History*, LXXV (September, 1979), 225–300; Karl J. R. Arndt, ed., *A Documentary History of the Indiana Decade of the Harmony Society, 1814–1824* (2 vols., Indianapolis, 1975, 1978).

20. Donald F. Carmony and Josephine M. Elliott, "New Harmony, Indiana: Robert Owen's Seedbed for Utopia," *Indiana Magazine of History*, LXXVI (September, 1980), 161–261.

21. Donald E. Pitzer, "Education in Utopia: The New Harmony Experience," *Indiana Historical Society Lectures, 1976–1977* (Indianpolis, 1978), 74–101; Dieter Jedan, "Joseph Neef: Innovator or Imitator?" *Indiana Magazine of History*, LXXVIII (December, 1982), 323–40.

22. Richard William Leopold, *Robert Dale Owen: A Biography* (Cambridge, Mass., 1940).

7: Pioneer Government and Politics

1. Quoted in Roger H. Van Bolt, "The Indiana Scene in the 1840s," *Indiana Magazine of History*, XLVII (December, 1951), 334.

2. George W. Geib and William J. Watt, "Indiana's Frontier Militia," William J. Watt and James R. H. Spears, eds., *Indiana's Citizen Soldiers: The Militia and National Guard in Indiana History* (Indianapolis, 1980), 27–31.

3. George Chalou, "Massacre on Fall Creek," *Prologue*, IV (Summer, 1972), 109–14. For a good fictional account see Jessamyn West, *The Massacre at Fall Creek* (New York, 1975).

4. Robert A. Trennert, Jr., *Indian Traders on the Middle Border: The House of Ewing, 1827–54* (Lincoln, Neb., 1981), 1–118; R. David Edmunds, " 'Designing Men, Seeking a Fortune': Indian Traders and the Potawatomi Claims Payment of 1836," *Indiana Magazine of History*, LXXVII (June, 1981), 109–22.

5. Glen A. Blackburn, Nellie Armstrong Robertson, and Dorothy Riker, eds., *The John Tipton Papers* (3 vols., Indianapolis, 1942). The introduction to this important published collection contains an excellent account of Tipton's career by Paul Wallace Gates.

6. John Lauritz Larson and David G. Vanderstel, "Agent of Empire: William Conner on the Indiana Frontier, 1800–1855," *Indiana Magazine of History*, LXXX (December, 1984), 301–28.

7. R. David Edmunds, *The Potawatomis: Keepers of the Fire* (Norman, Okla., 1978), 239–72.

8. Bert Anson, *The Miami Indians* (Norman, Okla., 1970), 177–233.

9. Hugh McCulloch, *Men and Measures of Half a Century* (New York, 1888), 102–103.

10. James A. Glass, "The Architects Town and Davis and the Second Indiana Statehouse," *Indiana Magazine of History*, LXXX (December, 1984), 329–47; Rebecca A. Shepherd, Charles W. Calhoun, Elizabeth Shanahan-Shoemaker, and Alan F. January, comps. and eds., *A Biographical Directory of the Indiana General Assembly*: Vol. I: *1816–1899* (Indianapolis, 1980). The intro-

duction to this volume contains a summary of the functions of the legislature.

11. Clyde F. Snider, "Indiana Counties and Townships," *Indiana Magazine of History*, XXXIII (June, 1937), 130–43.

12. David J. Bodenhamer, "Law and Disorder on the Early Frontier: Marion County, Indiana, 1823–1850," *Western Historical Quarterly*, X (July, 1979), 323–36.

13. Quoted in Pamela J. Bennett and Shirley S. McCord, eds., *Progress after Statehood: A Book of Readings* (Indianapolis, 1974), 386.

14. A good summary of the era's politics is contained in the introduction to Dorothy Riker and Gayle Thornbrough, eds., *Indiana Election Returns, 1816–1851* (Indianapolis, 1960). See also Frederick D. Hill, "William Hendricks: Popular Nonpartisan," *Their Infinite Variety: Essays on Indiana Politics* (Indianapolis, 1981), 1–45.

15. Calvin Fletcher to Michael Fletcher, February 23, 1823, Gayle Thornbrough and Paula Corpuz, eds., *The Diary of Calvin Fletcher* (9 vols., Indianapolis, 1972–1983), I, 89.

16. The most sustained attempt to explore this shift is David Walter Krueger, "Party Development in Indiana, 1800–1832" (Ph.D. dissertation, University of Kentucky, 1974). Krueger perhaps overstates the rapidity and strength of party formation. See also John D. Barnhart and Donald F. Carmony, *Indiana: From Frontier to Industrial Commonwealth* (4 vols., New York, 1954), I, 181–99, 388–407.

17. John William Miller, "The Pioneer Newspapers of Indiana, 1804–1850" (Ph.D. dissertation, Purdue University, 1975); John W. Miller, *Indiana Newspaper Bibliography* (Indianapolis, 1982).

18. Bernard Friedman, "William Henry Harrison: The People against the Parties," in Ralph D. Gray, ed., *Gentlemen from Indiana: National Party Candidates, 1836–1940* (Indianapolis, 1977), 3–28.

19. *Indiana Farmer and Gardner*, I (November 15, 1845), quoted in Richard Lyle Power, *Planting Corn Belt Culture: The Impress of the Upland Southerner and Yankee in the Old Northwest* (Indianapolis, 1953), 78–79.

20. Roger H. Van Bolt, "The Hoosier Politician of the 1840's," *Indiana Magazine of History*, XLVIII (March, 1952), 23–36; Roger H. Van Bolt, "Hoosiers and the Western Program, 1844–1848," *Indiana Magazine of History*, XLVIII (September, 1952), 255–76.

21. Barnhart and Carmony, *Indiana*, II, 83–104, provides a good general discussion. See also Charles Kettleborough, ed., *Constitution Making in Indiana*. Vol. I: *1780–1851* (Indianapolis, 1916), 222–425.

22. Logan Esarey, *A History of Indiana from Its Exploration to 1850* (3rd ed., Fort Wayne, 1924), 519. The constitution of 1851 with amendments and annotations is printed in *Here Is Your Indiana Government* (21st ed., Indianapolis, 1983), 132–50.

23. Wilbur D. Peat, *Indiana Houses of the Nineteenth Century* (Indianapolis, 1962), 50.

24. Angelina Maria Lorraine Collins, *Mrs. Collins' Table Receipts: Adapted to Western Housewifery* (New Albany, 1851).

25. *The Journals and Indian Paintings of George Winter, 1837–1839* (Indianapolis, 1948).

26. *Indianapolis Journal*, November 2, 1847.

27. Samuel Merrill to Mina Merrill, June 9, 1854, Samuel Merrill Papers (Indiana Historical Society Library, Indianapolis).

28. John B. Dillon, *The History of Indiana from Its Earliest Exploration by Europeans, to the Close of the Territorial Government in 1816* (Indianapolis, 1843), 2.

8: Making a Living, 1850–1920

1. Detailed treatment of the Indiana economy in these years is found in Emma Lou Thornbrough, *Indiana in the Civil War Era, 1850–1880* (Indianapolis, 1965), 318–460; and Clifton J. Phillips, *Indiana in Transition: The Emergence of an Industrial Commonwealth, 1880–1920* (Indianapolis, 1968), 132–323. Statistical data in this chapter derive largely from these sources and from the published reports of the United States Census Bureau.

2. Carl Abbott, "The Plank Road Enthusiasm in the Antebellum Middle West," *Indiana Magazine of History*, LXVII (June, 1971), 95–116.

3. John Stover, "Iron Roads in the Old Northwest: The Railroads and the Growing Nation," *Transportation and the Early Nation: Papers Presented at an Indiana American Revolution Bicentennial Symposium* (Indianapolis, 1982), 135–56; Victor M. Bogle, "Railroad Building in Indiana, 1850–1855," *Indiana Magazine of History*, LVIII (September, 1962), 211–32; George W. Hilton, *Monon Route* (Berkeley, Calif., 1978); Carl Abbott, "Indianapolis in the 1850s: Popular Economic Thought and Urban Growth," *Indiana Magazine of History*, LXXIV (December, 1978), 293–315.

4. Quoted in Thornbrough, *Indiana in the Civil War Era*, 347, 356.

5. George W. Hilton and John F. Due, *The Electric Interurban Railways in America* (2nd ed., Stanford, Calif., 1964), 275–86. The nation's only remaining interurban in the late twentieth century was the South Shore, linking South Bend and the Calumet with Chicago. William D. Middleton, *South Shore: The Last Interurban* (San Marino, Calif., 1970).

6. Nick Salvatore, "Railroad Workers and the Great Strike of 1877: The View from a Small Midwestern City [Terre Haute]," *Labor History*, 21 (Fall, 1980), 522–45.

7. Errol Stevens, "Heartland Socialism: The Socialist Party of America in Four Midwestern Communities, 1898–1920" (Ph.D. dissertation, Indiana University, Bloomington, 1978). Chapter three treats the Socialist party in Elwood.

9: Hoosiers Together, 1850–1920

1. Statistical data derive largely from the published United States census reports. More detailed treatments of many of the subjects of this chapter are found in Emma Lou Thornbrough, *Indiana in the Civil War Era, 1850–1880* (Indianapolis, 1965), 461–704; and Clifton J. Phillips, *Indiana in Transition: The Emergence of an Industrial Commonwealth, 1880–1920* (Indianapolis, 1968), 361–585.

2. Quoted in Emma Lou Thornbrough, *The Negro in Indiana: A Study of a Minority* (Indianapolis, 1957), 66–67.

3. The popular vote by county on Article XIII is recorded in Charles Kettleborough, ed., *Constitution Making in Indiana*, Vol. II: *1851–1916* (Indianapolis, 1916), 617–18.

4. Darrel E. Bigham, "Work, Residence, and the Emergence of the Black Ghetto in Evansville, Indiana, 1865–1900," *Indiana Magazine of History*, LXXVI (December, 1980), 287–318.

5. Quoted in Darrel E. Bigham, *Reflections on a Heritage: The German Americans in Southwestern Indiana* (Evansville, 1980), 7. See also Juliet Anne Niehaus, "Ethnic Formation and Transformation: The German-Catholics of Dubois County, Indiana, 1838–1979" (Ph.D. dissertation, New School for Social Research, 1981), 56–152.

6. Powell A. Moore, *The Calumet Region: Indiana's Last Frontier* (Indianapolis, 1959), 347–86; Dean R. Esslinger, *Immigrants and the City: Ethnicity and Mobility in a Nineteenth-Century Midwestern Community* [South Bend] (Port Washington, N.Y., 1975), 116–23. For the East European Jewish community on the Indianapolis South Side, see Judith E. Endelman. *The Jewish Community of Indianapolis: 1849 to the Present* (Bloomington, 1984), 57–110.

7. Maurice G. Baxter, "Encouragement of Immigration to the Middle West During the Era of the Civil War," *Indiana Magazine of History*, LXVI (March, 1950), 25–38; Clifford H. Scott, "Fort Wayne German-Americans in World War II: A Cultural Flu Epidemic," *Old Fort News*, 40 (no. 2, 1977), 3–18.

8. Baroness Alexandra Gripenberg, quoted in Ralph D. Gray, ed., *The Hoosier State: The Modern Era* (Grand Rapids, Mich., 1980), 23; Booth Tarkington, *The Magnificent Ambersons* (New York, 1919), 3. See also Timothy J. Sehr, "Three Gilded Age Suburbs of Indianapolis: Irvington, Brightwood, and Woodruff Place," *Indiana Magazine of History*, LXXVII (December, 1981), 306–32.

9. Meredith Nicholson, "Indianapolis: A City of Homes," *Atlantic Monthly*, XCIII (June, 1904), 839, 841; Robert G. Barrows, "Hurryin' Hoosiers and the American 'Pattern': Geographic Mobility in Indianapolis and Urban North America," *Social Science History*, V (Spring, 1981), 197–222; Robert G. Barrows, "Beyond the Tenement: Patterns of American Urban Housing, 1870–1930," *Journal of Urban History*, 9 (August, 1983), 413–15.

10. Charles Kettleborough, ed., *Constitution Making in Indiana*. Vol. I: *1780–1851* (Indianapolis, 1916), 346.

11. In addition to the discussion of education in Phillips, *Indiana in Transition*, 386–436, see also Wayne E. Fuller, *The Old Country School: The Story of Rural Education in the Middle West* (Chicago, 1982), 120–27. Fuller ascribes larger negative consequences to what he regards as "Indiana's autocratic township district" system than are perhaps warranted.

12. Quoted in Thornbrough, *Indiana in the Civil War Era*, 484.

13. Quoted in Charles W. Moores, *Caleb Mills and the Indiana School System* (Indianapolis, 1905), 620–21.

14. Quoted in Phillips, *Indiana in Transition*, 396.

15. Ronald D. Cohen and Raymond A. Mohl, *The Paradox of Progressive Education: The Gary Plan and Urban Schooling* (Port Washington, N.Y., 1979).

16. James J. Divita, *Slaves to No One: A History of the Holy Trinity Catholic*

Community in Indianapolis on the Diamond Jubilee of the Founding of Holy Trinity Parish (Indianapolis, 1981).

17. Genevieve C. Weeks, *Oscar Carleton McCulloch, 1843–1891: Preacher and Practitioner of Applied Christianity* (Indianapolis, 1976).

18. Grover L. Hartman, "The Hoosier Sunday School: A Potent Religious/ Cultural Force," *Indiana Magazine of History,* LXXVIII (September, 1982), 215–241.

19. Arthur W. Shumaker, *A History of Indiana Literature* (Indianapolis, 1962), especially 3–15; Howard H. Peckham, *Indiana: A Bicentennial History* (New York, 1978), 155–67.

20. Wes D. Gehring, "Kin Hubbard's Abe Martin: A Figure of Transition in American Humor," *Indiana Magazine of History,* LXXVIII (March, 1982), 26–37; David S. Hawes, ed., *The Best of Kin Hubbard: Abe Martin's Sayings and Wisecracks* (Bloomington, 1984).

21. Edward Eggleston, *The Hoosier School-Master: A Novel* (1871, reprint edition, Bloomington, 1984), 5.

22. Chris Smith, "A Plea for a New Appreciation of Popular History: John Clark Ridpath, a Case Study," *Indiana Magazine of History,* LXXVII (September, 1981), 205–230; John Braeman, "Charles A. Beard: The Formative Years in Indiana," *Indiana Magazine of History,* LXXVIII (June, 1982), 93–127; Lana Ruegamer, *A History of the Indiana Historical Society, 1830–1980* (Indianapolis, 1980), 77–134; Suellen M. Hoy, "Governor Samuel M. Ralston and Indiana's Centennial Celebration," *Indiana Magazine of History,* LXXI (September, 1975), 245–66.

23. John Edward Hasse and Frank J. Gillis, *Indiana Ragtime: A Documentary Album* (Indianapolis, 1981), contains a good brief history and marvelous recordings.

10: The Politics of the Civil War Era, 1850–1873

1. The best general treatment of mid-nineteenth century politics is Emma Lou Thornbrough, *Indiana in the Civil War Era, 1850–1880* (Indianapolis, 1965), 38–273

2. Patrick W. Riddleberger, *George Washington Julian: Radical Republican* (Indianapolis, 1966), 45–145.

3. Quoted in Thornbrough, *Indiana in the Civil War Era,* 104. For the large support of the war effort from Quakers, see Jacquelyn S. Nelson, "The Military Response of the Society of Friends in Indiana to the Civil War," *Indiana Magazine of History,* LXXXI (June, 1985), 101–30.

4. James R. H. Spears, "Hoosier Militiamen and the Civil War," William J. Watt and James R. H. Spears, eds., *Indiana's Citizen Soldiers: The Militia and National Guard in Indiana History* (Indianapolis, 1980), 51–79; Alan T. Nolan, *The Iron Brigade: A Military History* (2nd ed., Madison, Wis., 1975); John W. Rowell, *Yankee Artillerymen: Through the Civil War with Eli Lilly's Indiana Battery* (Knoxville, Tenn., 1975). Conditions of wartime service are described in dozens of Civil War letters published in the *Indiana Magazine of History.* See, for example, Lorna Lutes Sylvester, ed., " 'Gone for a Soldier': The Civil War

Letters of Charles Harding Cox," *Indiana Magazine of History*, LXVIII (September, 1972), 181–239.

5. Kenneth M. Stampp, *Indiana Politics during the Civil War* (Indianapolis, 1949).

6. The best account of Morton is Lorna Lutes Sylvester, "Oliver P. Morton and Hoosier Politics during the Civil War" (Ph.D. dissertation, Indiana University, Bloomington, 1968).

7. Gilbert R. Tredway, *Democratic Opposition to the Lincoln Administration in Indiana* (Indianapolis, 1973).

8. Quoted in Stampp, *Indiana Politics during the Civil War*, 147.

9. Quoted in Thornbrough, *Indiana in the Civil War Era*, 111.

10. Lorna Lutes Sylvester, "Oliver P. Morton and the Indiana Legislature of 1863," *Their Infinite Variety: Essays on Indiana Politicians* (Indianapolis, 1981), 121–54.

11. Frank L. Klement, *The Copperheads in the Middle West* (Chicago, 1960); Robert H. Abzug, "The Copperheads: Historical Approaches to Civil War Dissent in the Midwest," *Indiana Magazine of History*, LXVI (December, 1970), 40–55.

12. William E. Wilson, "Thunderbolt of the Confederacy, or King of Horse Thieves," *Indiana Magazine of History*, LIV (June, 1958), 119–30.

13. Ralph D. Gray, "Thomas A. Hendricks: Spokesman for the Democracy," Ralph D. Gray, ed., *Gentlemen from Indiana: National Party Candidates, 1836–1940* (Indianapolis, 1977), 119–39.

11: The Indiana Way of Politics, 1873–1920

1. Charles S. Hyneman, C. Richard Hofstetter, and Patrick F. O'Connor, *Voting in Indiana: A Century of Persistence and Change* (Bloomington, 1979), 83–119. Clifton J. Phillips, *Indiana in Transition: The Emergence of an Industrial Commonwealth, 1880–1920* (Indianapolis, 1968), 1–131, provides a detailed account of political developments.

2. For biographical essays on Indiana's presidential and vice-presidential candidates see Ralph D. Gray, ed.. *Gentlemen from Indiana: National Party Candidates, 1836–1940* (Indianapolis, 1977).

3. Quoted in Richard Jensen, *The Winning of the Midwest: Social and Political Conflict, 1888–1896* (Chicago, 1971), 1.

4. Quoted in ibid., 27.

5. Rebecca Shepherd Shoemaker, "James D. Williams: Indiana's Farmer Governor," *Their Infinite Variety: Essays on Indiana Politicians* (Indianapolis, 1981), 195–221.

6. Melvyn Hammarberg, *The Indiana Voter: The Historical Dynamics of Party Allegiance During the 1870s* (Chicago, 1977).

7. Jensen, *Winning of the Midwest*, 58–88, 178–208; Paul Kleppner, *The Cross of Culture: A Social Analysis of Midwestern Politics, 1850–1900* (New York, 1970); Philip R. VanderMeer, *The Hoosier Politician: Officeholding and Political Culture in Indiana, 1896–1920* (Urbana, Ill., 1985), 104–20.

8. Quoted in Emma Lou Thornbrough, *Indiana in the Civil War Era, 1850–1880* (Indianapolis, 1965), 301.

9. Frank A. Cassell and Marguerite E. Cassell, "Pride, Profits, and Politics:

Indiana and the Columbian Exposition of 1893," *Indiana Magazine of History*, LXXX (June, 1984), 93–121.

10. VanderMeer, *The Hoosier Politician*, 9–49.

11. Charles W. Calhoun, "Republican Jeremiah: Walter Q. Gresham and the Third American Party System," *Their Infinite Variety*, 223–63; James H. Madison, "Charles Warren Fairbanks and Indiana Republicanism," Gray, ed., *Gentlemen from Indiana*, 173–88; John Braeman, *Albert J. Beveridge: American Nationalist* (Chicago, 1971).

12. Quoted in Braeman, *Beveridge*, 100.

13. Quoted in Randall W. Jehs, "Thomas R. Marshall: Mr. Vice President, 1913–1921," Gray, ed., *Gentlemen from Indiana*, 232; Suellen M. Hoy, "Samuel M. Ralston: Progressive Governor, 1913–1917" (Ph.D. dissertation, Indiana University, Bloomington, 1975), 236.

14. Genevieve C. Weeks, *Oscar Carleton McCulloch, 1843–1891: Preacher and Practitioner of Applied Christianity* (Indianapolis, 1976), 165–218; Mina J. Carson, "Agnes Hamilton of Fort Wayne: The Education of a Christian Settlement Worker," *Indiana Magazine of History*, LXXX (March, 1984), 1–34; Robert G. Barrows, " 'The Homes of Indiana': Albion Fellows Bacon and Housing Reform Legislation, 1907–1917," *Indiana Magazine of History*, LXXXI (December, 1985), 309–50.

15. Quoted in Jensen, *Winning of the Midwest*, 187–88.

16. Jan Shipps, "J. Frank Hanly: Enigmatic Reformer," Gray, ed., *Gentlemen from Indiana*, 239–68.

17. Pat Creech Scholten, "A Public 'Jollification': The 1859 Women's Rights Petition before the Indiana Legislature," *Indiana Magazine of History*, LXXII (December, 1976), 347–59.

18. Quoted in Thornbrough, *Indiana in the Civil War Era*, 260.

19. Jane Stephens, "May Wright Sewall: An Indiana Reformer," *Indiana Magazine of History*, LXXVIII (December, 1982), 273–95; Nancy Baker Jones, "A Forgotten Feminist: The Early Writings of Ida Husted Harper, 1878–1894," *Indiana Magazine of History*, LXXIII (June, 1977), 79–101.

20. Nick Salvatore, *Eugene V. Debs: Citizen and Socialist* (Urbana, Ill., 1982); Errol Wayne Stevens, *"The Papers of Eugene V. Debs*: A Review Essay," *Indiana Magazine of History*, LXXX (September, 1984), 264–70; Errol Stevens, "Heartland Socialism: The Socialist Party of America in Four Midwestern Communities, 1898–1920" (Ph.D. dissertation, Indiana University, 1978).

21. Walden S. Freeman, "Will H. Hays and the Politics of Party Harmony," *Their Infinite Variety*, 327–51.

12: The People since 1920

1. Statistical data here and elsewhere come largely from the published reports of the United States Census Bureau, particularly the decennial reports, and the annual *Statistical Abstract*. More detailed treatment of some of the themes of this chapter is found in James H. Madison, *Indiana through Tradition and Change: A History of the Hoosier State and Its People, 1920–1945* (Indianapolis, 1982), 13–25, 263–306, 336–69.

2. George W. Geib, *Indianapolis: Hoosiers' Circle City* (Tulsa, Okla., 1981), 136–140; James B. Lane, *"City of the Century": A History of Gary, Indiana* (Bloom-

ington, 1978), 282–305; Richard M. Dorson, *Land of the Millrats* (Cambridge, Mass., 1981), 165–212. For the expanding urban influence in rural Indiana see Donald T. Zimmer, *Change in Rural Indiana: A History of Rush County, Indiana, 1920 to 1980* (Rushville, Ind., 1984).

3. Theodore Caplow et al., *Middletown Families: Fifty Years of Change and Continuity* (Minneapolis, 1982), 37; David A. Caputo, "The New Federalism: Its Impact on Indiana Cities—An Attitudinal Survey," James A. Papke, ed., *Indiana's Revenue Structure: Major Components and Issues* (West Lafayette, Ind. [1982]), 124–30.

4. See the series "Boom Town," *Indianapolis Star*, September 23–26, 1984; Robert V. Kirch, "Metropolitics of the 1971 Indianapolis Unigov Election: Party and Race," *Indiana Academy of the Social Sciences Proceedings*, VIII (1973), 133–40.

5. Francisco Arturo Rosales and Daniel T. Simon, "Mexican Immigrant Experience in the Urban Midwest: East Chicago, Indiana, 1919–1945," *Indiana Magazine of History*, LXXVII (December, 1981), 333–57; Dorson, *Land of the Millrats*, 109–64; Juliet Anne Niehaus, "Ethnic Formation and Transformation: The German-Catholics of Dubois County, Indiana, 1838–1979" (Ph.D. dissertation, New School for Social Research, 1981), 193–217; Darrel E. Bigham, *Reflections on a Heritage: The German Americans in Southwestern Indiana* (Evansville, Ind., 1980), 19–27.

6. Matthew E. Welsh, *View from the State House: Recollections and Reflections, 1961–1965* (Indianapolis, 1981), 45; Theodore Caplow et al., *All Faithful People: Change and Continuity in Middletown's Religion* (Minneapolis, 1983), 166–69; Judith E. Endelman, *The Jewish Community of Indianapolis: 1849 to the Present* (Bloomington, 1984), 189–254.

7. Grover L. Hartman, *A School for God's People: A History of the Sunday School Movement in Indiana* (Indianapolis, 1980), 89–96, Grover L. Hartman, "Retrospect and Prospect—The Indiana Council of Churches at Age Thirty-Five" (mimeograph draft, 1977, in author's possession).

8. *Minutes of the Indiana Annual Conference of the Methodist Episcopal Church 1926* (n.p., n.d.), 388.

9. Robert S. Lynd and Helen Merrell Lynd, *Middletown: A Study in American Culture* (New York, 1929), 315; Caplow et al., *All Faithful People*, 280; Mitchell K. Hall, "A Time for War: The Church of God's Response to Vietnam," *Indiana Magazine of History*, LXXIV (December, 1983), 285–304. Recent church and denominational membership data are in Bernard Quinn et al., *Churches and Church Membership in the United States* (Atlanta, 1982), 14–15.

10. Kenneth T. Jackson, *The Ku Klux Klan in the City, 1915–1930* (New York, 1967), 144–60.

11. Emma Lou Thornbrough, *Since Emancipation: A Short History of Indiana Negroes, 1863–1963* (n.p.,n.d.).

12. William W. Giffin, "The Political Realignment of Black Voters in Indianapolis, 1924," *Indiana Magazine of History*, LXXIV (June, 1983), 133–66.

13. Max Parvin Cavnes, *The Hoosier Community at War* (Bloomington, 1961), 108–79.

14. Thornbrough, *Since Emancipation*, 60; Emma Lou Thornbrough, "The History of Black Women in Indiana," *Indiana Historical Society Black History News & Notes*, 13 (August, 1983), 5–6.

15. Welsh, *View from the State House*, 94–95, 191–96.

16. Matthew E. Welsh, "Civil Rights and the Primary Election of 1964 in Indiana: The Wallace Challenge," *Indiana Magazine of History*, LXXV (March, 1979), 1–27.

17. Indiana Public Education Survey Commission, *Public Education in Indiana* (New York, 1923).

18. James H. Madison, "John D. Rockefeller's General Education Board and the Rural School Problem in the Midwest," *History of Education Quarterly*, 24 (Summer, 1984), 181–99

19. *Winchester Democrat*, January 8, 1923.

20. Indiana School Study Commission, *An Evaluation of the Indiana Public Schools* (Indianapolis, 1949), 348–51.

21. Roland E. Young, "The History of School District Reorganization in the State of Indiana" (Ed.D. dissertation, Indiana University, 1968), 88–278; Welsh, *View from the State House*, 123–32.

22. William R. Wilkerson, *Indiana School Finance Study: Summary Report* (n.p., 1978), 3–4; Indiana Farm Bureau, *School Statistical Report, 1983* (Indianapolis, 1983), 12.

23. Robert H. Salisbury, "State Politics and Education," Herbert Jacob and Kenneth N. Vines, *Politics in the American States: A Comparative Analysis* (2nd ed., Boston, 1971), 413–14; Morton J. Marcus, "Educational Attainment and Retention in Indiana," *Indiana Business Review*, 57 (September, 1982), 2–5; Indiana Department of Commerce, *An Assessment of Indiana's Educational Attainment Levels* (Indianapolis, 1982); Indiana University Institute for Social Research, *The Report of the 1976 Indiana Social Indicators Survey* (n.p., 1976), 19; Robert G. Lehnen and Carlyn E. Johnson, *Financing Indiana's Public Schools: An Analysis of the Past and Recommendations for the Future* (Indianapolis, 1984), 62–80.

24. Thomas D. Clark, *Indiana University, Midwestern Pioneer*. Vol. III: *Years of Fulfillment* (Bloomington, 1977).

25. Bob Williams, *Hoosier Hysteria!: Indiana High School Basketball* (South Bend, Ind., 1982), 38–53, 234–57; Irving Leibowitz, *My Indiana* (Englewood Cliffs, N.J., 1964), 163–69.

26. *Indiana Year Book, 1925*, p. 322.

27. William J. Watt, *Bowen: The Years as Governor* (Indianapolis, 1981), 107–125.

28. Examples include: Jessamyn West, *The Friendly Persuasion* (New York, 1945); Kurt Vonnegut, Jr., *God Bless You, Mr. Rosewater* (New York, 1963); Ross Lockridge, Jr., *Raintree County* (Boston, 1948); Jean Shepherd, *In God We Trust: All Others Pay Cash* (New York, 1966); Dan Wakefield, *Going All the Way* (New York, 1970).

29. R. E. Banta, ed., *Hoosier Caravan: A Treasury of Indiana Life and Lore* (2nd ed., Bloomington, 1975); A. L. Lazarus, ed., *The Indiana Experience* (Bloomington, 1977); Donald E. Thompson, comp., *Indiana Authors and Their Books, 1917–1966* (Crawfordsville, 1974); Donald E. Thompson, comp., *Indiana Authors and Their Books, 1967–1980* (Crawfordsville, 1981).

30. Eli Lilly, *Prehistoric Antiquities of Indiana* (Indianapolis, 1937); Glenn A. Black, *Angel Site: An Archaeological, Historical, and Ethnological Study* (Indianapolis, 1967); Lana Ruegamer, *A History of the Indiana Historical Society, 1830–1980* (Indianapolis, 1980).

31. Corbin Patrick, "Literature and the Arts," Donald F. Carmony, ed.,

Indiana: A Self-Appraisal (Bloomington, 1966), 233–45; Thomas M. Slade, ed., *Historic American Buildings in Indiana* (Bloomington, 1983).

32. Duncan Schiedt, *The Jazz State of Indiana* (Pittsboro, Ind., 1977); Hoagy Carmichael, *The Stardust Road* (Bloomington, New York & Toronto, 1946; repr. 1983).

13: The Economy since 1920

1. The Indiana economy is treated in more detail in James H. Madison, *Indiana through Tradition and Change: A History of the Hoosier State and Its People, 1920–1945* (Indianapolis, 1982), 153–262. In addition to the sources cited, statistical data in this chapter derive from the published United States census reports and the annual *Statistical Abstract*.

2. James Sanford Rikoon, "The White Plains, Indiana, Threshing Ring, 1920–1943," *Indiana Magazine of History*, LXXX (September, 1984), 227–63.

3. Earl L. Butz, "Agriculture—An Industry in Evolution," in Donald F. Carmony, ed., *Indiana: A Self-Appraisal* (Bloomington, 1966), 56.

4. *Indianapolis Star, Indiana's Economic Revolution* (Indianapolis, 1983), 18–19.

5. Eleanor Arnold, ed., *Party Lines, Pumps, and Privies: Memories of Hoosier Homemakers* (n.p., 1984).

6. Robert S. Lynd and Helen Merrell Lynd, *Middletown: A Study in American Culture* (New York, 1929), 114; Alan R. Raucher, "Paul G. Hoffman, Studebaker, and the Car Culture," *Indiana Magazine of History*, LXXIX (September, 1983), 209–30; Thomas J. Schlereth, *US 40: A Roadscape of the American Experience* (Indianapolis, 1985).

7. George W. Hilton, *Monon Route* (Berkeley, Calif., 1978); *Indiana Transportation Fact Book* (Indianapolis, 1982), 67–69.

8. Wallace Spencer Huffman, "Indiana's Place in Automobile History," *Indiana History Bulletin*, 44 (February, 1967), 11–44; Ralph D. Gray, *Alloys and Automobiles: The Life of Elwood Haynes* (Indianapolis, 1979), 167–202.

9. *Indiana's Economic Resources and Potential* (3 vols., Bloomington, 1955), Vol. I, Section 3, p. 50.

10. Morton J. Marcus, "Structure and Performance of the Indiana Economy: An Overview," James A. Papke, ed., *Indiana's Revenue Structure: Major Components and Issues* (West Lafayette, 1983), 6–12; "Indiana Regional Reports," *Indiana Business Review*, 57 (June, 1982), 2–14; *Indiana Business Review*, 59 (May–June, 1984), *passim*.

11. *In Step with the Future: Indiana's Strategic Economic Development Plan* (n.p., [1984]), 48.

12. Indiana Department of Commerce, *An Economic Development Profile of Indiana* (Indianapolis, 1982), 23–25, 188; Indiana Department of Commerce, *The Cyclical Behavior of the Indiana Economy: Description, Explanation and Implications* (Indianapolis, 1983), *passim*.

13. *In Step with the Future*, 19–25; Indiana Department of Commerce, *Economic Development in Indiana: Retrospect and Prospect* (Indianapolis, 1982), *passim*.

14. The series appeared in the *Indianapolis Star* between August 21 and September 5, 1983, and was later reprinted in booklet form.

15. Richard L. Pfister, "A Mid-Year Review of the Indiana Economy," *Indiana Business Review*, 59 (May–June, 1984), 4.

16. Hugh S. McLaughlin, "The Banking Structure in Indiana and Neighboring States," *Indiana Business Review*, 59 (January–February, 1984), 15–24; *Indianapolis Star*, March 20, 1984, January 3, 1986.

17. Indiana Environment Management Board, *Report on the Environment* (Indianapolis, 1977); *Indiana State Board of Health Bulletin* (Winter, 1984), 8–9; William J. Watt, *Bowen: The Years as Governor* (Indianapolis, 1981), 66–71.

18. Gary L. Bailey, "The Terre Haute, Indiana, General Strike, 1935," *Indiana Magazine of History*, LXXX (September, 1984), 193–226.

19. Dallas Sells, "Organized Labor," Carmony, ed., *Indiana: A Self-Appraisal*, 116–27; Indiana Department of Commerce, *Indiana Manufacturing Labor Costs Relative to Other States* (Indianapolis, 1982); *In Step with the Future*, 59.

14: The Politics of a State

1. Indiana *Senate Journal*, 1923, p. 6. For interwar politics generally see James H. Madison, *Indiana through Tradition and Change: A History of the Hoosier State and Its People, 1920–1945* (Indianapolis, 1982), 26–152.

2. Hugh Emmons, quoted in Madison, *Indiana through Tradition and Change*, 51.

3. Bert Morgan to Will Hays, May 29, 1924, Will Hays Papers (Indiana Division, Indiana State Library, Indianapolis).

4. *Inaugural Address of Governor Paul V. McNutt of Indiana* (Indianapolis, 1933).

5. Iwan Morgan, "Fort Wayne and the Great Depression: The Early Years, 1929–1933," *Indiana Magazine of History*, LXXX (June, 1984), 122–45

6. For a marvelous example of the hardship of the Depression and the human response to the New Deal see the oral history interview conducted by Thomas Krasean in Ralph D. Gray, ed., *The Hoosier State: Readings in Indiana History: The Modern Era* (Grand Rapids, Mich., 1980), 333–42.

7. *Indiana House Journal*, 1936, p. 101.

8. Iwan Morgan, "Factional Conflict in Indiana Politics During the Later New Deal Years, 1936–1940," *Indiana Magazine of History*, LXXIX (March, 1983), 29–60.

9. William B. Pickett, "The Capehart Cornfield Conference and the Election of 1938: Homer E. Capehart's Entry into Politics," *Indiana Magazine of History*, LXXIII (December, 1977), 251–75; Iwan Morgan, "Fort Wayne and the Great Depression: The New Deal Years, 1933–1940," ibid., LXXX (December, 1984), 348–78.

10. Charles Francis Fleming, *The White Hat: Henry Frederick Schricker, A Political Biography* (n.p., 1966), 3–4, 60–105: F. Gerald Handfield, "An Oral History Approach to the Administration of Governor George N. Craig: 1953–1957," *Indiana Academy of Social Sciences Proceedings*, XIV (1979), 101–107.

11. Irving Leibowitz, *My Indiana* (Englewood Cliffs, N.J., 1964), 15–30; Dale R. Sorenson, "The Anticommunist Consensus in Indiana, 1945–1958" (Ph.D. dissertation, Indiana University, 1980); Michael Paul Poder, "The Senatorial Career of William E. Jenner" (Ph.D. dissertation, University of Notre

Dame, 1976); Russell Pulliam, *Publisher: Gene Pulliam, Last of the Newspaper Titans* (Ottawa, Ill., 1984), especially 105–29.

12. Charles S. Hyneman, C. Richard Hofstetter, and Patrick F. O'Connor, *Voting in Indiana: A Century of Persistence and Change* (Bloomington, 1979), 17–25.

13. *Congressional Quarterly Weekly Report*, September 3, 1983, p. 1798.

14. William R. Shaffer and David A. Caputo, "Political Continuity in Indiana Presidential Elections: An Analysis Based on the Key-Munger Paradigm," *Midwest Journal of Political Science*, 16 (November, 1972), 700–11.

15. Matthew E. Welsh, *View from the State House: Recollections and Reflections, 1961–1965* (Indianapolis, 1981), 98.

16. Hugh Willoughby, *Amid the Alien Corn: An Intrepid Englishman in the Heart of America* (Indianapolis, 1958), 141; *Modernizing Our State Government: Selected Papers from a Conference Held at The Center for Continuing Education, University of Notre Dame, March 20, 1970* (n.p., n.d.), 57, 26.

17. Neal R. Peirce and John Keef, *The Great Lakes States of America: People, Politics, and Power in the Five Great Lakes States* (New York, 1980), 256–57.

18. Paul Kleppner, "Searching for the Indiana Voter: A Review Essay," *Indiana Magazine of History*, LXXVI (December, 1980), 346–66; John D. Cranor, et al., *A Summary Report: A 1980 Survey on Voting and Citizen Attitudes in Indiana* (Muncie, 1980), 33, 59–60.

19. For overviews of Indiana government see William P. Hojnacki, ed., *Politics and Public Policy in Indiana: Prospects for Change in State and Local Government* (Dubuque, Iowa, 1983); Philip S. Wilder, Jr., and Karl O'Lessker, *Introduction to Indiana Government and Politics* (Indianapolis, 1967); and the biennial volumes, which first appeared in 1944, *Here Is Your Indiana Government*, published by the Indiana State Chamber of Commerce.

20. Joseph A. Schlesinger, "The Politics of the Executive," Herbert Jacob and Kenneth N. Vines, eds., *Politics in the American States: A Comparative Analysis* (Boston, 1971), 210–37; Frank James Munger, "Two-Party Politics in the State of Indiana" (Ph.D. dissertation, Harvard University, 1955), 87–127.

21. Welsh, *View from the State House*, 83.

22. Citizens Conference on State Legislatures, *The Sometime Governments: A Critical Study of the 50 American Legislatures* (New York, 1971), 49, 210–13.

23. James L. McDowell, *The Emperor's New Clothes?: Legislative Reform in Indiana* (Terre Haute, 1976), 6–15.

24. Kenneth Janda et al., "Legislative Politics in Indiana," James B. Kessler, ed., *Empirical Studies of Indiana Politics: Studies of Legislative Behavior* (Bloomington, 1970), 33–42.

25. Welsh, *View from the State House*, 141–73.

26. William J. Watt, *Bowen: The Years as Governor* (Indianapolis, 1981), 35–43; Patrick D. O'Rourke, "Property Taxation," James A. Papke, ed., *Indiana's Revenue Structure: Major Components and Issues* (West Lafayette [1982]), 91–103.

27. *New York Times*, March 4, 1984; Papke, ed., *Indiana's Revenue Structure*, 1–3.

28. The general trends in Indiana's relationship with the federal government are sketched in James H. Madison, "The American Constitution and the Old Federalism: Views from the Hoosier State" (Bicentennial of the United

States Constitution Lecture Series, Poynter Center, Indiana University, Bloomington, 1985).

29. *Laws of the State of Indiana, 1947* (2 vols., Indianapolis, 1947), II, pp. 1509–10.

30. *Indianapolis Star*, September 23, 1951, quoted in Kan Ori, "Basic Ideas in Federal-State Relations: The Indiana 'Revolt' of 1951" (Ph.D. dissertation, Indiana University, 1961), 53.

31. Quoted in Ori, "Basic Ideas in Federal-State Relations," 200–201.

32. Richard E. Dawson and Virginia Gray, "State Welfare Policies," Herbert Jacob and Kenneth N. Vines, eds., *Politics in the American States*, 452–54.

33. Watt, *Bowen*, 66–75, 115–16, 248–50; Kay Franklin and Norma Schaeffer, *Duel for the Dunes: Land Use Conflict on the Shores of Lake Michigan* (Urbana, Ill., 1983); J. Ronald Engel, *Sacred Sands: The Struggle for Community in the Indiana Dunes* (Middletown, Conn., 1983).

34. Watt, *Bowen*, 13; State Planning Agency, *Integrating Federal and State Programs in Indiana* (Indianapolis, 1976), 9; Theodore Caplow et al., *All Faithful People: Change and Continuity in Middletown's Religion* (Minneapolis, 1983), 4.

35. *New York Times*, April 8, 1984.

15: Hoosiers Past and Present

1. Good summaries of the possibilities are found in Howard H. Peckham, *Indiana: A Bicentennial History* (New York, 1978), 11–13; and Raven I. McDavid, Jr., and Virginia McDavid, "Cracker and Hoosier," *Names*, 21 (September, 1973), 161–67.

2. Richard Lyle Power, "The Hoosier as an American Folk-Type," *Indiana Magazine of History*, XXXVIII (June, 1942), 107–22.

3. Meredith Nicholson, "Indianapolis: A City of Homes," *Atlantic Monthly*, XCVIII (June, 1904), 836. For Nicholson's denial of this stereotype see his *The Hoosiers* (New York, 1900).

4. Dillon Bustin, *If You Don't Outdie Me: The Legacy of Brown County* (Bloomington, Ind.,1982); Lorna Lutes Sylvester, " 'Down in the Hills o' Brown County': Photographs of Frank M. Hohenberger," *Indiana Magazine of History*, LXXI (September, 1975), 205–44, LXXII (March, 1976), 21–62.

5. Irving Leibowitz, *My Indiana* (Englewood Cliffs, N.J., 1964), 291. See also Peckham, *Indiana*, 187–95; and, for a more negative assessment, John Bartlow Martin, *Indiana: An Interpretation* (New York, 1947), 268–83.

A Guide to Further Reading

The notes to this book provide good beginnings for further reading and research on specific subjects. The starting points for more intensive study are the volumes in *The History of Indiana*: John D. Barnhart and Dorothy L. Riker, *Indiana to 1816: The Colonial Period* (Volume I, Indianapolis, 1971); Emma Lou Thornbrough, *Indiana in the Civil War Era, 1850–1880* (Volume III, Indianapolis, 1965); Clifton J. Phillips, *Indiana in Transition: The Emergence of an Industrial Commonwealth, 1880–1920* (Volume IV, Indianapolis, 1968); and James H. Madison, *Indiana through Tradition and Change: A History of the Hoosier State and Its People, 1920–1945* (Volume V, Indianapolis, 1982). Two volumes in this series are yet to be published: one dealing with the decades since World War II and the other covering the years from 1816 to 1850. For the pioneer period there is much useful information in R. C. Buley, *The Old Northwest: Pioneer Period, 1815–1840* (2 volumes, Indianapolis, 1950).

Many of the general accounts of Indiana's history are now outdated in scholarship and style, but several continue to be useful in various ways. The best of the older works is John D. Barnhart and Donald F. Carmony, *Indiana: From Frontier to Industrial Commonwealth* (4 vols., New York, 1954). Book-length essays that interpret Indiana include Howard Peckham, *Indiana: A Bicentennial History* (New York, 1978); William E. Wilson, *Indiana: A History* (Bloomington, 1966); John Bartlow Martin, *Indiana: An Interpretation* (New York, 1947); and Irving Leibowitz, *My Indiana* (Englewood Cliffs, N.J., 1964). Also useful are the essays gathered in Donald F. Carmony, ed., *Indiana: A Self-Appraisal* (Bloomington, 1966). Dwight W. Hoover, *A Pictorial History of Indiana* (Bloomington, 1980), and Patrick J. Furlong, *Indiana: An Illustrated History* (Northridge, Calif., 1985), provide a brief narrative along with excellent illustrations of Indiana's past. Finally, in *The Hoosier State: Readings in Indiana History* (2 vols., Grand Rapids, Mich., 1980), Ralph D. Gray introduces essays and documents that testify to the variety of subject matter and approach in the state's history.

As the notes to this book indicate, one of the most important sources of Indiana history is the *Indiana Magazine of History*. This journal is published quarterly by the Department of History, Indiana University, in cooperation with the Indiana Historical Society. Three twenty-five-year general indexes provide access to material in the magazine from the first issue in 1905 through 1979. For issues since 1979 there is an annual index in each December issue.

Much of the richness of the state's historical resources is due to the Indiana Historical Society, located at 315 West Ohio Street, Indianapolis. It supports publications, lectures, meetings, special projects, and a large library of printed and manuscript material. The Society also supports genealogical work in cooperation with the Genealogy Division of the Indiana State Library. The Indiana State Library is another institution central to the cause of history. Located at 140 North Senate Avenue, Indianapolis, it maintains a large collection of Indiana newspapers, books, government documents, and manuscripts. Also located in the Indiana State Library and Historical Building is the Archives Division of the Indiana Commission on Public Records, the primary source of state government records. And at 140 North Senate also are the offices of the Indiana Historical Bureau, which provide a variety of services and publications: especially useful is the *Indiana History Bulletin*, which publicizes current activites in state and local history.

In Bloomington, the Indiana University Library, including the Lilly Library, has large collections of printed and manuscript sources and a good Indiana newspaper collection. Also in the Indiana University Library are hundreds of Ph.D. dissertations relating to Indiana. Quick access to these and other dissertations is provided in Betty Jarboe and Kathryn Rumsey, comps., *Studies on Indiana: A Bibliography of Theses and Dissertations Submitted to Indiana Institutions of Higher Education for Advanced Degrees, 1902–1977* (Indianapolis, 1980). Finally, attention should be drawn to the many good local libraries in Indiana. From Gary to Fort Wayne to Madison to Evansville there are libraries that have collected, preserved, and made available material to study Indiana history.

Index

Adams, John, 46
Adams, John Quincy, 133
Ade, George, 188
Agriculture: in pioneer era, 67–70, 74–97, 141–42; 1850 to 1920, 147–53; since 1920, 263–66
American Home Missionary Society, 103, 104
American Legion 289, 290, 295, 303
American Protective Association, 186
Amherst, Jeffrey, 18
Anderson sit-down strike, 285
Angel Mounds, 5, 6
Anti-Saloon League, 224, 225, 239, 290
Antislavery. See Slavery
Archaic tradition, 4
Architecture, 259–60
Art: and George Winter, 141; 1850 to 1920, 190; since 1920, 259
Automobile: and transportation, 268–72, 273; manufacture of, 275, 285

Bacon, Albion Fellows, 223
Badin, Stephen, 99
Badollet, John, 51
Baker, Conrad, 175
Ball Brothers, 162
Ball State University, 252
Banks, in pioneer era, 87–89, 137; since 1920, 282
Baptists, 100, 102
Barnhart, John D., 259
Barrows, Robert, 177, 178
Basketball, 191, 254–256
Bayh, Birch, 304
Beard, Charles, 190
Beecher, Eunice, 103, 105
Beecher, Henry Ward: in Lawrenceburg, 102–103; in Indianapolis, 104, 105, 106, 115, 136–37
Beveridge, Albert, 220–21, 222–23, 228, 289
Birth control, 64, 120
Birth rate, 64, 234
Black, Glenn, 258
Black Hawk War, 122, 125

Blacks, in pioneer era, 107–108; 1850 to 1920, 169–73, 176–77, 206; since 1920, 241–47, 255–56, 292–93
Board of State Charities, 223–24
Bowen, Otis: and property tax, 236, 312; election of, 304, 309; and federal government, 316–17
Branigin, Roger D., 304
Brant, Joseph, 26
Brethern churches, 100
Bridge, John, Jr., 123
Bright, Jesse D., 194, 195
Brookville land office, 63
Brown County, 190, 319
Bruté, Bishop Simon, 99
Buffalo Trace, 60, 80
Buley, R. C., 259
Burns Harbor, 272
Butler, Charles, 84
Butler University, 184
Butz, Earl, 265

Camp meetings, 101–102
Canals, 82–86, 153
Cannelton Cotton Mill, 92, 93
Capehart, Homer E., 300, 303, 304
Carmichael, Hoagy, 191, 260–61
Carmony, Donald F., 259
Catholics: in pioneer era, 99; 1850 to 1920, 185–86; and Ku Klux Klan 292–94
Central Canal, 83
Central Normal College, 183
Chapman, George and Jacob, 135
Chautauqua, 187
Chickasaw Indians, 13
Child labor, 164–65
Christian Church. See Disciples of Christ
Cities and towns: in pioneer era, 93–97; 1850 to 1920, 162, 175–79; since 1920, 235–37
Civil rights, 1960s, 240
Civil War: military course of, 197–98
Clark, George Rogers, 22–26, 29
Clarksville, 29
Climate, 9

Coal mining, 165, 276, 283–84
Coffin, Levi, 107
Colfax, Schuyler, 209
Colleges and universities: in pioneer era, 110, 111; 1850–1920, 184; since 1920, 252–53
Collins, Angelina, 141
Columbian Exposition, 1893, 218
Columbus, 259
Conner, John, 41
Conner, William, 41, 124
Conscription, Civil War, 201
Constitution of 1816, 50–54
Constitution of 1851: and debt, 86; framing of, 138–40; and blacks, 169–70; and education, 179
Cotton, Fassett A., 183
Corydon 37, 47, 51, 52
Costigan, Francis, 141
County agricultural agent, 150
County government: in pioneer era, 127, 128, 130–31; 1850 to 1920, 215, 218; and roads, 153–54, 269
Courts, in pioneer era: 122–23, 130: since 1920, 307. *See also* Indiana Supreme Court
Craig, George N., 302–303, 309
Cranstone, Lefevre, 178
Crawfordsville land office, 63
Crime: in pioneer era, 53, 122–23, 130; and state police, 273. *See also* Lynching
Crispus Attucks high school, 242, 243, 255–256
Croghan, George, 16–17

Dale, George, 293
Darby, William, 122
Debs, Eugene V., 227
Delawares, 124
Democratic party: in pioneer era, 88–89, 133–38; 1850 to 1920, 194–96, 200–207, 209–22; since 1920, 243, 288–317
Dennis, Philip, 40
DePauw University, 110, 184
Dependent peoples: in pioneer era, 130–31; in Progressive era, 223–24; in Great Depression, 296–97; and Jenner Amendment, 315–16
Detroit, 24
Dillin, Hugh S., 315
Dillinger, John, 273
Dillon, John B., 141, 190
Disciples of Christ, 100
Divorce legislation, 226
Dix, Dorothea, 130

Dodd, Harrison H., 204
Douglass, Frederick, 108
Dreiser, Theodore, 189–90, 258
Dubois County, 173, 238
Dudley, William W., 210
Durbin, Winfield, 171
DuValle, Reginald, 191

Earlham College, 110, 184
Early, Jacob D., 90
Education: in pioneer era, 53, 108–115; 1850 to 1920, 179–84; since 1920, 247–53; and blacks, 172, 242 244–45, 246
Eggleston, Edward, 181, 188–89
Elections: in 1820s, 133–34; 1840, 135–36; 1862 210–202; 1864, 204; 1888, 209–210, 212; 1896, 219; 1924, 239; 1932, 295; 1964, 245–46, 304; 1970s, 307
Eli Lilly and Company, 162, 275
Employers' Association of Indianapolis, 166
English, William H., 209
Esarey, Logan, 140, 259
Evansville: and Wabash and Erie Canal, 84; German-Americans in, 174, 238; blacks in, 170, 171
Ewing, George W., 123, 125, 126
Ewing, William G., 123, 126

Fairbanks, Charles Warren, 209, 220, 225
Fall Creek massacre, 122–23
Fallen Timbers, Battle of, 30–31
Family life, 63–64, 108, 141–42
Fire protection, 176
Fisher, Carl G., 154
Flatboats, 77
Fletcher, Calvin, 94, 115, 132
Fort Dearborn, 41–42, 45
Fort Knox, 29
Fort Ouiatanon, 13
Fort Sackville, 23, 24, 25
Fort Wayne, 9, 11, 13, 30, 32, 63, 94, 122
Fort Wayne, Treaty of, 43
France: in North America, 12–18
Franklin College, 110, 184
French and Indian War, 17–18
French Lick, 191, 225
French settlers, 23, 27, 37, 99, 123
Fur trade, 12–13

Gary, 178, 184, 235–36
Gary Roosevelt High school, 242, 243, 255
Gas, natural, 160–61
Gates, Ralph F., 302–303

General Assembly: in pioneer era, 47, 53, 127, 136, 139; in 1863 crisis, 202; and Ku Klux Klan, 294; since 1940, 309–311
General Education Board, 247–248
German-Americans, 99, 100, 173, 175, 238
Goodrich, James P., 221, 228
Gougar, Helen M., 226
Grand Army of the Republic, 205
Grange, 149, 151, 157, 212
Great Britain: and empire, 18; and Indian resistance, 30, 31, 43; and War of 1812, 44–46
Greenback movement, 151, 165, 212
Greenville, Treaty of, 30–31
Gresham, Walter Q., 220

Hall, Basil: sketch by, 65
Hall, Baynard Rush, 68, 82
Halleck, Charles, 303, 315
Hamilton, Allen, 87, 94, 123, 125
Hamilton, Henry, 21–22, 23, 24
Hammarberg, Melvyn, 213
Hamtramck, John Francis, 29, 30
Handley, Harold W., 302–303, 311
Hanly, J. Frank, 225, 228
Hanna, Samuel, 87, 123
Hanover College, 110, 184
Harmar, Josiah, 29–30
Harmonists, 116–17
Harper, Ida Husted, 226
Harrison, Benjamin: and election of 1888, 209, 210; and election of 1876, 212, 215; and Republican factionalism, 220
Harrison, William Henry: as territorial governor, 37–40, 41, 43, 43–45, 46–50; and 1840 election, 135–36
Hartke, Vance, 303
Hatcher, Richard, 221, 228, 236, 246
Haynes, Elwood, 268, 275
Health: on frontier, 71–72; public, 222–23; and environment, 283
Helm, Leonard, 23
Hendricks Thomas A., 206, 209
Hendricks, William, 131-32, 134
Henry, Patrick, 22, 23
Herschell, William, 147
Highways. See Roads
Hindostan, 95
Historic Landmarks Foundation, 260
Historic preservation, 259–60
Hohenberger, Frank: photographs by, 216, 254
"Hoosier Group," 190, 259
Hoosier School-Master, 181, 188

House Concurrent Resolution Number 2, 1947, 313–14, 316
Housing reform, 223
Hovde, Frederick L., 252
Hubbard, Kin, 188
Hudnut, William H., III, 237
Hurty, John N., 222

Immigrants; in pioneer era, 99, 139–40; 1850 to 1920, 173–75; since 1920, 237–38, 292
Indiana Arts Commission, 261
Indiana Civil Rights Commission, 245
Indiana Colonization Society, 107
Indiana Committee for the Humanities, 261
Indiana Council of Churches, 238
Indiana dunes, 316
Indiana Farm Bureau, 265–66, 290, 303, 311
Indiana Farmer, 149
Indiana Gazette, 37, 134
Indiana Gazetteer, 62
Indiana Historical Bureau, 259
Indiana Historical Society, 190, 259
Indiana Library Association, 185
Indiana Magazine of History, 190, 259
Indiana Medical College, 71
Indianapolis: in pioneer era, 63, 80, 90, 91, 94, 95, 141; and economy, 154, 155, 158, 162, 166; blacks in, 170, culture in, 190–91; and urban change, 235, 236–37; and Ku Klux Klan, 241
Indianapolis Benevolent Society, 223
Indianapolis Charity Organization Society, 223
Indianapolis 500-mile race, 154, 191, 256
Indianapolis Museum of Art, 259
Indianapolis newspapers, 135, 155, 173, 220, 280 , 303, 314–15
Indianapolis Steam Mill Company, 91–92
Indiana Public Service Commission, 157, 273, 282
Indiana Railroad Commission, 157
Indiana State Board of Health, 222, 283, 316
Indiana state fair, 149, 150
Indiana State Federation of Labor, 166
Indiana State Federation of Organized Charities, 223
Indiana State Library, 185
Indiana State Medical Society, 72
Indiana State Museum, 258
Indiana State Teachers Association, 181, 183, 311

Indiana State University, 183, 184, 252
Indiana Supreme Court, 180, 222
Indiana University: in pioneer era, 110,
  111; 1850 to 1920, 184; medical school,
  223; basketball team, 242; since 1945,
  252
Indiana University-Purdue University,
  Indianapolis, 236
Indiana Vocational Technical College,
  253
Indiana Women's Rights Association, 226
Indians: and French and British, 10–19;
  and Revolution, 21–22, 23, 24, 27; and
  white settlement, 27–31, 37–46; and
  trade, 123–24; removal of, 122–26;
  paintings of, 141
Infant mortality 64, 171, 223, 247
Internal Improvements Act of 1836, 83–
  86, 137
Interurbans, 157–58; map of, 159
Irish-Americans, 99, 174
Irvington, 177

Jackson, Andrew, 124–25, 133, 137
Jackson, Ed, 290, 293, 294
Jefferson, Thomas, 22, 37, 40
Jeffersonville land office, 42, 63
Jenner, William E., 303, 315
Jenner Amendment, 315
Jennings, Jonathan: in politics, 47, 49, 50,
  54, 131–32; at constitutional conven-
  tion, 51
Jensen, Richard, 213
Jews: in pioneer era, 99; since 1920, 238
John Birch Society, 303
John Herron Art Institute, 190
Johnston, John, 41, 122–23
Jordan, David Starr, 184
Julian, George, 195, 200, 206

Kankakee Valley, 7
Kansas-Nebraska Act, 195
Kaskaskia, 22–23
Keelboats, 77
Kekionga. See Fort Wayne; Miami Indians
Kentucky: settlement in, 28–29
Kern, John W., 209
Kirk, William, 40
Kleppner, Paul, 213
Knights of Labor, 165–66
Knights of the Golden Circle, 204
Know-Nothing movement, 175, 185, 194,
  195
Knox County, 34

Ku Klux Klan, 237, 238, 240, 241, 289–
  95, 319

La Balme, Augustin de, 24–25
Labor: 1850 to 1922, 163–67; since 1920,
  284–86
La Demoiselle, 17
Lafayette, 80, 90
Lake County, 162–63, 237. See also Gary
Land: sales of, 31–33, 35, 42, 61, 63; and
  Indian removal, 124–26
Lane, Henry S., 198
Langlade, Sieur de, 17
Lanier, James F. D., 94, 141, 203
La Salle, Robert Cavelier de, 12
Law: in pioneer era, 127–28; and blacks,
  170; and state police, 273
Lawrenceburg, 102–103
League of Nations, 289
League of Women Voters, 283, 290, 299
Libraries, 120, 184–85, 259
Lieber, Richard, 257–58
Lilly, Eli, 258, 259
Lilly Endowment, 237
Lincoln, Abraham: on Indiana frontier,
  60, 77, 108; sumbook of, 109; and 1860
  election, 196
Lincoln, Nancy, 71
Lincoln, Thomas, 60, 64
Lind, Jenny, 191
Literacy, 111–13, 179, 180
Literature, 187–190, 258
Little Turtle, 25, 30, 40, 43
Lochry, Archibald, 25–26
Lockridge, Ross, Jr., 258
Logansport Indian agency, 124
Log cabins: construction of, 64–65
Lugar, Richard, 237, 304
Lutherans, 100
Lyles settlement, Gibson County, 116
Lynching, 171, 241
Lynd, Robert and Helen, 240

McCarthy, Joseph, 303
McCarty, Nicholas, 91
McCoy, Isaac, 126
McCray, Warren T., 289, 290
McCulloch, Hugh, 126
McCulloch, Oscar C., 186, 223
Maclure, William, 117
McNutt, Paul, 285, 295–302, 305; pic-
  tured, 296
Madison: in pioneer era, 80, 81, 95; pork
  packing in, 90, 91; decline of, 175

Madison, James, 50, 54
Madison and Indianapolis Railroad, 83, 85, 154
Manufacturing: in pioneer era, 89–93; 1850 to 1920, 158–63; since 1920, 274–81
Marion County, 130
Marion (Grant County) lynching, 171, 241
Marshall, Thomas, 209, 221, 228
Medicine: on frontier, 71–72. *See also* Health
Menominee, 125
Merchants, 87
Methodists, 100–102, 103, 185
Mexican-Americans, 237
Miami Indians: culture of, 10; and Europeans, 16–18, 18–19; and Revolution, 21–22, 24; and white expansion, 29–30, 40, 41, 43, 45–46; removal of, 124–26
Michigan Road, 80, 81, 82
Militia: in pioneer era, 43, 44, 45, 53, 122; and Evansville riot, 171
Miller, J. Irwin, 259
Milligan case, 201
Mills, Caleb, 113, 115, 179, 182
Mills, grain, 89–90, 160
Minton, Sherman, 301
Mississippian tradition, 5
Monon Railroad, 154, 272
Montgomery, Wes, 260
Moravian missionaries, 40
Morgan, John Hunt, 203, 204
Morton, Oliver P.: and immigrant recruitment, 175; and Civil War, 198–205; pictured, 199; and Reconstruction, 206–207
Mounds State Park, 5
Muncie, 240
Music, 190–91, 260–61

National Association for the Advancement of Colored People, 243, 244
National Road, 81, 82, 153
Natural gas boom, 160–61
Neef, Joseph, 117
New Albany, 95
New Albany and Salem Railroad. *See* Monon Railroad
New Deal, 266, 269, 283, 297–302
New Harmony: and Harmonists, 116–17; and Owenites, 117, 120; illustration, 118–19
New Purchase Treaty, 46, 61, 63, 124

Newspapers: in pioneer era, 134–35; black, 173; and Ku Klux Klan, 293, 294
New York Central Railroad, 155
Nicholson, Meredith, 177, 188, 319; pictured, 188
Nineteenth Indiana Regiment, 197
Noble, James, 123, 132
Northwest Ordinance, 33–35, 46–51
Northwest Territory, 31–35

Oberholtzer, Madge, 294
Oliver, James, 175
Oliver plow, 148, 149
Orange County courthouse, illustration, 216
Ordinance of 1787. *See* Northwest Ordinance
Ordinance of 1785, 31–32, 35
Orr, Robert D., 304, 309, 312
Ouiatanon, 13
Owen, Robert, 117, 120
Owen, Robert Dale, 120, 140

Paleo-Indian tradition, 4
Parry, David M., 166
Patronage: in pioneer politics, 124, 134; since 1920, 272, 273, 298–99, 305–307
Peckham, Howard, 187
Pennsylvania Railroad, 155
Physiographic regions: map of, 8
Pigeon Roost massacre, 45
Plank roads, 153
Political parties. *See* by name of party, e.g., Democratic party
Pontiac's Rebellion, 18–19
Populist party, 219
Pork packing, 90–91
Porter, Gene Stratton, 188
Posey, Thomas, 50, 54
Potawatomis: culture of, 10; and Europeans, 18–19; and Revolution, 21–22; and Fort Dearborn massacre, 42, 45; and Michigan Road, 81; removal of, 124–25
Poverty. *See* Dependent peoples
Prehistoric peoples, 3–6
Presbyterians, 102–104, 105
Prisons, 130
Proclamation of 1763, 19, 21
Progressive party, 221
Progressive reform, 220–26
Prohibition. *See* Temperance
Prophet, The, 43
Public health. *See* Health

Pulliam, Eugene C., 303
Purdue University, 149–50, 184, 252, 265

Quakers: and antislavery, 49, 99–100, 107; and Indians, 40; and Civil War, 343n
Quayle, Dan, 304
Quebec Act, 21

Racism: and constitution of 1851, 140; 1850 to 1920, 169–73; since 1920, 240, 241–47; and Ku Klux Klan, 289–95
Railroads: in pioneer era, 85, 91; 1850 to 1920, 153–57, 165; since 1920, 272
Ralston, Samuel, 221, 228
Randolph, Thomas, 47
Ransom, Willard, 244
Rapp, George, 116–17
Ray, James B., 81, 134
Reconstruction, 205–207
Reed, Isaac, 104
Religion: in pioneer era, 98–108; 1850 to 1920, 185–87, 224–25; and voting behavior, 213–14; since 1920, 238–41; and Ku Klux Klan, 291–92
Republican party: 1850 to 1873, 194–96, 199–207; 1873 to 1920, 209–22; since 1920, 243, 288–317
"Revolt" of 1951, 314–16
Rhea, James, 45
Richardville, Jean Baptiste, 41, 45, 125
Richmond, watercolor of, 178
Ridpath, John Clark, 190
Right-to-work law, 286
Riley, James Whitcomb, 179, 188, 189, 227; pictured, 188
Ristine, Richard O., 312
Rivers, 9, 75–80, 153, 184, 272–73
Roads: in pioneer era, 80–82; 1850 to 1920, 153–54; since 1920, 269
Robertson, Oscar, 256
Roberts settlement, Hamilton County, 116
Robinson, Solon, 61
Rodeheaver, Homer, 187
Roosevelt, Franklin D.: and New Deal, 295–302; pictured, 296
Roosevelt, Theodore, 225
Rose Polytechnic Institute, 184
Rural life: 1850 to 1920, 151–53; since 1920, 266–67

Sabbath observance, 103, 105, 186, 239
St. Clair, Arthur, 30, 34

St. Mary's, Treaty of. *See* New Purchase Treaty
Say, Thomas, 117
Schliemann, Heinrich, 226
School Reorganization Act of 1959, 250
Schools. *See* Education
Schricker, Henry F., 301, 302
Scott, John, 62
Settlement houses, 223
Sewall, May Wright, 226
Shakers, 116
Shepherd, Jean, 258
Shumaker, Arthur, 187
Shumaker, Edward S., 225, 239
Sissle, Noble, 260
Slavery: in territorial politics, 47, 49; and constitution of 1816, 53–54; opposition to, 106–107; and politics, 194–96; and emancipation, 200–201
Slocum, Frances, 125
Smith, Hamilton, 92
Social Gospel, 186
Socialism, 166–67, 227
Social welfare. *See* Dependent peoples
Sons of Liberty, 204
South Shore interurban, 341n
Spanish-American War, 220
Sports, 191, 254–56
Stanton, Wayne, 316
State parks, 256–58
Steamboats, 77–80
Steam power, 91–92
Steele, Theodore C., 190, 259
Stephenson, D. C., 294
Stout, Elihu, 37
Studebaker Company: illustration, 161; and immigrants, 175; and auto manufacture, 275, 276
Sullivan, Reginald: pictured, 296
Sunday, William S., 187
Sunday schools, 109, 186–87

Taggart, Thomas, Jr.: pictured, 296
Taggart, Thomas, Sr., 221, 228
Tarkington, Booth, 177, 188, 189, 258
Taxation: in 1930s, 298; since 1940, 236, 311–13
Tecumseh, 43–45, 122
Temperance: in pioneer era, 105–106; in 1850s, 194–95; before 1920, 224–25; in 1920s, 239
Terre Haute: land office at, 63; pork packing in, 90; and 1935 general strike, 285
Terre Haute Journal, 182

Thames, Battle of, 45
Thomas, Mary F., 226
Thompson, Maurice, 188
Tippecanoe, Battle of, 44
Tipton, John: and Indians, 123–24, 125;
  and politics, 134
Townsend, M. Clifford, 300
Township government: in pioneer era,
  127, 128, 131; and roads, 153–54, 269;
  and education, 180, 182, 248–50, 342n;
  and relief, 297
"Trail of Death," 125
Transportation: rivers, 75–80; roads, 80–
  82; and town development, 93–94;
  1850 to 1920, 153–58; since 1920, 268–
  74
Treaty of Paris, 1783, 26–27
Tucker v. *State*, 302
Turnout, electoral. *See* Voting
Two Percent Club, 299, 305

Underground railroad, 107
Unigov, Marion County, 237
Unions. *See* Labor
United Auto Workers, 285
United Mine Workers, 166
United States Steel, 162–63
Universities. *See* Colleges
University of Notre Dame, 110, 184, 256
University of Southern Indiana, 252–53

Vanderburgh County, 173
Van Nuys, Frederick: pictured, 296; and
  factional politics, 300
Vawter, Will, sketch by, 42
Vincennes: French fort, 13; and Clark expedition, 23–24; settlement at, 29, 34,
  37; land office at, 42, 63
Vincennes, Sieur de, 13–14
Vincennes University, 252
Vocational education, 183–84
Vonnegut, Kurt, Jr., 258
Voting: in Indiana territory, 47; and constitution of 1816, 53; by blacks, 107,
  206; and partisan loyalty, 138; and constitution of 1851, 139–40, 170; influences on, 209–18; reform of, 210–11;
  for women, 225–26; and turnout, 290,
  305, 307–308; in 1930s, 299–301

Wabash and Erie Canal, 82, 83, 84–85,
  153
Wabash College, 110
Wakefield, Dan, 258
Walker, Madame C. J., 172
Wallace, George, 245–46, 316
Wallace, Lew, 188
War of 1812, 44–46, 50, 59
Watson, James E., 289
Wayne, Anthony, 30, 41
Welfare, Social. *See* Dependent peoples
Wells, Herman B, 252
Wells, William, 41–42, 45
Welsh, Matthew: and civil rights, 245–46;
  as governor, 303–304, 309; and patron-
  age, 305, and taxes, 311–12; and fed-
  eral aid, 316
West, Jessamyn, 258
West Baden, 191, 225
Whig party: and banks, 88–89; in pioneer
  era, 133–38; in 1850s, 194
Whitcomb, Edgar, 304, 309
Whitewater Canal, 83, 85
Whitewater Valley, 37
Wiley, Harvey W., 222
Williams, James D., 212
Williams, Jesse L., 82, 83
Willis, Raymond E., 301
Willkie, Wendell L., 301
Wilson, William E., 259
Winchester Democrat, 249
Winona Lake, 187
Winter, George, 141
Wirt, William A., 184
Women: on frontier, 63–64, 69–71; and
  constitution of 1851, 140; on farms,
  152; as workers, 165, 172; as teachers,
  182–83; in Civil War, 198; in Progres-
  sive era, 225–26
Woodland tradition, 4–5
Woodruff Place, 177
World War II: and blacks, 243–44, and
  manufacturing, 276
Wright, Frances, 120
Wright, Joseph A., 194
Wylie, Andrew, 111
Wyneken, Frederich C. D., 100

Yohn, Frederick C., painting by, 25

Editor: Roberta L. Diehl
Book designer: Sharon L. Sklar
Jacket designer: Sharon L. Sklar
Production coordinator: Harriet Curry
Typeface: Baskerville/Palatino
Typesetter: J. Jarrett Engineering, inc.
Printer: Haddon Craftsmen